THE INSIDER'S *Arizona* GUIDEBOOK

FEATURING ARIZONA PARKWAYS, HISTORIC & SCENIC ROADS AND AMERICA'S BYWAYS®

Text by David N. Mitchell
With Additional Text by *Arizona Highways* Staff

Photography by *Arizona Highways* Contributors

ARIZONA HIGHWAYS
BOOKS

The Insider's Arizona Guidebook

Text: David N. Mitchell

Additional Text: *Arizona Highways* Staff and as indicated

Photographs: *Arizona Highways* Contributors

Photography Editor: Richard Maack

Copy Editors: Evelyn Howell, Beth Deveny

Maps: © 2006 DeLorme. Topo USA® 6.0

Interns/Researchers: Brie Iatarola, Brandon Quester, Casey Lynch, Clint Van Winkle, Jayme Cook, Kim Hosey

Book Designer: Jodi Deros (with assistance by Monique Maloney) for ATOMdesign

Assistant Book Designer: Ronda Johnson

Production Coordinator: Annette Phares

Book Editor: Bob Albano

Library of Congress Control Number 2006926839

ISBN 13: 978-1-932082-24-1

ISBN 10: 1-932082-24-7

First printing, 2006, in the United States of America. Second printing, 2006, in Singapore.

Published by the Books Division of *Arizona Highways*® magazine, a monthly publication of the Arizona Department of Transportation, 2039 West Lewis Avenue, Phoenix, Arizona 85009. Telephone: (602) 712-2200. Web site: www.arizonahighways.com

Publisher: Win Holden

Editor: Peter Aleshire

Managing Editor: Bob Albano

Associate Editor: Evelyn Howell

Director of Photography: Peter Ensenberger

Production Director: Kim Ensenberger

Production Assistants: Diana Benzel-Rice, Ronda Johnson, Annette Phares

This book was partly funded by the America's Byways program of the Federal Highway Administration (www.byways.org) and was published in cooperation with the Transportation Enhancement Group of the Arizona Department of Transportation (www.azdot.gov/Highways/EEG/enhancement_scenic_roads).

AMERICA'S
BYWAYS®

Contents

[Sage and cinders surround Wukoki Ruin at Wupatki National Monument.]

[Woods Canyon Lake on the Mogollon Rim east of Payson is the centerpiece of a recreation area that includes fishing and camping.]

David Muench

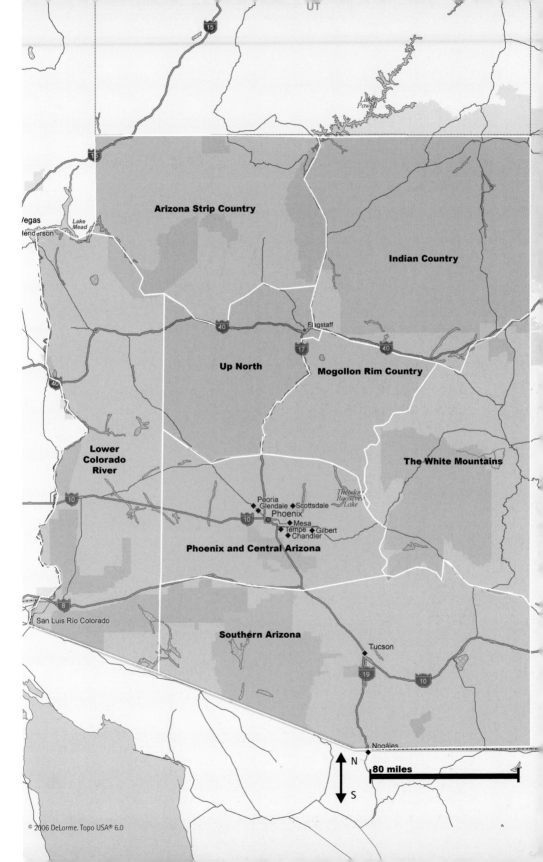

Using 'The Insider's Arizona Guidebook'

Ralph Lee Hopkins

In computer-speak, this page would be labeled "Read Me First." Here, we, the "Insider" aka *Arizona Highways*, explain the book's organization.

After acquainting readers with some of Arizona's best attractions, and its landscape, ancient and modern peoples, and plants and animals, the book highlights nine regions (see preceding Table of Contents and Page 11). Each regional chapter includes trips on scenic or historic drives and Where To Go lists of attractions and organizations that provide travel-related information.

The featured drives include roads with designations from related state and federal programs—Arizona Parkways, Historic & Scenic Roads and the national America's Byways® . One of those drives, Red Rock Scenic Road in the Sedona area, carries the national program's top designation of All-American Road. Across America, only 27 roads measure up to that designation. In addition, four roads in the Arizona Parkways, Historic & Scenic Roads collection are among the country's 99 National Scenic Byways. They include the Coronado Trail Scenic Byway, Historic Route 66, Kaibab Plateau-North Rim Parkway, and Sky Island Scenic Byway.

The book also presents a History on the Go section (Page 376) that summarizes information on historical markers placed along highways. Finally, Special Interest entries (Page 399) provide detailed information about statewide activities such as professional sports, golfing, and casinos.

A caveat: Operating hours of attractions such as museums range from seven-days-a-week, all-day-long to limited days and hours. Some reduce their schedules in the hot months, while others close entirely. If we do not specify a schedule for a particular attraction, you can assume it's open seven days from 8 or 9 in the morning to at least mid-afternoon. We've noted schedules with particularly limited hours. It's best to call first to verify operating hours—and our listings include the phone numbers.

When it flows, the Grand Falls of the Little Colorado River provides a dramatic scene. ▲ A hiker takes a break at the base of one "Up North" mountain, and prairie sunflowers decorate the meadow below another. ▶

Christine Keith

Robert G. McDonald

Spider Rock, an 800-foot sandstone pillar, towers above Canyon de Chelly. ▲
Riders tour Monument Valley. ▶

Introduction
All That Is Arizona

No one knows Arizona like we do. With an insider's perspective gained from more than 80 years of chronicling the Grand Canyon State's natural and man-made attractions, we offer this guide to the places we love. We draw on history, culture, and lore to help you enjoy both our icons and lesser-known places and events ranging from the indescribable Grand Canyon in the north to the grasslands of Sonoita in the south; from the ponderosa pines and snows of Flagstaff to the paloverde trees and desert marigolds of Tucson; from the dramatic and stark Navajo and Hopi canyons, plateaus, and mesas to the lush desert of Saguaro National Park; from the refuges protecting wildlife to the mud and stone ruins that housed our earliest residents. Our introduction touches on peoples, history, landmarks, plants, animals, and geology. Deeper in the book we map out scenic drives that take you into the countryside, and we list scores of places you should visit. We hope you'll know Arizona—and love it—as much as we do.

George Stocking

Kerrick James

[The Santa Rita Mountains south of Tucson brim with watery
retreats like this one in Madera Canyon.]

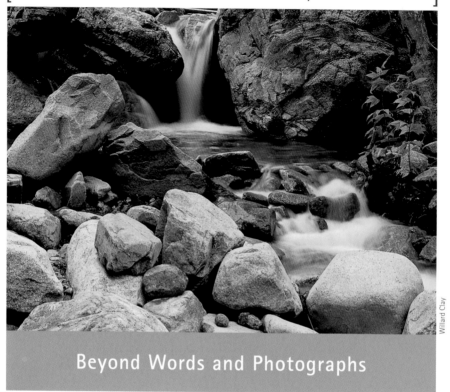

Willard Clay

Beyond Words and Photographs

1 t is a humbling reality that no thousands of words, no dozens of photographs, no documentary films, no paintings can truly and totally convey all that is Arizona, the sweep of its geologic and human history, the diversity of its plants and animals, the oh-wow landmarks created by Nature and by mankind. How does one convey all the traits of the Grand Canyon, the pungent perfume of creosote bush after a rain, or the tranquilizing morning coo of the mourning dove?

Skilled writers, photographers, painters, and poets have tried. They have not failed, yet neither have they fully succeeded. That is not their fault; in many instances, Nature alone has triumphed over science and the arts of communication. In other cases, the magnitude of human struggle and achievement elicits empathy and admiration but defies complete description. Experiencing the total magnificence of Arizona, even for those of unremitting secular persuasion, is a spiritual phenomenon, an epiphany. From the blindingly spectacular Grand Canyon on the north to the claustrophobic but compelling Kartchner Caverns to the south and from the aboriginal architectural achievements of the Casa Grande Ruins National Monument to the sprawling modernity of Phoenix, this state is a permanent Fourth of July display of color, character, charisma, charm, and, oh yes, cactus.

Thus, you must see it and sense it for yourself. Short of that, and forsaking humility for hubris, we think the next best thing is this book that exposes readers to where to go and what to see and do in Arizona.

Arizona is a show-and-tell state, and this is a show-and-tell book, but it is far more than a mere celebration or a coffee table picture book. The index summarizes the scope of these useful, wide-ranging discussions that, we believe, will contribute mightily to the reader's appreciation and understanding of the many features of this state, past and present.

The nine regions in order of their arrangement in this book (see map on Page 5) break down this way:

- Phoenix and central Arizona including metro Phoenix in Maricopa County and Pinal County sans the Casa Grande area.
- Tucson and southern Arizona; the low desert and tall mountain ranges covering the south-central and southeast counties of Pima, Santa Cruz, and Cochise; the Casa Grande area of Pinal County; and the Safford area of Graham County.
- The lower (between Yuma and Lake Mead) Colorado River area encompassing Yuma and La Paz counties plus Mohave County south of the river.
- The Grand Canyon and the Arizona Strip, largely western Coconino County and northern Mohave County.
- Flagstaff and Sedona and the central and northern mountain ranges including Coconino and Yavapai counties (Prescott) and the northern tip of Navajo County along Interstate 40.
- The communities of Payson and others along the magnificent Mogollon Rim, generally covering the southeast portion of Coconino County, the northwest portion of Gila County, and the southern part of Navajo County.
- The White Mountains, everybody's favorite getaway area including the southeastern portion of Navajo County, the southern part of Apache County, the east section of Gila County, the northern chunk of Graham County, and Greenlee County.
- Indian Country, sprawling in Coconino, Navajo, and Apache counties.
- Old Route 66 and its historic-designated sections, which in segments runs the width of the state between Lupton on the east, through Flagstaff, and on to the quaint (and touristy) village of Oatman.

■■■

Along the way, this book also offers easily digestible examinations of:

- Our people, from the prehistoric to today. The influences of conquering Spaniards, courageous Indians, determined Mormons, rugged settlers, gutsy U.S. Army soldiers and intrepid explorers are given their due.
- Our natural landmarks and wonders created by wind, water, volcanoes,

Names and Numbers

A somewhat skewed picture of Arizona drawn from its names and numbers:

Official state symbols: Cactus wren (official state bird), paloverde (tree), saguaro cactus blossom (flower), gemstone (turquoise), neckwear (bola tie), fossil (petrified wood), mammal (ringtail), reptile (Arizona ridge-nosed rattlesnake), fish (Apache trout), amphibian (Arizona tree frog). Unquestionably the only state to have officially embraced the charms of dead wood and a deadly rattler.

Statehood: Became the 48th on February 14, 1912. February 14, of course, also is Valentine's Day.

Some famous Arizonans, past and present: labor leader Cesar Chavez; U.S. Sens. Barry Goldwater and John McCain, U.S. Rep. Morris Udall and his brother Stewart, a congressman and Interior Secretary; Indian leaders Cochise and Geronimo (who would be called tribal chairmen today) and Indian outlaw the Apache Kid; U.S. Supreme Court Justices Rehnquist and O'Connor; singer-actor Rex Allen, actor Lynda Carter, singer Linda Ronstadt, and jazz musician and composer Charles Mingus; and Kerri Strug, Olympic gymnast; and many others.

Capital: Phoenix. Very big. Now the nation's fifth-largest city. Replaced earlier Territorial capitals of Prescott and Tucson.

Size: 114,000 square miles, in only 364 of which you could drown.

Highs and lows: 12,633 feet (Humphreys Peak near Flagstaff) and 70 feet (the Colorado River south of Yuma); 127 degrees in June of 1994 at Lake Havasu City on the western border, and -40 (that's minus) degrees in January of 1971 at Hawley Lake in eastern Arizona's White Mountains.

Population: Closing in on 6 million, not counting coyotes. Median age of people is 34.

[The Arizona flag represents a copper star from a blue field in the face of a setting sun. It has 13 rays in the upper half. ▲]

Approximate average per capital personal income: $30,000, give or take a few bull or bear markets.

Big league sports: Arizona Diamondbacks (baseball), Phoenix Suns (basketball), Phoenix Mercury (women's basketball), Arizona Cardinals (football) and Phoenix Coyotes (hockey). Don't plan to watch any of these teams' games when stopping over in Bisbee. You must head for Phoenix for that, although major league baseball spring training camps are sprinkled around elsewhere.

Best and worst souvenirs: Best, your photos and memories. Worst, a small desert creature trapped for eternity in a plastic paperweight.

and uplift as well as those ancient and modern monuments crafted by mankind.

- Our dependence on increasingly scarce water for commercial survival and on air conditioning for private comfort. Life today in the state's large cities and small towns does not escape our survey.
- Our plants (can you say saguaro?), our animals, forests, weather, canyons, and caverns. Add to that some mountains, some myths, some cowboys and Indians, a gunfight or two, some ranchers, a few politicians, some miners, and even some things minor.

In the spirit of candor, it should be noted that the fact-packed text probably does not come as close to the truth as the dozens of color photographs that do capture, however ephemeral, the magical realism of this Southwestern desert state, the most impressively varied of the nation's 50. It is the photos that prove what the words can claim: that, for example, springtime in the Sonoran Desert in the southern part of the state is a wildfire of purple and white and pastel flowers and golden blankets of California poppies, desert marigolds, daisies, and blooming paloverde trees. Or that sunrises and sunsets are consistently as stunning in any season as the sky and leaf display during autumn in New England.

Too rhapsodic? Only if you are a demented ascetic or a determined avant-gardist. Only if you prefer Berg to Bach, would rather read Chomsky than Cheever, stare at Kandinsky instead of Vermeer. In the end, this book fits loosely into the genre of the hopelessly romantic, a worshipful exploration tempered only by a plethora of useful information.

And speaking of facts: Those in this book are almost all derived from a combination of personal experience and from a variety of other sources, mostly books and articles by scholars and veteran writers with expertise in everything from aboriginals to zoology. It has been said, accurately, that all current human knowledge and accomplishment is based on the efforts of those who went before us—without the abacus, no calculator; without the monkish Mendel, no sheepish Dolly; without Fleming's moldy dishes, no anthrax-healing Cipro. So it is here.

■■■

And that's what some of this book is about: A sampling of Arizona's delectable delights as seen and experienced from two dozen always-scenic and usually historic drives that will lead you from the indescribable Grand Canyon in the north to the grasslands of Sonoita in the south, from the ponderosa pines and snows of Flagstaff to the paloverde trees and desert marigolds of Tucson, from the dramatic and stark realities of the Navajo Reservation (the Rez) to the lush succulents (cacti are succulents but not all succulents are cacti) of Saguaro National Monument, from sand dunes to ski hills.

(If some of those words sound a little queer and funny to your ear, try pal-o-VER-dee, TOO-sahn and suh-WARH-oh.)

You won't need a humongous SUV for these drives or Vibram-soled Scarpas for the walks. Cowboy boots or tennies are OK, as are shorts and sandals or blue jeans. There are few protocols in this come-as-you-are state. A word of warning, however, about those shorts: In summer, especially in the southern part of the state, leaning against your vehicle can quite literally brand you. It's a furnace outside, and the decibels of air conditioning and evaporative cooling can be heard almost everywhere.

[Golden willow, walnut, and sycamore trees line Sabino Creek near Tucson.   ]

Randy Prentice

And incidentally, if you wish to leave your car, this book will help you find some short walks nearby, some colorful towns, some amazing side drives, a lot of history, and a bit about the birds, the beasts (like mountain lions), the beastettes (like lizards), the rocks, and the flora.

■■■

Back to the subject of deserts. Forget, for the most part, about endless stretches of sand. That's the Gobi of Central Asia, or the Sahara in North Africa. You are in the North American desert, which, in irregular fashion, takes in 500,000 square miles of chunks of eastern Oregon, Utah, Nevada, western Colorado, southwestern Wyoming, southeastern California, most of western and southern Arizona, southern New Mexico, southwest Texas, and several states in Mexico including Sonora, Chihuahua, Coahuila, Durango, the Baja peninsula, and more. That massive area breaks down into four distinct, smaller deserts: the Sonoran, the Chihuahuan, the Mojave (or Mohave in Arizona), and the Great Basin. Part of northern Arizona is in the Great Basin, and you also can find fringes of the Chihuahuan and Mohave here, but it is the Sonoran that takes up the most acreage, and, in the minds of many, is the most varied and beautiful. For a primer on the Sonoran, by the way, don't miss the Arizona-Sonora Desert Museum near Tucson.

Don't look for signposts telling you when you're in the desert portion of the state or which desert you reached. There are technical definitions of each desert, and those definitions vary somewhat, but in general, there are two major criteria: moisture, or the lack thereof, and heat, or the abundance thereof. If you consistently measure no more than 10 inches of rain in a year, chances are you are in a desert. As for heat, it's not a sure sign because scientists talk about warm deserts, cool deserts, and cold deserts (the Arctic tundra, for example), but make no mistake, heat counts.

■■■

Now, let's return to a bit more introduction to Arizona.

This combination of text and photos seeks to provide a blend of city and country. Space is devoted to where to go, what to do, and what to see in the state's two biggest urban areas, metropolitan Phoenix and Tucson, as well as to its medium-sized cities such as Flagstaff or Yuma and smaller communities. The scenic and/or historic routes segment of each chapter is particularly worthwhile if you prefer to do your summer sightseeing while sitting inside a fridge on wheels. Regions and their byways are designated on accompanying maps.

For example, in the chapters devoted to the southern and southeastern areas of the state, you will find a discussion of the Sky Island Scenic Byway, an officially designated byway that will take you into the Santa Catalina Mountains in the Coronado National Forest on the northern edge of Tucson. Following what is locally called the Mount Lemmon Highway, you will climb from the desert floor's 2,400 feet to about 9,000 feet. There, you will see grasslands, oak woodlands, ponderosa pine forests, and spectacular views of the Sonoran Desert below as well as the only ski hill in this region of Arizona. In summer, the drive offers a cool respite from the heat below. You can fish for trout, pick berries, hike, climb, find lodging, or pitch a tent in a campground. Should tenting be your choice, remember to zip the entrance shut unless, of course, you think a skunk would make a fun bedmate. Read all about it, including how Mount Lemmon got its name.

A second example: In the north-central portion of the state is the wondrous red rock scenery surrounding the community of Sedona, site of many a cowboy movie, of psychic energy-supplying vortices (or so some believe), of good fudge, great restaurants, abundant shopping, hair-raising Jeep tours, hikes, and the homes of more artists than Paris in the 1920s. Winding out of Sedona is

[Brittlebush and hedgehog cacti brighten Apache Trail.]

David Muench

another of our drives, this one the Sedona-Oak Creek Canyon Scenic Road leading you north to the Mogollon Rim (MOE-gee-on) and within shouting distance of Flagstaff. The views during the drive up Oak Creek Canyon Road are ... well, you simply must see them for yourself, but our photos and text will give you guidance.

And speaking of guidance, there is an additional abundance of it to be found at various spots created by man. There are no better instructions about Nature than those that can be found at the Arizona-Sonora Desert Museum outside of Tucson or the Boyce Thompson Arboretum between Globe and Phoenix. Indian arts and crafts and artifacts (try the Heard Museum in Phoenix or the Northern Arizona Museum in Flagstaff) and cowboy lore can be found everywhere, and there is an unparalleled discussion and display of the very important mining industry's history to be found at a mining museum in Bisbee. You're English, you say, and can't locate a decent dish of porridge? Sorry, but we can offer you your London Bridge now imported from London to Lake Havasu City or a Shakespearean festival in Sedona.

The list is endless, but the point is this: History, culture, and lore, as well as Nature, are the handmaidens of any sightseeing in Arizona. And on those days when the visitor would rather clear the lungs than cramp the brain with more facts, there are outfitters available to guide you down the Colorado River in a raft or canoe or into a remote, prehistoric building site; there are ski instructors to improve your downhill technique; there are countless bike and hiking trails to be taken solo; and, of course, there is shopping, guided or unguided.

This book is intended to make your task of discovery easy and to be helpful for your looking pleasure, regardless of what part or parts of the state you have selected.

As you begin any exploration in this state, expect sensory overload from exposure to this most gorgeous of deserts and pine forests. Your eyes will recognize the intensity of the light and the exuberant colors, both primary and pastel, that distinguish the sunrises and sunsets, your ears will become attuned to the morning's coo-like sound of the dove and the sheep-like baahing of the mysterious Sonoran spadefoot toads after an afternoon's monsoon rain, and your nose will twitch to the delightful fragrance of the aptly named creosote bush after a sprinkling.

OK, fill your water jug and move out. Or, if you're not staying, we say both *bienvenidos* and *adios*. We think you'll be back, and you will be welcome. ᛤ

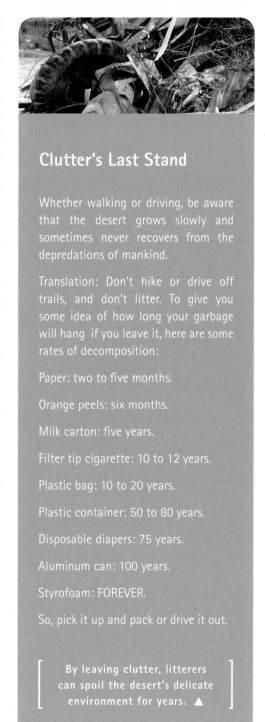

Clutter's Last Stand

Whether walking or driving, be aware that the desert grows slowly and sometimes never recovers from the depredations of mankind.

Translation: Don't hike or drive off trails, and don't litter. To give you some idea of how long your garbage will hang if you leave it, here are some rates of decomposition:

Paper: two to five months.

Orange peels: six months.

Milk carton: five years.

Filter tip cigarette: 10 to 12 years.

Plastic bag: 10 to 20 years.

Plastic container: 50 to 80 years.

Disposable diapers: 75 years.

Aluminum can: 100 years.

Styrofoam: FOREVER.

So, pick it up and pack or drive it out.

[**By leaving clutter, litterers can spoil the desert's delicate environment for years.** ▲]

Our Plants and Creatures

H ere's a Cliffs Notes version of some of the state's most common and best-known flora and fauna that you are likely to encounter, depending on the time of year and where you are.

Birdwatchers: If you are in the mountains, look for chickadees, mountain bluebirds, hummingbirds, jays, ravens, red-tailed hawks, and more jays. On the mesas lower down, look for golden eagles, mourning doves, handsome magpies, wrens, and pinyon jays. Dropping down to the low desert, you can't miss cactus wrens, the state bird, nesting in extremely prickly cholla (that's CHOY-yah) cactus, Gila woodpeckers, the Woody Allen of cuckoos known as the roadrunner, and the delightful and distinctive Gambel's quail (look for the curved head plume).

There are at least two dozen hot spots for birding with the biggest cluster of them just south and just north of Tucson. Included among those are Aravaipa Canyon, Catalina State Park, Sabino Canyon Recreation Area, Madera Canyon, Ramsey Canyon, San Pedro Riparian National Conservation Area, Patagonia-Sonoita Creek, Sycamore Canyon, and Buenos Aires National Wildlife Refuge. To the immediate north of Phoenix are Red Rock State Park and Dead Horse Ranch State Park.

Reptiles, snakes, lizards, and other things that go bump in the night: In the venomous-do-not-handle category are diamondback rattlers, sidewinders, and

G. C. Kelley

Tom Vezo

Arizona's southeastern mountains are home to this broad-billed hummingbird. ◀ The roadrunner will eat fruit and insects — although it prefers lizards. ▲ The cactus wren, Arizona's state bird, makes its home in the arms of a cholla cactus. ▼

Neil Weidner

A Fine Spider

The tarantula, that big, fine spider that is commonplace in the desert, can bite if provoked, but the effects are roughly the same as a bee sting. Furthermore, it does not (repeat: does not) jump and attack despite what you might think after watching a James Bond movie or other Hollywood nonsense.

A true scene: An Arizona newcomer sitting poolside under a shady ramada at a home outside downtown Tucson and watching a tarantula stroll across the concrete and up and down the eagerly outstretched bare arms and legs of several quite unafraid but enchanted staff members of the Arizona-Sonora Desert Museum.

A tarantula is a peaceful, solitary creature that walks slowly, has to ambush its prey, usually at night, and is exceedingly sensitive to heat, dryness, and cold winter rain. It needs a good hole to survive bad weather and predators, particularly tarantula hawks, those large, black wasps with orange wings and the ability to paralyze a tarantula with a sting and turn the spider into a living host for the wasp's grubs.

Note to romantics: The male tarantula has a miserable love life. According to Dr. Kevin Wright, a Phoenix zoo specialist, they get lustful during summer, leave their holes at night and go searching for a receptive female. The male lives only a short time after it becomes sexually mature "so it no longer worries about hiding from predators." Talk about dying for love.

[The tarantula is a gentle desert resident that is sensitive to heat, dryness, and cold rain. It hunts mostly at night. ▲]

the reclusive Sonoran coral snake with its distinctive and colorful bands. In the same look-but-don't-touch category are the Gila monster (generally shy and some-what reclusive), certain centipedes, black widow spiders, some scorpions, and the much-maligned (and unfairly so) tarantula, a spider that rarely bites and causes no serious damage if it does.

Speaking of rattlers, their distinctive, rattling sound is less likely to be heard in December, January, and February, but don't bet on that. They find their prey (birds, rodents, lizards, rabbits, etc.) by sensing its heat. But it's a dog-eat-dog world, and that dirty dog of a coyote is a rattler's enemy, as are roadrunners, hawks, and some other brother reptiles such as the king snake.

Lizards: You can't miss them, in town or out. One Tucson woman liked them so much she fished them out of her swimming pool and revived them with gentle, resuscitative pressure from a forefinger (but no mouth-to-mouth). With the exception of the Gila monster variety, they are harmless and wonderfully varied, ranging from the short-horned one called the horned toad to whiptails, geckos, collards, chuckwallas, and more. The Gila monster, with its generally black and coral beaded skin, is the largest and only venomous lizard in the United States and can grow to as much as 2 feet in length. Bless your luck if you get to see one in the wild and admire it all you wish, but unless it is tranquilized and you are a veterinary dentist, keep your hands out of its mouth, because its venom moves into the bite wound from glands at the base of its teeth. Do not harm the Gila. It is protected by law.

[A slow-moving Gila monster ventures out to sun itself.   ]

John Cancalosi

Other beasts, big and small: You may consider yourself most fortunate if you spot a mountain lion, but the chances are good that you might spot a buffalo in wildlife refuges and national parks. Also, and ranging free in many areas: bobcats, coatimundis, mule deer, elk, pronghorn antelope, bighorn sheep, bears, porcupines, chipmunks, marmots (listen for their whistle), jackrabbits, and kangaroo rats. If somehow you don't see any or all of these, you need only stand in one spot in the desert for an hour or so before the ubiquitous coyote lopes past. He won't challenge your Akita for turf, but you would do well to protect your toy poodle and your kitten. There also are some ugly fellows called javelinas that look like wild pigs but are, technically, peccaries. In gangs, they can be a mean adversary.

If, in your desert hiking you encounter what you think is a big turtle that is seriously lost and desperately in need of a pond, think otherwise. It is, doubtless, a desert tortoise that survives the harsh, dry desert by spending much of its time in a burrow dug under a shrub or in a cave. The desert tortoise can live to 60 years or longer, so pay your respects to your elder and do not—do not—pick it up or try to take it home.

Special animals: Efforts have been underway for several years in Arizona and elsewhere in the Southwest to preserve the existence of certain threatened, even officially endangered, creatures, among them the massive California condor, the gray wolf, and the Sonoran pronghorn antelope (called an antelope but not really related to antelope at all). Condors are

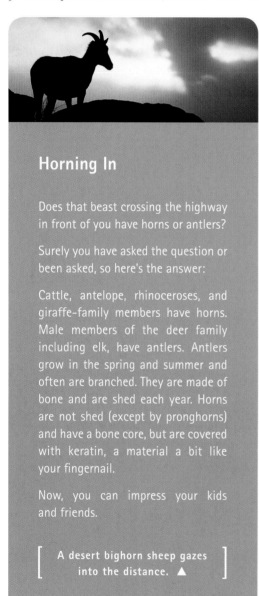

George H. H. Huey

Horning In

Does that beast crossing the highway in front of you have horns or antlers?

Surely you have asked the question or been asked, so here's the answer:

Cattle, antelope, rhinoceroses, and giraffe-family members have horns. Male members of the deer family including elk, have antlers. Antlers grow in the spring and summer and often are branched. They are made of bone and are shed each year. Horns are not shed (except by pronghorns) and have a bone core, but are covered with keratin, a material a bit like your fingernail.

Now, you can impress your kids and friends.

[A desert bighorn sheep gazes into the distance. ▲]

being released in the wild in several spots including certain cliffs in northern Arizona. The gray wolves, which once howled and prowled across North America, were hunted into near extinction by the 1930s. The wolves were reintroduced in 1995 in many areas and have generally prospered under the protection of federal law. Still in big trouble are the pronghorns, which once roamed the West and Southwest by the millions. By the end of 2002, however, the pronghorn, largely confined to a 5,000-square-mile chunk of Sonoran Desert in southern Arizona and another chunk in adjoining Mexico, had dropped to a miniscule 21 in Arizona and only several hundred in Mexico, according to the Defenders of Wildlife organization. The villains: hunters and habitat destruction by humans. There is some small hope: A square-mile breeding pen is planned to keep four female and one male pronghorn in and predators and hunters out.

As for plant life, the desert in spring is, in the view of many, better than the best English garden. It is blossom time, a festival of colorful wild-flowers including asters, locoweed, zinnias, penstemon, blue lupine, sacred datura, and brittlebush. When you drive past what looks to be a sea of yellow, chances are you are looking at California poppies or desert marigolds. For the red-green color blind, a field of golden poppies mixed with blue lupine cannot be matched, even by a Van Gogh or a Gauguin.

[The antelope jackrabbit lives in wilderness and urban areas.]

C. K. Lorenz

Cacti, of course: Or cactus if it's only one and if that makes you more comfortable. If you have no interest in being technically correct, go ahead with "cactuses." Lots of folks do. The giant, multi-ton, long-lived saguaros, which grow up to 50 feet and bloom in May, lead the Hall Of Prickly Fame list, followed by the dramatic and huge organ pipe cactus. Cholla is even more common than coyotes and comes in several varieties—Christmas, tree, cane, teddy bear, etc.—that are not recommended as an adversary in hand-to-hand combat. Almost as common are several varieties of the prickly pear. Tucked in and among the prickly pears are wonderful barrel cacti, pincushions, hedgehogs, and fishhooks.

Paul Gill

[
Aspen trees and sunflowers decorate the Hochderffer Hills near
Humphreys Peak in the San Francisco Mountains near Flagstaff.
]

Some others often thought of, erroneously, as cacti: Included are the crucifix-
ion thorn, the yuccas, the octopus-like ocotillo (o-ko-TEE-yo), and century plants
(no, the latter don't live for 100 years, but at the end of their long lives they do
shoot up a spectacular stalk before toppling over.).

Trees and shrubs: Sagebrush, rabbit brush, catclaw acacia, mesquite, the beautiful paloverde (the state's official tree) with its green bark and spring blooms of
gold, saltbush, jojoba (ho-HO-bah).

As mentioned earlier but to repeat, there are cacti and there are succulents.
All cacti are succulents, but not all succulents are cacti. Succulents are plants
that can survive long dry spells and usually have fleshy, moisture-holding leaves
or other appendages. A cactus is distinguished by the fact that it must have an
areole, a depression usually with short hairs called glochids, bristles, spines, or
long hairs.

Depending on elevation, the state's plant life is divided among six main life
zones beginning at the bottom—below 4,500 feet—in a zone called the Lower
Sonoran, which offers creosote bush, jojoba, paloverde trees, mesquite trees,
ironwood trees, and cacti. The other five zones are the Upper Sonoran at 4,500

to 6,500 feet with grasslands, sagebrush, pine, oak, and juniper; the Transition between 6,500 and 8,000 feet with ponderosa pines; the Canadian from 8,000 to 9,500 feet with Douglas fir, some spruce, and aspen; the Hudsonian from 9,500 to 11,500 feet with stunted spruce, fir, and bristlecone pines; and the Alpine, above 11,500 feet with lichens, sedges, grasses, and alpine wildflowers. Driving from bottom to top of most mountain ranges will lead the driver through several of these life zones.

Thus endeth the lecture and the mere taste from this amazing stew of the wild and the wonderful. Please help yourself to any size portion that pleases your travel palate. ⋀

A Gathering of Terms

At one time or another, you probably have read or referred to the poetry of the word applied to a bunch of larks: An exaltation, as in an exaltation of larks. Very, very nice, so what about congregations of some of Arizona's other creatures?

Courtesy of the Northern Prairie Wildlife Research Center, here are a few:

Bats come in colonies, but it's a sloth or a sleuth of bears, a gang or an obstinacy of buffalo, a herd of deer, a gang of elk, a tribe of goats, a labor of moles, a pack or splan or barren of mules, a prickle of porcupines, a colony or warren of rabbits, a dray of squirrels, a pack of wolves, a wake of buzzards, a cover of coots, a murder of crows, a dule of doves, a convocation of eagles, a charm of finches, a cast of hawks, a party of jays, a tiding of magpies, a parliament of owls, a bevy of quail, an unkindness of ravens, a flight of swallows, a rafter of turkeys, an army of frogs, a nest of snakes, a hover of trout, an intrusion of cockroaches, and a cloud of gnats or grasshoppers.

Rarely usable in Arizona (except for fat farms – oh, OK, spas): A bloat of hippopotamuses.

[Convergent ladybugs (they actually are beetles) sometimes are referred to as colonies when they cluster by the thousands during their brief life span. ▲]

An Ancient Sentinel

I supposed our old friend, a saguaro on the edge of our property east of Mesa, was 150 years old when it died. Nobody kept records. No one was even close to being alive when it was born. We knew it for only the last five years of its life. Scarred. Gnarled. Some folks thought it was ugly. It had lost a part of one arm some decades ago, I guess. No one could remember.

It was tall, maybe 25 feet, majestic, towering over its companions. It had befriended many, mostly birds—cactus wrens, woodpeckers. And now it was dying. And there was nothing Joyce or I could do.

Called the Sentinel of the Desert, the giant saguaro, more than any other plant, defines the Sonoran Desert. Like snowflakes, no two of these cacti have the same shape. It grows a scant few inches a year at most. Its water storage system allows it to withstand scorching summer heat and sometimes-lengthy droughts. Its whitish inner core is cool to the touch, quite moist, with the consistency and feel of a freshly cut cantaloupe. I've heard that the wild ones (as opposed to the cultivated ones) don't begin to sprout arms until they are nearly 70 years old. As the arms mature, they generally don't stray too far from the trunk, growing vertically upward. Some, however, begin to grow upward, then twist and grow downward. Some just grow downward, looking rather limp.

Most are scarred from constant bouts with the weather, birds that use their arms as homes, animals that desperately nibble on them in times of drought, and vicious vandals who use them for target practice. Sometimes, because of age or rot, an arm or part of an arm will drop off.

In late May or early June, white flowers and then edible, purple fruit appear at the tips of the arms, several on each tip. Birds, frequently bats, spread the seeds, thus continuing life's renewal process.

My mute old friend had a circumference of about 4 feet and four arms, the longest of which was some 12 feet. About 18 months before it died, rot splotches began to develop on the main trunk. They pooched out in a kind of inverted blossom. Shortly thereafter, a black liquid started to ooze from the rotting portions. Then it dripped and emitted an odor similar to a mix of mild skunk smell and tar. That's when the death watch began.

The ooze attracted all manner of gnats, flies, and bees. As the months passed, more splotches formed, more ruptures dripped. Then, we could look through the

Mike Dant, father of two, was a high school teacher, administrator, and amateur ironist in the Arizona cities of Scottsdale and Mesa for much of his adult life. He is now retired and living with his wife, Joyce, a well-known landscape artist, in Santa Fe, New Mexico.

> By MIKE DANT

Nick Berezenko

The many arms on these blooming saguaros near Roosevelt Lake indicate
they probably started growing decades before the lake was impounded
in the early 1900s.

splotches and see daylight on the other side. It was only a matter of time until
it would collapse, unable because of its widespread but shallow root system to
sustain the top-heavy weight.

In the dead of a calm late-winter night, about 2 a.m., Joyce awakened me.
"Michael, I think I heard the cactus die. Let's go see." We dressed, found the flashlight, and trekked down the driveway.

It had fallen. About 4 feet up from the ground, the trunk had splintered. It
just lay there, collapsed, helpless, dead. Ugly slivers of spine protruded from the
break, belying the plant's natural grace. It had succumbed to the ravages of age,
of myriad storms and dry spells, and of the generations of birds that created their
nests in its arms.

"I heard it fall, Michael. It sounded like it just gave up. It was tired of fighting,"
Joyce said. She gently stroked the trunk, knelt down and carefully stroked its great
arms between the spines. "I'm sorry," she whispered. And she wept. ▥

Our People ... Then and Now

H uman existence in Arizona probably got its start about...well, about...oh, go pick your own expert.

"The earliest evidence of humans in the Southwest has been radiocarbon-dated at about 11,500 years ago," declares journalist-writer Lawrence W. Cheek in a reference to so-called Paleo Indians discussed in his book *A.D. 1250.*

Too precise, says popular historian Marshall Trimble in his *Arizona, A Cavalcade Of History.* The fact is that "Paleo Indians or First Americans were known to roam this land more than 10,000 years ago" although Arizona's recorded history did not begin until the Spaniards arrived in the 1500s.

We can agree that they shall be—and are—called Paleo Indians, these first hunters who mostly ate mammoth steaks. However, the possibility exists that they might have lived here as long as 30,000 years ago, asserts respected historian and anthropological scholar Bernard L. Fontana in *A Guide To Contemporary Southwest Indians.*

Nah, "Arizona's history began more than 12,000 years ago," declares the state's official Blue Book, when the first inhabitants came from Asia across the Bering Strait land bridge. That's official, so there.

Well, what's a few hundred or a few thousand years among non-academic friends? We move on in our brief chronology to successor groups including, in

[
Sinagua Indians and other Ancestral Puebloans are believed to have lived at what is now the Wupatki National Monument. ▼ This cliff dwelling was built and occupied by Salado Indians in the 1300s. ▶
]

David W. Lazaroff

order of appearance on the Arizona big screen, other Indian groups, Spaniards, Mexicans, and American explorers and settlers, including Mormons.

Those first Paleo Indians gave way around 5,500 B.C. to hunter-gatherers called the Archaic People, who liked wild plant salads along with their rabbit and snake stews. Other cultures followed, and it is the architectural remains of their tenures—famous names such as Casa Grande Ruins, Keet Seel, Betatakin, Canyon de Chelly's White House Ruin, etc.—that hold immense fascination for travelers. The prehistoric ruins that abound throughout the state and the region draw thousands upon thousands of visitors annually so it is worthwhile to mention at least the major groups whose pit houses, cliff dwellings, pueblos, and other forms of dwellings are most likely to be encountered.

Whatever they might have called themselves, they later were named the Anasazi (a term more recently replaced by Ancestral Puebloans), the Sinagua, the Mogollon, the Hohokam, and the Salado. Depending on where you are in the state, you will encounter the remnants of one or more of these civilizations that, in turn, flowered and collapsed, their survivors probably absorbed into other cultural groups such as the current pueblo Indians in New Mexico as well as the Navajo, the Apache, the Hopi, and other tribes.

George H. H. Huey

Today, there are dozens of Indian groupings in the Southwest, functioning under such familiar names as Navajo, Hopi, Apache, Zuni, Pima, and Ute and less familiar ones such as Chemehuevi, Hualapai, Jemez, Maricopa, Mojave, Yaqui, and Tohono O'odham (formerly Papago). The Apaches alone break up into the San Carlos Apaches, the Tonto, the White Mountain, the Jicarilla, the Chiricahua, and the Mescalero.

The word "Indian," incidentally, seems to have originated with early European explorers who thought they had reached India. It stuck, however, and attempts to replace it with words such as "Native American" or "First People" have not met with great acceptance, even among Indians themselves.

Moving on, the next to arrive, in the 16th century (1540), were the Spaniards who came up from the south (what is now Mexico) on strange beasts called horses. They also carried guns and swords and boasted a written language. They came in search of gold and territorial expansion and in the service of God, the Spanish king, and glory. A lot of huffing and puffing by Spanish explorers and priests followed as they tramped through the desert and up and down mountains in search of the Seven Cities of Cibola, supposedly seven cities north of Mexico that were exceedingly wealthy and had coffers of gold and silver. They weren't and they didn't, but that failed to stop the Spaniards from making a huge and permanent impression on the region. It is not uncommon to hear a resident insist that he or she is of Spanish heritage, not Mexican, and the power of the Roman Catholic church in the region traces directly to the forceful proselytizing of the Spanish missionaries who came with—and occasionally without—horse-mounted soldiers.

The names of Spanish explorers are the stuff of legend and can be found today in virtually every Arizona town: on street signs, town names, hotels, cafes, restaurants, casinos, etc. Names such as Cabeza de Vaca, Coronado, Antonio de Espejo, Juan de Onate, Father Eusebio Kino, de Anza, de Vargas, de Niza. Not all of them left behind fond memories of their presence. After they eventually left and their missions collapsed, many of the Indians returned to their original beliefs.

But the Spaniards hung in there. Eventually, they became embroiled in a whopping war with the Mexicans who wanted independence from Spain and won it in the Mexican War of Independence, which ended with the Treaty of Cordoba in 1821. The Mexican flag was then raised at Tucson, the only big settlement in Arizona at the time.

A series of Indian wars followed as did major American exploration of Arizona. That turmoil culminated in—you guessed it—another war, this one the Mexican-American war, which came to an end of sorts in 1848 with the Treaty of Guadalupe Hidalgo. Under that treaty, Mexico gave the United States a big chunk of land including all of what is now Arizona north of the Gila River. In return, the United States gave Mexico $15 million, a splendid example of tax dollars at work. Establishing boundaries, however, was a problem that was not resolved until 1853 with the so-called Gadsden Purchase of 30,000 square miles that made all of Arizona part of U.S. territory.

The takeover of Texas by the United States in 1845 persuaded our leaders to confiscate all of the Southwest and California, including Arizona. After moving soldiers to the Rio Grande (no, no, not the Rio Grande River; that's redundant), President James K. Polk declared the war on Mexico in 1846. A group of Mormons on its way to join the battle for ownership of California (then owned by Mexico), raised the first American flag over Tucson in that year.

It was in this land in the 1850s, then, that military posts were set up to protect stagecoaches from attacks by Apaches who were, in turn, trying to protect their hunting lands. Small silver-mining camps began to show up along the Colorado and Hassayampa rivers and south of the Gila River.

Following the beginning of the American Civil War in 1861, Arizona settlers from the South called a convention in Tucson and made Arizona a Confederate territory. But it did not have much of an effect on Arizona. The Confederacy did send a force to take the New Mexico Territory, but it was beaten in New Mexico. On February 24, 1863, President Abraham Lincoln approved the creation of the Territory of Arizona. Tucson was the capital of Arizona from 1867 to 1877. The capital was then moved back to Prescott, which had been the first capital, and finally, in 1889, the capital was moved to Phoenix.

During all of these years, there washed over the land a wave of American settlers in search of furry animals, gold, silver, copper, timber, ranch land, and a route to the gold fields of California.

Statehood eventually arrived—in 1912—making Arizona the 48th star on the U.S. flag.

As the state's Blue Book puts it, Arizona at the beginning of the 20th century "was still a wild place. Violence was a way of life in this corner of the Old West." Never mind that Arizona is not a geographic corner of anything except one of the four corners on the spot where four states share a boundary line. It is, nonetheless, accurate to say that shootings, shootouts, train and stagecoach robberies, brothels, saloons, and sunburned, uncombed ruffians abounded. It's better now. No stagecoaches, for one thing. ◫

[White House Ruin, an Ancestral Puebloan dwelling in Canyon de Chelly, still has remains of nearly 60 rooms.]

Tom Danielsen

Tom Till

The Best Ruins

Let's go over some old ground, so to speak.

The dominant prehistoric cultures in Arizona and the region hit their developmental peak in the 1200s, but they were largely gone—due to drought, migration, absorption into other cultures, death, etc.—by the time the Europeans rode in during the 1500s. No one knows with any certainty what these cultures called themselves, but the names they are known by these days are:

The Sinagua: Translates from the Spanish as "without water." Existed in the northern and central parts of Arizona, mostly between Flagstaff on the north and the Verde River on the south. Set up a trading system.

The Ancestral Puebloans (or Anasazi): Anasazi translates as "ancient enemy" from the Navajo language. Existed in the region of the Four Corners of Arizona, New Mexico, Utah, and Colorado. Nice pots and baskets.

The Hohokam: Or "those who have gone" in Tohono O'odham. Hung out in the Salt and Gila river valleys and built 500 miles of irrigation canals by hand. Bulldozers and ditching machinery came along later. A lot later.

The Mogollon: Based along the Mogollon Rim and among the mountains of central Arizona. More good pots and a sewer system of sorts.

The Salado: Named for the Salt River, or Rio Salado in Spanish. Home was in the Tonto Basin east of Phoenix. Still more good pots.

That's the big five. For an up-close-and-personal look at how they lived, here are some of the best places to visit:

[Pots rest at Keet Seel Ruin in Navajo National Monument. ▲   ]

Wupatki National Monument, near Flagstaff: Sinagua. Four pueblos, one of which is two stories high.

Walnut Canyon National Monument, near Flagstaff: Sinagua. Pueblos and cliff dwellings in a picturesque canyon.

Montezuma Castle and Montezuma Well, near Camp Verde: Sinagua. A 65-room "castle" built into a limestone cliff and reached by a pleasant, short walk. The well is 5 miles northeast and is a deep limestone sink fed by a spring and used to water Sinagua crops. Misnamed. Montezuma never saw it, never heard of it.

Navajo National Monument, near Tonalea on the Navajo Reservation: Ancestral Puebloan. Astonishing cliff dwellings, called Betatakin and Keet Seel, but reached in their scenic canyons only by substantial hikes or by horse. There is an easily accessible overlook for Betatakin.

Canyon de Chelly, near Chinle: Ancestral Puebloan. Now home to Navajo families. Strikingly beautiful and dramatic canyon with prehistoric dwellings tucked into the canyon walls just about anywhere you look. With a tour guide you can drive or hike or take a horse along the canyon floor.

Casa Grande Ruins National Monument, near Coolidge: Hohokam. An amazing, four-story "great house" and probably built as an observatory. Excellent museum adjoins as do several smaller structures and a ceremonial ball court.

Tonto National Monument, near Roosevelt: Salado. You have to walk to get to them, but the two cliff dwellings are worth it—and good for you.

Besh-Ba-Gowah Archaeological Park, in Globe: Salado. Not well known but easily reached and explored if you are in the city of Globe for any reason.

Casa Malpais, outside of Springerville: Mogollon. No visitor center but a self-guided tour of this beautifully sited pueblo is possible. A guide is even better. Overlooks the Little Colorado River and sports a great kiva and masonry walls.

A final, cautionary note: The cliché that when you have seen one you have seen them all does not apply in the case of these phenomenal windows on the past. Visiting them can become addictive.

A Diverse Land

T he reservoir of adjectives seems almost too shallow to meet the needs of those seeking to describe the variety and complexity of Arizona's surface, its geology and the impact of the natural forces including wind, water, volcanism, uplift, tilt, earthquakes, and erosion.

For those with a little determination, a little curiosity, and an attention span longer than 30 seconds, a Geologic Highway Map of Arizona, published by the Arizona Geological Society and the Arizona Geological Survey, is splendid and available for a fee by writing AGS, 416 W. Congress St., Tucson, AZ 85701; (520) 770-3500.

Marc Muench

From that map's text and color-coded graphics, you can learn such things as:

- Faults are common in the state except in the northeast, but have been inactive for the most part for millions of years. However, fault movements and volcanic eruptions of the past 30 million years have combined with erosion and sediment deposition to create the current landscape.

- The worst geologic hazards in the state are flooding and subsidence, the latter largely due to withdrawal of ground water. Flooding does the worst damage.

- To see old volcanoes head for the San Francisco volcano field near Flagstaff. Prehistoric people were living there the last time one blew its top.

- Mining has always been a big business in Arizona, courtesy of Nature's deposits. Chief among the valuable ores has been copper, but gold, silver, turquoise, molybdenum, and uranium also have played major roles. We lead the nation in copper production and molybdenum output. We rank third in gemstones, fourth in silver, fifth in pumice and mica, and almost nobody cares how we rank in bentonite.

For those of statistical bent, the state's 15 counties cover 114,000 square miles. The geographic center is Yavapai County 55 miles east-southeast of Prescott. Arizona is 400 miles by 310 miles. Its highest point is 12,600 feet (a mountain outside of Flagstaff), its lowest is 70 (the Colorado River on the western border).

A major chunk of Arizona land is devoted to six of the country's 155 national forests. In this state, the forests offer everything from downhill skiing to white-water rafting, from refuges for certain wild animals, such as the re-introduced gray wolf and the California condor, to fishing, camping, biking, and hiking.

As an example, consider the Coronado National Forest with headquarters in Tucson. This particular forest, immensely popular in the southern and south-eastern part of the state, covers 1.7 million acres and has 15 mountain ranges that leap up from the low, flat, surrounding desert. These mountains, called sky islands, range from 3,000 to 10,720 feet above sea level and offer gorgeous vistas, cooler temperatures, an ever-changing panorama of vegetation, and a variety of wildlife.

It is much the same in the other forests of the state, which include: The Apache-Sitgreaves, Coconino, Kaibab, the Prescott, and the Tonto.

Other government agencies own and control vast areas of the state. In fact, nearly 85 percent of the state is owned by the state, the Indians, or the federal government.

One can choose his or her landscape of preference including big and snowy mountain ranges, hot and flat and sandy deserts, flowering and cacti-rich des-erts, verdant forests of towering pines, endless grasslands, prairie vistas, canyons great and small, gorgeous gorges, raging rivers, small trout streams, rangeland, plateaus, mountain rims, sky islands, slick rock by the mile, dunes by the acre.

And that doesn't cover buttes. Or, for that matter, our mesas, limestone caves, and dried up inland seas dating back 170 million years. Arizona's beauty: some-times grand, sometimes gentle, usually startling. Pick your place. ⚐

[
A diverse land: A skier races through deep powder near Flagstaff, ◄ and a mountain-bike rider makes his way over slick rock near Sedona less than 40 miles away. ▼
]

Dugald Bremner

Tony Marinella

Acres of Fun

Arizona encompasses some 30 million acres of land designated for fun and relaxation. For those of you familiar with a common comparison of huge, almost incomprehensible, acreages to a site more readily grasped—that's a lot of football fields.

Here in these place, visitors can take a hike or ride a bike or trod trails in snowshoes; camp overnight or for weeks (in your tent or a Forest Service cabin), or just hang out for a few hours; fish and hunt, or view creatures with no intent to take them; get lost (figuratively or literally) in wilderness areas or stroll along a nature trail; and take in sites that preserve history and culture and explain nature and science.

To fully appreciate the plethora of public land in Arizona, consider the six national forests in Arizona and remember these A-B-Cs: Adios, adage. Begone, bromide. Can the cliché. The truth is that you can see the forests AND the trees.

Yes, these big, national woods in Arizona are full of trees: firs with their flat needles, spruce with their square ones, mountain oaks with their size far less than their cousins' elsewhere, aspen with their quaking foliage, ponderosa pines smelling like vanilla, other pines with other odors, pungent cedars and junipers, and, always at lower elevations, mesquite and paloverde. But the forests also provide a vast canopy sheltering an equally vast assortment of life in addition to trees: pot growers, meth and myth makers, naked nymphs, bearded elves, furry bunnies, big carnivores, hikers, skiers, campers, forest rangers, tree-hugging environmentalists, tree-taking loggers and cattle-raising ranchers, terrain destroying ATVers, lecturers, arborists, hunters, botanists, biologists, map makers, fishermen, spelunkers, hermits, and miscellaneous crazies.

A leap of faith might be required to spot a naked nymph or bearded elf, but there is nothing to stop ye of little faith, Darwinians all, from seeing

[Aspens cover the mountainside in gold. ▲   ]

and enjoying the overwhelming beauty and pleasures of the forests, their privacy, their serenity, their rivers, their lakes, their canyons, their gentle rains and violent storms and, of course, their trees.

In all, our half-dozen national forests, all administered by the U.S. Department of Agriculture's Forest Service, comprise more than 11 million acres, and that total does not count the huge tracts of land and spectacular sites and sights under the control of the National Park Service, Bureau of Land Management, Bureau of Reclamation, U.S. Fish and Wildlife Service, and others.

Each forest offers many amenities, but not all can be found in every forest or in every campground. Best to call ahead but, in general, the offerings you might find could include a fee area, disabled access, interpretive exhibits, visitor information, bathrooms, drinking water, showers, dump stations, electric hookups, developed campsites, primitive camping, picnic areas, hiking trails, bicycle trails, equestrian trails, self-guided tours, historical and archaeological sites, wildlife viewing, scenic view areas, hunting, swimming, hot springs, canoe and raft facilities, fishing, boating facilities, winter sports and playgrounds.

As we said earlier, the national forests are only part of the scenic wonders of the state and do not encompass such outstanding offerings as the National Park Service's Canyon de Çhelly National Monument, the Casa Grande Ruins, the Fort Bowie National Monument, the Glen Canyon National Recreation Area including Lake Powell, the Grand Canyon National Park, the Hubbell Trading Post, Lake Mead National Recreation Area, Montezuma's Castle, the Navajo National Monument, Saguaro National Park, Walnut Canyon and on and on. Still more attractions fall under the aegis of the Navajo Nation, the U.S. Bureau of Land Management, the state Game and Fish Department, and the Arizona State Parks unit. Dozens of publications ranging from many offered by *Arizona Highways* to a listing and map of recreation and historic sites put out by the Arizona Council for Enhancing Recreation and Tourism (ACERT) are available.

That's just an overview. If you have never gone hiking off trail and seen and heard a solitary flutist or lutist seated on a rock or against a tree and playing a soulful melody, if you've never rounded the bend of a trail and spotted a herd of elk in a meadow, if you've never taken off your Levi's and boots and waded in the transparent waters of a creek and had a big trout brush against your leg, well ... it's time. The public lands of Arizona await you. (See Where To Go at the end of this chapter for contact information.)

[Besides recreational sites, the San Francisco Peaks hold spiritual value.]

Kate Thompson

Great Landmarks by Nature and Mankind

Antelope Canyon: Outside of Page in the Lake Powell region. Short and spectacular so-called slot canyons (upper and lower). Brilliant colors as sunlight filters through holes and cracks in the red sandstone walls. A short, easy walk in the upper; a little demanding in the lower.

Arcosanti: A creation of architect Paolo Soleri that stands incomplete in the desert just off the Interstate 17 near Cordes Junction, 65 miles north of Phoenix. A curious experiment in urban architecture that, if ever finished, might house several thousand souls.

Biosphere 2: Another curious experiment, this one near Tucson. Huge, enclosed ecological system created to study various environments—all under glass. Some scientists got together inside when it started up and tried to live there. Didn't work. Eventually, its operation was taken over by Columbia University, but the school backed out of that in 2003, and its unknown future is just that—in the unknown future. In teen argot, it's still a cool place.

Canyon de Chelly: Tucked into the Navajo Reservation, this beautiful canyon features spectacular cliff walls and prehistoric Indian ruins.

Casa Grande Ruins National Monument: An amazing, four-story Hohokam structure, now protected from the weather by a canopy. Might have been an ancient astronomical observatory. Somewhat near, but not in, the city of the same name.

Glen Canyon National Recreation Area: Home to Lake Powell, a massive, scenic wonder created by mankind's construction of the Glen Canyon Dam. One of its visitor centers, the Carl Hayden center just outside of the town of Page, offers awesome views of the huge dam that killed much of Glen Canyon and that is said by some to have provoked the modern environmental movement.

[At Walnut Canyon National Monument, one of the ruins peeks out from the cliff face. ▲]

Grand Canyon: One of the world's greatest natural wonders, largely created by Colorado River erosion and flash floods over thousands of years. You can hike into it, ride a mule in and out, camp, or rent accommodations. Or you can simply look down and across from multiple vista points. There are six lodges on the South Rim, but accommodations are more sparse on the North Rim, which is 10 miles from the South Rim as the eagle flies or 215 miles as the SUV drives.

Hubbell Trading Post National Historic Site: Oldest continuously operating trading post on the Navajo Reservation. Astonishing collection of genuine, hand-woven Indian rugs for sale. Near the town of Ganado.

Kartchner Caverns: Immense limestone cave 50 miles southeast of Tucson. Remarkable structures inside, and the cave is still growing.

Kitt Peak: A national observatory atop a mountain 90 minutes of driving from Tucson. Features clear sky and what is said to be the world's largest group of optical astronomical telescopes.

Lake Mead National Recreation Area: Big lake and 1.5 million acres of wonderful wilderness in northwestern Arizona and southern Nevada.

Montezuma Castle National Monument and Montezuma Well: In the beautiful Verde Valley north of Phoenix is this Sinagua dwelling of five stories and 20 rooms tucked into a limestone recess above a creek. The Aztec emperor had nothing to do with it. Montezuma Well, several miles away, is a limestone sink formed when a cavern collapsed. The constantly replenished water was used by Hohokam and Sinagua people for irrigation.

Navajo National Monument: Outstanding Ancestral Puebloan (or Anasazi) community ruins, such as Betatakin and Keet Seel, can be found in this monument area on the Navajo Reservation in the northeastern part of the state.

Organ Pipe Cactus National Monument: This vast assortment of Sonoran Desert cacti and other plants, plus six varieties of rattlesnakes, can be seen in utterly natural settings west of Tucson. The monument covers more than 330,000 acres, most of it wilderness. Monster organ pipe cactus, saguaros, and elephant trees abound.

Petrified Forest National Park: Near Holbrook. Said to have the world's largest collection of petrified wood plus the colorful badlands of the Painted Desert. The park covers nearly 100,000 acres. Leave the wood alone. It's the law.

Phelps Dodge Morenci Open Pit Copper Mine: To the far northeast of Tucson is this 3-mile rim-to-rim mine, a massive hole created by man digging for copper.

Picacho Peak: Distinctive small peak in a tiny range just a short distance northwest of Tucson. It was the site of the westernmost battle of the Civil War.

Pipe Spring National Monument: This oasis with four springs was home to Mormons who settled there and created a ranching operation. The main house is a virtual fort with high walls and gun ports.

Saguaro National Park: The ultimate in viewing for fans of the saguaro, the state's largest cactus species. About 15 miles outside Tucson.

Sunset Crater: A volcano that blew up in 1065 and covered the region with black cinders. Near Wupatki National Monument (Sinagua), equally attractive because of its four ancient pueblos and its proximity to more volcanoes and ruins.

Tonto National Monument: Cliff dwellings of the prehistoric Salado people. As good as ruins get.

Tumacacori National Historical Park: Site of Jesuit missions dating to the late 1600. In the center of the mission is a Franciscan church built in the early 1800s. Has a traditional high mass in April and October and a marvelous Christmas fiesta. Near Tubac between Nogales and Tucson.

Tuzigoot National Monument: Another ruin, this one built around 1100 A.D. by the Sinagua people. Near Clarkdale.

Walnut Canyon: Yes, still another Sinagua ruin, this one near Flagstaff and very big. Involves a somewhat-strenuous climb in the canyon that has more than a score of cliff-dwelling homes. It's a 200-foot climb down and again up, all at 7,000 feet of altitude.

Yuma Territorial Prison: A lot of very bad men and women were incarcerated in this hellhole. Best appreciated for its gothic nature if seen on a sunny day in July or August. Small but excellent museum adjoins.

Chuck Lawsen

Sunset Crater's cinder cone rose to its height of 1,000 feet with the volcano's last major eruption in 1180.

Kerrick James

Not To Miss

Bisbee: Historic mining town in the Tucson region featuring endless fascinations including an excellent mining museum, a mine tour, and shops and shops and shops.

Hopi Mesas: Home of the Hopi tribe, smack dab in the middle of the Navajo Nation. Renowned for its splendid artists and craftsmen.

Jerome: Old mining town and artists community clutching the side of a mountain in the Flagstaff-Sedona region.

Lake Havasu City: London Bridge, or much of it, moved to this western border town in the Yuma-Lower Colorado River region. Brought here, piece by piece, from the Thames River and cost $2.5 million to do so.

Nogales: In southern Arizona, the twin to its sister city just across the border in Mexico, where there's shopping and margaritas.

Oatman: Old mining community southwest of Kingman and known for the free-roaming wild burros, the progeny of beasts of burden abandoned long ago by miners. The burros now prowl the streets looking for and getting handouts, mostly carrots purchased by tourists. They can be cantankerous–both the burros and the tourists, not the carrots.

Page: Clean northern town that owes its existence to the creation of Lake Powell, which it adjoins. DO NOT miss seeing and hiking the short and spectacular Antelope Canyon (upper and lower) not far out of town.

Prescott: Another community full of history and, once upon a time, saloons. Good college town with many cultural advantages. Lovely town square.

Quartzsite: Tiny town north of Yuma that balloons into what surely is the world's largest collection of RV dwellers—and dealers—in January. Acres upon acres of parked recreation vehicles containing visitors with a passion

[English-themed shops line the shore at Lake Havasu City. ▲   ]

for rock and mineral shows and wandering through acres of flea markets.

Sedona: Dramatic red rocks and oodles of fancy shopping, fancy restaurants, fancy artists, and crystal gazers. Bring money.

Summerhaven: A little community atop cool Mount Lemmon rising above a hot desert and Tucson below. A delightful place to stop for a beer and view.

Tombstone: Site of the O.K. Corral shootout involving the Earps. Need more be said?

Tubac: Near Tucson. First permanent white settlement (1752) in what is now Arizona. Once a bastion for those under Indian attack, now a tiny version of Sedona with more art galleries and shops than you comfortably can fit into a day's touring.

Window Rock: Headquarters of the sprawling Navajo Nation on the east side of the state and home to a remarkable rock with a big hole (window) in it.

Tubac Presidio State Historic Park's "living history" program explores the region's diverse roots. ▼ Snow dusts the San Francisco Peaks and the Lomaki Ruin at Wupatki National Monument. ▶

Randy Prentice

Our Hot and Cool Sides

T raveling in southern Arizona and need to temporarily lose five pounds so you can fit in those suit pants for tonight's fancy how-de-do in the hotel ballroom? Here's how . . . guaranteed. Find the nearest par-3 golf course, play nine holes in 107 degrees (if you stop sweating, quit instantly and get medical help), then find the scales in the hotel gym. Bingo. Five (at least) pounds in plenty of time to enjoy the air-conditioned cool of the ballroom or, for that matter, your bedroom, your bathroom, the bar, the gym, even the broom closet should you wish to hide from your companion or the house detective.

Now let's get real. Almost single-handedly, some would argue, air-conditioning accounts for Arizona's skyrocketing population growth. Yeah, well, there's also lots of great land, wonderful vistas, big mountains, beautiful desert, casual people, big money to be made, but it is undeniable that it was air conditioning that made it all comfortable and, therefore, even more desirable.

Basically, there are two kinds of A/C: The standard air conditioner known as refrigeration and evaporative cooling, called swamp cooling or a swamp box. Virtually everyone knows about standard air conditioners, whether giant machines

Robert G. McDonald

in big structures or small ones stuck in windows of apartments. Because they duct warmer air across a cold, heat-absorbing refrigeration apparatus and send the cool air back into the space to be cooled, they work even in high humidity. Evaporative cooling, on the other hand, barely works when humidity is thick as gravy. In dry, hot air, however, it's another matter, and you can guess what kind of air blows around the desert.

In days of yore, there were several non-evaporative ways to escape the worst of the late spring, all summer, and early fall heat of the desert. Among them: 1) Get in the shade and stay there. 2) If moderately wealthy, drive your loved ones to the top of the nearest mountain and leave them to camp out in a cabin until you could join them on the weekend. 3) Move to Fairbanks, Alaska, in late May and stay there until late October. Alternatively, as the Indians—veterans of living in the desert—knew, you could pour water on your head and let the dry wind cool you; or, you could soak a blanket in water and hang it up in the ramada so the breeze blew through the blanket and onto your face and body. Those last two are evaporative cooling. As the water evaporates, it cools the air and you. Simple and cheap. The problem is that you or the blanket have to stay wet.

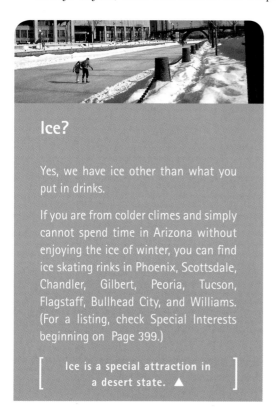

Ice?

Yes, we have ice other than what you put in drinks.

If you are from colder climes and simply cannot spend time in Arizona without enjoying the ice of winter, you can find ice skating rinks in Phoenix, Scottsdale, Chandler, Gilbert, Peoria, Tucson, Flagstaff, Bullhead City, and Williams. (For a listing, check Special Interests beginning on Page 399.)

[Ice is a special attraction in a desert state. ▲]

The answer, purportedly first proposed in 1934 by inventor A.J. Eddy, a resident of boiling-hot Yuma: Build (buy, these days) an evaporative, or swamp, cooler equipped with delightful-smelling, old-fashioned straw or aspen pads or the more modern ones made of artificial materials. Add a pump, a fan, a bunch of tubes and some other doodads and stick it on your roof. Then duct it into the residence, pump water into the pads, let in fall through the pads to a tray below and be recirculated. Meanwhile turn on the cooler's fan so it blows air through the water-soaked pads and into the house. Sit back and watch the temperature drop 10 to even 20 degrees. It requires a little cheap water and very little expensive electricity, and it remains in extensive use today, particularly in homes, less so in commercial establishments. One other advantage is that it is possible, even necessary, to leave your doors and/or windows cracked open instead of claustrophobically closed, the latter condition a cost-saving requirement for refrigeration.

As to Arizona weather in general:

In short, there is snow in the north and at the higher elevations and heat in the south and west. In winter, count on snow in the White Mountains and in Flagstaff and farther north but think about having Christmas dinner on a blanket outdoors at midday in Tucson or Yuma. In summer, you will get all the Vitamin D and too much of a sunburn just about anywhere but particularly to the south, the east, and the west of far northern Phoenix. If you must have a holiday picnic on July 4 and prefer that your frankfurters cool off after the grill, head north—far north. Or find a big, shady ramada and pack a 5-gallon container of water.

Rain? Not much but most of it comes during what are appropriately but meteorologically inaccurately called monsoon seasons. There are two of them. One is in summer, roughly between July and September, that brings brief but intense storms that begin in the Gulf of Mexico. The other is in winter, roughly between December and March, that produces longer-lasting but gentler storms that originate in the Pacific ocean. The monsoon seasons bring with them life-saving rain but life-threatening floods in the arroyos and spectacular but lethal lightning in the skies. It's one of the few states where a rainy, cloudy day makes people happy.

Rainfall in some areas such as Phoenix ranges from 7 to 16 inches annually, considerably less than that in others. Sun? Lots of it, averaging 221 days a year of mostly cloudless sky. Some years it seems more like 360. ⫴

[The lift at Arizona Snowbowl carries skiers up the San Francisco Peaks.   ]

A Word on Shopping

1 n this chapter we have discussed some trivial topics such as our ancestors, our history, our geology, our weather, things like that. Now let us briefly take up what really matters: SHOPPING.

Obviously, it can be done anywhere in the state. Phoenix or Tucson? Of course. These are big cities with all the usual quality and discount stores and malls, art galleries, and museum shops that can be found in any such metropolitan area. Small places? Yes, those, too, in small towns and settlements. And even in make-shift stands at stopping points all over Indian reservations with some beautiful, handcrafted work arranged on blankets. For the true shop-'til-you-droppers, the do-not-miss spots are:

Nogales, Sonora, Mexico: Just across the border below Tucson. Bargains, bargains, bargains. But do not hesitate to ... bargain over price. Rugs, booze, jewelry, hats, belts, purses, carvings, glassware, chessboards and pieces. On and on. But haggling is part of the ritual, so memorize this statement to be said after hearing the first price offering:

"It's very nice work, but I really don't want to afford that price. Thank you very much."

Arizona Office of Tourism

Arizona Office of Tourism

Kokopelli's Many Traits

Almost anywhere you shop, in posh and poufy places or cluttered curio stands, you will find Kokopelli. He comes to you in statuary, wall hangings, metal sculptures, pins, tie clasps, bracelets, necklaces, and earrings, and on T-shirts, sweatshirts, and bathing suits, whatever.

Kokopelli is a mythic figure known to many Indian tribes. He is generally depicted as a humpbacked flute player (or a guy carrying a primitive backpack full of seeds).

Depending upon which fiction or non-fiction book or which anthropologist or novelist you read, he also is: A rain priest, a snow melter, a trader, a planter of crops, a minstrel, a magician, a trickster, an entertainer, a bird owner, a bringer of prosperity, and most entrancing of all, a stud who is invited to unfailingly impregnate women of whatever tribe he is visiting.

You can't miss him. But remember, to many people he is a revered figure whose likeness doesn't belong on bric-a-brac.

> Shopping includes "in" spots and places that carry Southwestern items like re-creations of the mythical Kokopelli.

Then slowly turn and begin to slowly stroll away. More often than not (the exceptions usually are the fancier stores, some of which even have signs stating that prices are final), a new, lower offer will be announced. Now the real haggling begins. What started at, say, $130, eventually will drop to, perhaps, $75. Or less. It's fun, and it is expected. Lots of junk including gaudy paintings on black velvet, but much of it is good junk. Everybody speaks English, and dollars are just as good as pesos.

Flagstaff: Lots of shops including a small but excellent gift shop at the Museum of Northern Arizona.

Tubac: Tiny, historic little community between Tucson and Nogales. Quality stuff. Heavy on art.

Sedona: Again, quality. Bring money.

Scottsdale: Phoenix area. See Tubac and Sedona.

Hubbell Trading Post: Rugs. Handmade. Hand-dyed. Genuine. Bring even more money.

Keams Canyon Trading Post (McGee's Indian Art Gallery) on the Hopi Reservation: Good place to buy a kachina from an experienced dealer.

The Arizona Office of Tourism has put together handy shopping primers on its Internet Web site: www.arizonaguide.com/section.aspx?sid=20

Some words of caution about two of the most popular items: Turquoise and Indian rugs.

Patronize trusted and knowledgeable dealers. According to one expert estimate, only about 5 percent of turquoise on the market is natural. That means it is not changed in any way except for shape. The rest can be plastic, waxed, dyed, ground up and mixed with glue or stabilized with a bonding element to increase its color and durability. Get a statement in writing from a reputable dealer. Stabilized turquoise is OK, but be sure you know that is what you are getting. As

Arizona Office of Tourism

[Flagstaff shopping takes you through a part of the town with the look
that it had a century ago.]

Arizona Office of Tourism

for rugs, a genuine, 4-by-6-foot new rug that could have taken months to weave might cost several thousand dollars. A large, old rug, in excellent condition, could run into many, many thousands of dollars. If it is genuine you want, stick with a recommended, reputable dealer-expert. Or you can get a cheap imitation in Nogales that will fool most of your friends, and it won't matter much if the moths like it too.

Less risky than turquoise and rugs is silver jewelry. Your own good judgment should suffice in most cases when buying that precious metal. Copper ornamentation such as a bracelet is commonplace and does not cost enough to worry about. Western art (paintings) is available everywhere and in an astonishing variety of quality and price. Unless you are contemplating your purchase as an investment as well as an aesthetic pleasure, let your personal taste and your pocketbook be the guides. ⧫

Where To Go
What To See
What To Do

These listings include governmental and other agencies that provide statewide information to assist travelers and tourists. Listings for chambers of commerce and tourist agencies for individual cities and areas can be found in the "Where To Go" sections in chapters covering the state's nine regions. The listings include the U.S. Forest Service, Bureau of Land Management, and the National Park Service.

Information

Arizona Office of Tourism: Features an events calendar, descriptions of regions and cities, and links to Internet sites with travel and tourist information. The calendar allows you to search by date, region, or city for events involving festivals, celebrations, nature and adventure, shopping and entertainment, culture and heritage, resorts and ranches, and golf and sports. 1110 W. Washington, Suite 155, Phoenix. (866) 275-5816. www.arizonaguide.com

Arizona Department of Transportation: ADOT provides information on road closures, construction delays, and other travel conditions 24/7. To access recorded information, call 511 (within Arizona only); or connect with www.AZ511.com

National Weather Service: Weather conditions, forecasts, the times for sunrises and sunsets, and other information are available online (www.wrh.noaa.gov/psr); or by calling an area office, including one based in Las Vegas, Nevada, that includes northwestern Arizona: Phoenix area, (602) 275-0073; Tucson, (520) 881-3333; Flagstaff, (928) 774-3303; Lake Mead, Lake Mohave, Lake Havasu City, and Kingman, (702) 263-9744.

Arizona State Parks: The state operates 29 parks and natural areas. Each facility focuses on recreation or historical preservation. 1300 W. Washington, Phoenix. (602) 542-4174. www.pr.state.az.us

Arizona Game and Fish Department: Information about hunting and fishing regulations, conservation, wildlife areas, off-highway vehicles, boating, and watchable wildlife. 2221 W. Greenway Road, Phoenix. (602) 942-3000. www.gf.state.az.us

[Lake Pleasant, north of Phoenix, catches the last rays of sunset.   ]

Arizona Indian Gaming Association: Information about Indian gaming in Arizona and links to each nation. (602) 307-1570. www.azindiangaming.org

Arizona Department of Commerce: Online community profiles and other information at http://new.azcommerce.com. Put cursor on "Site Selection" to open a drop-down window for choices.

***Arizona Highways*:** The award-winning travel magazine's Internet site (www.arizonahighways.com) features articles, photographs, trip planners, links to Arizona topics, and other information. Copies of the magazine, books, calendars, and other products with an Arizona flavor can be purchased online; by calling toll-free (800) 543-5432; by calling (602) 712-2200 within Arizona; and from the magazine's gift shops at 2039 W. Lewis Ave., Phoenix, and in Terminal 4 at Sky Harbor International Airport.

U.S. Public Lands

Public Lands Information Center: The center serves as a central source of information on lands and facilities managed by governmental agencies. (877) 851-8946 or (505) 345-9498. www.publiclands.org

Apache-Sitgreaves National Forests: Sprawls over 2 million acres and is noted for being at high elevations (9,100 feet at some camping areas), and for its 24 lakes and 450 miles of streams. This splendid country in east-central Arizona was named for a Capt. Lorenzo Sitgreaves, a government topographical engineer who conducted an expedition across the state in the early 1850s, and for the Apache people. Headquartered in Springerville. (928) 333-4301. www.fs.fed.us/r3/asnf

Coconino National Forest: Covering 1.8 million acres, the forest is part of the world's largest contiguous stand of ponderosa pines. It's diverse terrain ranges from Sedona's famous red rocks and vortices to alpine tundra and the state's biggest ski hill. Headquarters: 1824 S. Thompson St., Flagstaff. (928) 527-3600. www.fs.fed.us/r3/coconino

Coronado National Forest: Totals nearly 1.8 million acres in southeastern Arizona and 69,000 acres in southwestern New Mexico and can brag about its 12 so-called sky islands, huge mountain ranges and peaks jutting out of the low desert floor. It is smack dab in the Sonoran Desert, the most gorgeous of the deserts in the view of some, but the forest elevations range up to nearly 11,000 feet and down to 3,000. Headquarters: 300 W. Congress St., Tucson. (520) 388-8300. www.fs.fed.us/r3/coronado

Kaibab National Forest: The Grand Canyon, Arizona's top attraction, splits the 1.6 million acres of northern and southern sections of this forest. For the record, it is pronounced KI-bab (rhymes with sky-bab). It boasts a rare squirrel of the same name and found only there. Headquarters: 800 S. 6th St., Williams. (928) 635-8200. www.fs.fed.us/r3/kai

Prescott National Forest: Covers 1.25 million acres in central Arizona and includes eight wilderness areas including the striking Granite Mountain Wilderness outside of Prescott. It borders three other national forests—Kaibab, Coconino and Tonto—with half of it west of Prescott in four mountain ranges and other half east of Prescott and including the headwaters of the Verde River. At its lowest elevations, it boasts Sonoran Desert vegetation. Headquarters: 344 S. Cortez St., Prescott. (928) 443-8000. www.fs.fed.us/r3/prescott

Tonto National Forest: Offers 2.8 million acres (fifth-largest forest in the nation) north of Phoenix, cool temperatures (cooler than Phoenix, at least) during summer's heat and abuts the Mogollon Rim. It was the home ground for author Zane Grey. It offers remarkable recreational opportunities and, partly for that reason, it is one of the most-visited forests in the United States with about 5.8 million visitors annually. Headquarters: 2324 E. McDowell Road., Phoenix. (602) 225-5200. www.fs.fed.us/r3/tonto

Bureau of Land Management: The BLM manages 12.2 million surface acres of public lands in Arizona. The agency has several field offices providing recreational information.. The state office is at One N. Central Avenue, Phoenix. (602) 417-9200. www.blm.gov/az
Listings for BLM field and similar offices follow:

Arizona Strip Field Office: Covers the area north of the Grand Canyon, including the Grand Canyon-Parashant National Monument. (435) 688-3200. www.blm.gov/az/azso.htm

[Backlit saguaro cacti march over Mazatzal Mountains slopes.]

Robert G. McDonald

Kingman Field Office: Northwest Arizona. (928) 718-3700. www.blm.gov/az/kfo/index.htm

Lake Havasu Field Office: Western Arizona. (928) 505-1200. www.blm.gov/az/lhfo/index.htm

Yuma Field Office: Southwestern Arizona. (928) 317-3200. www.blm.gov/az/yfo/index.htm

Tucson Field Office: Southern Arizona. (520) 258-7200. www.blm.gov/az/tfo/index.htm

Safford Field Office: Southeastern Arizona. (928) 348-4400. www.blm.gov/az/sfo/index.htm

San Pedro Project Office: Southeastern Arizona. (520) 439-6400.

Lower Sonoran and Hassayampa field offices: Central Arizona. (623) 580-5500. www.blm.gov/az/pfo/index.htm

National Parks Service: See individual listings in "Where To Go" sections throughout the book. www.nps.gov

Permits and Reservations

Golden Eagle Passport: This is an annual ticket for the pass owner and accompanying passengers in a private vehicle to enter most facilities and sites operated by the Bureau of Land Management, Fish & Wildlife Service, Forest Service, and National Park Service. The Golden Eagle does not cover fees for camping, boat launching, nor concessionaires' charges. It can be purchased at entry gates and visitors centers or online: www.publiclands.org/recpermits/recpermits.php?plicstate=AZ www.natlforests.org/partnership_goldpass.html

Day-use Passes: Areas such as red rock country (Sedona area) in the Coconino National Forest and the Santa Catalina area (Tucson) of the Coronado National Forest require passes for functions such as parking, hiking, and picnicking. They are available at Forest Service rangers stations or online at the Internet sites operated by each forest. They also are available at the Public Lands Internet site.

Reservations: The National Recreation Reservation Service handles reservations for campgrounds and other outdoor recreation facilities and activities for the Forest Service, Army Corps of Engineers, National Park Service, Bureau of Land Management, and Bureau of Reclamation. (877) 444-6777 (toll free); (877) 833-6777 (TDD); (518) 885-3639 (international). www.ReserveUSA.com. The National Park Service offers reservations at http://reservations.nps.gov

Over Phoenix, sunset infuses a summer monsoon cloud with bright hues. ▲
The Phoenix skyline stands out against sunset's glow. ▶

Phoenix and Central Arizona

Valley of the Sun and Beyond

Stretching over a day's worth of miles and eras' worth of time, this chapter focuses on the hub of metropolitan Phoenix and extends to places with the flavors of prehistoric, Old West, and modern-day cultures. Here, you can luxuriate in resort comfort, enjoy the outdoors within an urban confine, and visit attractions focusing on just about any interest you may have – beads, collectibles, and antiques; mines and railroads; Western, Indian, and modern art; professional and collegiate sports; plants of the desert and birdwatching; great architecture; and so much more. Besides Phoenix and its attached cities and communities, this chapter covers towns and places like Wickenburg and the nearby Vulture Mine; the Pioneer Arizona Living History Museum with displays and re-creations; Tortilla Flat along the Apache Trail; Globe, Miami, and Superior in mining country; and two drives steeped in scenry and history.

George Stocking

Chuck Lawsen

Phoenix: Urban, Urbane, and Outdoorsy

P hoenix. Ah, Phoenix. The real West.

Well, yes. In spots, but this shore isn't no cow town nowadays, although you are likely to spot a lot of genuine hombres in roughout cowboy boots (dudes prefer snakeskin and the gals tend toward boots with multi-color, floral sidewalls). As any one of the nation's other major population enters—New York, Chicago, Dallas, or, especially, Los Angeles—the sprawling metropolitan area of Phoenix is a splendid example of modernity and, more significantly, synergism: The total effect of this vast complex that dominates the entire state, as well as central Arizona, is greater than merely adding up its parts.

Speaking of L.A., residents of that city and its cosseted suburbs might notice that in Phoenix, unlike their hometown, not every other vehicle is a Lexus. Phoenix prefers chromed and pampered Ford 150s with crew cabs and 4WD. Two western cities, two cultures.

[Brittlebush blossoms add color to the Hedgepeth Foothills at Thunderbird Park.]

Chuck Lawsen

Although Phoenix is smack dab in the middle of a desert, that does not mean you'll be struggling through sand in your flip flops, searching for the nearest waterhole. (Come to think of it, Phoenix does offer plenty of golfing in and out of some coarser, yellowish sand traps, and there are plenty of waterholes, some lovely, some lowdown.)

The fact is that there is so much to admire and enjoy inside this pulsing Big City and along its wide, clean, downtown streets designed in an easy-to-master grid. And you always have the option of driving 15 to 30 minutes to a trailhead where you can hike or ride a mountain bike or a horse through some beautiful, saguaro-festooned desert mountains and return to a restful massage and a soak in an herbal tub at one of the many spas in the area. Or if it's water you want, a slightly longer drive will take you to any number of fine, fish-filled lakes or streams.

When you say Phoenix, you are not merely describing the city proper, a sun-

Kerrick James

[Spring training in the Cactus League. ▲ A family enjoys the terrain
and a light show while hiking in Carefree. ▼]

Don B. Stevenson

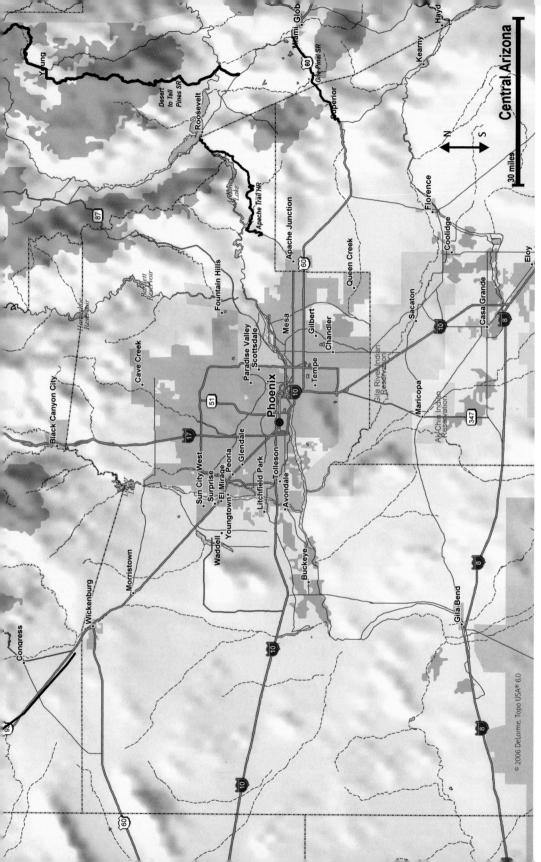

Central Arizona

N

S

30 miles

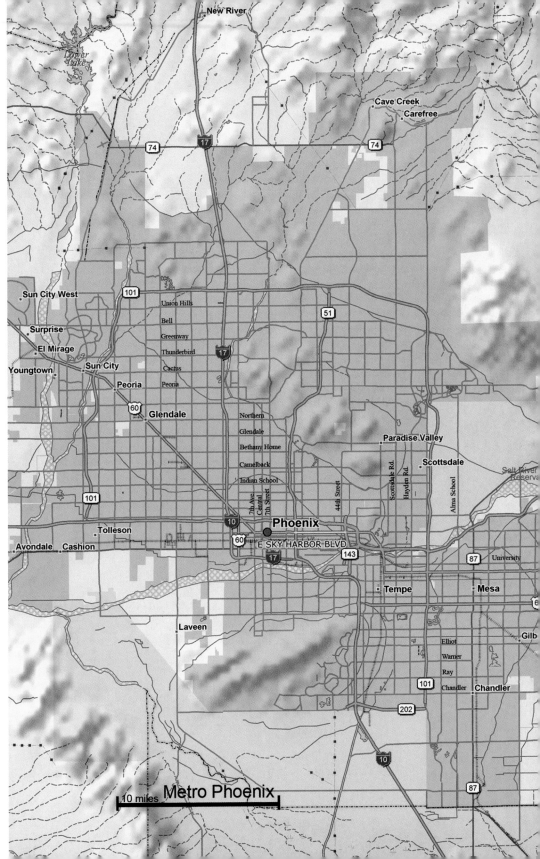

David H. Smith

[Shopping in Glendale includes about 70 antique shops and specialty stores.]

drenched, sweating, air-conditioned, multi-lingual, multi-ethnic, traffic-jammed, civilized, sophisticated, raw community of some 1.5 million humans living on 450 square miles and accompanied by uncounted numbers of dogs, cats, horses, and even an occasional irreverent rooster who refuses to yield to the cry of the city for reasonable silence during the very early morning hours.

Nosiree. You also are saying Maricopa County with something on the order of 3.5 million people living in communities of varying size, significance, and attractiveness. Just to mention a few of them, they include:

Wickenburg: Here or near here you'll find the Desert Caballeros Western Museum, the Del E. Webb Center for the Performing Arts, a nature park, old mines that you can tour, and one end of the Joshua Forest Scenic Parkway.

Sun City and Sun City West: Everyone has heard of these, the essence of retirement communities. Northwest of Phoenix off the interstate. Countless shopping malls, golf courses, and entertainment facilities tailored to the retired. Lots of square dancing for those who care and plenty of Pilates or yoga classes for sagging abs, stiffening spines, and weakening knees. Heavy traffic in all-purpose electric golf carts and lots of respectable, middle-to-upper-middle-class homes that look a lot like the other respectable middle-to-upper-middle-class homes in

Richard Maack

The Sublime

If you've got the money, honey, Phoenix has the sublime.

This book in not in the business of recommending specific restaurants or lodging, but the historic and fabled Biltmore hotel is worth singling out because it was Phoenix's first resort and because it remains a fine example of the many luxury spas and resort accommodations available to those who are not on a nickel and dime (or even dollar) budget.

Located at 2400 E. Missouri (within walking distance of the fancy shopping center called the Biltmore Fashion Park at Camelback and 24th Street), this renowned hotel, known for its beauty and excellent service, was crowned the "Jewel of the Desert" when it opened in 1929 with the help of a consulting architect you might have heard of, Frank Lloyd Wright. Over the decades, it was the honeymoon hotel for countless famous couples including Clark Gable and Carole Lombard (he lost his wedding ring on the golf course but it was found by a concierge who returned it) and Ronald and Nancy Reagan.

A year after it opened, it was purchased by William Wrigley Jr., a Chicagoan who made a big wad of money by persuading people to chew gum, spit, and play baseball. The Wrigley family owned the venture for next 43 years. They also built an adjacent mansion that now can be toured.

Just a small sampling of what it offers: A 39,000-square-foot conference center, historic cottages, 738 guest rooms, world-class restaurants, a pool complex with a 92-foot-long water slide and 213 cabanas, an 18-hole putting course, a 22,000-square-foot spa and fitness center offering everything from Pilates to power yoga, a gigantic ballroom, and immaculately groomed grounds.

Ranking right up there with the Biltmore for size and luxury is the J.W. Marriott Desert Ridge Resort & Spa at 5350 E. Marriott Drive, a complex on nearly 320 acres with 869 rooms and 81 suites. There are at least a dozen others in the same general class and any one of them would satisfy even the most sybaritic traveler.

The Arizona Office of Tourism maintains a comprehensive, statewide list of accommodations. (See Where To Go beginning on Page 80.)

[**The Biltmore was Phoenix's first resort.** ▲   ]

the same nice and clean block and in the adjoining nice and clean block. Most of them occupied by reasonably comfortable seniors who like the abundance of stock brokerages, medical clinics, and assisted care facilities just a block or two away and the relative absence of anyone under 55 years or so.

Sun City opened in 1960 with deed restrictions that require at least one resident of each household to be at least 55. It sprawls over nearly 9,000 acres, 1,200 of them comprising golf courses. Another chunk is occupied by 350 clubs and civic organizations plus seven recreation centers. The annual income of its residents has been estimated to total about a billion dollars, much of that in the form of investment returns and Social Security. The population is nearly 45,000.

Sun City West opened in 1978 about two miles away from the original Sun City and offers roughly the same features, although slightly fewer residents.

Carefree/Cave Creek: Sister communities of roughly 8,000 people 15 miles northeast of Phoenix and tucked into the foothills among spectacular scenery, particularly huge granite boulders that provide the foundations for many beautiful, architecturally astonishing homes. There is a re-creation of an old western town and a fine museum, ample shopping, nearby lakes, and scenic drives. Well worth the traveler's time, but to see the many big, creative homes, get off the main road onto the side roads leading to and through the residential sections.

Peoria: Settled in the 1880s by families from, duh, Peoria, Illinois, this city began booming with the creation of nearby Sun City in the 1960s and now boasts a population of nearly 130,000.

Fountain Hills: A smallish (about 22,000 population) planned community nearly 20 miles northeast of Phoenix and notable for what is claimed to be the world's tallest, man-made, continuously running fountain.

Glendale: More than a quarter-million people live in this city that borders Phoenix on the northwest. It was established in 1892 and is a commercial and industrial hub, but also a historic one that has been dubbed "Arizona's Antique Capital" with more than 70 antique and specialty shops, many of them packed into its Catlin Court Historic District. It also offers more than 60 parks and five golf courses.

Scottsdale: Lots of art galleries, heavy on the Western and Southwestern landscape theme, and lots of capital gains. Arizona's version of Santa Fe in New Mexico, but much bigger, hitting close to 225,000 population. Same level of urbanity and sophistication, however, and home to Frank Lloyd Wright's Taliesin West, as well as to first-class shopping in first-class malls.

Mesa: Whoo boy, hard to call a community of nearly a half-million people a suburb, but that is what it is. It was founded in 1878, but nobody in those days imagined the impact of modern commerce, namely aerospace, aviation, agribusiness, electronics, manufacturing, business services, etc. There is now a ballet, a symphony, chorale groups, a Shakespearean company, an arts center, an aquatics center, 20 golf courses, and 55 parks. That list of attractions does not include the nearby lakes, and, in the Usery Mountain Regional Park and the Lost Dutchman State Park, the huge number of hiking trails and camping facilities.

Tempe: Roughly in the center of the metro area and bordered by the other big population centers of Phoenix on the west, Scottsdale to the north, Mesa on the east, and Chandler on the south. Tempe, with 160,000 or more residents, is home to Arizona State University, a highly respected research and educational institution with more than 44,000 students. A good place to go for entertainment, including an annual spring and fall Festival of the Arts.

Chandler: How can you beat a town that is home to an ostrich race and ostrich festival in March? Not only that, it is home to a world-class hotel, the San Marcos, built in 1913; a top-notch museum dedicated to farming, Indians, and early

Richard Maack

Southwestern Cultures

Chances are you are part of the herd that has heard of the Heard, famous for its permanent collection of 75,000 or more objects that represent the cultures of the Southwest from prehistory to today. It offers a Hohokam pit house, Pima basketry, Mogollon, Salado and Sinagua pottery, kachinas galore, and more and more and more. It was founded by a prominent couple, Dwight and Maie Heard, who came to Phoenix in 1895. It opened in 1929. You can find it at 2301 N. Central Ave. in the heart of central Phoenix just north of McDowell Road.

When you go there, you will find a big, sprawling but utterly charming, unostentatious grouping of low-lying, white, tile-roofed, southwestern-style architecture fronted by a delightful, sculpture-filled courtyard, which, in turn, is fronted by a green lawn. The gift shop is full of eye candy, expensive eye candy.

[The Heard's architecture is as distinguished as its collections. ▲]

Arizona; a railway museum; and lots of shops offering Western antiques. It also is home to nearly 200,000 people, many of them employed by high-tech industries such as Motorola and Intel.

Apache Junction: Although this town of about 35,000 people is in adjoining Pinal County rather than Maricopa, it is only 30-odd miles from Phoenix and is the gateway to the impressive Superstition Mountains (Lost Dutchman Mine, maybe) and the remarkably scenic mountain drive called the Apache Trail. If strip malls are to your taste, so is Apache Junction.

And that doesn't include other communities such as El Mirage, Youngtown,

Litchfield Park, Avondale, Gilbert, Paradise Valley, and still more, but you get the idea.

Anything and everything one might ever want or need is available here in the metro area, some for free and some quite costly. Just in the city of Phoenix alone, there are, by one recent tally, 20,000 hotel and motel rooms (55,000 in the 9,200-square-mile metro Maricopa County area), the fifth-busiest airport in the world (Sky Harbor with service to 108 domestic and international destinations on 1,300 daily flights), 47 art galleries, 11 libraries, 16 museums, 138 parks, more than 1,200 clubs and organizations, a symphony hall that seats 2,500 people, opera and ballet companies, dozens of golf courses stretching for 18 holes in all directions, and all the big league professional sports including the Diamondbacks (MLB), the Cardinals (NFL), the Suns (NBA), the Coyotes (NHL), and the Mercury (WNBA).

[**Chase Field plays host to the Arizona Diamondbacks' home baseball games.**]

David H Smith

For would-be residents, the living choices are endless: mobile home parks, elaborate and expensive gated neighborhoods, solid middle-class subdivisions, struggling barrios. For visitors, in addition to the thousands upon thousands of motel rooms, there are luxury hotels and pricey spas, B&Bs, and park-your-RV or pitch-your-tent communities. Wherever you go, even to the home of old friends from "back East," you are bound to find a swimming pool and, not far away, a sign urging everyone to conserve water. Counter-intuitive? Should be banned? Absolutely, but this is still the Wild West, the wellspring of rugged individualism—at least a vestige of same.

The city of Santa Fe in New Mexico is called the "City Different." Seattle is the "Emerald City." Phoenix is the heart of the "Valley of the Sun," so named for good reason. For one, it is in a valley, one with splendid mountain ranges in any direction. For another, it gets sun. The average daily high temperature in January is a pleasant 66 degrees, but it starts climbing until it reaches 105 in July. And that's just the average high. The residents don't complain until they have endured two weeks of 110 degrees or higher. It happens all the time. Rain? On average, 8 inches a year, but probably less during the past several years of drought. Snow? Oh, please. Expecting to see a snowball in Hell has a greater chance of realization.

For history fans, a brief synopsis of Phoenix: This fifth-largest city in the United States, and the state's capital, was founded in 1867 and incorporated in 1881. The founder was Jack Swilling, who created a canal company that diverted irrigation water from the Salt River. The population ballooned during WWII when the military began building airfields in the area and defense companies followed.

Angela Reaburn

'Lost' Hopi Art

Seven decades passed before the bronze *Hopi Flute Player*, designed by Hopi artist Emry Kopta (1884-1953), was cast into sculptural life. Today the flutist silently plays amid the serene fountain courtyard of the Arizona State University Music Building in Tempe.

Commissioned in 1933, the artwork languished until 2003 for lack of funding. It was designed for the Public Works of Art Project initiated by President Franklin D. Roosevelt. Kopta's original plaster model was digitally enlarged, cast by Arizona Bronze of Tempe, and placed—finally—in the courtyard in accordance with the wishes of the Hopi Tribe.

[The *Hopi Flute Player* emerged from obscurity. ▲]

It is called Phoenix after the mythic Egyptian bird that symbolizes rebirth and rising from the ashes, an acknowledgement by the English adventurer and scholar Darrel Duppa, who gave the city its name, that it was rising on the ruins of a prehistoric Indian culture called Hohokam.

And rise it did. In its first two decades, it grew so big that it took over from Prescott as the Territory's capital and remains the state capital today. Its astonishing growth was made possible largely after a large supply of Salt River water was made available with the construction of the Roosevelt Dam in 1911.

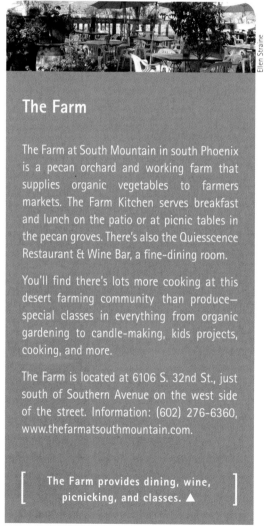

Ellen Straine

The Farm

The Farm at South Mountain in south Phoenix is a pecan orchard and working farm that supplies organic vegetables to farmers markets. The Farm Kitchen serves breakfast and lunch on the patio or at picnic tables in the pecan groves. There's also the Quiesscence Restaurant & Wine Bar, a fine-dining room.

You'll find there's lots more cooking at this desert farming community than produce—special classes in everything from organic gardening to candle-making, kids projects, cooking, and more.

The Farm is located at 6106 S. 32nd St., just south of Southern Avenue on the west side of the street. Information: (602) 276-6360, www.thefarmatsouthmountain.com.

[The Farm provides dining, wine, picnicking, and classes. ▲]

The suburbs followed, in all their variety. It would take an entire book just to list and briefly summarize all the other books that have been written about the delights and disasters of the metropolitan area, but we first will offer some capsules of the major attractions and then move on to descriptions of two scenic or historic drives in central Arizona that are related in geography but have quite separate and distinct histories based on copper, water, and cowboys.

Parting notes ...

All those palm trees: Nope, not native. Brought to the state from Egypt.

About that hiking in the city, which we mentioned earlier: Arizona with its vast spaces, even surrounding its biggest cities, is a hiking paradise. In the Phoenix area, a 1.2-mile-long trail (one way) that switchbacks up to the 2,600-foot summit of Piestewa Peak in the Phoenix Mountains Preserve draws about a half-million people annually. It ranks just under Bright Angel Trail in the Grand Canyon as the state's most popular, and Phoenix offers even more. Find Squaw Peak Drive just west of 24th Street, and go to the first ramada on the left to find the trailhead. Alternatively, there is a steep climb to the 2,700-foot summit of Camelback Mountain that offers a 360-degree view of the metro area. You can find the trail through Echo Canyon Park just east of Tatum Boulevard, south of McDonald Drive.

Remember: Take water. They are called city hikes, but that does not mean they can't be killers. **⚑**

[A rock climber clings to one of Camelback Mountain's red sandstone cliffs.   ]

Apache Trail Historic Road

Route	State Route 88, east of Phoenix between Apache Junction and Theodore Roosevelt Dam and Lake.
Mileage	Apache Junction to Tortilla Flat and Roosevelt Dam and Lake, 42 miles. Roosevelt to Globe, 30 miles.
Time to allow	Three hours at least, more if frequent stops and a visit to the Tonto National Monument are included.
Elevation	Roughly 1,700 feet at Apache Junction to 3,000 feet at Fish Creek Hill.
Overview	A close look at the incredible Superstition Mountains at the start of this ancient trail that follows the Salt River to the impressive Roosevelt Dam and Lake. A winding, narrow, mostly gravel, road goes precipitously up-and-down along and above steep canyons.

Welcome to amiable, inoffensive Apache Junction, eastern appendage of Phoenix and home to strip malls.

Also, and more to the point, it's the gateway to the justifiably famous Apache Trail Historic Road along which are the fabled Superstition Mountains, the Lost Dutchman State Park, a white-knuckle chunk of mountain driving, a chain of lakes formed by the Salt River, and, at trail's end, 44 miles away, Roosevelt Lake and the big dam that started the whole process of so-called reclamation back in 1911. Just beyond the lake and the end of the trail is the amazing Tonto National Monument and its cliff dwellings. (See Where To Go.)

State Route 88 running northeast out of Apache Junction soon hits a frontier remnant, the little community of Tortilla Flat (no, it has nothing to do with John Steinbeck), which is the official start of the historic road. Portions of the road thereon will test any flatlander's IQ for ever getting on it and his or her VQ (vertigo quotient) for staying on it.

After Apache Junction and before Tortilla Flat on State 88, however, are a couple of worthy attractions, one natural, one not: The Superstition Mountains and the ersatz but well-done Goldfield Ghost Town, a re-creation of an old western mining town. (See Where To Go for additional details on both.)

Goldfield is located near the original town of Goldfield, which was an 1890s boom town of several thousand people, three saloons, a hotel, boarding house, general store, and 50 or so gold mines. In 1895 heavy rains flooded the mines in a rather permanent way, and by 1899 Goldfield was a ghost town. Its touristy replacement looks genuinely antique and authentic. Visitors can get a steak, pan for gold, take a realistic mine tour, and examine the "world's oldest mule-power'd drill" from 1890.

Back on the road less than a half-mile farther and 5 miles out of Apache Junction is Lost Dutchman State Park. The park is a beautifully maintained and popular campsite named after the fabled Lost Dutchman gold mine, which is still lost somewhere in the overwhelmingly rugged, monstrous, and beautiful Superstition Mountains that backdrop the park. There are 35 campsites on paved roads in the park, a dump station, showers, ramadas, picnic tables, and water but no electricity. You'll pay a fee for overnight camping, and you can camp there for two weeks. A quarter-mile native plant trail near the ranger station offers labels describing some of the desert plants. A Forest Service road nearby leads to trails, which, in turn, lead into the Superstition Wilderness.

[The Apache Trail winds steeply through 40 miles of desert scenery.]

Kerrick James

Barrels of ink and decades of futile searching have been expended on the subject of Jacob Waltz, a German (or Deutchman) and his supposed Lost Dutchman gold mine. Variously described as a scoundrel, liar, and drunk, Waltz claimed to have rediscovered a rich gold mine first found, supposedly, by a wealthy Mexican cattle rancher named Miguel Peralta. Waltz said it was located somewhere near Weaver's Needle. Look for the thumb-shaped spire on your right near Milepost 203. The needle purportedly casts a shadow over the mine opening. Waltz died in Phoenix in 1891, and his mine passed into quasi-history alongside the Loch Ness Monster. But don't let cynicism stop you from continuing the search.

The highway now leads upward on a winding mountain road to a view down into a canyon and a watery jewel called Canyon Lake, the first of a chain of man-made lakes along the Salt River.

At lake level is a marina and, 2 miles and a couple of narrow bridges farther, the old and tiny settlement of Tortilla Flat with an eatery, a saloon, a post office, and a old, outdoor bathtub with a sign alleging that "Wyatt Earp were washed heah." Probably not. Tortilla Flat was introduced to Arizona as a freighters camp in the early 1900s when Theodore Roosevelt Dam was being built.

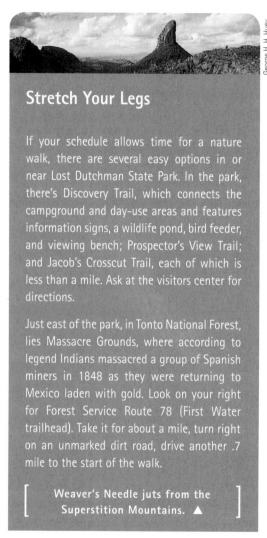

George H. H. Huey

Stretch Your Legs

If your schedule allows time for a nature walk, there are several easy options in or near Lost Dutchman State Park. In the park, there's Discovery Trail, which connects the campground and day-use areas and features information signs, a wildlife pond, bird feeder, and viewing bench; Prospector's View Trail; and Jacob's Crosscut Trail, each of which is less than a mile. Ask at the visitors center for directions.

Just east of the park, in Tonto National Forest, lies Massacre Grounds, where according to legend Indians massacred a group of Spanish miners in 1848 as they were returning to Mexico laden with gold. Look on your right for Forest Service Route 78 (First Water trailhead). Take it for about a mile, turn right on an unmarked dirt road, drive another .7 mile to the start of the walk.

[Weaver's Needle juts from the
Superstition Mountains. ▲]

Coming up, with 22 miles still to go to Roosevelt Lake, is the beginning of road to be driven with a 10- to 15-mph speedometer reading, wide eyes, and a tight grasp on the steering wheel. The Fish Hill Creek scenic vista is next, with a sign revealing that you are about to drive down— that's down as in steeply downhill—an aboriginal trail through country that has been, not unfairly, compared to the Alps. This section of the highway was modernized to permit hauling of supplies to the then-abuilding Roosevelt Dam. The words to quite literally live by are "gear down, look up." Should your vehicle slip off the washboarded road, it will plummet down hundreds of feet and, absent a big helicopter, become a permanent part of the scenery. You, too.

Next up is an overview of 17-mile-long, 266-foot-deep Apache Lake, the deepest of the chain of lakes created by the damming of the Salt River. A shaded vista point offers informative signs. For about 10 miles the drive continues to flank the lake and its marina and resort and offers a view of the Mazatzal Mountains on the opposite side of the road. The now upward and angst-inspiring drive resumes until suddenly . . .

Theodore Roosevelt Dam. Large. Very large. You have to see this sucker to believe it, but because the historic Apache Trail route ends here, we'll quit with just the facts, ma'am.

Roosevelt Dam was completed in its original form in 1911, at a cost of 41 lives, and renovated in 1986-1996 to cope with potential flooding and increase its storage capacity. It was the first of the great reclamation dams built across rivers—the Salt in this case—by busy federal beavers determined to deal with the issues of flood control and making water reliably available for generating power and farming throughout the arid Southwest and West. The lake created by the dam, Roosevelt Lake, has a storage capacity of 1.8 million acre feet, and its waters cover 20,000 acres, including what was once the old town of Roosevelt. (An acre-foot of water, incidentally, is the amount of water needed to cover one acre with one foot of water.) The dam construction is a concrete-covered masonry gravity arch 357 feet high, 21.6 feet thick at top, 196 feet at the base.

Above and just beyond the dam is a steel, traffic bridge described elaborately as "longest two-lane single span steel arch bridge in North America" stretching 1,080 feet across the lake and painted blue to match the lake.

This bridge and dam, created to serve the needs of western expansion, put a clamp on the Salt, whose once-wild magnificence begins with the snow melt high in the White Mountains of Arizona and the resulting runoff that forms the Black and the White Rivers. The confluence of those lesser streams is the start of the Salt, whose controlled water now feeds desert cities and farms.

Coda: Fishing in Roosevelt Lake, or any of the other three lakes along the route, is said to be good if you have a taste for bass and crappie.

Many possible stops at marinas on the lakes formed out of the Salt. ▥

George H. H. Huey

Tonto National Monument

State Route 88 joins State Route 188 just beyond Theodore Roosevelt Dam and Roosevelt Lake. A turn on State 88 toward Globe leads quickly to exciting cliff dwellings of the prehistoric Salado people. A moderate climb (gaining 350 feet in elevation) up a good and self-guiding trail takes the visitor to one of these ancient sites overlooking Roosevelt Lake.

You can prowl the rooms and see the original construction materials including the ancient support timbers (unfortunately marred with the initials of modern morons). A ranger will point out places on the Salado-built walls within the big, natural cave where the finger traces of those assigned to smooth the mortar—the children (little and lowest on the wall), women (thin and midway up the wall) and men (biggest and bluntest and highest)—can still be seen. The Salado lived in this area between 1150 and 1450 A.D. when they mysteriously departed.

[The lower ruin of a cliff dwelling at Tonto National Monument. ▲]

Gila-Pinal Scenic Road

Route	U.S. Route 60.
Mileage	Globe-Miami to Superior and Florence Junction, 39 miles.
Time to allow	Two to four hours.
Elevation	3,500 to 1,300 feet.
Overview	This drive, together with the Apache Trail Scenic Road (see Page 70), forms a loop beginning and ending at the eastern edge of metro Phoenix. The drive encompasses a short but surprisingly dramatic exposure to rolling lands, deep canyons, fascinating rock outcrops, panoramic views, the history of copper mining, and a splendid arboretum.

T he nonpareil attraction of this particular road epic is mostly green, grows from the ground, and smells good. And no, it's not a UFO-wrecked Martian using green Irish Spring soap.

Give up? OK, it's the astonishing Boyce Thompson Arboretum State Park, an Edenic desert garden between Superior and Florence Junction. But we will come to that eventually as we traverse the actual, official scenic drive. It is called the Gila-Pinal Scenic Road and runs roughly westish (or eastish if you are headed in the reverse) for 40 miles along U.S. Route 60 between the towns of Globe-Miami and Superior-Florence Junction. The highway signs that spring up just west of Globe specify that the scenic part has begun.

Globe is a good place to start, especially for anyone who has just come south on State Route 88, another scenic byway, from the tiny and once-violent hamlet of Young, but the distances between Globe and Phoenix or any other point along this route are so short that a driving investment of two hours will suffice to put the driver at any starting point that is desired.

So back to Globe. This is copper mining country, big time, with the names of the huge mining firms of Phelps Dodge and Broken Hill Properties (of Australia and usually referred to as BHP Copper). Note the words Broken Hill, because that is what this area is: a bunch of hills broken up by miners to get at the early gold and silver and, eventually, the copper secreted there. The man-made mountains of mine tailings are sometimes as big as the ones made by Nature.

Almost as impressive is the absence of parking meters in the downtown.

Globe, said to have gotten its name from a large piece of silver shaped like a globe and found in a local mine, was determined by prospectors as early as 1864 to be full of minerals, and the first copper mining began in 1878. But 600 or so years before that, in the 13th century, the Salado Indians showed up and began constructing pueblos near the banks of Pinal Creek. Besh-Ba-Gowah, a now-abandoned pueblo on the southern edge of what is now Globe, is one of several pueblos constructed in the 13th century. The Salado civilization disappeared in the 1400s, and the area apparently was mostly uninhabited until the 1600s when the Apache people made it a homeland. Besh-Ba-Gowah translates as "place of metal" or "metal camp" in Apache. The ancient and partly restored ruin and its adjoining museum and gift shop are open, at a modest admission price, to visitors who wish to prowl its some 200 rooms defined by walls of stone cobbles held in place by adobe.

On U.S. 60 leading west out of Globe toward nearby Miami is the Gila County Historical Museum, just across the road from the massive Old Dominion Copper Mine, which was closed

San Carlos Apache Cultural Center

Apache History

Not far from Globe, a side trip will take you to the San Carlos Apache Cultural Center, which Peridot offers a spiritual, cultural, and historical view of the Apache people, strictly from the tribe's perspective. Exhibits interpret the lives and ceremonies of the San Carlos people through words and artifacts, displaying grinding stones, arrowheads, clay pottery, cradleboards, bows and arrows, and a saddlebag.

The subjugation of the nine bands that make up the Apache tribe is depicted without romance, including the practice of paying bounty on scalps. The center's gift shop sells beadwork, Apache violins, woven-twine burden baskets, and wood carvings of mountain spirit dancers.

The center is located in Peridot on U.S. Route 70, about 20 miles east of Globe. Information: (928) 475-2894.

[Tightly woven baskets are decorative and functional. ▲]

during the Great Depression. The museum contains the original mine rescue station, constructed on this spot in the 1920s to cope with mine disasters. It also has an Indian Room, a Ranch Room, a buggy, several old typewriters, a telephone switchboard, and a glass cabinet containing the personal detritus of those days including "Dyspepsia Tablets" and a box delicately labeled "Lydia E. Pinkham's

Sanative Wash," the purpose of which the woman at the desk delicately denied any knowledge.

Next door is the Greater Globe-Miami Chamber of Commerce visitors center, fronted by a sign identifying the now-flooded Old Dominion Mine across the street and noting that the black cliff along the nearby creek is slag from smelter operations and the white sand along the roadside is mine tailings. Remember: slag is black, tailings are light. Such knowledge will help you stand out in cocktail party conversations.

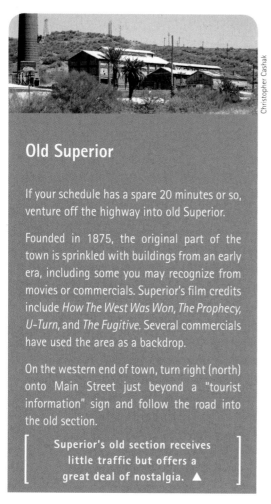

Christopher Cashak

Old Superior

If your schedule has a spare 20 minutes or so, venture off the highway into old Superior.

Founded in 1875, the original part of the town is sprinkled with buildings from an early era, including some you may recognize from movies or commercials. Superior's film credits include *How The West Was Won, The Prophecy, U-Turn,* and *The Fugitive.* Several commercials have used the area as a backdrop.

On the western end of town, turn right (north) onto Main Street just beyond a "tourist information" sign and follow the road into the old section.

[Superior's old section receives little traffic but offers a great deal of nostalgia. ▲]

On the way out of Globe, mountains on both sides of the road and nearby, have been disemboweled—or created—by miners. The vivid, dramatic scars of the brutal surgery remain.

The Gila-Pinal Scenic Road begins at Milepost 240 just west of the mining town of Miami, originally a mining camp named Mima in honor of miner Black Jack Newman's fiancée, Mima Tune, but later changed to Miami because of a lobbying effort by miners who hailed from Miami, Ohio. (More party conversation.)

Two mileposts farther is a crossing over Bloody Tanks Wash, where, in 1864, some militiamen captained by King Woolsey conducted a peace conference with some Apache Indians, gave them some tobacco and food . . . and then killed them. Thus the name.

Superior is about 17 miles away from Miami along a remarkable drive through gorgeous canyons, big boulder fields, spectacular spires, small bridges, and a slightly claustrophobic tunnel. Superior, with many vacant retail buildings, does not live up to the usual meaning of its name, but that's not its fault. It got its name from the Arizona and Lake Superior Mining Company, as in Lake Superior in Michigan.

Just on the western outskirts of Superior, still on scenic U.S. 60, is the

Buckboard City Café where, depending on the menu of the season, you might be offered a Sweat-Hog breakfast tortilla wrap of jalapeno peppers, sausage, green chile pepper, and cheese for 6-plus dollars or a luncheon of South-Westy burger with more green chile and jalapeno for about the same price. And don't forget the Monster Taco, a taco the size of the Schwarzenegger's forearm. What you also can get—for free—is entrance to an adjoining, tiny (8- by 17-foot) shack roofed by 1,800 empty beer cans and billed as the "World's Smallest Museum," a claim that is not likely to be disputed.

Inside, the marketers' affinity for world records continues with a display of the "World's Largest Apache Tear," a 1,600-carat nodule of shiny obsidian and member of a family of gemstones that, according to legend, got their name from tears shed by the loved ones of some Apaches who rode their horses off a mountain and into death's grip rather than accept defeat by U.S. Calvary. The tears turned to stone when they hit the ground. Actually, they're just a kind of lava, but that's soooo not romantic. Also on display: a box of 10-cent Peter Paul Almond Joy candy bars, the "World's Largest Fake Zippo Lighter, " an incongruous 1984 Compaq computer, and lots and lots of other old, um, stuff. Also: photos of several politicians, including Arizona's maverick U.S. Senator John McCain, the campaign-spending foe who probably would be amused to know he qualifies as a museum piece.

What the heck, it's free, although donations are suggested.

Just beyond the museum is an historical marker noting the existence nearby of Picket Post Mountain, a rugged outcrop south of the highway that was used as a lookout and heliograph station during frontier wars with the Apaches.

Golden barrel cacti welcome visitors to Boyce Thompson Arboretum,
a collection of desert plants from around the world.

Kerrick James

[
Boyce Thompson Arboretum, an Arizona state park, offers
2 miles of winding trails.
]

The officially scenic route is now near its end—at Milepost 214, somewhat short of Apache Junction and the inescapable Phoenix—but the wonders of the drive have not ended. The last—and in some ways the best—is a cultivated desert wonderland, a living garden known as the Boyce Thompson Arboretum State Park, which can be found at Milepost 223, 3 miles west of Superior in scenic Queen Creek Canyon. It is, in its quiet way, a miniature (350 acres) botanical display of more than 3,000 desert plants that is the equal of the much larger, indigenous splendors of the entire drive.

This mostly out-of-doors oasis was founded in the 1920s by a mining mogul, Col. William Boyce Thompson, who built the 26-room Picket Post House overlooking what now is the arboretum. The arboretum is now an Arizona state park.

The wonders of these desert plants from throughout the world, growing in a natural setting, were immediately apparent to those visitors who lucked out by showing up there in April of 2001; garden staff told them that a rare, tall Chilean cactus called a *Puya berteroniana*, which had been on the property for at least 15 years, had bloomed for the first time, possibly the first time anywhere in the United States. The bees knew it. Do not despair if it is not blooming when you visit. Among other exotics you will see, probably for the only time in your life unless you travel the Baja peninsula, is a pair of big boojums, a plant that merits the same awe accorded to saguaros and organ pipe cacti.

There is a bookstore heavy on desert gardening. The store is backed up by an interpretive center and a variety of displays.

Outside the entrance to the main visitors center of the arboretum in some months are long tables containing collections of for-sale cacti and other succulents

Wes Holden

ranging from tall to tiny and including ones with such exotically descriptive names and appearances as the brain cactus, hens and chickens, and chubby toes.

The main, 1.5-mile, self-guided walking trail leads through an amazing variety of different deserts and their plants, including those from South America, Africa, Asia, Australia, the Mediterranean, and America's Southwest. Along the way are a small desert lake and amenities such as benches equipped with a fine mist sprayer to cool the hiker, vending machines, telephones, toilets, water fountains, side trails, bird and butterfly areas, first aid station, gift shop, display greenhouses, a drovers' wool shed, a network of side trails, and on and on.

It is a restful, shady, birdsong-filled escape that requires about two hours for a decent look but really is worth at least a full day's time and attention. It is open every day from 8 a.m. to 5 p.m. except Christmas Day. There is an admission charge.

Back on U.S. 60, the way west leads to Apache Junction, one of the many suburban suction cups on one of the tentacles of the Phoenix octopus. **AH**

Baking With Beans

Among the special areas in the Boyce Thompson Arboretum is one dedicated to desert legumes and their importance to aboriginal peoples in the days when legumes were worth a great deal more than a hill of beans.

Early Mojave Indians of the lower Colorado River, for example, considered mesquite beans an important food source. Roasted in ashes, the young mesquite beans have been described as "tender like a string bean."

That information was provided by an Arizona State University anthropology professor, Kenneth M. Stewart, writing in a 1968 edition of a Museum of New Mexico scholarly journal, *El Palacio*. The article also offers "an informant's" account of this ancient Mojave recipe for mesquite bean cake:

"They pounded the mesquite beans to a powder, then added a little water to make a ball. A fire was built, and when it burned to ashes they scraped off the sand. They put the ball of mesquite powder there and left it out in the sun until it got hard. They'd put mesquite bean skin over it to cover it. When it gets hard, it binds in and holds it together. Then they would break off little chunks and eat it when they wanted to. They would also put it in water and drink it."

Oh, yummy.

[The arboretum nourishes aboriginal ways with beans. ▲]

Where To Go
What To See
What To Do

Besides Phoenix, these listings cover communities (listed alphabetically) in central Arizona beyond metropolitan Phoenix, including Ak-Chin Indian Community, Gila River Indian Community, Globe-Miami, San Carlos Apache Tribe, and Superior; north metropolitan Phoenix, including Carefree/Cave Creek, Fort McDowell Yavapai Nation, and Fountain Hills; East Valley of the Sun, including Apache Junction, Chandler, Gilbert, Mesa, Queen Creek, Salt River Pima-Maricopa Indian Community, Scottsdale, and Tempe; and West Valley of the Sun, including Glendale, Goodyear, and Litchfield Park.

BEYOND METROPOLITAN PHOENIX

Ak-Chin Indian Community

Information: The community, located south of metropolitan Phoenix, has headquarters at 42507 Peters and Nall Road, Maricopa. It includes Tohono O'odham and Pima Indians. (520) 568-2227. www.ak-chin.nsn.us

Him Dak Eco-Museum: Exhibits focus on the Ak-Chin "way of life." Closed weekends. Donations. 4685 N. Eco-Museum Road, Maricopa. (520) 568-9480.

Casino: See "Casinos" in Special Interests beginning on Page 399.

Gila River Indian Community

Information: Consisting of nearly 375,000 acres south of Phoenix, the Gila River Indian Reservation of the Pima and Maricopa Indians is the largest in the metropolitan area. The reservation features a museum, heritage park, golf courses, a world-class drag-and-boat racing facility, a 500-room deluxe resort complex, and three casinos. Based in Sacaton. (520) 562-6131. www.itcaonline.com/tribes_gila.html

Gila River Arts & Crafts Center: Basket and pottery making demonstrations, tours, Indian dance groups, restaurant and museum. Sacaton. (480) 963-3981. www.gilaindiancenter.com

Firebird International Raceway: The world-class facilities accommodate the super stars of drag racing. Professional races, including boat races at

The Arizona Science Center draws kids and adults alike with its interactive displays. ▲

Firebird Lake, take place year round. 20,000 S. Maricopa Road, Chandler; (602) 268-0200. www.firebirdraceway.com

Rawhide at Wild Horse Pass: 1880s Western theme town with stunt shows, dining, saloon, special events. $. Take Exit 162 from Interstate 10 southeast of Phoenix. Entry free. (480) 502-5600; (800) 527-1880. www.rawhide.com

Casinos: See "Casinos" in Special Interests beginning on Page 399.

Globe-Miami

Globe-Miami Chamber of Commerce: Information on annual events such as December's Festival of Lights, antiquing, area wildflowers, and touring historic buildings. Also features a guide for lodging and dining. (928) 425-4495. www.globemiamichamber.com

Antiques: The combined towns of Globe and Miami can count more than 26 antique shops among their businesses. Specialties range from mining collectibles to glassware and furniture. Contact the Globe-Miami Chamber of Commerce (see previous listing).

Besh-Ba-Gowah Archaeological Park: Large community of reconstructed Salado Indian ruins, with visitors center and museum that bring Salado culture into vivid relief. In December it's lit up by luminarias. $. Jess Hayes Road, Globe. (928) 425-0320. www.globemiamichamber.com/custom2.asp?pageid=600

Copper Spike Railway: The historic, 38-passenger railroad car named Spike, built in 1930, travels from Apache Gold Casino (seen listing below under San Carlos Apache Tribe) to Copper Spike Station in downtown Globe. Not handicap accessible due to its age. Tickets available at Apache Gold Casino or the station. Call for schedule. $. (928) 425-0235. www.copperspike.com

Gila County Historical Museum: Exhibits include Salado Indian artifacts dating from about 1125 to 1400, artifacts from the Old West and Globe history, antique furniture, and old mining equipment. Museum is partly housed in the original fire and rescue station from the Old Dominion Mine. Sponsors annual Apache Days street fair, usually the third weekend in October. Free. 1330 N. Broad St., Globe. (928) 425-7385.

Bullion Plaza Cultural Center and Museum: Housed in a grammar school that was built in 1923 and now listed on the National Register of Historic Places. Showcases Miami and Gila County history. Fri.-Sat., 11 a.m.-3 p.m. 1000 Plaza Drive, Miami. (480) 983-8611.

Cobre Valley Center for the Arts: Dance studio, artist studios, art gallery, frame shop, gift shop, theater and exhibitions housed in the historic county courthouse. 101 N. Broad St., Globe. (928) 425-0884. www.cobrevalleyarts.org

Mining Country Boomtown Spree: Action-packed weekend that includes the Arizona State Mining Championships, the 10K Copper Crawl, a parade, live entertainment, a street dance, car shows, arts and crafts. April. Downtown Miami. Contact Globe-Miami Chamber of Commerce listed above.

Bustle & Boots Square Dance Festival: October. Free. Gila County Fairgrounds, Globe. (928) 425-3392 or (928) 405-0451

San Carlos Apache Reservation

Information: The tribe's reservation encompasses nearly 2 million acres in portions of Gila, Graham, and Pinal counties. Headquartered in San Carlos, east of Globe. (928) 475-2579. www.sancarlosapache.com

San Carlos Apache Tribe Wildlife and Recreation Department: (928) 475-2343; (888) 475-2344. www.sancarlosrecreationandwildlife.com

San Carlos Apache Culture Center: Exhibits documenting Apache culture and history. Also features artwork by current Apache artists. Gift shop. Closed weekends. $. Located just east on U.S. Route 70 from the State Route 170 junction, near Milepost 272. (928) 475-2894.

San Carlos Lake: Fish off 158 miles of shoreline, thanks to Coolidge Dam, which was dedicated by President Calvin Coolidge. Fishing permit required. (928) 475-2343; (888) 475-2344.

Mount Turnbull All-Indian Rodeo: Rodeo plus Apache dances, crafts, foods. April. Bylas. (928) 475-3131.

Powwow: At Apache Gold Casino. March. Free. (800) 272-2438. www.apachegoldcasinoresort.com

Casino: See "Casinos" in Special Interests beginning on Page 399.

Superior

Superior Chamber of Commerce: Information about the area's history and attractions; maps. (520) 689-0200. www.superiorazchamber.net

Boyce Thompson Arboretum State Park: Relax and enjoy nature of the desert variety along the many trails. $. Call for summer hours. Located 3 miles west of Superior off U.S. Route 60. (520) 689-2811; (520) 689-2723. http://arboretum.ag.arizona.edu; www.azstateparks.com/Parks/parkhtml/boyce.html

Picket Post House: The 7,021-square-foot, red-brick mansion was built by the founder of the nearby Boyce Thompson Arboretum. Col. William Boyce Thompson lived in the 28-room house from 1923 until his death in 1930. The house also is known as the Castle on the Rock. Call for hours. $. Reached from the arboretum-park. (520) 689-2845.

Bob Jones Museum and the Superior Historical Society: Named after former Superior resident and the 6th governor of Arizona (1939-41), the museum's top local-history exhibit is a life-sized miner display. Wed. and Fri., 1 p.m.-4 p.m.; Sat.-Sun., 10 a.m.-4 p.m. Free. 300 W. Main St., Superior. (520) 689-5733.

World's Smallest Museum: No bigger than a wood shed, this privately operated roadside attraction claims to display the world's largest Apache tear, a merikanite obsidian, among other quirky items and found-art sculptures. Closed Tuesdays. Free. On U.S. Route 60, Superior. (520) 689-5857. www.worldssmallestmuseum.com

Wickenburg

Information: See listings on Page 206.

CENTRAL METROPOLITAN PHOENIX

Information: The Greater Phoenix Convention & Visitors Bureau and the Downtown Phoenix Visitors Information Center sponsor an online warehouse of information, including listings for dining and lodging, maps, transportation services, and an events calendar. (877) 225-5749; (602) 452-6282. www.phoenixcvb.com

Phoenix Zoo: Four trails lead visitors through themes of Africa, Arizona, the tropics, and children's interests. Includes Harmony Farm. Each Christmas season the zoo is lit by more than 2 million lights. $. Call for summer and holiday hours. At Papago Park, 455 N. Galvin Parkway. (602) 273-1341. www.phoenixzoo.org

Desert Botanical Garden: A 145-acre collection of cactus, succulents, and desert flowers. Wildflower and nature trails. Special events include jazz concerts and night walks. $. Call for summer hours. At Papago Park, 1201 N. Galvin Parkway. (480) 941-1225. www.dbg.org

Camelback Mountain-Echo Canyon Recreation Area: Steep, precarious hiking trails. Rock climbers favor the cliffs. McDonald Drive and Tatum Blvd. (602) 261-8318. www.phoenix.gov/PARKS/hikemain.html

Papago Park: Walking and mountain biking trails among red sandstone buttes. Fishing lagoons and picnic ramadas. Encompasses the zoo and botanical garden. Van Buren St. and Galvin Parkway, Phoenix. (602) 262-4837; (602) 261-8318. www.phoenix.gov/PARKS/hikemain.html

South Mountain Park: Hiking and biking. Scenic drive to city overlook. Petroglyphs. South Mountain Environmental Education Center, 10409 S. Central Ave. (602) 534-6324. www.phoenix.gov/PARKS/hikemain.html

Piestewa Peak: Hiking trails and picnic ramadas. Take Glendale Ave. or Lincoln Drive to Piestewa Peak Drive (between 22nd and 23rd streets) and go north about 1 mile. (602) 256-3220; (602) 261-8318. www.phoenix.gov/PARKS/hikemain.html

Museo Chicano: Focuses on Mexican arts and the Hispanic culture. $. Closed Monday. 147 E. Adams St. (602) 257-5536. www.museochicano.com

Pueblo Grande Museum and Archeological Park: Site of a Hohokam platform mound from about 1150, the museum is dedicated to the Hohokam and their ruins. Gift shop, tours, and picnic areas. $. 4619 E. Washington St. (602) 495-0900. www.phoenix.gov/PARKS/pueblo.html

George Washington Carver Museum and Cultural Center: Housed in Phoenix's first African-American high school, the museum gives insight into the life of early African-American pioneers and prominent national and local figures. Sculpture garden, art, and exhibits. Closed Sunday; call for Saturday hours. $. 415 E. Grant St.(602) 254-7516. www.gwcmccphx.org

Phoenix Police Museum: Police memorabilia from a real cruiser to an early 1900s jail cell. Free. Mon., Wed., and Fri., 9 a.m.-3 p.m. 101 S. Central Ave., Suite 100. (602) 534-7278. www.phoenixpolicemuseum.com

Phoenix Civic Plaza: Downtown Phoenix's convention and entertainment center with outdoor fountains and sculptures. 111 N. Third St. (800) 282-4842; TTY (602) 495-5048. www.phoenix.gov/CIVPLAZA/plazaidx.html

Heard Museum: Internationally renowned for its extensive collections of Indian artifacts and fine art, the Heard has an emphasis on the cultures of the Southwest. $. 2301 N. Central Ave. (602) 252-8848; gift shop, 252-8344. www.heard.org

Heritage Square: Victorian-era city block encompassing museums, shops, eateries, and homes from the original Phoenix town site. Includes 1895 Rosson House, Teeter House Tea Room, Arizona Doll and Toy Museum. $. Call for hours. 115 N. Sixth St. Recording, (602) 262-5029; (602) 262-5071. www.phoenix.gov/PARKS/heritage.html

Arizona Science Center: Hands-on exhibits and interactive demonstrations; planetarium; and giant-screen Werks theater. $.

600 E. Washington St. in Heritage Square Park. (602) 716-2000. www.azscience.org

Phoenix Museum of History: Wander through Phoenix-area history from prehistoric times through life in the 1930s. $. Closed Monday. 105 N. Fifth St. in Heritage Square Park. (602) 253-2734. www.pmoh.org

Phoenix Art Museum: Houses more than 16,000 pieces, from Renaissance to contemporary Southwestern to Asian and Latin American. $. Closed Monday. 1625 N. Central Ave. (602) 257-1222. www.phxart.org

State Capitol Museum: Copper-domed original capitol was built in 1899 when Arizona was a territory. Includes old governor's office and the House and Senate chambers. Free. Closed weekends. 1700 W. Washington St. (602) 542-4675. www.lib.az.us/museum

Arizona Mining and Mineral Museum: Colorful ore samples from Arizona's copper mines, plus more than 3,000 minerals on display. Free. Closed Sunday. 1502 W. Washington St. (602) 255-3791.

[Visitors can tour the Rosson House, a restored 1895 historic Phoenix home in the downtown area.]

George Stocking

Mystery Castle: Eccentric home built over 16 years from found objects. $. Reservations required. Closed June-September. 800 E. Mineral Road in South Mountain Park. (602) 268-1581.

Arizona Military Museum: Recalls Arizona's military history as far back as the Spanish conquistadors. Weapons, archives, military helicopter. Free. Open weekend afternoons. Enter through National Guard gate at 5636 E. McDowell Road. (602) 267-2676; (602) 253-5378.
www.az.ngb.army.mil/museum/museum.htm

Hall of Flame: Displays of fire-fighting apparatus dating as far back as 1725. $. 6101 E. Van Buren St. (602) 275-3473. www.hallofflame.org

Shemer Art Center: 1920s Santa Fe-style house showcasing local and national artists. Free. Closed Sunday. 5005 E. Camelback Road.
(602) 262-4727; TTY (602) 262-6713.
www.phoenix.gov/PARKS/shemer.html

Dodge Theatre: Offers top popular concerts and touring comedy shows. 400 W. Washington St. in downtown Phoenix. $. (602) 379-2888.
www.dodgetheatre.com

Orpheum Theatre: Events include touring Broadway musicals, opera, ballet, and symphony concerts. 203 W. Adams St. in downtown Phoenix.
(602) 262-7272. http://phoenix.gov/STAGES/orpheum.html

Phoenix Symphony Hall: The Orpheum Theatre, 203 W. Adams St. in downtown Phoenix, is the main box office for Symphony Hall on the Phoenix Civic Plaza. Events include touring Broadway musicals, opera, ballet, and symphony concerts. (602) 262-7272. Symphony Hall is home to the Phoenix Symphony Orchestra, (602) 495-1999. Arizona Opera, (602) 266-7464 and Ballet Arizona, (602) 381-1096. Online ticket information at http://phoenix.gov/CIVPLAZA/stages.html

Phoenix Theatre: Presents plays and musicals. Home to Main Stage, Cookie Company, Nearly Naked Theatre, and the Shakespeare Company. 100 E. McDowell Rd. Box office, (602) 254-2151.

The Herberger Theater Center: Offers dance performances and plays. Home to Actors Theatre, Arizona Theatre Company, Center Dance Ensemble, and Childsplay. $. 222 E. Monroe St. in downtown Phoenix. Performances and tickets: (602) 252-8497; www.ticketmaster.com

Celebrity Theatre: Intimate venue that shows popular touring concerts and comedy acts and includes a rotating center stage. $. 440 N. 32nd St., Phoenix. Performances and tickets: (602) 267-1600;
www.celebritytheatre.com

Arizona Jewish Theatre Company: Professional theater in an intimate setting. Playhouse on the Park is located on the first floor inside the Viad Corporate Center, 1850 N. Central Ave., on the southwest corner of Central Ave. and Palm Lane in Phoenix. Performances and tickets: (602) 264-0402. www.azjewishtheatre.org

U.S. Airways Center: Home of the Phoenix Suns. Sports and entertainment arena shows top music acts, ice skating revues, and, of course, professional sports. 201 E. Jefferson St. in downtown Phoenix. Ticket information: (602) 379-7800; www.ticketmaster.com

First Friday Art Walk: Downtown Phoenix comes alive with art and live entertainment for a carnival-type experience that features artists of skill levels from the aspiring to the professional. Free shuttle bus service. First Friday of every month. Free. Starts at central branch of Phoenix Public Library, just south of McDowell Road on Central Ave. Brochure with gallery listings available at library. (602) 256-7539. www.artlinkphoenix.com

Downtown Phoenix Public Market: Products from around the state: vegetables, flowers, fruit, baked goods, and gifts. Southeast corner of Central Ave. and McKinley St. Sat., 8 a.m.-1 p.m. and the first Friday of each month, 6 p.m.-10 p.m. (602) 493-5231. www.foodconnect.org

World Championship Hoop Dance contest: The best Indian hoop dancers from the United States and Canada compete for bragging rights. February. $. Heard Museum, 2301 North Central Ave., Phoenix; (602) 252-8848; www.heard.org/hoop.php

NORTH METROPOLITAN PHOENIX

Carefree / Cave Creek

Carefree/Cave Creek Chamber of Commerce: The tone of these two communities ranges from Old West to poshy resorts and golf courses. The chamber has extensive information on the area's history, lodging and dining, attractions, and events. (602) 488-3381. www.carefree-cavecreek.com

Lake Pleasant Regional Park: Boating, fishing, water skiing, and swimming in a desert reservoir. Camping, picnicking, and hiking too. $. Carefree Highway west of Interstate 17. (928) 501-1710. www.maricopa.gov/parks

Cave Creek Regional Park: County park with trails for hiking, biking, and horseback riding. Rodeo arena. Tent and RV camping. $. 37019 N. Lava Lane, Cave Creek. (623) 465-0431. www.maricopa.gov/parks

Carefree Sundial: The copper landmark is the third-largest working sundial in the Western hemisphere. Sundial Circle, downtown Carefree.

Spur Cross Ranch Conservation Area: County park trails for hiking, biking, and horseback riding. No camping. Wildlife viewing, especially along the lush streamside habitat of Cave Creek, which flows seasonally. $. 44000 N. Spur Cross Road, Cave Creek. (480) 488-6601. www.maricopa.gov/parks

Gateway Desert Awareness Park: Hiking and horse trails lace this town park for a close-up look at the desert. Playground, ramadas, barbecues, pond. Cave Creek. (480) 488-1400. www.cavecreek.org/index.asp?SID=26

Cave Creek Museum: Showcases the history of the surrounding foothills with Indian, mining, and geological exhibits. October-May; call for hours. Free. 6140 E. Skyline Drive, Cave Creek; (480) 488-2764.

Cave Creek Mistress Mine: Rock shop, museum, and self-guided tours of the 1883 gold mine. Free. 45402 N. Seven Springs Road, 10 miles northeast of Carefree. (480) 488-0842.

Pioneer Arizona Living History Museum: Reconstructed frontier town alive with old-time skill demonstrations and Old West re-enactments. Pioneer Road off Interstate 17 north of Carefree Highway. $. Closed part of year. (623) 465-1052. www.pioneerarizonavillage.com

Fort McDowell Yavapai Nation

Information: Located about 25 miles northeast of central Phoenix. The 40-square-mile reservation, consisting of desert land with the Verde River running through it, offers a variety of enterprises for tourists and fun-seekers, such as a casino, resorts, a golf course, and backcountry adventures by horse or Jeep. For a listing, visit the tribe's Internet site. Headquartered in Fountain Hills. (480) 837-5121. www.ftmcdowell.org

Casino: See "Casinos" in Special Interests beginning on Page 399.

Fountain Hills

Fountain Hills Chamber of Commerce: It's Internet site includes a visitors guide, lodging and dining listings, and calendars of events and art shows. (480) 837-1654. www.fountainhillschamber.com

Fountain Hills Fountain: Touted as one of the "world's highest fountains," the town's centerpiece shoots a stream of water 560 feet into the air. Operates daily at the top of each hour 10 a.m.-9 p.m. Free. Avenue of the Fountains north of Shea Blvd.

River of Time Museum: Exhibits focus on the history, prehistory, culture, and environment of the lower Verde Valley. Call for hours. $. 12901 N. LaMontana Blvd., Fountain Hills. (480) 837-2612. www.riveroftimemuseum.org

McDowell Mountain Regional Park: Scenic drives and trails for hiking, biking, and horse riding in the lower Verde River Basin. Tent and RV camping. $. North of Fountain Hills on McDowell Mountain Road. (480) 471-0173. www.maricopa.gov/parks

Phoenix

Adobe Dam Regional Park: Home of Waterworld Safari aquatic park (open Memorial Day weekend-Labor Day weekend). Plus golf course, kart racing track, scale trains park, and model planes airfield, all run by various clubs. $. Call for hours of various activities. 23280 N. 43rd Ave., Phoenix. (623) 465-0431. www.maricopa.gov/parks

Ben Avery Shooting Facility: Shooting range open Wed.-Sun., 7 a.m.- 7 p.m. $. 4044 W. Black Canyon Blvd., Phoenix (north of the Carefree Highway and west of Interstate 17). (623) 582-8313. www.basfaz.com

North Mountain Park: Hiking trails and picnic ramadas. Visitors center at 12950 N. Seventh St., Phoenix. (602) 495-5540. www.phoenix.gov/PARKS/hikemain.html

Deer Valley Rock Art Center: Landscape of petroglyph-adorned boulders, with some of the petroglyphs dating to 3000 B.C. Visitor center, gift shop and tours. Hours vary; $; 3711 W. Deer Valley Road; (623) 582-8007

EAST VALLEY OF THE SUN

Apache Junction

Information: Recreational activities in and around Apache Junction include a dog-racing track, Jeep tours, an annual Renaissance Festival, and boat cruises and other water sports on nearby lakes. (602) 982-3141; (800) 252-3141. www.apachejunctioncoc.com

Lost Dutchman State Park: Hiking and camping at the foot of the Superstition Mountains. $. East of Apache Junction off State Route 88. $. (480) 982-4485. www.pr.state.az.us/Parks/parkhtml/dutchman.html

Goldfield: A theme park based on a re-created ghost town, with a saloon and an underground mine and narrow-gauge train. $. 4650 N. Mammoth Mine Road, off State Route 88 east of Apache Junction. (480) 983-0333. www.goldfieldghosttown.com

Arizona Renaissance Festival: Six-course "pleasure feasts," shows, re-enactments and an artisan marketplace at this huge annual gathering. February-April. $. 2601 E. Highway 60, Apache Junction. (520) 463-2700. www.royalfaires.com

Chandler

Information: The local chamber of commerce has compiled guides for dining and enjoying area attractions and events. (480) 963-4571; (800) 963-4571. www.chandlerchamber.com

Dugan's Dairy Farm Tours: A carton of milk for each guest. $. Early October to mid-May; closed Sun-Mon. 2471 S. Dobson Road. (480) 899-8795. www.dugansdairy.com

Arizona Railway Museum: Free. 399 N. Delaware St., Chandler. (480) 821-1108. www.azrymuseum.org

Chandler Center for the Arts: presents touring musicals, jazz, comedy, ballet, Chinese acrobatics, and more. Home to the San Marcos Symphony. 250 N. Arizona Ave., downtown Chandler. Mon.-Fri., 10 a.m.-5 p.m.; Sat., noon-5 p.m. (480) 782-2680. Online at www.ticketmaster.com

Ostrich Festival: Ostrich races, ostrich burgers, rides, live entertainment, arts and crafts. March; $; Tumbleweed Park, 2250 S. McQueen Road, Chandler. Call chamber of commerce for more info, (480) 963-4571. www.ostrichfestival.com

Firebird International Raceway: The world-class facilities accommodate the super stars of drag racing. Professional road and water races take place year round. 20000 S. Maricopa Road, Chandler; (602) 268-0200. www.firebirdraceway.com

Gilbert

Gilbert Riparian Preserves: City water reclamation effort produced two urban wetland parks. Bird watching galore. The 110-acre Riparian Preserve at Water Ranch is located east of Greenfield Road on Guadalupe Road; walking and biking paths and small fishing lake. The 72-acre Neely Ranch Preserve is south of Guadalupe Road on Cooper Road with entrance at the fire station; butterfly and hummingbird garden. Free. Gilbert. (602) 696-1195; (480) 503-6744. www.riparianinstitute.org

Mother Nature's Farm: Pick peaches and apples in the summer, pumpkins in the fall. Pumpkin patch, hayrides, animals. $. 1663 E. Baseline Road, Gilbert. (480) 892-5874. www.mothernaturesfarm.com

Gilbert Historical Museum: View the past of this once-rustic farming community, housed in a charming old schoolhouse. Free. Tues., Thurs., and Sat., 9 a.m.-4 p.m. 10 S. Gilbert Road. (480) 926-1577. www.gilbertmuseum.com

Gilbert Days: The annual week-long event has a rodeo, Pony Express ride re-enactment, parade, rides, and entertainment. March. (480) 892-0056. www.gilbertpromotionalcorp.org

Mesa

Mesa Convention and Visitors Bureau: Provides visitor information on topics such as lodging and dining, area attractions, golf, and online maps. (480) 827-4700; 800-283-6372; www.mesacvb.com

Salt River Tubing: Float down the Salt River on a rented inner tube. April-October. $. Call for shuttle schedule. Usery Pass Road. (480) 984-3305. www.saltrivertubing.com

Mesa Southwest Museum: Ponder local history and prehistory, from animated dinosaurs to Hohokam petroglyphs to movie memorabilia. $. 53 N. MacDonald St. (480) 644-2230. www.cityofmesa.org/swmuseum

Arizona Museum for Youth: Interactive museum opening the world of art for children to age 12. $. Closed Monday. 35 N. Robson St. (480) 644-2468; recording, (480) 644-2467. www.cityofmesa.org/amfy

Mesa Arts Center: Sculptural multi-level city complex of performing arts theaters, galleries, art studios, and outdoor public spaces. Mesa Contemporary Arts gallery, $. Closed Monday. 1 E. Main St. (480) 644-6501 or box office, (480) 644-6500. www.mesaartscenter.com

Sirrine House: Fully restored 1896 Victorian home operated by the Mesa Southwest Museum. Free. October-March, Sat., 10 a.m.-5 p.m.; Sun., 1-5 p.m. 160 N. Center St. (480) 644-2760; (480) 644-2230.

Park of the Canals: City park where you can view remnants of ancient canals dug by the Hohokam. 1710 N. Horne St. (480) 644-2351.

Mesa Historical Museum: Quaint collections of local artifacts spell out the story of this city's settlement. $. Closed Monday. Summer hours vary. 2345 N. Horne St. (480) 835-7358. www/mesaaz.org

Confederate Air Force Museum: War planes—many from World War II—on display with related memorabilia. $. Falcon Field at McKellips and Greenfield roads. (480) 924-1940. www.cityofmesa.org/airport/commemorativeairforce.asp

Mesa Amphitheatre: Part of the Mesa Convention Center, it shows touring rock and alternative music concerts. 201 N. Center St. The box office is at 263 N. Center St. (480) 644-2560. www.cityofmesa.org/cencntr

Arizona Scottish Highland Games: Pipes and drums, games, live entertainment, food, and various Scottish themed activities. February; $. www.arizonascots.com

Usery Mountain Regional Park: Trails for hiking, biking, and horseback riding. Tent and RV camping. Archery range. $.Ellsworth Road. Mesa. (480) 984-0032. www.maricopa.gov/parks/usery

Queen Creek

Queen Creek Chamber of Commerce: (480) 888-1709. www.queencreekchamber.org

San Tan Historical Society: Exhibits and displays about Queen Creek, Chandler Heights, Combs, and Higley history. Free. Sat., 9 a.m.-1 p.m. and Tues., 9 a.m.-noon. 20740 S. Ellsworth Road. (480) 987-9380.

Schnepf Farms: Gardens and orchards for picking produce. Country store and bakery. Special events. $. October-May. 22601 E. Cloud Road. (480) 987-3333. www.schnepffarms.com

San Tan Mountain Regional Park: Set in the lower Sonoran Desert, the day-use only park has trails for hiking, biking, and horseback riding. $. 6533 West Phillips Road. (602) 506-2930. www.maricopa.gov/parks/santan

Salt River Pima-Maricopa Indian Community

Information: Community headquarters are in Scottsdale. Enterprises include two casinos, golf courses, and a trap and skeet range. (480) 850-8000. www.saltriver.pima-maricopa.nsn.us

Hoo-hoogam Ki Museum: This small museum focuses on the cultures of the two tribes that live in the community, the Pima and the Maricopa. Closed weekends. Free. 10005 E. Osborn Road. (480) 874-8190. www.saltriver.pima-maricopa.nsn.us/history_culture/kimuseum.htm

Casinos: See "Casinos" in Special Interests beginning on Page 399.

Scottsdale

Scottsdale Convention & Visitors Bureau: The bureau has compiled information, including maps, online and in booklets on all of the types of attractions that draw visitors to Scottsdale, including arts and culture, shopping, spas, nightlife, golf, lodging and dining. (480) 421-1004. www.scottsdalecvb.com

Scottsdale Civic Center Mall: Manicured, 21-acre promenade with sculptures, fountains, gardens, and walkways linking to venues like the Scottsdale Center for the Performing Arts and the Scottsdale Museum of Contemporary Art. The annual Scottsdale Arts Festival is held here in March. The complex extends between First Avenue and Second Street and Brown Avenue and 75th Street. www.scottsdaleaz.gov/Parks/_maps/ScottsdaleMallMap.asp

Scottsdale Museum of Contemporary Art: Five galleries showcase changing exhibitions of visual arts. Includes an outdoor sculpture garden. $. Scottsdale Civic Center Mall , 7374 E. Second St. 480-874-4666. www.smoca.org

Scottsdale Center for the Performing Arts: Performances include modern dance, plays, music, and Indian dances and music. Scottsdale Civic Center Mall, 7380 E. Second St. (480) 994-2787. www.scottsdalearts.org; www.scottsdaleperformingarts.org

[Scottsdale's Taliesin West, once Frank Lloyd Wright's winter home, welcomes the public.]

David H. Smith

Public art tour: The Scottsdale Cultural Council has fashioned three self-guided tours of public art. www.scottsdalepublicart.org/tour.php

Scottsdale art walks: Local galleries each Thursday evening sponsor walks, sometimes laced with live music and other entertainment. Free. Downtown Scottsdale. (480) 990-3939. www.scottsdalegalleries.com

Heard Museum North: Rotating exhibits and a gallery shop are featured at this satellite site of the world renowned Heard Museum. $. 34505 N. Scottsdale Road. (480) 488-9817. www.heard.org

Scottsdale Historical Museum: Focuses on the history of Scottsdale with permanent and changing exhibits. Free. Gift shop. 7333 E. Scottsdale Mall. (480)-945-4499. www.scottsdalemuseum.com

Sylvia Plotkin Judaica Museum: Includes a reconstructed Tunisian synagogue. Donations. Tues.-Fri., 10 a.m.-3 p.m. Temple Beth Israel, 10460 N. 56th St. (480) 951-0323. www.spjm.org

Taliesin West: Legendary architect Frank Lloyd Wright's winter home still runs as a school. A variety of tours are available, including some at night, to campus sites such as Cabaret Cinema, Music Pavilion, Seminar Theater and Wright's private office. $. 12621 N. Frank Lloyd Wright Blvd. (480) 860-8810 for recorded tour information. (480) 860.2700, ext. 494/495 for reservations. www.franklloydwright.org

Kerr Cultural Center: An Arizona State University venue, it offers diverse musical performances and plays. 6110 N. Scottsdale Road. $. (480) 596-2660. www.asukerr.com/home.shtml

WestWorld of Scottsdale: Showcases equestrian events, specialty auto events, and dog shows. 16601 N. Pima Road. (480) 312-6802. www.scottsdaleaz.gov/westworld

Barrett–Jackson car auction: Millions of dollars trade hands at this world-class automobile auction. January. $. WestWorld, Scottsdale. (480) 421-6694. www.barrett-jackson.com

Cosanti: Eclectic home and studio of visionary architect Paolo Soleri. Donations. 6433 E. Doubletree Ranch Road. (480) 948-6145. www.cosanti.org/expCosanti

McCormick-Stillman Railroad Park: A 1-mile track carries visitors throughout the park. The train is a reproduction of a narrow gauge railroad (5 inches to 1 foot). Other attractions include a carousel, 2 Navajo hogans, historical exhibits, and picnic area. Admission free. $ for rides. 7301 E. Indian Bend Road. (480) 312-2312. www.therailroadpark.com

Indian Bend Wash: Greenbelt extending 7.5 miles from Indian Bend Road almost to the Salt River. Trails for biking, running, and skating. Includes Eldorado Park, 2311 N. Miller Road at Oak St. (480) 312-7922.

Parada del Sol Rodeo Festival: Scottsdale Jaycees sponsor a rodeo festival and parade in March. WestWorld and Old Town Scottsdale. (480) 990-3179. www.scottsdalejaycees.org/paradadelsol

House of Broadcasting Museum: Dedicated to Arizona broadcasting history. Free. 7150 E. Fifth Ave. (602) 944-1997; www.houseofbroadcasting.com

Tempe

Tempe Convention & Visitors Bureau: Tempe is home for the main campus of Arizona State University and many other attractions. The bureau has assembled information on both university and town attractions and events. (480) 894-8158; (800) 283-6734. www.tempecvb.com

Old Town Tempe: Vintage buildings preserve the past along Mill Ave. between First St. and University Drive Stroll among eclectic shops and eateries. Downtown Tempe.

Tempe Town Lake: Fish, rent a watercraft, boat with your own craft, take a rowing class, or lounge on an excursion tour. Wide paved paths on the shore great for skating and biking. Extends from Priest Drive to Rural Road/ Scottsdale Road between the Rio Salado Parkway and State Loop 202. Operations center, southwest corner of Mill Ave. and Curry Road, (480) 350-8625. www.tempe.gov/lake

Arizona Historical Society Museum at Papago Park: The Tempe branch of the state's oldest history museum features imaginatively designed displays. $. 1300 N. College Ave. (480) 929-0292. www.arizonahistoricalsociety.org

Tempe Historical Museum: Traces city history from 1871. Free. 809 E. Southern Ave. (480) 350-5100. www.tempe.gov/museum

Petersen House Museum: 1892 Victorian pioneer ranch home. Donations. 1414 W. Southern Ave. (480) 350-5151; (480) 350-5100. www.tempe.gov/museum/aphm.htm

Arizona State University Art Museum: Five galleries in Arizona State University's fine arts center include Latin American and early American art. The Nelson Fine Arts Center also holds the Galvin Playhouse, the University Dance Laboratory, and sculpture courts. Free. Southeast corner of 10th St. and Mill Ave. (480) 965-9011. http://asuartmuseum.asu.edu

Grady Gammage Auditorium: On the campus of Arizona State University. Offers cultural events, including Broadway shows, modern dance, music, and dramas.1200 S. Forest Ave. on the corner of Mill Ave. and Apache Blvd. (480) 965-3434. www.asugammage.com/home.shtml

WEST VALLEY OF THE SUN

Glendale

Glendale Office of Tourism: Glendale ranks as Arizona's fourth-largest city, but it retains elements of small-town charm. As the hub of the West Valley, the Glendale visitors center, information packets, and Internet site highlight accommodations, shopping (including antiquing), attractions, dining, festivals, adventure, sports, and arts for several neighboring communities, including Avondale, Buckeye, El Mirage, Goodyear, Litchfield Park, Peoria, Sun City, Sun City West, Surprise, Tolleson, Wickenburg, and Youngtown. Visitors center at 5800 W. Glenn Drive, Suite 140. (623) 930-4500; 877-800-2601. www.visitglendale.com

Luke Air Force Base: Largest fighter training base in the Western world. Public monthly tours. Biennial air show. (623) 856-5853. www.visitglendale.com/directions.php

Bead Museum: Exotic collection of beads and personal ornaments from ancient and modern cultures. Beading classes, workshops; museum store. $. 5754 W. Glenn Drive. (623)931-2737. www.thebeadmuseum.com

Historic Sahuaro Ranch Museum: Vintage 1800s fruit ranch converted to museum and art gallery. Peacocks roam the lush grounds. Donations. Closed June-late September. 9802 N. 59th Ave. (623) 930-4200. www.sahuaroranch.org

Cardinals Stadium: Home of the Arizona Cardinals of the National Football League. Located along Glendale Avenue just off Loop 101. www.azcardinalsstadium.com; www.visitglendale.com/sports.php

Glendale Arena: Home the Phoenix Coyotes (National Hockey League) and Phoenix Sting (Professional indoor lacrosse) and hosts musical acts and performances. 9400 W. Maryland Ave. (623) 772-3200; (623) 772-3800. www.glendalearenaaz.com

Glendale Chocolate Affaire: The early Valentines treat offers horse-drawn carriage rides, music, activities and lots of chocolate. February. Downtown Glendale. www.visitglendale.com/signature_events.php

Tolmachoff Farms: Children can frolic in this place where they can pick produce and walk in a six-acre corn maze and tour the farm. Country store.

$. 5726 N. 75th Ave., Glendale. (623) 386-1301, (888) 386-1301.
www.tolmachoff-farms.com

Goodyear

Southwest Valley Chamber of Commerce: 289 N. Litchfield Road.
(623) 932-2260; (623) 932-9057. http://southwestvalleychamber.org/

Estrella Mountain Regional Park: Trails for horseback riding, biking, and
hiking. Golf course, picnic sites, rodeo arena, ball fields. Wetlands area and
catch-and-release fishing along the Gila River. $. Estrella Parkway and
Vineyard Ave. (623) 932-3811. www.maricopa.gov/parks/estrella

Litchfield Park

Wildlife World Zoo: Extensive private collection of exotic animals,
including tigers, giraffes. Aviary. $. 16501 W. Northern Ave. (623) 935-9453.
www.wildlifeworld.com

Peoria

Peoria Sports Complex: Major League Baseball spring training.
16101 North 83rd Ave. (623) 773-8700. www.peoriaaz.com

Phoenix

Cricket Pavilion: Huge, open-air amphitheater in west Phoenix that stages
music acts. $. 2121 N. 83rd Ave., (602) 254-7200. http://cricket-pavilion.com

Surprise

West Valley Art Museum: Focuses on ethnic dress, textiles, and
ethnographic arts, as well as exhibiting Arizona artists. $.17420 N. Avenue
of the Arts (114th Ave.). (623) 972-0635. www.wvam.org

Sun City West

Sundome Center for the Performing Arts: An Arizona State University
venue for performing arts.19403 R.H. Johnson Blvd. Check Gammage
auditorium for information. (480) 965-3434.
www.asugammage.com/home.shtml

Waddell

White Tank Mountain Regional Park: Scenic drives and trails for
hiking, biking, and horseback riding. Camping. $. Olive Ave. and State Route
303, Waddell (on the metropolitan area's far-west side). (623) 935-2505.
www.maricopa.gov/parks/white_tank

Mount Graham rises among the Pinaleno Mountains. ▲
Water cascades through Ramsey Creek in southeast Arizona. ▶

Southern Arizona
In All Directions From Tucson

A survey of southern Arizona starts with the multicultural, scenic, and recreational pleasures of Tucson and then stretches from Ajo on the west to the border with New Mexico on the east, Casa Grande on the north, and the Mexican border on the south, across tall mountain ranges and low desert in all or parts of five counties. Cruise the Patagonia-Sonoita Scenic Road and other scenic drives, delve into Kartchner Caverns, browse the shops of Bisbee, and explore the wild history of Tombstone. Hiking, bird-watching, and historical rambling are all on this region's menu.

David Muench

David Muench

Changing City ... Unchanging Desert

Once upon a time many years ago, a husband and wife, beset by blue fingers in winter and red mosquito welts in summer, left their Midwestern home one dreary, snowy day in search of a place that was neither snow-swept nor bug-infested.

Eventually they chugged into southern Arizona and Tucson. There, under a benign, early March sun, they took a motel room, put on their bathing suits, and plopped into the motel's unheated outdoor pool, an act that would have earned them a stay in a nuthouse back in their home state. They also struck up a conversation with some fellow bathers who had just shed their parkas after a morning of downhill skiing an hour away.

Skiing and sunbathing an hour apart? Could Sir Thomas More, the man of all seasons, have envisaged a more perfect Utopia, one with all seasons perfect? After shrugging off remarks that Tucson's summer temperatures reach the triple digits, the couple relocated.

In the decade of the 1990s, this city grew at about a 17 percent rate that raised its population to about 487,000 people. Since then, Tucson has topped the half-million mark. Its malls, its subdivisions, and its commercial activities have spread across many miles. Its pace has quickened; its traffic has thickened. Roads that once led a short distance into the vast desert now lead to a subdivision. But all the while this has been happening, the magnificent Sonoran, the most beautiful and varied of the world's deserts, has hung onto much of its ecological and aesthetic purity.

It is, in short, a changing city in a seemingly unchanging desert.

Sabino Canyon, once a favorite riparian wilderness in the Santa Catalina Mountains but too close to the expanding city for its own good, is now traveled by trams loaded with sun-screened tourists; but Madera Canyon in the more distant Santa Rita range remains a quiet sanctuary for birds and a non-motorized delight for hikers. The subdivisions now sprawling westward still yield to forests of saguaros more magnificent than any skyline of expensive homes.

For decades, what has not changed in any substantive way except for paving is a wondrous road that leads a to the top of a magnificent mountain. It is called the Mount Lemmon Road by residents and the Sky Island Scenic Byway by officials. We shall drive it in this chapter. As for the city and its other attractions, it can be said that a day of looking and visiting simply will not do. Better a week starting, perhaps, with a cruise along the simple grid that forms the street pattern of this cosmopolitan but relaxed community, followed by drives to any or all of the natural and man-made attractions in the immediate area.

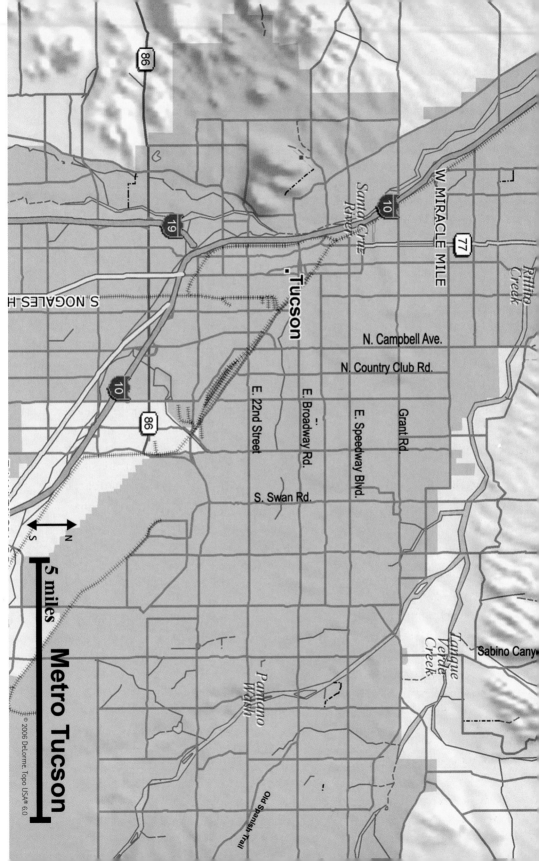

George H. H. Huey

Organ Pipe National Monument

We've harped a lot about plants; now, let's take up the organ.

State Route 86 west out of Tucson will eventually lead the traveler to the tiny community of Why and the intersection with State Route 85 heading south and into the Organ Pipe Cactus National Monument. It's a long, hot drive in the warm months, but it is worth it.

State 85 leads to the monument's visitors center about 5 miles north of the border town of Lukeville. The center is an ideal jumping-off spot for exploration of a fascinating sliver of this 330,000-acre chunk of volcanic desert populated by ocotillo plants and more than two dozen species of cactus including saguaro, cholla, gray-bearded senita (or "old man" cactus), and the marvelous organ pipe.

Why is it called organ pipe? Because each one resembles a collection of pleated organ pipes rivaling the saguaro in height. Organ pipe and senita cacti cannot be found growing naturally anywhere else in the United States.

If you have the time, the stamina, and the inclination—and plenty of water—consider a somewhat strenuous, 4.1-mile-loop hike along the Bull Pasture Trail and into the Ajo Mountains. The trailhead is 11 miles from the start of Ajo Mountain Drive that begins off State 85 just across from the visitors center.

[Saguaro and jumping cholla cactus abound at the
Organ Pipe Cactus National Monument. ▲]

■ ■ ■

The region treated in this chapter sprawls across southern Arizona. Tucson, one of the state's two big cities, is the obvious geographic, population, and cultural center, but the area stretches from Ajo on the west to the border with New Mexico on the east, Casa Grande on the north, and the Mexican border on the south, across the tall mountain ranges and low desert of five counties.

Thus, once the traveler has enjoyed that panoply of Tucson pleasures, there are several more days of glorious driving to be found all directions from the city, starting with the Patagonia-Sonoita Scenic Road on state routes 82 and 83 and including stops in Bisbee to see its once-monstrous mining operations, now defunct; the unveiled mysteries of Kartchner Caverns; the O.K. Corral in Tombstone where, as you may have heard, several guys died in a gunfight; Indian strongholds where famous chiefs fought the U.S. Army; the rock formations of the Chiricahua Mountains; a cowboy museum in the town of Willcox along with that town's part-time population of migrating sandhill cranes; and more canyons and water worlds full of birds and birders than anyone could reasonably hope for in this amazing basin-and-range country.

■■■

But we digress. Let us return to Tucson, which, you will note, is frequently misspelled as "Tuscon." Although there are some fine Italian restaurants in the town, you need not speak Italian nor need you assume that you have mistakenly landed in Tuscany. It's TOO-sahn, not TUCK-son and most assuredly not TUS-can.

It sometimes seems to be a bipolar city: a surging entrepreneurial spirit signaled by constant new construction combined with a laid-back attitude that commands your attention to an afternoon nap and a big Mexican late lunch on a shady restaurant patio. It's "get it done yesterday" and "worry about it mañana." It's big business but conducted in shorts and sandals. It is famous for relaxing retirement, fat farms, spas, and golf but often at prices that demand the pocketbook of a hard-charging capitalist. It has every ultra-modern convenience and every latest fad shop, but it is set in a gorgeous, primitive desert ringed by four unchanging mountain ranges. It is hot below and cool above.

Essentially, Tucson's culture blends those of Indians, Spanish, Mexicans, and Anglos. The state's second-largest city, it sits at 2,400 feet above sea level and offers an average high temperature in January of 65 degrees, in July of 100 degrees. A little more than 11 inches of rain falls in an average year, and the rare snowfall has a lifespan of about eight hours with the exception of snowmen created by thrilled residents of all ages.

The city officially was founded in 1775, but the first Spanish mission, San Xavier, was established in 1700. Indian villagers and farmers had made the area home for 2,000 years. Mexico governed it from 1821 until 1854 when it became part of the United States with the Gadsden Purchase. It was, at one time, the Territorial capital.

■■■

The focus of the rest of this chapter centers on three officially designated routes: the Sky Island Scenic Byway, the Patagonia-Sonoita Scenic Road, and the Swift Trail Scenic Parkway. They are the hubs of this travel wheel rolling through southeastern Arizona, but the spokes of beauty and history and dramatic scenery extend for miles beyond the actual routes themselves. We'll go along for the ride. ∭

Dale Schicketanz

Remains of barracks at Fort Bowie. ▲ Adventurers explore a back road in Saguaro National Park. ▼

Ralph Lee Hopkins

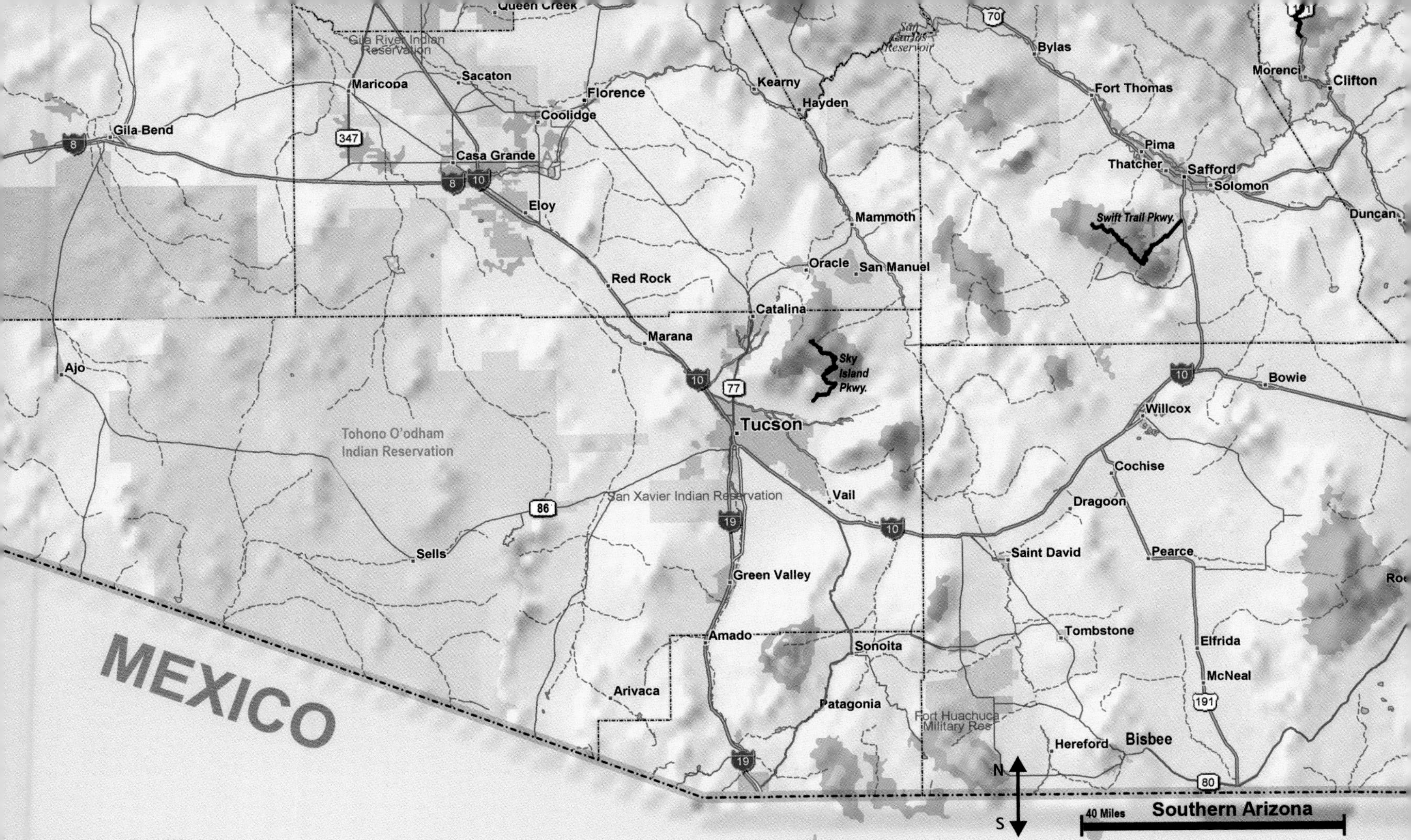

© 2006 DeLorme. Topo USA® 6.0

MEXICO

Southern Arizona

40 Miles

N   S

Sky Island Scenic Parkway

Route   Tucson to Summerhaven via Catalina Highway.

Mileage   25 miles one way.

Elevation 2,400 feet to above 9,100 feet. Snow in winter.

Overview   Officially designated as an Arizona Parkway and
               a National Scenic Byway, this paved, two-lane
               highway runs from the lower Sonoran Desert and
               climbs, bends, and rolls to the alpine village of
               Summerhaven atop Mount Lemmon in the Santa
               Catalina Mountains. Enroute are great views of
               mountains and valleys, rock formations and a
               variety of environments offering cool summer
               temperatures, camping, fishing, hiking, berry-
               picking, picnic sites, and even a small ski hill.

It must sometimes seem to visitors to Tucson that all roads lead to Mount Lemmon, and there's a reason for that: There is only one road, but it has several aliases including the Hitchcock Highway, the Catalina Highway, the Sky Island Scenic Parkway, and, quite sensibly, the Mount Lemmon Road.

It is an officially designated scenic drive that is short on distance but long on vistas and outdoor revelry. It can begin with a breakfast burrito in almost any café in the low desert of Tucson at 2,400 feet and end 25 miles or so later with homemade pie in the sky at another café, this one at nearly 9,200 feet in the mountain town of Summerhaven, just a short schuss away from skiing on the southernmost ski hill in the United States.

About those various names:

The road, a classic example of mountainous switchbacks, leads up the south face of the Santa Catalina range, a majestic set of crags and domes and one of five ranges (the Santa Catalinas and Tortalitas on the north, Rincons east, Tucsons west, Santa Ritas south) that surround Tucson. The name of the range, according to some accounts, might have come from that famed Jesuit priest-explorer, Father Eusebio Kino who, in the late 1600s, is reported to have dubbed a nearby Indian rancheria "Santa Catarina de Cuytoabucam."

As for Mount Lemmon, in 1881 a botanist named John G. Lemmon and his bride, Sarah, were taken into the Catalinas by a guide named Emerson Stratton.

Out of gallantry to Mrs. Lemmon, Stratton is said to have christened this particular peak with her name.

The origin of the road names Catalina Highway and Mount Lemmon Road are obvious. The other two – Hitchcock Highway and Sky Island Scenic Parkway – are not, which requires a further paragraph of etymological excavation. Hold the groans.

Access to the mountaintop in the early 1900s and earlier was by a rugged trail, and what few residents made their home there were supplied by pack trains. In the 1930s and 1940s, prison laborers created part of a road and, after World War II, a local editor (and postmaster) named Frank Harris Hitchcock persuaded the bureaucrats of the day to complete the road to the top. In 1951 the road was surfaced and is now a two-lane paved passage through some gloriously dramatic scenery as it climbs from the saguaros below to the ponderosa pines above.

So much for how it got its name of Hitchcock Highway. As for the ponderous appellation Sky Island Scenic Parkway, "sky island" is a poetic term for a mountain range abruptly jutting up from flat desert. For the record, the road is not part of the state of Arizona's scenic road system, but if that ruins anyone's enjoyment of this drive, he or she is urged to seek therapy.

[The Catalina Highway twists past spectacular rock forms.]

Randy Prentice

So how to find this road of many names? One easy way, assuming the driver is on Interstate 10 coming south into Tucson, is to exit on Grant Road, head east on Grant to Tanque Verde Road, then left to the Catalina Highway (that's the Mount Lemmon Road) leading into the eastern end of the Catalinas and then left again. At that point, the community of Summerhaven is 25 miles and some melodramatic scenery away. The climb on this road begins quickly, as do the resulting views down into the valley where Tucson reclines flatly and fatly across the desert. This is, by the way, a toll road, and a fee is charged at Milepost 3 for use of some facilities along the way. A straight drive-through, however, costs nothing.

Before starting out, check the gas gauge. Despite the fact that this road and these mountains are hugely popular with the locals seeking respite from the heat as well as with tourists and skiers, there are no gas stations. And unlikely as it might seem to someone leaving the valley floor in June, July, August, or

September, take along a sweater and even a raincoat. In late fall and winter, raid the closet for boots, parkas, and gloves and the garage for tire chains. There might be snow.

Hundreds of thousands of people make this drive annually, and among them are the specialists: botanists, geologists, anthropologists, zoologists, ornithologists, climatologists, and all sorts of other scientists. Collectively, their dissections have revealed just about all anyone could want to know about the anatomy of this range.

A miniscule sampling of their lore that was derived from painstaking observation and evisceration:

Rocks. The Catalina Mountains are, in the main, a big pile of nice gneiss and grand granite. Those rocks are the oldest, dating back perhaps 1.5 billion years. The 200-square-mile range itself came to be at least 20 million years ago and since then has been elaborately carved by erosion. The U.S. Forest Service says the Catalinas "are unrewarding for mineral collectors" although some old mine sites have produced quartz, hematite, mica, pyrite, copper minerals, red garnets, and even minor amounts of gold, just to name a few.

Fossils. Not good either. Although, along the east and northeast flanks of the mountains corals, brachiopods, and trilobites can be found.

Birds. Lots of same and quite varied because of the changes in moisture and habitat due to climbing elevation. There are turkey vultures, kites, hawks, falcons, quail, turkeys, sandpipers, pigeons, doves, owls of all kinds, swifts, nighthawks, hummingbirds, woodpeckers, flycatchers, swallows, magpies, and crows.

Trees. Douglas and white firs, aspens, maples, ponderosa and white pines, madrone, among others. In 1998, University of Arizona tree-ring researchers found a then-678-year-old Douglas fir near the top and said it was the oldest living tree ever found in this range. How did they determine its age? Why, they bored a pencil-sized hole into the tree, pulled out a tube of wood and counted its growth rings, each one designating a year.

Animals. The usual list of suspects including those old mountain standards, skunks, bears, deer, squirrels, an occasional mountain lion, and many, many more. It's a zoo out there, but if you prefer to see your wild animals in a safer setting, head for the Arizona-Sonora Desert Museum in Tucson. As for the bears, Arizona Game and Fish authorities suggest taking all the usual precautions: Clean the campsite, clean pots and pans, don't eat in the tent, leave no food odors anywhere, put food in the car trunk or suspend it from a tree if in the back country. In short, if something, including you, smells, there's a possible problem.

On the road again, the eyes of a botanist are not required to spot the obvious changes in flora, starting with the saguaros below and moving onward and upward into scrub oak and, finally, pines, aspens, and firs near the top. Near mileposts 5, 11, and 12 are rest areas, campgrounds, picnic sites, and trailheads.

Not long after the climb begins, a left turn onto East Prison Camp Road (remember the prisoners who built part of the early road?) leads in less than a mile to the Gordon Hirabayashi Recreation Site, a charming, small campground with a rest room, good shade, a horse corral, a dozen campsites, a mostly dry creek, a startling, stately cypress tree, and some fine fragments of earlier stone walls.

Back on the main path, a sign marks the first of several falcon-nesting sites, although spotting a nesting falcon is roughly akin to nailing Jell-O on your living room wall.

Shortly before Windy Point Vista, at about mileposts 13 and 14, the rock outcrops sculpted by Nature's forces become an omigosh affair. At Milepost 15 is what could be called Duck Rock or Platypus

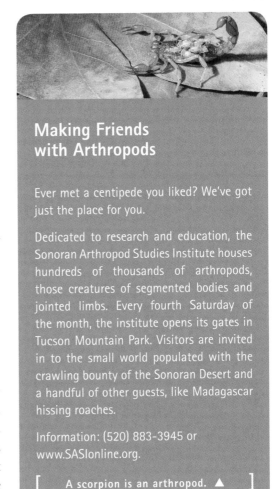

Making Friends with Arthropods

Ever met a centipede you liked? We've got just the place for you.

Dedicated to research and education, the Sonoran Arthropod Studies Institute houses hundreds of thousands of arthropods, those creatures of segmented bodies and jointed limbs. Every fourth Saturday of the month, the institute opens its gates in Tucson Mountain Park. Visitors are invited in to the small world populated with the crawling bounty of the Sonoran Desert and a handful of other guests, like Madagascar hissing roaches.

Information: (520) 883-3945 or www.SASIonline.org.

[A scorpion is an arthropod. ▲   ]

Point but is actually Goosehead Rock. One look will tell you why. Next up, near Milepost 17, is a turnoff to Rose Canyon Lake, a campground, picnic area, and lake, although the word "lake" somewhat overstates the magnitude of this seven-acre pond that is stocked with trout and people with fishing rods. Camping here costs by the vehicle per night. Roughly three mileposts farther is the Forest Service's Palisades visitors center offering telephones, rest rooms, maps, and a few interpretive displays.

Just before the village of Summerhaven is the turnoff leading 2 miles to the small but charming Mount Lemmon Ski Valley and its ski hillock and chairlift. It is open all year, and rides on the lift are available. (See Mount Lemmon Ski Valley entry in the Where To Go section at the end of this chapter.) It is a tiny facility despite its claim of 15 runs, four of them expert, seven of them intermediate, the rest beginner. The runs are short and many of them are precipitous. The snow pack isn't always great—in fact, it sometimes barely exists—but for those short on time and long on desire, it beats driving several hours north to Sunrise Resort in the White Mountains or the Snowbowl in Flagstaff.

Back down to the main road, Summerhaven and almost the end of the drive are just ahead. Beyond is the road's end and Marshall Gulch, which offers a picnic area and a nice hike. Summerhaven, although victimized earlier this decade by a forest fire, is, in the words of one resident, a "forest paradise in the middle of the desert," a literally cool village where you can get and enjoy a bowl of steamy chili in August at the Alpine Lodge and a slice from any one of 14 kinds of pie at the Mount Lemmon Café. Cabins are crowded tightly together in a sort of architectural mosh pit, and some can be rented, sometimes for prices that could put a debit dent in a modest checking account.

Drivers and their passengers are now confronted with two alternatives: Turn around and drive back down to Tucson or backtrack from Summerhaven for a short distance to Forest Service Road 38, otherwise signed "Control Road," and take it off the backside of Mount Lemmon down its even more inspirational north face to the town of Oracle and the much-publicized Biosphere 2.

The argument for turning around is that the vistas can be revisited without twisting the neck, and it's an easy, downhill coast. The argument for the latter is … uh … well … it's something to do if you are bored, don't want to see Tucson again, and have plenty of gas, good tires, a spare, water on board, a vehicle with four-wheel drive and ample clearance, and passengers with patience and a sense of adventure.

Early on, the sign off the backside says this is a "primitive road not maintained for passenger cars." Believe it. In fact, it is a twisty, winding, dusty, bumpy, rock-embedded, one-and-a-half lane washboard of a dirt road with forks but few if any signs and, eventually, some nice vistas and an abundance of century plants that have sent their stalks heavenward. Best advice if you are driving a sedan or there is any doubt in your mind: Don't. Best advice if you like a small adventure in driving that would give AAA advisors spasms: Do. ∭

Hikers make their way up the Butterfly Trail in the Santa Catalina Mountains, capped by Mount Lemmon.

Randy Prentice

Patagonia-Sonoita Scenic Road

Route	Any direction you wish to go to see most of southeastern Arizona and some backtracking. Primary routes are Interstate 10; state routes 83, 82, 80, 90, 92, 186, and 181; and U.S. Route 191. The official route, however, is along State 82 and 83.
Mileage	Tucson to Nogales, 63 miles. Nogales to Patagonia, Sonoita, I-10, and Tucson, 68 miles.
Elevation	2,400 feet at Tucson, about 5,000 at Sonoita, nearly 9,000 in the Chiracahua peaks.
Overview	A trip that can be started in any direction and one that will lead, within minutes, to something that is either remarkably beautiful, starkly dramatic, or iconically historic. There are wonderful caves (Colossal and Kartchner), marvelous mountains (Santa Ritas, Whetstones, Dragoons, Chiracahuas), historic communities (Tombstone, Bisbee, Douglas, Benson, Willcox), canyons (Texas), and Indian hangouts dating to the old Wild West (Cochise's Stronghold). It's all in a beautiful desert, and it can be done any time of year in a day or, better, two or three.

1 If you permit it, the thing about this trip could be THE THING.

Big, bright-yellow billboards with those two bold-black words appear with even greater frequency than gift shops on major routes in this area of southeastern Arizona but particularly along Interstate 10. The building housing THE THING is at Interstate 10's Exit 322, about 18 miles east of Benson roughly where the interstate runs through a jumble of rocks and rock formations known as Texas Canyon. This Barnumesque phenomenon has been there for decades, nay, generations. Locals mostly ignore it.

Should you also, for whatever reason, choose to do just that, ignore it, there

Continued on Page 114

A Relaxing Haven

Driving a rental car from Phoenix to Tucson at night is to experience the urbanizing American pit of speeding semis and riotous light and sound. East of Tucson, traffic abates and life improves. Hope ignites in the desert south of Benson on State Route 80 and swells to happy anticipation in Tombstone. Then, four hours after leaving Phoenix, we honk joyfully in the Mule Pass Tunnel, the gateway to Bisbee, hidden in the Mule Mountains pretty much outside the real world.

So in our second visit from Wisconsin in less than a year, here is our take: Bisbee is a relaxing haven from which to visit other nice southeastern Arizona destinations including Tombstone, Fort Huachuca, the Coronado National Monument, Arizona's wine country, Chiricahua National Monument, Cochise Stronghold, Kartchner Caverns, and birdy canyons.

Paul G. Hayes, an expert in the raising of chickens, retired after a career as an acclaimed science and environmental journalist for the Milwaukee Journal *(now the* Journal-Sentinel*). He spends his days hunting, fishing, hiking, teaching, collecting esoteric oddments, and, in this instance, writing about his travels to what is becoming one of his favorite destinations, the historic mining town of Bisbee.*

> By PAUL G. HAYES

But Bisbee outranks them as the cozy center without which we would not schedule the trip. Its jewelry and arts and crafts shops are special, but the antiquing is unmatched for eclecticism and value. In one shop, I found steel eagle emblems that once adorned the famous pickelhauben, or spiked helmets, of the Kaiser's imperial German army. I badly needed one for an emblem-less pickelhaube in my possession and found that $25 per emblem was cheap enough. But when the antique dealer offered all three for $45, I peeled off two twenties and a five in a second. Immediately after unpacking at home, I fitted my pickelhaube with a gray eagle, made a gift of the gilded eagle to a delighted 14-year-old collector, and stashed the third.

My wife, Philia, found a green, yellowware bowl that fit her kitchen for much less than she would have paid in Wisconsin. If we'd driven instead of flown, an old typewriter would have made the trip back to Wisconsin in the back seat. The Remington No. 7, patented in 1897, is a direct descendant of the world's first workable typewriter invented by Milwaukee's own Christopher Lapham Sholes. Priced at 60 bucks or roughly three dollars a pound, the typewriter cost less per pound than Milwaukee's famous bratwurst.

Walking and hiking are outstanding. Start anywhere and walk in any direction and you either are climbing or descending. Good advice is to set aside ample time, wear quality walking shoes and heavy jeans for pushing through some prickly cover, and carry water. We didn't do any of these things, a strategy that caused occasional pain.

Leaving the comfy old Copper Queen Hotel, we turned left, then left again onto Brewery Avenue. We passed yards of barking dogs, fences decorated with hubcaps, and guys out fixing cars in their yards. One of these kindly pointed us toward a gulch, which led to an old concrete reservoir. We picked through the dry bed of the watercourse above the reservoir and then climbed cross-country to the top of a ridge. Philia wrote in her journal: "At the ridge, we found narrow trail and overlooks of stretched-out old Bisbee, then the copper pit. Agave, manzanita, pearly everlasting, beautiful grasses everywhere, especially on north slopes behind Bisbee. Lovely walk."

Picking our way down the rocky hillside, we soon were walking down narrow steps between restored miners' houses and into the center of Bisbee. Three hours; good photos. Now a ravenous appetite leads to Bisbee's food, which can vary from good soups and sandwiches, coffee house pastry-based fare to top level, pricey spreads. Bisbee appetites frequently lead to Café Roka, reputed among the state's best, an experience of mellow wines and rich entrees. Get reservations – and the duck.

Bisbee residents are nothing if not quaint. Who knows what a native Bisbeean looks like; most miners dispersed when the mine closed decades ago. Outside the mining museum we met no one directly linked to mining days. Those folks who stand out are the spaghetti-western wannabes, complete with hairy faces, flinty eyes, black slickers and clunky spurs, sharing the sidewalks with long-braided, barefoot hippie moms now edging up on Social Security. Cowboy, hippie or in-between, Bisbeeans seem laid back, friendly, and content, which is your destiny too, once you emerge from Mule Pass Tunnel. ʎΙΙ

[
Bisbee introduces visitors to mining with excursions like the
Copper Queen Mine Tour.
]

Tony Marinella

Continued from Page 111

remains the problem of the curiosity of the more credulous younger set in the vehicle. Suggestion: Tell them what a local newspaper reporter, Douglas Kreutz, recounted of his investigation into THE THING back in November 1973. It appears to be a mommy mummy with a baby mummy. One major problem, however, is that the mommy mummy is about 6 feet long (Kreutz is, or used to be when younger, 6 feet 2 inches tall) and the people indigenous to this part of the country some 5,000 to 10,000 ago, deprived as they were of multivitamin pills, were much shorter than that. Kreutz also reported that an anthropological scholar had been refused permission to examine the purported remains.

A Madera Canyon waterfall cascades in the Santa Rita Mountains.

Willard Clay

So let us pick up the route of the Patagonia-Sonoita Scenic Road on State routes 83 and 82. Head east out of Tucson on I-10 to Exit 281 where you pick up State 83, which runs south to the community of Sonoita where it intersects with State 82 leading on to Patagonia and, finally, Nogales, the end of the official route.

A worthwhile stop just off I-10 about 2 miles before you reach the turnoff to 83 is Colossal Cave Mountain Park, featuring a big "dry" cave that has served as a shelter and storage area of the aboriginal Hohokam Indians and, much later, for train robbers. It is reached from Exit 279.

The scenery along State 83 is beautiful, basic basin-and-range country, a panorama of small valleys and big hills with the towering Santa Rita Mountains, snow-capped in winter, just ahead. The terrain ranges back and forth among various forms of plant life: prickly pear cactus, then scrub oak, then grasslands so abundant they could feed the world's herbivores, then yuccas and piñon-juniper forest, the various populations depending on the ever-changing elevation. In spring, it's a wonderland of wildflowers. The entire journey of 60-plus miles from near Tucson to Nogales wanders through this sometimes pastoral, sometimes dramatic scenery to its end in Nogales, where, in late fall and early winter, the traveler is greeted on Grand Avenue by sculpted pyracantha bushes bursting with orange-colored berries that are popular with robins bent on a bender (or so it is said).

In the tiny community of Sonoita, State 83 intersects with State 82, which, in turns, leads on to Nogales. But before that, take a left on Upper Elgin Road in Sonoita to Elgin about 5 miles away and in the heart of Arizona's wine country, an incongruous mix of yuccas, vineyards, and propane-powered wind generators that keep the frost from the vines at 4,700 feet of elevation. It is home to a dozen or so boutique wineries.

David H. Smith

A Mountain of Attractions

Besides antiquing, there are many other attractions worth mentioning to visitors to the mountain town of Bisbee that began as a mining camp in 1880 and is now an artists' colony, a retirement community, and a Victorian-era tourist attraction that often reminds visitors of San Francisco.

Underground mine tour: There has been no mining of consequence in the city since 1975. That works to the advantage of travelers who can take a Queen Mine tour, a drafty, chilly ride in open cars along a narrow rail line running along an underground tunnel into the dormant mine and its shafts where grimy, gutsy guys once extracted the ore with sledge hammers and steel spikes to make the holes to hold the dynamite that would release the ore- bearing rock. The tours last about an hour. Advice: Wear a coat. The year-round temperature inside the shaft is 47 degrees. Although you will be decked out in miner's helmet, yellow slicker, and miner's lamp that add style, of a sort, they offer no warmth.

Museum: The non-profit Bisbee Mining and Historical Museum, a Smithsonian affiliate, offers 120 years of Bisbee history with excellent exhibits.

Birding: Birds everywhere, many of them migrants from Mexico here for short stays. Go to the Bisbee Chamber of Commerce and Visitor Center on Subway Street for advice on how to go birding in the San Pedro Riparian Conservation Area, the Whitewater Draw, or just about anywhere in the Mule, Huachuca, and Chiricahua mountains. There are two birding festivals—one in May that includes tours, seminars, and vendors, and another one, the Southwest Wings Birding and Nature Festival, in August.

July 4 entertainment: Overwhelming. Everything from a run from the not-too-distant Continental Divide through a canyon and into the historic district of the town to a parade, to a mine mucking and hard-rock drilling contest, to fireworks to the famous coaster races. The coaster races, which spawned the nationally famous soapbox derbies of years past, are once again limited to kids and a 300-pound weight limit. There was a time after World War II when

▶

[The tour leader (in front) once worked in the Queen Mine. ▲   ]

grown men got into this amazing downhill roll and began producing coasters weighing up to 1,000 pounds and capable of negotiating the 3-mile course in fewer than three minutes. Some serious injuries and at least one fatality ended that folly.

Brewery Gulch Daze: Held every Labor Day weekend, this party brings together a mix of locals and out-of-towners in a wide-open, shoes-optional, small-town street festival. Visitors can entertain their kids at carnival-style booths, play waterball or something called "human foosball," dance to live music or enjoy a drink from the open-air balcony of the Stock Exchange bar, while watching a parade of pets dressed in ridiculous outfits or a waitperson contest in which contestants balance pitchers and water cups on trays and run an obstacle course. All the while, chili cooks brew their recipes beneath makeshift tents. The aroma is intense. Brewery Gulch is a street once home to more than 20 bars and brothels. Additional information: (520) 432-5421; www.bisbeearizona.com

The pits: There are two spectacular open-pit copper mines, one the Sacramento Pit and the other the famous, 300-acre Lavender Pit. Essentially, they are huge, terraced holes in the earth that start wide and get smaller and smaller in diameter as they get deeper and deeper. Both are shut down now, but it's worthwhile just to gaze into them and marvel at what man can do to Mother Earth if money is involved.

Miscellaneous: A chocolate tasting in February; a three-day bicycling event in April; an antique show in May; tours of historic homes in November or December, and trolley tours just about any time (call the Warren-Bisbee Railway at (520) 220-4192 for trolley reservations).

(See Where To Go, beginning on Page 130, for details on these and other Bisbee and southeastern Arizona attractions and events.)

For a modest sum, two of the wineries offer daily, year-round wine tastings; the others less frequently. Major offerings include cabernet sauvignons, chardonnays, colombards, merlots, sauvignon blancs, pinot noirs, Rieslings, white ports, clarets, and syrahs. Non-snobs (or snobs with a sense of humor and adventure) can enjoy a taste (or a bottle) of some whimsical labels from Sonoita Vineyards including "Arizona Dry," described as light, dry, and crisp with hints of oak – good with fish; or "Arizona Sunset," a semi-sweet blush "good on picnics;" or "Sonora Blanca," sweet, delicate and "good with cheesecake." At the nearby and more flamboyant Village of Elgin Winery, the number one seller is "Tombstone Red," a blend of red and white that "goes great with scorpion, tarantula, and rattlesnake meat," assuming one can find a fat scorpion or a balding tarantula. That same winery, however, also offers a $295 bottle of Reccieto, called Regalo.

The co-owners of the Village of Elgin Winery are Gary and Kathy Reeves, also known, mostly to themselves, apparently, as Kathryn, Lady Ellam, and Garrison, Lord Ellam. Lord Ellam, aka Gary, a stocky man in his mid-40s, alleges that he is a Scot and a former earl and member of the British House of Lords. He is given to dry, good humor and the occasional wearing of kilts. He also has a creative imagination and claims to have size 14 feet with which, he says, he stomps his own grapes for his own red wines (the grapes for whites go into a press). His accent, which might pass for Scottish, comes and goes.

Uh-huh, sure. But whatever one wishes to believe of all that—and some of his winemaker peers in the region are deeply and openly skeptical—the fact remains that the lord and his lady, ersatz or not, produce some genuinely wonderful wines and some highly entertaining conversation.

He might also still have Gizmo, a fine house cat who likes everybody and treats them, as proper cats do, like members of its staff.

[A harvester spends the morning cutting grapes in Elgin's Renzi Vineyards.   ]

Dave Bly

Jeff Snyder

A Hideaway

The American Museum of Natural History in New York operates the Southwestern Research Station in the quiet folds of the Chiricahua Mountains primarily for researchers. However, as space permits – frequently in the spring and fall, occasionally in the summer – other guests may stay at the station and enjoy outstanding scenery amid woodlands, a multitude of birds and other wildlife, and great hiking trails.

The station provides comfortable cabins and a main house with a library, a lounge with a fireplace, and a family-style dining room where chefs serve up home cooking. Outside, a swimming pool, volleyball court, and horseshoe pit offer relaxing diversions.

To find the getaway, take State Route 80 from Douglas northeast to Rodeo, New Mexico; go 2 more miles (you'll cross back into Arizona) to Portal Road and turn left (west) and go 7 miles to Portal. Drive up the mountain another 5 miles (the road is paved) until you see on your left an in-ground pool, an expanse of grass and a cluster of buildings. Turn left, cross a wash, and turn left again at the station's gate. For information: (520) 558-2396; http://research.amnh.org/swrs

[**Volcanic tuff formations inspire the imagination at the Chiricahua National Monument.** ▲]

Another winery, the Sonoita Vineyards, was created in 1983 by a fellow with a somewhat more prosaic but unquestionably legitimate title of Dr., as in Ph.D. He is Gordon R. Dutt, a retired professor of soil sciences at the University of Arizona who has been described variously as "a sort of an Indiana Jones character" and by a *Washington Post* writer in 1986 as perhaps the "father of viticulture in a state better known for whiskey-drinking cowboys than Chablis-sipping oenophiles."

Dutt's wines are distinct from those of Lord Ellam's—two of Dutt's were selected for the inauguration of President George Bush The First—and a dedicated taster could do worse than to go to those and others for a sampling of the differences. The settings are equally different: The Village of Elgin Winery is a set of rough-hewn structures —the main building is a single-story, tin-roofed structure with sun-blackened wood siding and is said to have been built in 1895 as a bordello. The complex is nestled near a creek amid big cottonwoods. The Sonoita Vineyards, on the other hand, is housed in a modern villa on a hilltop and offers a 360-degree view of the surrounding almost Tuscan-like landscape of distant mountains, adjacent rolling hills, grasslands, and white oaks. Sonoita Vineyards, managed by Kreg Mosel, also offers a winery tour, a tractor-drawn vineyard tour, and the option of a catered lunch in an upstairs room seating 65.

Dutt, incidentally, offers the explanation for why fine wines can be produced in an area more noted for cactus. The soil in this spot, he says, is almost identical to the acidic, red clay soil of Burgundy's Côte d'Or, a region famous for its quality red wines. That he wraps his wines in a label of the landscape, painted by Tucson artist Barbara Smith, is testimony to his taste for fine art.

Good times to visit: April for a blessing of the vines, August for a wine fest, and November for the new harvest and new releases. For exact dates, call Sonoita Vineyards, (520) 455-5893; or the Village of Elgin Winery, (520) 455-9309.

After sipping your fill, it's time for the designated driver to turn around and head back to Sonoita and the intersection that leads on State 82 to the delightful hamlet of Patagonia, with its oak grasslands at more than 4,000 feet and its bird watching. The community has a small selection of restaurants, a bank, churches, a library, parks, a swimming pool, gas station, galleries, shops, a small grocery, and some lodging. From there, it is a short shot to the end of the trip in Nogales and the Mexico border.

While traveling through this grassland paradise, there are countless southeastern Arizona side trips within 90 minutes driving time and leading to the historic towns of Tombstone (remember the OK Corral), Bisbee, and Douglas; magnificent mountain ranges, especially the Chiracahuas; Indian hideouts, particularly Cochise's; astounding rock formations; the Willcox playa with its sandhill crane migration; a cowboy museum dedicated to actor Rex Allen; and much, much more.

The ranching communities of Sonoita and Elgin came into existence with the arrival of a Benson-to-Nogales Railway in 1882 and are set in high, rolling grasslands dominated by major mountains. They have been the setting for several movies including *Oklahoma, Red River,* and, more recently, *Tin Cup* and *The Young Guns.* Patagonia was founded in 1898 and by some stretch of linguistic imagination is said to have gotten its name from the Spanish meaning "the place where the big-footed animals hold forth." It originally was a shipping center for cattle and silver and lead ore. The last ore was shipped in 1959, and the rail line closed in 1962. The old depot became a town hall, and a park and gazebo are a focus of the town's public life.

As the trip continues along 82 past Patagonia and toward Nogales, there is at least one more "must see" site, the Patagonia Lake State Park just 7 miles past Patagonia.

Hidden away in these rolling hills is this 265-acre, man-made lake established in 1975 as a state park and a great place to find deer in the surrounding hills, great blue herons on the shoreline, and crappie, bass, bluegill, and catfish in the waters. Trout? They are stocked every three weeks from November until late February.

The lake area, like many of the canyons in the area, is a bird watcher's Nirvana, with trails offering views of loons, grebes, pelicans, cormorants, herons, egrets, ibises, geese, ducks, vultures, hawks, eagles, falcons, turkeys, quail,

Randy Prentice

A Cavalcade of Sites

A diverse mixture of towns and attractions sprinkle southeastern Arizona like a juxtaposed dusting of snow on cactus. Among them are sites from the old West, mining towns, border towns, a world-renowned cave hidden below a mountain for a half-million years before two cavers discovered it in 1974, and a fort and stronghold that recall the Apache Wars of Territorial Arizona, and a wonderland of rocks.

Tombstone

You've seen it in the movies, you've seen it on TV, but until you go there, you've not really seen it, podnuh.

Tombstone, "the town (stifle that gag reflex) too tough to die" (from a 1932 headline in the *St. Louis Dispatch*). The O.K. Corral, near where the Earps and the Clantons and the McLaurys conducted their inglorious but much-celebrated gunfight for 30 seconds and 25 shots in 1881. The Bird Cage Theatre, the wildest, wickedest combination of honky-tonk, poker den, theater, and whorehouse in America in the 1880s. Boot Hill Graveyard, the final resting place for the good, the bad, and the unknown of the town in the 1880s.

You bet it's touristy. Without tourists, the too-tough-to-die town would be dead. With or without them, is it ever historic. That's a statement, not a question. There is little to match the sensation of actually standing in the real dirt of the famous corral and watching a re-enactment of the gunfight (which actually took place behind the corral). Or walking among the graves in Boot Hill and reading the epitaphs over the graves of dead gunfighters, abandoned women, Chinese laborers, victims of drunken brawls, and just plain people. Or strolling around the genuine Bird Cage and down the stairs to gaze at a high-stakes poker table set on a dirt floor within almost arm's reach of "cribs," small rooms with a bed where prostitutes serviced the players.

It's a thick veneer of civility overlaying a rich history of overactive libidos, overarching egos, and matchless machismo. Lots of shops, restaurants, and

[Historic Bisbee spreads through Tombstone Canyon. ▲   ]

plovers, sandpipers, gulls, doves, pigeons, owls, roadrunners, nighthawks, swifts, hummingbirds, trogons, kingfishers, woodpeckers, flycatchers, larks, crows, jays, nuthatches, wrens, warblers, tanagers, cardinals, towhees, meadowlarks, finches, and sparrows. There also are facilities including a beach; picnic area with ramadas, tables, and grills; a creek trail; boat ramps, a marina and supply store; and a campground with hookups, rest rooms, showers, and a dump station.

[
A male Gila woodpecker perches on
a saguaro blossom in Tucson.
]

Tom Vezo

The park, just off State Route 82, sits between 3,800 and 4,200 feet of elevation and has vegetation of the Upper Sonoran Desert, which is mostly desert grassland. The Sonoita Creek flows along the edge of the park for nearly 3 miles. A bird list supplied by the Arizona State Parks names more than 200 birds to be seen there at varying times of year and in varying abundance. Bird-watching tours on pontoon boats are available, one per day usually but more available upon request and reservation. Scheduled tours are Wednesdays, Saturdays, and Sundays at 9 a.m. The boats hold eight passengers and the fee is per person. Call (520) 287-2791 or (520) 287-6965.

After that, it is time for the final, short run into Nogales and, just across the border, some fine shopping if you have a taste for bargaining and, despite the wine bottles purchased earlier in the day, a jug of 100 percent blue agave tequila. ▥

saloons along the genuine boardwalks; motels; friendly clerks; free parking. All the literature you could ever want telling you about Wyatt Earp, who died in 1929 at age 80 in Los Angeles; his shotgun-toting friend, Doc Holliday; and Doc's gossipy prostitute girlfriend, Big Nose Kate Elder. The world's largest rose tree covers 8,600 square feet and still is growing.

It's the bawdy, brawling, turbulent West that once was. Nobody need apologize for enjoying the spectacle. And, in passing, it is worth noting that there's still a fight going on about the most-touted gunfight in Tombstone's history. The town newspaper, the famed *Tombstone Epitaph*, in November of 2001 carried a front-page headline reading: "Group debates O.K. Corral gunfight facts." Seems there

▶

is some disagreement about whether or not Tom McLaury was armed during the gunfight. A relative of one of the Clantons says he wasn't. Either way, Tom died in the battle.

How to find Tombstone? Hard to miss. Head south from Interstate 10's Exit 304 just east of Benson or north from Bisbee, both directions on State Route 80.

Kartchner Caverns

In 1974, about 50 miles southeast of Tucson, two cavers who weren't afraid of the dark began poking around a sinkhole in the limestone hills at the base of the Whetstone Mountains . They were searching for a cave, any cave, and they found a beaut.

In the bottom of the sinkhole, they discovered a narrow crack leading into the hillside and a flow of warm, moist air reeking of bat guano, just the sort of thing that makes a spelunker's heart pound. Several hours of crawling, wiggling, twisting, squirming, and sledge hammering later, they entered into a black world of stalactites (hang from the ceiling), stalagmites (rise from the floor), helictites, soda straws (thin-walled, hollow tubes), and bacon and fried eggs (mineral formations that look remarkably moist and edible but aren't unless you have steel teeth).

What they had found was a big, half-million-year-old "living" cavern 2-and-a-half miles long with two football field-sized rooms filled with extraordinary colors and formations including the largest column ever found in cave-rich Arizona—a 58-foot monster now named Kubla Kahn. They had lucked out, because the limestone-laden Whetstones have been combed for years by cavers who know that when water seeps through limestone, it dissolves the rock and forms underground cavities. Sinkholes, depressions in the ground created when cavities collapse, are a good sign of a cave, but no one had found this one until Randy Tufts and Gary Tenen came along.

Legitimately fearful that the cavern would be harmed by souvenir hunters and graffiti idiots if word of its existence got out, they kept their discovery relatively secret until 1978, when they revealed it to the owner of the land, a science teacher and school superintendent named James Kartchner. The Kartchner family eventually decided that it would be too expensive to develop the cave and, in 1984, decided to sell it to the state, which could afford to create a state park. Finally, after 14 years of secrecy, the state purchased the cave for slightly more than $1.6 million.

Kartchner Caverns, which opened as a state park in 1999, offers paved trails, guided tours of the caverns and the area above ground, a 23,000-square-foot informational center with fine displays, a picnic area, vending machines, an auditorium with videos, and a tram. The cave is still "living," meaning it is still damp and dripping, its formations still growing. The temperature averages 68 degrees and the humidity 99 percent. Paleontologists have found the skeletons of an 80,000-year-old sloth, a 34,000-year-old horse, and an 11,000-year-old bear (that's the age of the skeletons, not the beasts, lest anyone wish to pick a nit).

During summer months, a fascinating area called the "Big Room" — 400 foot long by 240 feet wide and now opened to the public — becomes a nursery roost for a thousand or so female myotis bats. The pregnant bats return to the caverns from Mexico around the end of April and give birth to a single pup in late July. Then, they all wing off for Mexico in about mid-September. Their nursery is off limits to visitors during the bats' residence.

The caverns, despite dim lighting, can be claustrophobic for some and, unless you are under 6 years old, a bit pricey. Entrance into the park costs per vehicle carrying four passengers (additional passengers are charged per person) and cave tours cost another fee per person for those 14 and older. Cave tours last about 75 minutes, 45 of those underground. It is a good idea to make reservations by calling (520) 586-2283. The park is 9 miles south of Interstate 10 (Exit 302), just off State Route 90.

Willcox

The town of Willcox, on Interstate 10 east of Tucson, provides access for interstate drivers to many of the historic wonders of southeastern Arizona, but it has its own fascinations, particularly the Rex Allen Museum and Theater, the Cowboy Hall of Fame (a separate exhibit located within the Allen Museum), and the Willcox Playa, a mostly dry lake bed that provides habitat for wintering and migrating birds including several thousand sandhill cranes.

For those too young to remember, Rex Allen was born in 1920 in Willcox and stayed there until he became one of the silver screen's singing cowboys. Rex and his horse, KoKo, starred in 19 movies for Republic Pictures in the 1950s. He also narrated more than 100 Disney films and hung around long enough to get pretty big on television. He died in 1999, and his ashes were scattered in the park across from the museum, also the site of KoKo's grave, according to the plaques and publicity.

The museum offers a large collection of Rex Allen memorabilia, including endless photos of him, his multi-hued silk cowboy costumes, his guns, his hats, his wife, his kids, his horse, his movie posters, his . . . well, you get the idea. And don't forget the annual Rex Allen Days celebration with parades, rodeos, stage shows, and dances, usually the first weekend in October.

The museum is on Railroad Avenue in downtown Willcox. Look for the bronze statue outside and across the street in the park or just stand and listen for the

▶

continuous tape of Rex singing. There's a pretty good barbeque joint a "historic" building or so away.

From October through late February, the Willcox Playa (which used to be a lake in prehistoric times) outside the city draws flocks of sandhill cranes that feed in nearby corn stubble and grassland. There is a Wings Over Willcox festival in mid-January to celebrate these birds, which are about 4 feet tall and have wingspans of 5 to 7 feet. They migrate from Utah, Idaho, Montana, and Wyoming, as well as Alaska and Siberia, and appear to be happy campers when they put down on this semi-secluded roosting area. Best time to see them: sunrise and late afternoon.

An Arizona Game and Fish Department Mexican Duck Nesting Area on Kansas Settlement Road outside of Willcox offers a good view of the cranes in flight.

Fort Bowie

This old ruin of a fort, now a national historic site, was established in 1862 and abandoned in 1894. It was named after commanding officer Col. George Washington Bowie and for more than 20 years was a nerve center for military operations by the Army against the Chiricahua Apache Indians in the so-called Apache Wars. That struggle ended with the surrender of wily Apache leader Geronimo in 1886. To get there, you have to walk a 1.5-mile foot trail that is open sunrise to sunset and that follows an old military road used by the soldiers who garrisoned the post. Along the way are the ruins of the Butterfield Stage station. There is a visitor center. To get to the trailhead on Apache Pass Road from Willcox, located on I-10, drive 22 miles south on State Route 186 to a graded dirt road leading east into Apache Pass.

Chiricahua Mountains

So many mountain ranges in southern and southeastern Arizona offer incredible scenery, day hiking, extending backpacking, and camping that it is difficult to single out one that must be visited. But we'll open ourselves up to argument by nominating the Chiricahua Mountains as our first choice, with the Santa Catalinas, the Whetstones, the Dragoons, the Rincons, the Santa Ritas, and several others not far behind. It's a bit like trying to pick the No. 1 college football team, so friendly disagreements are welcome.

How to get there: There are several routes, but an easy one is from Willcox on Interstate 10 southeast on State Route 186 to the turnoff to the Chiricahua National Monument.

For those who have no interest in getting more than 50 feet from the vehicle or who simply want an overview of this incredible range with its astounding rock formations and big vistas, there is an 8-mile, paved scenic drive from the visitor center to the crest and Massai Point, where there is a nature trail. The drive climbs through oak and juniper and pine forests and reaches an overlook offering greats views of the park, desert valleys, and various peaks. There are roadside pullouts permitting closer examination of rock formations and other natural features.

More than 20 miles of trails go past those fancy rocks—with names such as Duck on a Rock, Totem Pole, and Big Balanced Rock—and explore forests or lead to a natural bridge and ledge of volcanic hailstones, the evidence of ancient eruptions. The trails range from 9 miles long to only a quarter-mile long.

The monument is in the range's northwest corner and features huge rock spires, stone columns, and balanced rocks perched on small pedestals. All this stone glory probably began nearly 30 million years ago when volcanic eruptions dumped hot ash, which cooled and became a 2,000-foot layer of volcanic rock called rhyolite. The range formed from this and was sculpted further by water and wind and ice.

With Mexico 50 miles south and the Sonoran and Chihuahuan deserts all around, the Chiricahuas remain cool, moist, forested, and full of wildlife (including comical-looking coatimundis), wildflowers, and exotic bird species.

The mountains were the home of the Chiricahua Apaches during the Apache Wars and at other times. Small wonder.

Cochise Stronghold

It's a natural fortress of granite rock formations used by the Chiricahua Apaches under the leadership of the famous Apache chief Cochise. It is popularly believed that the old warrior is buried somewhere in this box canyon, where he and his followers often hid from pursuing soldiers during the Apache Wars, which he and Geronimo fought in their ultimately futile attempts to stem a tide of pioneers. There is a long (5-mile) hiking trail and short one (a quarter-mile) leading out from the beautifully forested camping area. Rock climbing, petroglyph viewing, picnicking and camping await the visitor. The stronghold is 19 miles southwest of Willcox off U.S. Route 191 and several miles along a gravel road.

Douglas

Just north of the Mexico border and the town of Agua Prieta and not far east of Bisbee on State Route 90 is the town of Douglas and one of its main claims to fame: the Gadsden Hotel, listed in the National Register of Historic Places. The hotel was built in 1907 and offers a splendid lobby adorned by Victorian chandeliers, Tiffany vaulted skylights, an Italian marble staircase, and a 42-foot stained-glass mural. It is at 1046 G Avenue and can be reached at (520) 364-4481. (See Where To Go, Page 147, for additional details.)

Swift Trail Parkway

Route	State Route 366 up a mountain beginning at U.S. Route 191 about 7 miles south of Safford and ending at Riggs Lake.
Mileage	35 miles.
Elevation	Somewhat of a roller coaster starting at 3,200 feet and ending at about 9,400 feet just below the top of Mount Graham in the Pinaleno Mountains, but with the certainty that the final portion of the route will be closed by winter conditions, generally between Nov. 15 and April 15.
Overview	The way to get above it all. Valley views, rugged canyons, and plenty of mountain driving.

The Swift Trail Parkway is short, 35 miles up a big mountain, 35 back down, but swift it's not. Slow it is.

This drive will demand quick braking as you take its many curves and hairpin turns. It is named for Theodore T. Swift, the first supervisor of the Coronado National Forest, who envisioned a scenic highway over the mountain and got it. He is memorialized by a bullet-pocked plaque mounted high up, too high up, on a big rock at one of the first stops on the drive, Wet Canyon Bridge.

If traveling in winter, it is good to know that those are not snowballs along the road into Safford. They are uncollected cotton from the abundant plantings in the adjacent cotton fields. Safford, founded in 1873, is at about 2,900 feet of elevation, and cotton is a major crop. Graham County, the county home of Safford, devotes more than 22,000 acres to the stuff, a number more than twice that of the population. For those with somewhat arcane interests, there are two cotton gins in the area, one in Safford and one in nearby Pima.

There's lots of entertainment—and plenty of motels and restaurants—in Safford, but we're here to climb a mountain by traveling the Swift Trail. To get to the start of the road up this nearly 11,000-foot peak, take U.S. Route 191 south out of Safford for about 8 miles and turn southwest on State Route 366, the start of the designated road (or trail). It is a 70-mile-plus trip that will take somewhere around four to five hours, even longer if you dally on any of the many side trips along the way.

Arizona State Parks

Warning: The road is entirely open April 15 to Nov. 14, snow permitting. The lower portion is usually accessible year-round but it is closed near the top, about where the pavement ends, during winter (Nov. 15 to April 15). The first 23 miles are paved, and 13 miles are graded dirt ending just beyond Riggs Lake, or Riggs Flat. (Fishing note: When Riggs Lake is snowed in and iced over, the Frye Mesa Reservoir is still open for trout fishing. It is located southeast of the nearby town of Thatcher.)

What is to be seen during this assault of Mount Graham's flanks? For starters, the traveler will pass through five of North America's seven life zones, all populated by a variety of animals and plants beginning in a desert of cactus, yucca, and mesquite, winding upward through oak grasslands, piñon-juniper woodlands, and eventually, pine forests. Near the route's end is Riggs, a small

Camping Like the Stars

Pampered campers soak in a stone-lined hot mineral bath at eastern Arizona's picturesque Roper Lake, a state park that lies minutes from the base of Mount Graham. In addition to 32-acre Roper Lake, the park offers campgrounds with rest rooms, showers, and water. There's also a boat launch and an RV dumping station.

You can spend your time hiking, fishing, boating, or picnicking. For campers with physical disabilities, the park offers reserved level sites and wheelchair-accessible showers and rest rooms.

And soaking in the hot springs? That's free —on a first-come basis—but limited to 15 minutes per soak when others are waiting. Swimwear required.

Information and reservations: (928) 428-6760.

[**A boat facility at Roper Lake State Park. ▲**]

reservoir with good trout fishing. Below but well along the route near a spot called Shannon Campground (one of many campgrounds along the way) is a rutted road to Heliograph Peak. Here the U.S. Army constructed a heliograph—a mirrored, sun-reflecting signal tower—to send signals during the 1880s military campaign against Geronimo's Apaches and to maintain military communications throughout southern Arizona.

To quote the U.S. Forest Service, the traveler "will experience the ecological equivalent of driving from Mexico to Canada, all in one leisurely afternoon on this sky-scraping, switchbacking mountain road." Mount Graham tops out at 10,717 feet, but the route, which starts at 2,900 feet, ends at 9,300.

The Pinalenos are, like the other mountain ranges of southeastern Arizona, called "sky islands." That's because they are surrounded by desert below and

Randy Prentice

Aravaipa Canyon Wilderness

You will need a permit to hike in this marvelous, 11-mile-long canyon, or any of its nine side canyons, to be found 60 miles west of Safford, but it is well worth the bother.

The canyon, quite narrow in parts, has a perennial creek running through it and colorful, 1,000-foot canyon walls, great scenery, wildlife, native fish, bighorn sheep, and 200 species of birds living in the cottonwoods and sycamores. It is an easy, mostly flat hike, but much of it involves wading in and out of Aravaipa Creek, a pleasant thing to do in the heat of summer.

The east entrance to the canyon can be reached by taking U.S. Route 70 out of Safford to a point 5 miles west of Pima. Then turn south on Klondyke Road (be alert for possible flooding) and go for 45 miles to the parking area. The west entrance is reachable by taking State Route 77 south from Winkelman to the Aravaipa Road at the Central Arizona College exit. Then follow Aravaipa Road 12 miles to the parking area.

Contact the U.S. Bureau of Land Management, Safford District, for more information. (928) 348-4400. www.blm.gov/az/sfo/index.htm

[**Aravaipa Creek runs through a wilderness.** ▲]

isolated from one another by those stretches of arid land at the base, quite unlike the forests that populate the ranges. The same description applies to Mount Lemmon in the Santa Catalina Mountains just north of Tucson.

In addition to the diverse scenery of this drive (you might want to go in fall for the vivid leaves), there are plenty of camping and picnicking facilities, fishing and boating, wildlife viewing (including a fine bobcat we saw skittering across the road), huge vistas of the various valleys below, hiking horseback riding, and mountain biking. It is cool at the top in summer, and the mountain is a popular escape spot for city dwellers.

There are many short side trips on the way up Mount Graham including Hospital Flat, a wildflowered meadow and the place where soldiers wounded in the Apache wars could recuperate, and Treasure Park where, according to legend, some Mexican bandits buried some gold. If you are remarkably fortunate, you might even see a Mount Graham red squirrel, a protected subspecies unique to this mountain.

Two of the many hiking trails deserve special mention: Arcadia Trail and Ladybug Trail.

The Arcadia offers remarkable views of peaks and canyons and is a designated National Recreation Trail, one of the best in the country. It winds in and out of fir, spruce, and aspen forests and even offers an area of wild raspberries. The trailhead is reached 22 miles up the Swift Trail to the Shannon Campground entrance, then by following the road through the campground to the trailhead at the turnaround. A mile from the trailhead is a way to Heliograph Trail. The Forest Service rates Arcadia as "more difficult."

The Ladybug starts near Ladybug Peak, a spot popular with congregations of those amusing, little orange and black-spotted beetles at various times of the year. The scenery along the trail includes fine overlooks into Jacobson Canyon and the Gila Mountains and Gila Valley. It is a steep trail and rated "most difficult." To get there, go 17 miles up Swift Trail to Ladybug Saddle, where the trailhead at the parking area on the left side of the road follows the Bear Canyon Trail to Ladybug.

For precise trail information and maps, contact the Safford Ranger District, (928) 428-4150.

A final thought about the Swift Trail Parkway, something to keep in mind if hiking, camping, or picnicking along the way: This is major bear country, said by some to be home to the West's largest concentration of black bears. Hang down your head, Tom Dooley, if you must, but hang high your food and anything else that smells, including your spouse's socks. Otherwise, like Tom, it's remotely possible, poor boy, you're gonna die.

On that cautionary note, we head slowly and in low gear back down the unrailed way we came. ∭

[**The Gila River in eastern Arizona winds through golden-leaved cottonwoods.**]

George Stocking

Where To Go
What To See
What To Do

These listings cover Tucson and southern Arizona. Communities south of Tucson include: Amado, Arivaca, Green Valley, Nogales, Patagonia, Sahuarita, Sonoita, Tubac, and Tumacacori. Communities southeast of Tucson include: Benson, Bisbee, Dos Cabezas, Douglas, Dragoon, Fort Grant, Fort Huachuca, Hereford, Huachuca Mountains, Pima, Pomerene, Safford, Sierra Vista, St. David, Sunsites, and Willcox. West of Tucson are Ajo and Sells. North and northwest of Tucson are Arizona City, Casa Grande, Eloy, Gila Bend, Marana, Oro Valley, Picacho, and San Manuel/Mammoth/Oracle.

TUCSON

Metropolitan Tucson Convention and Visitors Bureau: A warehouse of information on attractions and special events, maps, and visitor and travel news. Ask about the "Tucson attractions passport," which offer discounts to more than 40 area attractions. (520) 770-2142. www.visittucson.org

Southern Arizona Attractions Alliance: A nonprofit, co-operative organization of regional attractions that promotes tourism. Sponsors an entrance-fee discount program called the "Tucson attractions passport." www.tucsonattractions.com

Southeastern Arizona Bird Observatory: Lists scores of bird-watching areas, including lodging and other facilities. www.sabo.org/index.htm

Arizona-Sonora Desert Museum: This 21-acre combination of zoo, natural history museum, and botanical garden summarizes the ecosystem of the Sonoran Desert, including caves and underwater life. $. 2021 N. Kinney Road. Take either Speedway Boulevard/Gates Pass Road or Ajo Way to Kinney Road and follow the signs. (520) 883-2702. www.desertmuseum.org

International Wildlife Museum: If the kids are restless on the way to the Arizona-Sonora Desert Museum, this museum along the way is bound to appeal to them as well as to adults. Unlike the Desert Museum, all the 400 species of mammals, birds, and insects here are stuffed. Exhibit areas feature displays and dioramas; educational movies; a gift shop and a restaurant. $. 4800 W. Gates Pass Road (520) 629-0100 Ext. 336. www.thewildlifemuseum.org

[A forest of saguaro cacti stands tall at Saguaro National Park. ▲]

Tucson Botanical Gardens: An assembly of 16 gardens in the heart of Tucson. $. 2150 N. Alvernon Way. (520) 326-9686. www.tucsonbotanical.org

Saguaro National Park: If you can't take a desert back-road trip, the next best thing is this park, divided into eastern (Rincon Mountains) and western (Tucson Mountains) units. Hiking trails and scenic drives meander throughout the units. Visitors center at each unit provides an excellent overview of the Sonoran Desert with detailed displays on the saguaro cactus and other plant and animal residents. $. For the east unit, about 17 miles east of downtown, take Speedway (Exit 257 from Interstate 10) east to Old Spanish Trail, turn right (southeast) and look for signs. (520) 733-5153. For the west unit, about 15 miles west of downtown, take Speedway west to Gates Pass Road and follow the signs. (520) 733-5158. www.nps.gov/sagu

Coronado National Forest: Many historic and recreational sites and natural wonders are scattered throughout this 1.8 million-acre forest with segments throughout southern and eastern Arizona, including Mount Lemmon north of Tucson. Some fees. Main office, 300 W. Congress St. (520) 388-8300. www.fs.fed.us/r3/coronado

[Boulders and granite crags pick up the afternoon
light in the Dragoon Mountains.]

Tom Danielsen

Sabino Canyon Recreation Area: Hiking and equestrian trails, picnicking, wildlife watching, and shuttle bus tours within a desert oasis and canyon. $. From Tanque Verde Road take Sabino Canyon Road north to the visitors center. Santa Catalina Ranger District of Coronado National Forest, (520) 749-8700.
www.fs.fed.us/r3/coronado/forest/recreation/camping/sites/sabino.shtml

Tucson to Mount Lemmon: The University of Arizona makes available a comprehensive guide produced by the Arizona-Sonora Desert Museum: http://eebweb.arizona.edu/courses/Ecol406R_506R/Guide_to_MtLemmon_highway_Sonorensis1994.pdf

Mount Lemmon Tourism Commission: Information on lodging, dining, and other topics. (800) 652-1542. www.mt-lemmon.com

Mount Lemmon Ski Valley: The southernmost ski area in the continental United States, it has a summit of more than 9,000 feet. Open year-round for snow skiing, picnicking, or ski lift rides. $. 10300 Ski Run Road. (520) 576-1400. ww.skitown.com/resortguide/stats.cfm/az02/Mt.Lemmon

Santa Catalina Ranger District: This Coronado National Forest district includes Mount Lemmon. (520) 749-8700. www.fs.fed.us/r3/coronado

Visitors stroll through Old Tucson Studios, where more than 60 movies have been filmed.

Tony Marinella

Tucson Mountain Park: A magnificent saguaro forest encompasses camping sites, scenic picnic areas, archery and pistol ranges, along with trails for hiking, bicycling, and horseback riding spread over 20,000 aces. The Arizona-Sonora Desert Museum, Old Tucson Studios, and Saguaro National Park (west unit) are located in or near the Pima County park. $. 8451 W. McCain Loop. (520) 883-4200; (520) 877-6000. www.co.pima.az.us/pksrec/natres/tucmts/tumtpk.html

Old Tucson Studios: You've seen this place in scores of movies. Put on your jeans and boots and Stetson and walk the dirt streets of this Old West theme park and movie studio that originated in 1939 with the filming of the movie *Arizona*, starring William Holden and Jean Arthur. Stepping out of its Western mode, it was a filming site for *The Bells of St. Mary's*, starring Bing Crosby and Ingrid Bergman. The false-front church and bell tower are still there. Since, some of Hollywood's biggest Westerns have been filmed here. Stunt shows, trail rides, guided studio tours, musical reviews, eateries, and shops. $. In Tucson Mountain Park, 201 S. Kinney Road. (520) 883-0100. www.oldtucson.com

Tohono Chul Park: This small but quite delightful urban oasis consists of 49 acres set smack dab amid some heavily trafficked streets and the freeway in the Tucson metropolis. You can hear the throaty bass of carsong if you try, but it's mostly drowned out by the soprano of birdsong. Tohono Chul ("Desert Corner" when translated from the Tohono O'odham language), is a private, nonprofit park that offers, among other features, short nature trails, undisturbed desert, birds galore, pools, plants labeled for what they are, a self-guided tour, numerous gardens, a research library, greenhouse, exhibit house, a café, a tea room, gift shops, and a shady, plant-choked courtyard. $. From Interstate 10, take the Ina Road exit and drive east approximately 5 miles to Paseo del Norte; turn left (north) and proceed to the first driveway on the right. (520) 742-6455. www.tohonochulpark.org

Colossal Cave Mountain Park: A 45-minute tour takes you six-and-a-half stories underground to explore stalactites, stalagmites, and helictites. Or saddle up for a trail ride, pan for "gems" at the replica mining sluice, walk through the butterfly garden, and visit a museum and history room that include a timeline and artifacts dating to about 900 A.D., when Hohokam Indians lived in the cave. $. 16721 E. Old Spanish Trail. (520) 647-7275. www.colossalcave.com. See Chili Cook-off below.

Reid Park Zoo: Before you complain about Arizona's heat, think of Boris and Kobe, the resident polar bears here. Like people, they stay cool with evaporative cooling (and occasional ice blocks and fishcicles). More than

400 animals and a walk-through aviary. $. 1030 S. Randolph Way. (520) 791-4022. www.tucsonzoo.org

Garden of Gethsemane: In World War I, Felix Lucero made a vow to God while lying injured on a battlefield in France: If he survived he would create religious sculptures. Lucero kept that vow. Works include a life-size sculpture of Jesus on the cross and a depiction of the Last Supper. Free. 602 W. Congress St. Tucson Parks and Recreation Department, (520) 791-4873 Ext. 108.

Arizona Historical Society Museum: Learn about Arizona history through the society's archives, educational programs, displays, and tours. One display replicates an underground mine; another the multi-cultural dimensions of southern Arizona in the 1870s. Closed Sunday. Donations. 949 E. 2nd St. (520) 628-5774. www.arizonahistoricalsociety.org

Arizona Opera: Has been entertaining audiences for more than 35 years with performances in Tucson (the Tucson Convention Center) and Phoenix (Symphony Hall). Season generally runs September to April. $. (520) 293-4336; (602) 266-7464. www.azopera.com

Arizona Theatre Company: Presents musicals and dramas in Tucson, Mesa, and Phoenix. Performances usually run September to May. $. (520) 622-2823; (602) 256-6995. www.aztheatreco.org

The Screening Room: Shows Indie, student, and rare films. Also hosts poetry nights and film festivals. $. 127 E. Congress St. (520) 622-2262. www.azmac.org/scroom

Arizona Friends of Chamber Music: Produces performances by national and international groups, highlighted by the annual weeklong Winter Chamber Music Festival. $. Tucson Convention Center's Leo Rich Theatre. (520) 577-3769. www.arizonachambermusic.org

Arts for All: Community theatre series, after-school art programs, and summer arts camp. $. 2520 N. Oracle Road. (520) 622-4100. www.artsforallinc.org

Borderlands Theatre: Focuses on "the Latino/Chicano voice" and presents shows with a Southwestern flair. $. El Centro Cultural de las Americanas, 40 W. Broadway Blvd. (520) 882-7406. www.borderlandstheater.org

Broadway in Tucson: Brings Broadway shows to downtown Tucson. $. Tucson Convention Center. (520) 903-2929. www.broadwayintucson.com

Center for Creative Photography: More than 60,000 photographic works by thousands of artists. Store, gallery, research center. Free. 1030 N. Olive Road. (520) 621-7968. www.creativephotography.org

La Pilita Museum Gallery: Located in a traditional adobe building in Tucson's Barrio Viejo (Old Neighborhood) next to El Tiradito Shrine (a national historic site), the gallery houses photos and oral histories of Tucson's barrios. Includes a *tiendita* (gift shop) and special events. Hint: Park at nearby Tucson Community and Convention Center. Mon.–Fri., 11 a.m.–2 p.m. Closed June–July. Donation. 420 S. Main Ave. (520) 882-7454. www.lapilita.com

Sonoran Glass Art Academy: A commercial glassblowing studio that offers glassblowing and flame-working classes and special events. $. 633 W. 18th St. (520) 884-7814. www.sonoranglass.org

Fox Tucson Theatre: The historic building is listed as a significant building on the National Register of Historic Places. Movies, special events, and live performances. $. 17 W. Congress St. (520) 624-1515. www.foxtucsontheatre.org

Tucson Jazz Society: Hosts performances and educational activities. $. (520) 903-1265. www.tucsonjazz.org

Tucson Symphony Orchestra: Performs musical programs and festivals for adults and children. $. Tucson Symphony Center, 2175 N. 6th Ave. (520) 792-9155; (520) 882-8585. www.tucsonsymphony.org

UA Presents: A department of the University of Arizona that brings performing arts to Tucson. 1020 E. University Blvd. (520) 621-3341. www.uapresents.org

Tucson Arts District Partnership: Information about downtown Tucson's art district and galleries. Also hosts art walks. 125 S. Arizona Ave. (520) 624-9977. www.tucsonartsdistrict.org

Tucson Puppet Works: The troupe performs "oversized puppet dramas" with hand, pole, and big-head puppets. Also hosts puppet workshops. $. (520) 770-1533. www.tucsonpuppetworks.com

Flam Chen: A pyrotechnic theater troupe that employs "circus tactics, martial arts weaponry." www.flam-chen.com

The Loft Cinema: First-run independent, foreign, and documentary films. Has showed *Rocky Horror Picture Show* every Saturday at midnight for nearly 30 years and hosts special events. $. 3233 E. Speedway Blvd. (520) 795-7777 (Show times); (520) 322-5638. www.loftcinema.com

The Invisible Theatre: Showcases new playwrights' productions, off-Broadway plays, and musicals in an intimate, 80-person theatre. $. 1400 N. 1st Ave. (520) 882-9721. www.invisibletheatre.com

Gaslight Theatre: Dinner theatre for the family. Also hosts a family concert series. $. 7010 E. Broadway Blvd. (520) 886-9428. www.thegaslighttheatre.com

Beowulf Alley Theatre Company: A professional company that combines classical and modern, edgy approaches to theatre. 11 S. 6th Ave. (520) 882-0555 (tickets and reservations); (520) 622-4460. www.beowulfalley.org

Ortspace Studios: Home to O-T-O Dance, a "flying modern dance company" that utilizes the trapeze. Workshops and classes. 7th St. and 7th Ave. in downtown Tucson. (520) 624-3799. www.orts.org

DeGrazia Gallery of the Sun: The largest and most complete collection of work by the late artist Ted DeGrazia is housed in this adobe gallery. Behind the gallery is DeGrazia's Mission in the Sun. Free. 6300 N. Swan Road. (520) 299-9191. www.degrazia.org

Arizona State Museum: Established in 1893, it is the oldest and largest anthropology museum in the Southwest and focuses on native cultures from mammoth hunters to present-day tribes. Closed on state-government holidays. Donations. University of Arizona, 1013 E. University Blvd. (520) 621-6302. www.statemuseum.arizona.edu

Fort Lowell Museum: The fort was established in 1873 as a base of operations against the Western and Chiricahua Apache Indians. The museum, housed in a reconstructed building of the commanding officers' quarters, details the history of the fort and the surrounding region. Wed.–Sat., 10 a.m.–4 p.m. Free. 2900 N. Craycroft Road. (602) 885-3832. www.arizonahistoricalsociety.org

Sosa-Carrillo-Fremont House: The historic 19th-century adobe house is named after Gov. John C. Fremont and two other distinguished families that occupied it. Exhibits on Tucson's Hispanic pioneer families and period room settings. Lectures, special events, tours, and a gift shop. Wed.–Sat., 10 a.m.–4 p.m. $. 151 S. Granada Ave. (520) 622-0956. www.arizonahistoricalsociety.org (click on "visit us," "AHS museums," "Tucson area." Also, http://oldpueblomoo.arizona.edu:7000/14352)

San Xavier del Bac Mission: Known as "the white dove of the desert" and filled with statues, murals, and other art, the church was built from 1783–1797 by Franciscan missionaries on a mission site established in the late 1600s by the Jesuit Padre Eusebio Kino. Still functions as parish church for the Tohono O'odham. Donations. 1950 W. San Xavier Road. (520) 294-2624. www.sanxaviermission.org

H.H. Franklin Auto Museum: Houses one of the nation's most complete collections of Franklin motorcars. Oct. 21–Memorial Day, Wed., Thurs., Fri., 10 a.m.–4 p.m. $. 3420 N. Vine St. (520) 326-8038. www.franklincar.org/body.htm

Gadsden Pacific Division Toy Train Operating Museum: 4,500 square feet of model train displays. Hosts annual toy train shows and swap meets in winter and summer. Call for hours. Donations. 3975 N. Miller Ave. (520) 888-2222.

Tucson Children's Museum: Kids can don firefighter's gear in the "Fire Station," create artwork in the "Art Studio," and explore exhibits such as Dinosaur Canyon and Ocean Discovery Center. $. 200 S. 6th Ave. (520) 792-9985. www.tucsonchildrensmuseum.org

Tucson Museum of Art and Historic Block: Museum galleries feature original work focusing on art of the Americas and the American West, and modern and contemporary art. The historic block includes five houses that were a part of the original walled fortress that marked Tucson's beginning. Historic block tours: Wed., Thurs., and Sat., 11 a.m. $. 140 N. Main Ave. (520) 624-2333. www.tucsonarts.com

Tucson Rodeo Parade Museum: Hundreds of buggies and wagons as well as a replica of Tucson's Main Street from the 1800s pay homage to Tucson's La Fiesta de los Vaqueros (Celebration of the Cowboys) parade, which is "the world's longest nonmotorized parade." Closed Sunday. Donation. Northeast corner of S. 6th Ave. and Irvington Road in the Tucson Rodeo Grounds. (520) 294-1280. See La Fiesta de los Vaqueros listing below.

History of Pharmacy Museum: Located throughout the University of Arizona's College of Pharmacy building, the museum contains more than 60,000 bottles, drug-related artifacts, store fixtures, drug containers, and

[The Pima Air and Space Museum houses more than 250 aircraft.]

Kerrick James

books. Closed weekends and holidays. Free. College of Pharmacy,
1703 E. Mabel. (520) 626-1427. www.pharmacy.arizona.edu/museum

Flandrau Science Center: Galaxies of entertainment and information are
at your disposal. The planetarium's shows use more than 30 projectors to
bring the universe into a theater equipped with reclining seats. Observatory
features a 16-inch telescope through which you can examine current
heavenly displays. Mineral museum, science store, heliochronometer (that's
a sundial). Hours extend into the night. $. University of Arizona,
1601 E. University Blvd. (520) 621-7827. www.flandrau.org

Trail Dust Town: A Wild West attraction that includes an arcade, stunt
shows, miniature train rides, gold panning, museum, a steak house, shops,
and a town square with gazebo. $. 6541 E. Tanque Verde Road.
(520) 296-5442. www.traildusttown.com

The T-Rex Museum: Hands-on interactive exhibits that use
"edutainment" to teach children about ancient reptiles and science. $.
100 E. Drachman St. (520) 792-2884. www.trexmuseum.org

Historic Stone Avenue Temple: Arizona's first synagogue, built in 1910.
Free tours Wed. and Thu., noon–4 p.m.; a living history program every third
Sat. 564 S. Stone Ave. (520) 670-9073.

University of Arizona Museum of Art: Houses more than 4,500
paintings, sculptures, prints, and drawings dating from the sixth
century B.C. to the present. Free. University of Arizona campus, near Park
Ave. and Speedway Blvd. (520) 621-7567. www.artmuseum.arizona.edu

Postal History Foundation: Visitors can buy any stamp that currently is
offered as well as view an extensive stamp collection that features the first
U.S. stamp ever issued. Includes a fully operational post office and section
of the original Naco, Ariz., post office. Mon.–Fri., 8 a.m.–2:30 p.m. Saturday
by appointment. Free. 920 N. 1st Ave. (520) 623-6652.
www.postalhistoryfoundation.org

Pima Air and Space Museum: Tram and walking tours. Features
President Kennedy's Air Force One, an SR-71 Blackbird, several B-36
Peacemakers (the nation's largest bomber ever built). Includes Arizona
Aviation Hall of Fame. Arranges tours of Davis-Monthan Air Force Base. $.
6000 E. Valencia Road. (520) 618-4800. www.pimaair.org. See Titan
Museum listing below under Sahuarita.

Davis-Monthan Air Force Base Tours: Weekdays, given by the Pima Air
and Space Museum of Davis-Monthan's Aerospace Maintenance and
Regeneration Center, which notes: "All tours are subject to cancellation
without notice due to mission requirements or for reasons of security." See

previous listing for Pima Air and Space Museum. $. Tour reservations, (520) 618-4800.

Tucson Gem, Mineral, and Fossil Showcase: Held throughout Tucson, this two-week event ranks among the largest marketplaces of its kind. Precious gems, minerals, fossils, beads, jewelry, and jewelry-making materials for purchase and viewing. February. $. (800) 638-8350.

Dillinger Days: An annual street festival that re-creates and commemorates the 1934 capture of the notorious John Dillinger gang with live entertainment, tours, lectures, re-enactments, and historic displays. Downtown. Free. (520) 884-5980. www.downtowntucson.org

Chili Cook-Off and Ranch Heritage Day: This spicy festival includes cowboy poetry and chili tasting. March. $. Colossal Cave Mountain Park. See Colossal Cave listing on Page 133. (520) 647-7275; (520) 647-7121. www.colossalcave.com

El Tour de Tucson: More than 5,500 cyclists of all skill levels take part in this perimeter event to raise money for charity. November. $. Tucson. (520) 745-2033. www.pbaa.com

Southwest Indian Art Fair: An annual gathering of hundreds of the nation's Indian artists exhibiting and selling their works in one of the Southwest's finest Indian art shows. Crafts, native foods, live entertainment, demonstrations. February. $. Arizona State Museum. (520) 621-6302. www.statemuseum.arizona.edu

International Mariachi Conference: Workshops, music, art, and the day-long Fiesta de Garibaldi are combined in this Hispanic cultural event. April. $. (520) 838-3908. www.tucsonmariachi.org

4th Avenue Spring/Winter Street Fair: One of the top visual arts fairs in the country with 400 arts and crafters, live entertainment, food, and children's activities. December and March. Free. On 4th Av. between 9th St. and University Blvd. (520) 624-5004. www.fourthavenue.org

Arizona International Film Festival: Screenings of hundreds of new works by independent producers plus workshops and other presentations. April. $. (520) 628-1737. www.azmac.org

NASCAR Weekly Racing Series: Stock car races. Dec.–Feb., Sat. $. Tucson Raceway Park. (520) 762-9200. www.tucsonracewaypark.com

La Fiesta de los Vaqueros (Celebration of the Cowboys): The four-day extravaganza features the "world's longest nonmotorized parade" and one of the top 20 rodeos in North America. February. Tucson Rodeo Grounds. $. (520) 741-2233; (800) 964-5662. www.tucsonrodeo.com

SOUTH OF TUCSON

Amado

Nogales–Santa Cruz Chamber of Commerce: See listing under Nogales on Page 141.

Fred Lawrence Whipple Observatory Visitors Center: The observatory, located in the Santa Rita Mountains off of Interstate 19 south of Tucson, is operated for solar system, galactic, and extragalactic astronomy. Visitors center exhibits pertain to astronomy and astrophysics, natural science, and cultural history. Closed weekends. Guided tours available mid-March–Nov., Mon., Wed., Fri. Reservations necessary. $. (520) 670-5707. http://cfa-www.harvard.edu/ep/flwo.html

Arivaca

Buenos Aires National Wildlife Area: More than 320 species of birds have been recorded at Buenos Aires, and a host of mammals and reptiles call the refuge home. A 10-mile drive allows visitors to view antelope in their natural environment. Hiking, primitive camping, horseback riding, and biking. Restrooms, drinking water, picnic tables, and brochures available at

[Afternoon light warms the hills above the border town of Nogales.]

Randy Prentice

refuge headquarters. Free. From Tucson, take State Route 86 (Ajo Way) 22 miles west to State Route 286 at Three Points. Turn left (south) and go 38 miles to Milepost 7.5. From Interstate 19, take the Amado/Arivaca Exit west, turn right at the T, and then left at the Cow Palace onto Arivaca Road. Drive west 35 miles on Arivaca Road to State 286 and turn left at Milepost 7.5. (520) 823-4251.
www.fws.gov/southwest/refuges/arizona/buenosaires

Green Valley

Green Valley Chamber of Commerce: Information about the area's numerous golf courses and other recreational opportunities and events. (520) 625-7575; (800) 858-5872. www.greenvalleychamber.com

Madera Canyon: A popular retreat for hikers and wildlife watchers in the Santa Rita Mountains south of Tucson off Interstate 19. Part of the Coronado National Forest, it boasts 240 species of birds, a creek, and a big shady trees at an elevation of 4,600 to 5,500 feet. Campground, picnic areas, nature trail, restrooms, drinking water, hiking trails, and an amphitheater. Donations. From Tucson, take I-19 south approximately 30 miles to the Continental Road Exit. Turn east and follow the signs 13 miles to Madera Canyon. Nogales Ranger District, (520) 281-2296. www.fs.fed.us/r3/coronado/forest/recreation/camping/sites/madera.shtml

Nogales

Nogales–Santa Cruz Chamber of Commerce: A central source of information about attractions in Santa Cruz County and Ambos Nogales, the name that applies to the cities of Nogales in Arizona and Sonora, Mexico. Especially helpful to bird-watchers and travelers to Mexico. 123 W. Kino Park Way. (520) 287-3685. www.nogaleschamber.com

Pimeria Alta Historical Society Museum: Just one block from the international border, visitors will learn about the history of southern Arizona and northern Sonora, Mexico. Library, archives, photo collection, self-guided tours, gift shop. Closed Sunday. Free. From last exit on I-19 turn east on Crawford. Museum is in old Nogales City Hall. (520) 287-5402.

Patagonia

Nogales–Santa Cruz Chamber of Commerce: 123 W. Kino Park Way, Nogales. (520) 287-3685. www.nogaleschamber.com

Patagonia–Sonoita Creek Preserve: Look for the 300 bird species observed at this park nestled between the Santa Rita and Patagonia mountains. Hikes, guided tours, visitors center. Closed Mon.–Tues. $. Take Pennsylvania Avenue south from town. (520) 378-4952.

Butterfly Garden: Hundreds of colorful butterflies migrate through this area during the summer. The park is lined with Arizona walnut, willow, and oak trees and has a gazebo. Free. South side of Richardson Town Park on McKeown Ave.

Patagonia Lake State Park: Water skiing, fishing, camping, picnicking, and hiking. A marina has boat rentals, fishing accessories, and a handicapped-accessible fishing dock. Stocked with rainbow trout in the winter, but also good for bass, crappie, bluegill, and catfish. Electrical hookups, visitors center. $. On State Route 82 about 7 miles south of Patagonia. (520) 287-6965. www.pr.state.az.us/Parks/parkhtml/patagonia.html

Sahuarita

Asarco Mineral Discovery Center and Mine Tours: The only place in Arizona that operates regularly scheduled tours of a working open-pit copper mine and mill. The center, which is adorned with more than 3.5 tons of Asarco copper, has a theater, picnic area, plus indoor and outdoor mining exhibits. Closed Sun. No fee for Mineral Discovery Center. Mine tour available Tues., Thurs., and Sat; call (520) 625-8233; (520) 625-7513. $. South on Interstate 19 to Exit 80, Pima Mine Road , then 200 feet west and turn left through the railroad crossing gate. Go south a quarter-mile and turn right into parking lot. www.asarco.com/AMDC

Titan Missile Museum: Only site that has a Titan II missile from the Cold War era still in its silo. One-hour tour descends several flights of stairs, passes through a massive bomb-blast door in the belly of the silo, and ends at the command center. Visitors center, gift shop. $. Take Exit 69 from I-19, turn west onto Duval Mine Road, and follow the signs. (520) 625-7736. www.pimaair.org

Sonoita

Las Cienegas National Conservation Area: A pristine area that's home to the historic Empire Ranch and scenic Cienega Creek. Biking, camping, hiking, horseback riding, hunting, picnicking, wildlife viewing. Free. From Tucson. go east on Interstate 10 and then south on State Route 83 to the wildlife area turnoff near Milepost 40. (928) 722-4289. www.blm.gov/az/nca/lascienegas/lascieneg.htm

Cave of the Bells: An "underground wilderness" in Coronado National Forest's Sawmill Canyon that has a naturally heated lake about 100 yards below the entrance. Visitors must contact park ranger for access; for weekend access, pick up key on Friday. $. Nogales Ranger District, (520) 281-2296 www.fs.fed.us/r3/coronado

Tubac

Tubac-Santa Cruz Visitors Center: Tubac is 45 miles south of Tucson on Interstate 19. The center is at 4 Plaza Road, Suite E. (520) 398-0007. www.toursantacruz.com/benefits.asp

Tubac Center of the Arts: Over 3,500 square feet of exhibit space, a members' gallery, performance stage, art library, and gallery shop. Closed June–Aug. Located at 9 Plaza Road. (520) 398-2371. www.tubacarts.org

Tubac Historical Society Library: More than 3,000 volumes dedicated to Arizona and the Southwest. Closed May–Sept. Donations. 5 Placita de Anza. (520) 398-2020.

Tubac Presidio State Historic Park: The presidio was founded in June 1752 after the Pima Indians surrendered to the Spaniards. Listed on the National Register of Historic Places, the park has an underground archaeology display, museum, and picnic area. $. (520) 398-2252. www.pr.state.az.us/parkhtml/tubac.html

Old Presidio Traders: A family-owned shop featuring work made by Zuni, Navajo, Hopi, Santa Domingo, Pueblo, Apache, and Tohono O'odham artists. Free. 27 Tubac Road. (520) 398-9333 or (866) 773-7434. www.oldpresidiotraders.com/index.html

Tubac Festival of Arts: This annual street festival showcases the work of hundreds of artists. February. Free. Downtown Tubac. (520) 398-2704.

Anza Days Cultural Celebration: Commemorates the 1775 Anza expedition that left from Tubac and founded San Francisco, Calif. Events in Tubac Presidio State Historic Park include arts and crafts, entertainment, and military re-enactments. October. $. (520) 398-2704.

Tumacacori

Tumacacori National Historical Park: Showcases two of the oldest Spanish colonial missions in Arizona, the San Jose de Tumacacori and Los Santos Angeles de Guevavi missions, both established in 1691. Also includes the San Cayetano de Calabazas mission established in 1756. Bookstore, museum, and visitors center. Self-guided and ranger-led tours; birding. On weekends, usually Sept.–June, demonstrators show visitors skills such as making tortillas, baskets, pottery, and paper flowers. $. During Anza Days (see Tubac listing) in October, visitors with reservations can attend (free) a historic High Mass or *Misa Mayor* similar to those celebrated in the 17th and 18th centuries. Participants are required to dress in Spanish or Indian attire. Reservations: (520) 398-2341. At Exit 29 on I-19, 45 miles south of Tucson and 19 miles north of Nogales. (520) 398-2341. www.nps.gov/tuma/home.htm

La Fiesta de Tumacacori: A traditional mariachi procession, a blacksmithing exhibit, piñatas, regional ethnic food, and live entertainment are features of this two-day event. December. Free. Tumacacori National Historical Park, 1891 E. Frontage Road (520) 398-2341.

SOUTHEAST AND EAST OF TUCSON

Cochise County: Touring information, www.discoverseaz.com; www.co.cochise.az.us/route/thingsto.htm

Benson

Benson Visitors Center: True to its railroad heritage, the Benson center is located in a replica of a 19th-century depot. Benson considers itself the "gateway to Cochise County" and the "home of Kartchner Caverns State

[
Kartchner Caverns' massive limestone formations boast
13,000 feet of passages.
]

Peter Ensenberger

Park." 249 E. 4th St. (520) 586-4293. The Internet site includes a shopping guide. http://bensonvisitorcenter.com

Kartchner Caverns State Park: Considered to be among the world's top 10 caves. Camping sites with electric hook-ups, water, dump station, restrooms, showers, interactive displays, several hiking and walking trails. $. Located 9 miles south of Interstate 10 (Exit 302) off State Route 90. Tour reservations recommended. (520) 586-2283. www.pr.state.az.us/Parks/parkhtml/kartchner.html or www.friendsofkartchner.org

San Pedro Valley Arts and Historical Society Museum: An old-time grocery store exhibit as well as antiques and displays that represent Benson's past. Rotating displays vary. A visitors center, lodging, restaurants, and RV park are nearby. Hours vary seasonally; closed in Aug. $. 180 S. San Pedro. (520) 586-3070.

Singing Wind Bookshop: As you enter the property, a sign directs visitors to close the gate behind them. That's because the bookshop is located on a working cattle ranch. The shop pays special attention to topics of the Southwest and poetry. Bring a picnic lunch, if you wish. 700 W. Singing Wind Road. From Interstate 10 Exit 304, go 2.25 miles north on Ocotillo Road and a half-mile east on Singing Wind Road. (520) 586-2425.

The Thing?: Colorful billboards for miles along Interstate 10 draw visitors to this wacky roadside tourist attraction. Museum, gift shop. $. 2631 N. Johnson Road. Take Interstate 10 to Exit 322 between Benson and Willcox. (520) 586-2581.

Bisbee

Greater Bisbee Chamber of Commerce: Information about Bisbee lodging, dining, shopping, and attractions. One Main St. (866) 224-7233; (520) 432-5421. www.bisbeearizona.com or www.discoverbisbee.com

Bisbee Mining and Historical Museum: Takes visitors on a journey through the early days of Bisbee and the mining activities that put the city on the map as one of the world's richest mineral sites. $. located at 5 Copper Queen Plaza. (520) 432-7071. www.bisbeemuseum.org

Muheim Museum Heritage House: Guided tours take visitors through the 19th-century home that was built by Joseph and Carmelita Muheim. Closed Wed.–Thurs. Donation. 207 Youngblood Hill. (520) 432-7698.

Copper Queen Mine Underground Tour and Lavender Open Pit Tour: Copper Queen tours last approximately 1 hour and 15 minutes and start throughout the day. Dress warmly, mine stays at 47 degrees. After exploring the Copper Queen Mine, visitors can tour the massive Lavender Open Pit. The 13-mile narrated bus tour takes visitors to the 1,000-foot-deep, 300-acre mine. $. Tours leave from the Queen Mine Tour Building located immediately south of Old Bisbee's business district, off the U.S. Route 80 interchange. (520) 432-2071 or (866) 432-2071. www.cityofbisbee.com/queenminetours.htm

Spring Art Auction: Bisbee hosts local and national artists in March at Copper Queen Plaza. (520) 432-3765. www.discoverbisbee.com

Brewery Gulch Daze: This annual event celebrates Bisbee's colorful past with a chili cook-off, waiter/waitress contest, horseshoe tournament, kiddie carnival, live entertainment. September. Free. Brewery Gulch, Bisbee. (520) 432-3554. www.discoverbisbee.com

Bisbee 1000 Stair Climb: Pits climbers against a towering flight of hillside stairs. Musicians play for the steppers as they struggle their way up the old miners route. And, for those who want something a bit more challenging, there is always the Barco Ice Man Challenge: Requires participants to carry an 8-pound block of ice, using antique tongs, up 153 grueling steps. Of course, this is after running the initial 1,000 steps. October. $. (520) 432-9162. www.bisbee1000.org

Southwest Wings: An annual birding and nature festival featuring speakers, exhibits, and field trips led by nature specialists; includes topics for beginners. August. $. Copper Queen Plaza in Historic Old Bisbee. (520) 678-8237. www.swwings.org

La Vuelta de Bisbee: Three-day bicycling event that speeds through Bisbee, Hereford, and Tombstone. April. $. (520) 432-5795. www.azcycling.com

Dos Cabezas

Fort Bowie National Historic Site: Established in 1862 during the Apache Wars. Wander the same grounds that once housed an imprisoned Geronimo. Free. From Willcox, drive east on Interstate 10 for 22 miles to the Bowie Exit, then south on unpaved Apache Pass Road and follow the signs. Or, take State Route 186 south from Willcox through Dos Cabezas to Apache Pass Road, turn left, and follow the signs to the Fort Bowie Trailhead. From there, it's a 1.5-mile walk to the site. (520) 847-2500. www.nps.gov/fobo

Frontier Relics Museum: Collection includes Civil War artifacts and mining gear. Call for hours. Donations. 14 miles south of Willcox on State Route 186. (520) 384-348.

Douglas

Johnson Historical Museum of the Southwest: Located on a portion of the Slaughter Ranch, once owned and run by ex-Texas Ranger John Slaughter, who also served two terms as Cochise County's (Tombstone) sheriff in the Wyatt Earp era. Registered as a National Historic Landmark, the ranch has several restored buildings, including a car shed with a restored 1915 Model T Ford, washroom, and icehouse. The ranch once served as an assembly area for U.S. troops campaigning against the infamous Pancho Villa. Self-guided tours, picnic area. Closed Mon.–Tues. $. From Douglas go east on 15th Street (which becomes Geronimo Trail) for about 17 miles to the ranch gate.
(520) 558-2574. www.slaughterranch.com

San Bernardino National Wildlife Refuge: Here you can hike and watch or photograph birds and animals. Over 270 species of birds; mule deer, whitetail deer, javelina, mountain lion, coyote, bobcat, gray fox, antelope, badger, and coatimundi. Open for dove, quail, and cottontail rabbit hunting in season. Always open for viewing. Free. Adjacent to the Slaughter Ranch.
(520) 364-2104.
www.fws.gov/southwest/refuges/arizona/sanbernardino.html

Leslie Canyon National Wildlife Refuge: Protects habitat for the endangered Yaqui chub and Yaqui topminnow. The 2,770-acre refuge at the southern end of the Swisshelm Mountains also protects a rare forest of velvet ash, cottonwood, and black willow trees. Refuge office: Go north from Douglas on U.S. 191 to a road that's .25 mile past Milepost 11 and turn left (west). Call for hours. (520) 364-2104.
www.fws.gov/southwest/refuges/arizona/sanbernardino.html#Welcome

Douglas Wildlife Zoo: The 5-acre, privately owned zoo has more than 120 species and a petting zoo. Some crowd favorites include a jaguar, monkeys, and miniature horses. $. From the junction of U.S. Route 191 and State Route 80 in Douglas, go west on 80 about 10 miles (go through Calumet), turn north on Plantation Road and go 1.7 miles. (520) 364-2515.

Douglas Art Association Gallery: Rotating exhibits by local artists displayed in 100-year-old building. Gift shop. Afternoon hours only June–Aug. Free. 625 10th St. (520) 364-6410.

Douglas/Williams House Museum and Genealogical Library: The two-story house, built by mining magnate Jimmy "Rawhide" Douglas in 1908, was occupied by the Douglas family until 1938. Now displays the regional history of the Douglas area and the house's period furnishings. Wed., Thurs., Sat., 1 p.m.–4 p.m. Donations. 1001 Ave. D. (520) 364-7370.

Dragoon

Amerind Foundation: A collection of Spanish Colonial Revival-style buildings on spacious grounds 64 miles east of Tucson in the jaw-dropping rock formations of Texas Canyon. The campus is an archaeological research facility and museum dedicated to the study of Native American culture and history. Thus, its name: Amerind is a contraction of "American Indian." It offers numerous and superb archaeological collections, displays of Indian cultures, and exhibits of beadwork, costumes, ritual masks, shields, weapons, snowshoe-making and Indian weavings. Closed Monday and major holidays. $. 2100 N. Amerind Road. From Interstate 10 between Benson and Willcox, take Dragoon Road (Exit 318) and go east about 1 mile. (520) 586-3666. www.amerind.org

Fort Grant

Graham County Chamber of Commerce: Provides information on

[Cottonwood and willow trees reflect fall colors in the San Pedro River.]

Tom Danielsen

recreational opportunities such as hiking, biking, birding, and the area's heritage. 1111 Thatcher Blvd., Safford. (888) 837-1841. www.visitgrahamcounty.com and www.graham-chamber.com/community.html

Fort Grant Historical Museum: Adjoining a state prison, the museum is housed in the lobby of the administration building off the prison grounds. The museum chronicles Fort Grant's past as a 19th-century military installation, state reformatory, and state prison. Closed Sat–Sun. Free. (520) 828-3393.

Fort Huachuca

Fort Huachuca Historical Museum: Operated by the U.S. Army. The fort once was the base for all four of the Buffalo Soldier regiments, museum displays explain the role the black-soldier units played. Gift shop. The nearby Army Intelligence Museum focuses on the history of Army communication and intelligence. (520) 533-5736. http://huachuca-www.army.mil/history/museum.htm

Hereford

San Pedro Riparian National Conservation Area: The San Pedro River cuts through the desert northward from Mexico into Arizona, creating a strip of green. For approximately 40 miles, the river is flanked by a conservation area ranging from 1 to 3 miles wide. Even if the flow is a only trickle at times, the river and its adjacent habitat overflow with recreational opportunities for nature enthusiasts. Wildlife watching — there are more than 400 bird, 82 mammal, and 45 reptile and amphibian species nestle among a variety of grasses and willow and cottonwood trees. Numerous trails attract hikers and riders astride horses and bicycles. Prehistoric mammoth kill sites and the ruins of a Spanish presidio also are within the boundaries. (See listings under Sierra Vista.) The best place to start indulging yourself in this strip is the San Pedro House, located where State Route 90 crosses the river about 8 miles east of Sierra Vista. Upstream lies Hereford the near the southern end of the area. Take State Route 92 about 9 miles south of Sierra Vista to Hereford Road and turn left (east). If you want to press farther south, take Palominas Road from Hereford Road for about 4 miles and you'll be back on State 92. Free. Run by the Bureau of Land Management. (928) 458-3559; (520) 439-6400. www.blm.gov/az/nca/spnca/sphouse.htm; www.sanpedroriver.org or http://eebweb.arizona.edu/courses/Ecol406R_506R/SanPedro_NG_Kingsolver_smaller.pdf

Huachuca Mountains

Coronado National Memorial: Commemorates Francisco Vasquez de Coronado Expedition of 1540–1542 in which he sought (but did not find because they were myth) the Seven Cities of Gold. Hiking, birding, biking, picnicking, and spelunking. Allow plenty of time to hike to Coronado Peak and to explore Coronado Cave. Guided tours, history and nature programs, horse trails, a museum, visitors center. Park is open from dawn to dusk, daily. $. Free. From Sierra Vista or Bisbee, take State Route 92 to Coronado Memorial Drive (signs will direct you) and then 5 miles to the visitors center. (520) 366-5515. www.nps.gov/coro/index.htm

Ramsey Canyon Preserve: A hot spot for watching birds and other wildlife, especially April through Sept. Distinguished by a spring-fed stream, waterfalls, and high canyon walls. 23 parking spaces available on first-come first-served basis. Open all year; hours vary with the season; guided walks available March 1–Oct. 31. $. From Sierra Vista, go south on State Route 92 for 6 miles to Ramsey Canyon Road; turn right (west) and go 4 miles. http://nature.org and click on "where we work." (520) 378-2785.

Our Lady of the Sierras Shrine: The shrine, located at an elevation of 5,300 feet in the Huachuca Mountains, has a 75-foot-tall Celtic-style cross, a 31-foot Madonna, grotto, chapel, waterfall and garden. Daily, 9 a. m.–sunset. From Sierra Vista or Bisbee, take State Route 92 to Prince Placer Road, which is between mileposts 333 and 334, and follow signs. Free. (520) 378-2950. www.ourladyofthesierras.org

Pima

Eastern Arizona Museum and Historical Society: Features pioneer and Indian artifacts. Open afternoons Wed.–Sat. Free. 2 N. Main St. (928) 485-9400.

Pomerene

Gammons Gulch Old West Town and Mining Camp: A working movie set located in the high desert of Cochise County that has been used for several productions. The town is open Sept.–May on Wed.–Sun. for tours, including a museum; June–Aug. by appointment. $. Located 12 miles from Interstate 10. Take Exit 306 to Pomerene road, which merges into Cascabel Road; go to East Rock Spring Road and turn west; Gammons Gulch is the first property on the left. (520) 212-283. www.gammonsgulch.com

Safford

Graham County Chamber of Commerce: Provides information on recreational opportunities such as hiking, biking, birding, the area's heritage, and special events. 1111 Thatcher Blvd., Safford. (888) 837-1841. www.visitgrahamcounty.com and www.graham-chamber.com/community.html

Roper Lake State Park: The park is divided into two sections: Roper Lake and Dankworth Pond. $. Located off U.S. Route 191, 6 miles south of Safford. Dankworth Pond is located 3 miles south of Roper Lake. (928) 428-6760. www.pr.state.az.us/Parks/parkhtml/roper.html

Hot Well Dunes Recreation Area: A destination for off-road vehicle enthusiasts who want to ride the dunes and then soak their bodies afterwards. Two hot tubs, grills, camping, fishing, picnicking. Operated by Bureau of Land Management, Safford office. $. From Safford, take U.S. Route 70 east for 7 miles to BLM's Haekel Road; turn right (south) and go 25 miles. (928) 348-4400. www.blm.gov/az/sfo/hot_well/hotwell.htm

Cotton Gin Tours: During the cotton harvest season Oct.–Jan., visitors can tour the two cotton gins that serve all of Graham County's fields. Call in advance. $. (928) 428-0714; (928) 485-9255.

Discovery Park: A science center with wildlife area, mining and agriculture museums, exhibits on astronomy, and tours of the Mount Graham International Observatory. Includes the Gov Aker Observatory with a 20-inch telescope. Two rides: a train ride around the grounds and the Shuttlecraft Polaris, which simulates a ride into space. Fri., 6–10 p.m.; Sat., 4–10 p.m. $. From U.S. Route 70 on the west side of Safford, take 20th Avenue 2.4 miles south to the entrance;. from U.S. Route 191 south of Safford, turn west on Discovery Park Boulevard to 20th Avenue, then turn left. (928) 428-6260. www.discoverypark.com

Mount Graham International Observatory: An observatory perched on the 10,720-foot summit of Mount Graham. Saturday tours mid–May–mid–Nov; arranged at Discovery Park (see listing above). http://mgpc3.as.arizona.edu

Graham County Historical Museum: Indian and pioneer relics, replica rooms and rotating displays. Mon., Tues. and Sat., 10 a.m.–5 p.m. Donations. 808 8th Ave., Safford. (602) 348-0470.

Sierra Vista

Sierra Vista Convention and Visitors Bureau: Includes information on area attractions including ghost towns, lodging, shopping, and birding. 1011 N. Coronado Dr., Sierra Vista. (520) 417-6960; (800) 288-3861. www.visitsierravista.com

San Pedro Riparian National Conservation Area: See listing above under Hereford.

Murray Springs Clovis Site: Numerous Ice Age fossils and tools were recovered from this San Pedro Riparian National Conservation Area site. Trails with exhibits about life in the late Ice Age. $. From Sierra Vista, go east on State Route 90 for 4 miles from the intersection of Fry Boulevard (90) and State Route 92 to Moson Road; go left (north) 1.1 mile to the entrance road on the right. (520) 439-6400. www.blm.gov/az/nca/spnca/murray.htm

Presidio Santa Cruz de Terrante: This 18th-century Spanish fortress is the most intact survivor of a network of defensive sites constructed by the Spaniards. Biking, hiking, horseback riding, and wildlife viewing are favored activities here. Year-round. Fee for backcountry camping. From Tucson, take Interstate 10 east to State Route 90; turn right (south) and go 20 miles to State Route 82; turn right (east) and go 9 miles to Kellar Road, then 2 miles north to the site. (928) 458-3559.

[
Tombstone Courthouse State Historic Park guides visitors
through the town's colorful past.
]

Laurence Parent

Lehner Mammoth-Kill Site: Ice-Age era kill site and camp where several important archeological finds have been made. Free. San Pedro Riparian National Conservation Area. (520) 458-3559.
www.blm.gov/az/nca/spnca/lehner.htm

Arizona Folklore Preserve: Established and run by Dolan Ellis, Arizona's official state balladeer, and his wife, Rose, it features performances by singers, songwriters, storytellers, and poets focus on Arizona's history, culture, people, events, and scenic attractions. Show times vary; call ahead. $. Take State route 92 south from Sierra Vista for 6 miles, turn right (west) on Ramsey Canyon Road, go 3.5 miles and turn left on Folklore Trail and follow signs. (520) 378-6165. www.arizonafolklore.com

St. David

Holy Trinity Monastery: A Benedictine monastery. The annual Festival of the Arts is held the second weekend in November. Guest retreats, art gallery, thrift store, RV area, conservatory, library, museum are on site. Tours available. $. From Tucson, east on Interstate 10 to Exit 304 in Benson, south on State Route 80 for 8 miles to St. David; monastery is south of St. David between mileposts 302 and 303. (520) 720-4016 ext 17. www.holytrinitymonastery.org/index.html

Sunsites

Cochise Stronghold: Rugged natural fortress was once the domain of the legendary Chiricahua Apache chief Cochise. Hiking, picnicking; campgrounds nearby. Some fees. From Tucson, Interstate 10 east to Exit 331; south on State Route 191 to Sunsites; right (west) on Ironwood Road. Coronado National Forest, Douglas Ranger District, (520) 364-3468. www.fs.fed.us/r3/coronado

Tombstone

Visitor Information: (520) 457-3929. www.tombstone.org

Tombstone Western Heritage Museum: Items from the early days of the "town to tough to die." $. Fremont and 6th St. (520) 457-3800.

Six Gun City Wild West Show: Western dinner theatre that pays homage to Tombstone's violent past. Performances daily at 11:30 a.m., 1 p.m., and 3:30 p.m. $. 5th and Toughnut St. (520) 457-3827.

Old Tombstone Tours: A 15-minute tour by stagecoach, covered wagon, or carriage. $. Allen St. in front of Tombstone Stage Stop and across from the Crystal Palace Saloon. (520) 457-3018. www.oldtombstonetours.com

Bird Cage Theatre/Museum: The 1881 brothel, saloon, and gambling house displays many relics from its infamous past. Visitors can try to count all the bullet holes on their self-guided tour. Gift shop. $. Allen and 6th St. (520) 457-3421.

Boot Hill: Famous 19th-century cemetery. Slain O.K. Corral cowboys and Old Man Clanton are among the infamous people laid to rest here. Gift shop. Donations. State Route 80 just north of Tombstone. (520) 457-9344 or (800) 457-9344.

Helldorado Days: For more than 75 years Tombstone has hosted the Helldorado Days celebration. Weekend event includes Old West storytelling, a beard and mustache contest, re-enactments, a parade, and carnival. October. $. www.helldoradodays.com

Rose Tree Museum: The star here is a white Lady Banksia rose planted in 1885 and still blooming. Covering more than 8,000 square feet, it's the focus of an annual event in April, when it blooms. Museum includes a mineral collection, Tombstone memorabilia, and antique household furnishings of the Macia family, long-time residents of Tombstone. Gift shop and book store. $. 4th and Toughnut Sts. (520) 457-3326.

Schieffelin Hall: The restored 1881 adobe building hosts the occasional show. Call for show times and events. Fremont and 4th St. (520) 457-3929.

St. Paul's Episcopal Church: The people, building materials, and fixtures associated with this adobe brick structure built in 1882 are a history lesson, but the church still serves a parish. Services every Sun. Donations. 3rd and Safford Sts. (520) 432-5402. www.1882.org

O.K. Corral: History tells us that a 30-second gunfight with Wyatt Earp, his brothers Morgan and Virgil, and Doc Holliday on one side, and the McLaurys and Clantons on the other, took place behind this site. But since the eruption on Oct. 26, 1881, the legendary shoot-out has been called the Gunfight at the O.K. Corral and that's where it is re-enacted daily at 2 p.m. $. Allen St., between 3rd and 4th St. (520) 457-3456. www.ok-corral.com

Tombstone Courthouse State Historic Park: The 1882 courthouse housed the sheriff's and other Cochise county government offices. In the back was a jail. Alongside, a gallows. It's now a museum. $. 3rd and Toughnut Sts. (520) 457-3311.
www.pr.state.az.us/tripguide/adventure/time.html

Tombstone Historama: A 26-minute multi-media show on the history of Tombstone narrated by Vincent Price. $. 310 E. Allen St. (520) 457-3456.

Pioneer Home Museum: Early 19th-century home of the Garland mining family. Call for tour. 804 E. Fremont St. Donations. (520) 457-3853.

Tombstone *Epitaph* Museum: Tombstone's *Epitaph* has been in circulation since 1880 and is one of the West's most famous publications. Original press, vintage newspapers, and other exhibits. Free. 5th St. around the corner from the Crystal Palace Saloon. (520) 457-2211.

Big Nose Kate's Saloon: Originally the Grand Hotel, this 1881 landmark welcomed the Clantons and McLaurys the night before the shoot-out at the O.K. Corral. Saloon and gift shop occupy the building now. $. 417 E Allen St. (520) 457.3107. www.bignosekate.com

Crystal Palace Saloon: The staff includes a Wyatt Earp impersonator and other costumed employees in this restored 19th-century saloon. Live music, dancing, drinks. $. 420 Allen St., Tombstone. (520) 457-361. www.crystalpalacesaloon.com

Helldorado Town: A Wild West theme park featuring live entertainment, a

[Site of an old volcanic eruption, Chiricahua National Monument now showcases hundreds of rock spires.]

Tom Danielsen

shooting gallery, the Beer Barrel Saloon, a mine shaft, and grub shack. $. 4th and Toughnut Sts. (520) 457-9035. www.helldoradotown.com

Schieffelin Monument: A stone memorial, in the shape of a miner's claim, marks the spot where Tombstone's founding prospector, Ed Schieffelin, was buried. Free. Two miles west of town on Allen St.

Ed Schieffelin Territorial Days: Annual festival featuring a fireman's muster, championship hose cart races, an all-pet parade, and mining displays. March. (888) 457-3929. www.tombstone.org

Wyatt Earp Days: Wild West extravaganza. Cook-off, live entertainment, gunfight re-enactments, fashion show, parade, and Wyatt look-alike contest. May. (520) 457-3291. www.wyattearpdays.com

Vigilante Days: Old West costume contest, 10K road race, chili cook-off. August. (520) 457-3197; (520) 457-3291. www.tombstone.org

Willcox

Willcox Chamber of Commerce / Museum of the Southwest: Museum of the Southwest and tourist center are housed in the city's chamber of commerce offices. Learn about farms where you can pick pumpkins, apples, or chilies. The museum has an exhibit focusing on the

[Sunset layers colors over Organ Pipe Cactus National Monument.]

George H. H. Huey

Apache chief Cochise. 1500 N. Circle I Road. (520) 384-2272;
(800) 200-2272. www.willcoxchamber.com

Rex Allen Cowboy Museum and Willcox Cowboy Hall Of Fame: The
star here is Rex Allen, a famous singing cowboy of Western movies and a
Willcox native. Westerns regularly are shown in the hall's theater. Ko Ko,
Allen's stallion, is buried in the park across the street next to a life-sized
bronze statue of the cowboy. Donations. 150 N. Railroad Ave.
(520) 384-4583. www.rexallenmuseum.org

Rex Allen Days: Annual celebration that honors the singing cowboy film
star is more than 50 years old. Food, entertainment, parade, tractor pulls,
softball tournaments, carnival, and rodeo. The proceeds from the weekend
go to a charitable organization. October. $. (520) 384-2272;
(800) 200-2272. www.rexallendays.com

Chiricahua Regional Museum and Research Center: Museum focuses
on Apache leaders Cochise and Geronimo. Also displays an extensive rock
and mineral collection. Closed Sun. $. 127 E. Maley St. (520) 384-3971.

Willcox Playa Wildlife Area: The enormous dry lake bed 7 miles
southwest of Willcox is a birding and photographic paradise. The area is a
stopover for thousands of migratory birds, including sandhill cranes. From
Willcox, take State Route 186 about 5 miles to Kansas Settlement Road.
Turn right (south) and go 3 to 5 miles. (520) 384-2272; (800) 200-2272.
www.gf.state.az.us/outdoor_recreation/wildlife_area_wilcox_playa.shtml

Wings Over Willcox Sandhill Crane Celebration: Birding and nature
festival focusing on the sandhill crane. Natural history tours, seminars.
Reservations needed. January. $. Willcox Chamber of Commerce,
(800) 200-2272. www.wingsoverwillcox.com

Southern Pacific Depot: Built in 1800 and restored for use as the Willcox
City Hall. Displays pioneer and railroad items. Closed Sat–Sun. $. 101 S.
Railroad Ave. (520) 384-6034. www.cityofwillcox.org

Chiricahua National Monument: Haven for hikers and birders. Fantastic
rock formations. The pioneer homestead, Faraway Ranch, offers view into
early life in the region. $. Exit Interstate 10 at Willcox and follow State
Route 186 36 miles to the monument. (520) 824-3560. www.nps.gov/chir

WEST OF TUCSON

Ajo

Ajo Chamber of Commerce: Provides information on attractions and
events. (520) 387-7742. www.ajochamber.com

New Cornelia Open Mine Pit: One of the world's widest (nearly 2 miles) mines. Although mining ceased in the 1980s, visitors can view the massive mine from an overlook and tour the visitors center to learn about mining operations. From the town Plaza, take La Mina Street southwest to Indian Village Road to the viewpoint. Open Oct.–May. (520) 387-7742.

Ajo Historical Society Museum: Located in the old Saint Catherine's Indian Mission, the museum display relics representative of Ajo's rich historical past such as gemstones, Navajo blankets, mining displays. Gift shop. Open Nov.–May; summer by appointment. $. 160 S. Mission Road. (520) 387-7105.

Cabeza Prieta National Wildlife Refuge: The Spanish name means "dark head." Seven desert mountain ranges and several valleys define the Cabeza Prieta area. Bighorn sheep, javelina, bobcats, mountain lions, Sonoran pronghorn, and a variety of birds are some of the animals living here. Remember, do not linger near water holes because wildlife likely won't approach them if you are there. Be well prepared if you plan to hike and camp in this primitive country. A short interpretive trail near the National Fish and Wildlife Service visitors center is fine for beginners. The center is located near the refuge's office on the west side of State Route 86 on the northern end of Ajo. You'll need an entry permit (free) and you must sign a "Military Hold Harmless Agreement." Most of the refuge lies in the air space of the Barry M. Goldwater Air Force Range, and low-flying aircraft cross the refuge to reach bombing and gunnery ranges. Permits are available at the office, or you can call to arrange for one to be mailed to you. Be sure to read the "tips for watching wildlife" section of the refuge's Internet site. (520) 387-6483. www.fws.gov/southwest/refuges/arizona/cabeza.html

Organ Pipe Cactus National Monument: Hiking and primitive camping. Ranger-led activities conducted Jan.–March. Visitors center exhibits explain the desert. $. On State Route 85, about 35 miles south of Ajo. (520) 387-6849. www.nps.gov/orpi

Fiddlers Contest and Piecemakers Quilt Show: Fiddles and quilts galore at this annual Ajo event. February. (520) 387-7742. See Old Time Fiddlers in Special Interest listings.

Sells

Kitt Peak National Observatory: Perched above the Sonoran Desert on the Tohono O'odham Reservation, the observatory has a diverse collection of telescopes. Guided tours, nightly observing programs. Picnic area. $. Kitt Peak is 56 miles southwest of Tucson. From Tucson, take State Route 86

(Ajo Way) to State Route 386; turn left and drive up the mountain 12 miles to the visitors center. (520) 318-8726. www.noao.edu/kpno

Tohono O'odham All-Indian Rodeo and Fair: Held annually in late January or early February. Showcases Tohono O'odham wranglers' riding and roping skills. Parade, craft exhibits, and Indian songs and dances. Contact the tribal office in Sells for information on dates and location. (520) 383-2588 Ext.5. www.itcaonline.com/tribes_tohono.html

NORTH AND NORTHWEST OF TUCSON

Arizona City

Gem and Mineral Show: February. Free. 13270 S. Sunland Gin Road. www.admmr.state.az.us

Casa Grande

Greater Casa Grande Chamber of Commerce: Distributes visitors information on attractions, events, lodging, shopping and other travel topics. (800) 916-1515; (520) 836-2125. www.casagrandechamber.org

Casa Grande Valley Historical Society and Museum: The museum grounds have the Rebecca Dallis Schoolhouse, Heritage Hall (a historic stone church) and 3,000 artifacts to explore. Closed mid-May to mid-Sept. $. 110 W. Florence Blvd. (520) 836-2223. www.cgvhs.org

Casa Grande Art Museum: Housed in the historic Kratzka House. Features sculpture, water-color, multi-media, and Western art by local, regional, and national artists. Open Sept.–May, Wed., Sat., Sun., 1 p.m.–4 p.m. Free. 319 W. 3rd St. (520) 836-3377.

Wuertz Farm: Gourd farm (2487 E. Route 287) open to visitors. Miniature donkeys and gift shop. Hosts annual gourd festival in February at the Pinal County Fairgrounds. (520) 723-4432; for RV camping call (520) 723-5242. www.wuertzfarm.com

Arizona State Open Chili Championship: Annually in March. Live entertainment, classic car show as well as arts and crafts. Free. Dave White Park, 2121 N. Thornton. (800) 916-1515. www.casagrandechamber.org/events/chilichamp.htm

Fiddlers Bluegrass Jamboree and Craft Bazaar: Fiddler and bluegrass musicians entertain at this multi-event festival. Arts and crafts, an RV display, trade show, and food. January. $. Pinal County Fairgrounds, 512 S. 11 Mile Corner Road. (520) 723-5242. See Old Time Fiddlers in Special Interest listings beginning on Page 399.

Historic Downtown Street Fair: Car show, historic bicycle tour, fine-art show, food, and entertainment. Free. January. (800) 916-1515.

O'odham Tash Indian Days Celebration: Held in February on President's Day weekend, this "celebration of the people" has an all-Indian rodeo, a pow-wow, parade, entertainment, food. (800) 916-1515; (520) 836-4723.

Cactus Fly-In: Hosted by the Arizona Antique Aircraft Association, the event, which has taken place for more than 45 years, showcases classics, warbirds, replicas, and homebuilt aircraft. March. Casa Grande Municipal Airport. (800) 916-1515 or (520) 836-2125. www.cactusflyin.org

Eloy

Eloy Chamber of Commerce: Maintains Internet links to area attractions. 305 N. Stuart Blvd. (520) 466-3411. www.eloychamber.com

Skydive Arizona: Billed as the "world's largest skydiving resort." RV hook-ups, bunk houses, camping, a sky dive school. 4900 N. Taylor Road, Eloy. (520) 466-3753. www.skydiveaz.com

Marana

Marana Chamber of Commerce: (520) 682-4314. www.maranachamber.com

Tour of the Tucson Mountains: The 50-and 100-kilometer bike tours take participants around the perimeter of the Tucson Mountains. A much shorter kids course is set up as well. April. $. Start and finish in Marana. (520) 745-2033. www.perimeterbicycling.com

Oro Valley

Catalina State Park: Trails, camping facilities with electrical hookups, equestrian center, picnic area, and visitors center. Daily, 5 a.m.–10 p.m. Visitors center hours, 8 p.m.–5 p.m. $. On State Route 77 (Oracle Road) at Milepost 81, just north of Oro Valley. (520) 628-5798. www.pr.state.az.us/Parks/parkhtml/catalina.html

San Manuel/Mammoth/Oracle

San Manuel/Mammoth/Oracle Chamber of Commerce: Oracle. (520) 896-9322. www.the-chamber.com/catsaddleoracle.htm

Acadia Ranch Museum: Housed in Oracle's oldest building, built around 1800. Local cowboy and mining histories and a collection of mastodon remains. Sat., 1–5 p.m. or by appointment. Free. 825 Mount Lemmon Road. (520) 896-9609. www.oraclehistoricalsociety.org/ohs/museum.html

Biosphere 2: The world-renowned glassed-in structure encloses a tropical savanna, ocean, mangrove forest, and desert. Guided tours "under the glass" and self-guided tours around the exterior. Daily, 9 a.m.–4 p.m. $. On State Route 77 (Oracle Road) at Milepost 96.5. (520) 838-6200. www.bio2.com

Oracle State Park: Environmental education park and wildlife refuge features approximately 15 miles of trails for hiking, cycling or horse riding; the 100-year-old Kannally Ranch House; a picnic area; nature programs for children. $. In the northern foothills of the Santa Catalina Mountains. (520) 896-2425. www.pr.state.az.us/Parks/parkhtml/oracle.html

Globe-Miami

Globe-Miami Chamber of Commerce: 1360 N. Broad St., Globe. (928) 425-4495. www.globemiamichamber.com

Antiques: The combined towns of Globe-Miami can count more than 26 antique shops among their businesses. Specialties range from mining collectibles to glassware.

[Biosphere 2 demonstrated the difficulty of replicating Nature's handiwork.]

Tony Marinella

Black Mountain looms over the winding Colorado River. ▲
Hoover Dam catches light at dusk in Lake Mead National Recreation Area ▶

Lower Colorado River
Yuma to Lake Mead

Locals sometimes refer to this stretch of the state as Arizona's West Coast, flanked by a waterway that's a river—the Colorado—rather than an ocean. You can explore it, as we do, by starting in Phoenix, traveling to southern Arizona (with waypoints along Interstate 10), and then following a route pioneered by Spanish explorers. When they reached what's now Yuma, they crossed into California, moved up a real coast, and established San Francisco. We, however, bear north out of Yuma to take in river cities and some areas east of them, such as the Joshua Forest Scenic Parkway and places like Wikieup, Nothing, and Wickenburg. And then, we're almost back in Phoenix.

Larry Ulrich

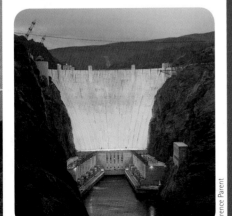

Laurence Parent

A Prison and Much More

I t's 2 o'clock on a cloudless midsummer's day, and you have just completed a trip that has brought you to an inferno. With a blowtorch wind in your face, you figure that you have done some bad things in your life, are now dead and enduring the first day of your eternity in a four-letter place. Or, maybe you took the wrong exit from the freeway and drove straight into another four-letter hotspot: Yuma.

It's hot. Really hot. Except in winter, when it's not.

To visualize the geography of the region under discussion in this chapter, it might help to think of one of those United Way thermometer displays that chart the progress of donations. At the bottom, or south, is a big bulb of red simulating mercury. A thin column of red rises north out of the bulb. On the map, that big bulb is Yuma north to Lake Havasu City, and the column of mercury rising out of there is a narrow strip paralleling the Colorado River—the boundary between Arizona's western edge and the eastern edges of California and Nevada—all the way north to Lake Mead and its creator, Hoover Dam, as well as the outskirts of Las Vegas.

The selection of a thermometer with a rising temperature as a graphic representation of the region may be apt but, at the same time, it is too one-dimensional and unfair.

The story is told of a Yuma man who died and dropped into the hellfire, then promptly dispatched a message to former, still-living Yuma neighbors asking for his blankets. And then there's the one about the coyote chasing the rabbit on an August day in Yuma, and they're both walking.

Very funny—except to Yumans. The fact is that although a 120-degree day there is not all that freakish during the peak of summer, Phoenix is a couple of degrees hotter on average than Yuma, the records show. Want a number or two? Yuma's average January high temperature is almost 69 degrees, in July almost 107. Precipitation hovers around 3 inches a year.

So why go there?

Answer: The city is not in the geographic center of the region under discussion, but it is the clean, airy, and modern cultural and population center with an astonishing number of exciting attractions in and around it. The population of about 90,000 (and growing rapidly) swells to about twice that number with winter visitors, many of them attracted to 13 area golf courses. Some even attend the ballets.

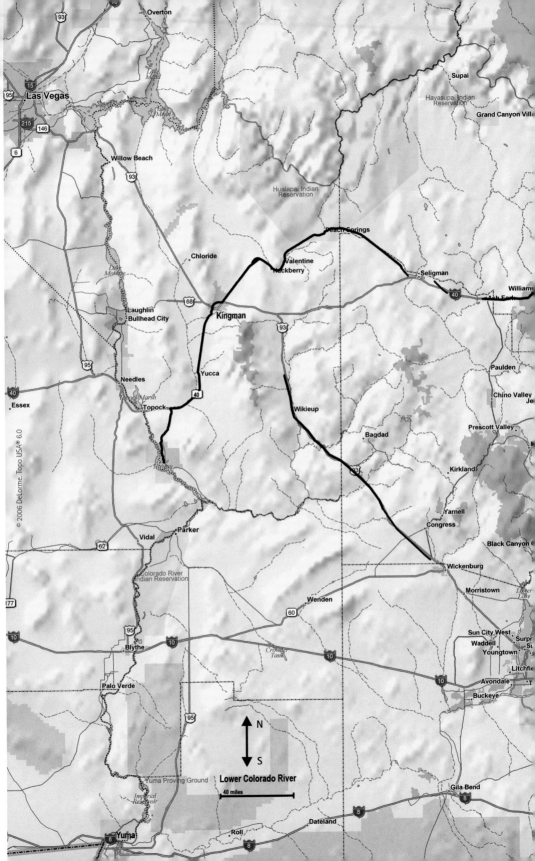

Lower Colorado River

N
S

40 miles

Among the best of Yuma's other attractions:

- The Colorado River, once wild, now tamed and offering several wildlife refuges, real sand beaches, and a colorful recorded history dating to the 16th century. That's when it was cutting its way south through the Grand Canyon to its confluence near Yuma with the Gila River and then on into Mexico. In spots in those days, it was once as wide as 15 miles. No longer. Dams took care of that.

- The Territorial Prison, a historic inferno from frontier days where, as freelance writer Leo Banks described in an article in *Arizona Highways*, you can stand in one of the tiny jail cells and "imagine what it must've been like there in the depths of August, five other guys with no fashion sense and bad attitudes lying on steel bunks around you." He didn't mention that it undoubtedly was arid, but there was no Arrid. On the other hand, lots of freelancers don't wear deodorant.

- Shopping in any or all of dozens of specialty stores that populate the city's shade-dappled and quite pretty downtown mall (featuring landmark pool hall-bar-restaurant Lute's Casino). Or go 7 miles southwest and across the border in Algodones, Mexico, where cheap but generally good dentists (150 by one count), eye docs (two dozen or so), and inexpensive prescription drugs at a dozen pharmacies compete for your dollar with dozens of shops jammed into eight square blocks and offering jewelry, pottery, glassware, leather goods, clothing, and handicrafts.

- The Yuma Crossing State Historic Park, site of the structure that was a major supply center for troops during the Indian Wars of the 1870s and the spot where travelers ferried across the river to get to California and its gold.

- Remnants of the Old Plank Road, built of planks during pioneer days to permit wagon travel over Arizona sands and used later by early autos.

- The Algodones Sand Dunes (sometimes called Imperial Sand Dunes), largely just across the border into California but fringing on the Yuma area. Covering an area about 5 by 40 miles with dunes reaching 300 feet in height, it is an immense expanse of shifting, golden sand dunes that date back 10,000 to 20,000 years. The active dune system is home to rare lizards and beetles as well as a few plants. Parts of the dunes are open to off-road vehicle recreationists, but an area known as the North Algodones Dunes Wildness is closed to the sand buggies. The dunes were the site of a battle scene in one of the *Star Wars* epics as well as scenes in many other American movies. The dunes are called the Great American Sahara and properly so. Good to look at from an overlook or to walk on for a short distance. Keep your tires on the road. From Yuma, you can reach the dunes via Interstate 8, along which are viewpoints. The area south of the interstate is reachable only by off-road vehicle. To tour the area north of the interstate, take the Olgiby Road Exit.

- Paddle-wheel boat rides on the river as well as boat trips and Jeep tours of big stretches of wildlife refuges on both sides of the river.
- Lettuce. It might not send your heart rate into dangerous territory, but the expanse of lettuce fields around the city outskirts, both the conventional iceberg and many specialty lettuces, is astonishing.
- Spring baseball training for the San Diego Padres.

Not to be forgotten is Jay Stokes, of Yuma, who made Ripley's "Believe It or Not" by parachuting 534 times from an airplane in 24 hours.

And that's just a sample. See Where To Go for additional details.

Sun glares through a gate at Yuma Territorial Prison State Historic Park.

Kerrick James

■■■

Moving on north from Yuma, the most popular destinations are the communities of Quartzsite (an RVer's version of Nirvana), Parker, Lake Havasu City (the historic London Bridge is there and isn't falling down), Bullhead City and, finally, Lake Mead formed by Hoover Dam, that gigantic obstruction in the throat of the river and nestled amid an astonishing, Alps-like setting of rippling and rugged mountain ranges and gorgeous gorges. (Kingman is along the way but is covered in the Route 66 chapter.)

Quartzsite: Normally a community of fewer than 3,500 people, this desert spot where Interstate 10 and State Route 95 intersect swells—according to some estimates—to a million people in the winter, primarily January and February. They come for the warm winter weather, cheap rent on RV spaces, gem and mineral sales and shows, RV sales and shows, and a swap meet atmosphere that stretches over thousands of acres.

Parker: State Route 95 goes north out of Quartzsite to Parker, one of countless, small, riverine communities that dot the length of the river and that offer boat ramps and other marine accoutrements as well as a café or two, a fast-food franchise, gasoline, camping areas, and the occasional sand beach.

Robert Herko

Yuma Territorial Prison

Imagine this: It is July 1876, exactly a century since America announced its national independence and that of all its people. You find all of that noble sentiment about freedom quite pointless, because you have been convicted of a felony and have been incarcerated in the newly finished Yuma Territorial Prison. The temperature is 108 degrees, and you are housed in a 9- by 12-foot cell with five other nasty guys, all walking around the rocky, dirt floor and sharing the hot, thick air and the one pot available for bodily needs and not a stick of deodorant in sight. You also are sharing the space with bedbugs, black widow spiders, scorpions, and cockroaches. You know that if you give the guards a bad time, you will end up in the "dark cell," a black cave containing a cage in which you will be chained, stripped to your underwear, and fed bread and water once a day. There is no bed or bedding nor are there toilet facilities in the dark cell. The human refuse of the men who were there before you has not been removed in the last three months, and the stench would make a gargoyle gag.

Scene shift: It is today, and you are a tourist standing inside the walls of this prison that is partly dug into a rock hill. You have read the blather about the prison having a library and good medical facilities and being humane "for its time," but as you stare into this heart of darkness, you can only echo Conrad's Mr. Kurtz: "The horror, the horror."

The prison, today one of the state's top attractions, opened on July 1, 1876, with seven inmates locked into cells they had dug out and built up themselves. In 1909, some 33 years and 3,069 prisoners (29 of them women) later, it was closed because of overcrowding. No one who had been imprisoned there mourned its passing.

Prisoners were sentenced for a variety of crimes including murder, rape, robbery, stage holdups, cattle rustling, horse stealing, drug peddling, whiskey selling, and, of all things, seduction. One woman was there as a convicted rapist. Among the prison's most famous alums was Buckskin Frank Leslie, a noted gunman, crack shot, and convicted murderer who once got his wife to

[Infamous men passed through Yuma Territorial Prison's sally port. ▲]

pose against a wall while he shot bullets around the outline of her body. She divorced him. Also on hand at one point was Pearl Hart, sentenced to five years in connection with a stage holdup. Courtesy of the distortions of the so-called "yellow journalists" of the time, Pearl became a celebrity lady bandit and, when she eventually was pardoned, she took a shot at becoming a theatrical star. She wasn't any better at that than at stage holdups. Her partner in the holdup, a man named Joe Boot, did better. While serving a 30-year term, he escaped, probably to Mexico, and was not heard from again. His escape was one of 26 successful ones, but only two of those were from within the prison confines.

To get to the prison, take Interstate 8 into Yuma, then Exit 1 to Giss Parkway and turn at Prison Hill Road. The number to call is (520) 783-4771.

Lake Havasu City: Continuing north on State 95 leads to this pleasant city of about 51,000 people (up from 15,500 in 1975) on the banks of Lake Havasu, a lake formed when the Parker Dam was completed across the Colorado River in 1938.

Not incorporated until 1978, Lake Havasu City was founded in 1964 by a chainsaw millionaire Robert P. McCulloch, Sr. He was flying over the Southwest looking for a motor testing site when he saw an abandoned military landing strip, bought it and, later on, imported the London Bridge and re-erected it over a channel off the river.

The city, beautifully planned and a vast change from the somewhat ramshackle environs of Quartzsite, sports more than 1,000 businesses, shopping, a regional hospital, a community college, several golf courses, a big marina, and, of course, the famous bridge.

Bullhead City: Next stop up State 95 is Bullhead City, the location of still another of the Colorado River dams, this one named Davis Dam. This tourism-based community is a seemingly endless strip of 2,000 shops, malls, and fast-food places plus some green and shady parks smack dab in the Mohave Desert. That's all perfectly pleasant but what catches the eyes is ... high rises. Really. Actual almost-skyscrapers. A mini-Manhattan. Nearly a dozen of them, rising out of the desert floor along the riverfront. But they are not in Arizona. They are a few hundred feet just across the river—in Bullhead's sister city, Laughlin, Nevada.

They are gambling casinos-resorts with somewhere around 12,000 rooms (and 6 million visitors some years), and they, in addition to the river, account in large measure for the nearly 40,000 people, including 14,000 who work in Laughlin, who have chosen to live in Bullhead City. The names on these preposterous towers plopped into the flat, hot desert tell the story: Edgewater, Flamingo, Riverside, a riverboat wheeler called *Colorado Belle*. It's all there, just across short, low bridges from Bullhead City.

As befits any tourism-based community, Bullhead City offers a county-run riverside campground, Davis Camp, that is large and convenient and set up for

RVs with full hook-ups, fishing pier, day-use group ramada, swimming beach, museum, wading area, dozens of small shade ramadas with places for parking and tents, and even resort homes that run cheaper in winter. Simple beach camping costs a vehicle fee plus a fee per pet per day. Reservations at (877) 757-0915.

Chloride: Off of U.S. Route 93 is this small, old mining town that dates to 1863 where gold, silver, lead, zinc, copper, and turquoise were found. Good shopping.

Willow Beach: On the way to Hoover Dam, also a short distance off U.S. 93 out of Kingman, is this delightful rest stop with an abandoned motel, a fish hatchery, and a strip along the Arizona shoreline from which it is possible to launch canoes and kayaks. The trip down to the river from the highway is modestly dramatic. Bring tortillas or crackers to feed the abundance of small birds and waterfowl that will cluster around your feet.

Hoover Dam and Lake Mead Recreation Area: The 726-foot, semi-circular dam with its pleasing Art Deco designs first began impounding the water of the Colorado River in 1935 when workers could buy a quart of milk for a dime, a gallon of gas for 18 cents, and a car for less than $600. Originally called Boulder Dam, it was renamed in 1947 to honor (pick one) (a) a vacuum sweeper, (b) a transvestite FBI director or (c) a Depression-era POTUS. It has been called a "towering icon of American ingenuity," but some environmentalists have called it other, less sycophantic things. Whatever you call it, the impressive dam, jammed between the walls of the Black Canyon, sucks up the power of the river to generate mega megawatts that are carried on power lines strung from dozens upon dozens of stick-figure, steel transmission towers anchored at improbable angles to the rocky, mountainous terrain. Whew. What a sentence. Take a breath; you'll need to know how to do that when you see this monument.

So pay your five bucks to park in the multi-level parking garage and go see the sights, take a "Discovery Tour," read the plaque at the grave of a stray puppy who wandered into the construction site and became a pet of the laborers until he was run over in 1941 by a truck under which he was snoozing, shop, eat, take photos, go to the visitors center but leave your pocket knife in the car, or take a motorized raft trip from the base of the dam out into the waters of the canyon (Black Canyon River Adventures, Boulder City, Nevada, (800) 455-3490).

The two major lakes are Mead and, farther south on the river, Lake Mohave, both part of the sprawling Lake Mead National Recreation Area. They are called lakes, but the unglamorous fact is that they are really just big aneurysms in the artery that is the river. Both are huge and provide an endless array of recreational opportunities for boaters, fisherpeople, swimmers, water-skiers, backcountry hikers, campers, and anyone who simply wants to sit under an umbrella on a sandy beach and drink a low-carb beer. A wealth of information is available from the Alan Bible visitors center four miles east of Boulder City, Nevada. (702) 293-8990. ⋀⋀

A River Runs Through It

Back in the good ole pioneer days, when—the myth makers would have us believe—men were men and women were women and both had bad bicuspids and big biceps, the Colorado River was a deep and roaring torrent of water providing river-area dwellers, travelers, would-be gold miners, and the military with bath water, a cooling dip on a hot day, water to drink and irrigate crops, occasional floods. Ferries provided passage across the river between Arizona and California paddle-wheel steamboats provided transportation of goods and people up and down.

These days, the river, though still a vital source of precious water for irrigation, has been tamed by dams constructed since the passage by Congress in 1902 of the National Reclamation Act. In fact, on the lower portion of the river above and through Yuma, it is so tame and so shallow in spots that even a canoe can hang up on the ever-shifting sandbars that dot the width and length of the stream.

For almost two-thirds of a century after 60,000 gold-seekers created the 1849 Gold Rush, those paddle-wheel steamboats provided inexpensive and efficient transportation. The first steamer was launched in 1852 and the last one was lost in 1916. The dams and the railroads killed them.

[A boy fishes from a dock at the Branson Resort along Parker Strip on the Colorado River.]

Don B. Stevenson

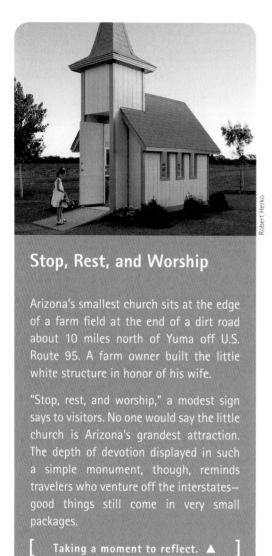

Robert Herko

Stop, Rest, and Worship

Arizona's smallest church sits at the edge of a farm field at the end of a dirt road about 10 miles north of Yuma off U.S. Route 95. A farm owner built the little white structure in honor of his wife.

"Stop, rest, and worship," a modest sign says to visitors. No one would say the little church is Arizona's grandest attraction. The depth of devotion displayed in such a simple monument, though, reminds travelers who venture off the interstates—good things still come in very small packages.

[Taking a moment to reflect. ▲   ]

If you can find it, the history of the steamboats is delightfully detailed in Richard E. Lingenfelter's *Steamboats On The Colorado River*, published and copyrighted in 1978 by the University of Arizona Press.

There are countless other ways to enjoy the river, particularly in cooler months when the jet ski and motorboat crowd is largely absent. One is a narrated river tour offered by Yuma River Tours that leads through the Imperial Wildlife Refuge and spectacular cliffs and rock sculptures just north of Yuma. They are conducted by Smokey and Judy Knowlton—she a Navy veteran, he an ex-boat dealer—and by Smokey's son, Ron. They also offer a boat ride several miles upriver, where they will leave you supplied with a canoe, paddles, life jackets and a four-hour (or longer) paddle back to Martinez Lake just outside Yuma.

For novice canoeists, a reassurance: There is no white water; the current is a meek 2 to 3 miles an hour in cooler months

If paddling using only your arms and lungs isn't your thing, there is the *Colorado King I* paddle boat, a big stern-wheeler that offers narration and all the amenities one might wish as well as its own paddling power, generally from October through May.

The Yuma River Tours can be reached at (928) 783-4400 in Yuma (1920 Arizona Ave.) and the *Colorado King* at (928) 782-2412. Both operations launch from Fisher's Landing at Martinez Lake. To get there, take U.S. Route 95 north out of Yuma for 22 miles to Martinez Lake Road, turn left and go 10 miles to the landing. ▥

Quartzsite = RV

A ttention, RV owners.

U.S. Route 95, the main road north out of Yuma, leads in 80 or so miles to Quartzsite, a small, sun-scorched chunk of unprepossessing desert that averages a high of 108 degrees in July and 71 in February and is occupied by a year-round, permanent population of somewhere between 600 and 3,400. The smaller figure is offered by one local tourism official who says the larger, official estimate is cockeyed because census takers failed to eliminate some of the winter visitors who hung on past the winter months.

So what about those winter visitors? Get ready to scoff. An estimated 2.2 million of them! That means a population on any given day in January, the biggest month, of about a million people, never mind dogs, cats, ferrets, gerbils, pythons, deodorized skunks, and assorted other pets they brought with them.

Who are these guys, these men with mostly white or no hair, big belt buckles disappearing under ample bellies and their women in pink or lavender shorts and matching Topsiders? They are, for the most part, seniors from throughout the nation and Canada who drove their recreational vehicles here for guaranteed warm weather in winter and lots of cheap and open space where they can park,

[Ocotillo, teddy bear cholla, brittlebush, and lupines bedeck the foothills of the Kofa Mountains.]

Jack Dykinga

play bridge, cook outdoors, attend musical jams, go to endless flea markets, swap meets and the world's biggest gem and mineral shows, look for quartz or turquoise in the surrounding mining country—and force the creation of a big sewer system to replace an overwhelmed septic network that was polluting the earth below.

Where do they stay? In a sea of RVs—small ones, big ones, huge ones—parked in scores of RV and mobile home parks spread over for 70 square miles in and around this tiny town. One of the parks is La Posa Long Term Visitor Area, an 11,400-acre chunk of flat, sparsely vegetated, Bureau of Land Management land. An RV owner can buy a seven-month permit to park in La Posa, which provides water, sewage disposal, and a community shower. Full details are available at www.blm.gov/az/yfo/laposa.htm.

By late April, the madness has subsided, and by summer it would be possible to stroll the circumference of the town in, perhaps, 15 to 30 minutes. In the peak of winter, the traffic is so dense that it can take an hour to circumnavigate the perimeter in a car. Drivers who get desperate even park in the arroyos.

Among other oddities in this former wagon stop—where Wyatt Earp is said to have tried, and failed to become constable—are a nudist colony outside of town, trees inexplicably decorated with shoes, bras, panties, and hats, and a camel statue marking a time in the 1800s when the Army experimented with the use of camels to haul supplies. Hi Jolly Days in Quartzsite is a tribute of sorts to one of the camel drivers, Hadji Ali, who was dubbed Hi Jolly by troopers. (See Quartzsite listing in Where To Go section.) ᴬᴴ

[A Titan II missile sits in a silo at the Titan Missile Museum south of Tucson.]

Tom Bean

Juan Bautista de Anza National Historic Trail

Route	Nogales to Tucson on Interstate 19; Tucson to Coolidge on Interstate 10 and state highways; Coolidge to Yuma on state highways and Interstate 8.
Mileage	Nogales to Tucson, 65 miles; Tucson to Coolidge, 70 miles; Coolidge to Yuma, 195 miles.
Time to Allow	Minimum two days, not including time you may spend in Nogales or Yuma.
Elevation	Not much. Less than 500 feet in most places.
Overview	Officially, the trail stretches from Nogales to Yuma. But here, we are first driving from Phoenix to Tucson and on to Nogales. That means a lot of driving along freeways through Sonoran Desert vegetation and vast flatlands now dedicated to irrigation and agriculture. There are big, historic rewards at both ends (Nogales and Yuma) and hours upon hours worth of exploring amazing prehistoric sites along the way. A hard-to-beat trip.

A popular way to get from southern Arizona to the Yuma region is a drive westward, and we are going to do it on the Juan Bautista de Anza National Historic Trail between Nogales and Yuma.

Beginning with shopping in Nogales, Mexico, the experience continues to embrace many historic and prehistoric sites. The scenery from the interstate and through the windshield might not be as consistently spectacular as that of other drives described in this book, but there are so many easily accessible sites just off and off-off the freeway that bypassing them deprives the traveler of unmatched pleasures. Gone would be the chance to experience North America centuries before the white man showed up (Casa Grande Ruins) and, leaping ahead, life in the Cold War era (a Titan missile silo).

During the Sonoran summer, the Juan Bautista de Anza drive is, frankly, a lot of hot air. Better you should go in winter. In late fall or during the winter, you can take this drive and plan with reasonable certainty to walk out into the desert on Thanksgiving or Christmas Day, spread a linen tablecloth under the chiaroscuro of bright sunlight and mesquite shade, and tie into a bottle of cold wine, a room-temperature turkey, and a slow-melting slice of pumpkin pie a la mode. It can be wonderful, and it certainly can't be done at that time of year on the North Rim of the Grand Canyon unless you are wearing some goose's clothing.

Willard Clay

[
Sunrise warms cholla and saguaro cacti below Baboquivari Peak
in Buenos Aires National Wildlife Refuge.
]

If you are destined or determined, however, to take this Dantean trial run of a two-desert inferno (Sonoran and Mohave) in the less hospitable months, be sure you have a wide-brimmed hat on your head, the windows up in your vehicle, an air conditioner under the hood, and an ice chest full of cold water in the back of your vehicle.

On the positive side of the argument for driving the route in summer, you will have the terrifying and realistic experience of sweating out what it was like to have been in the Yuma Territorial Prison in July or August.

(A tip for travelers that may not bear the Martha Stewart seal of approval but has worked well over the centuries: If the air conditioning system in the car fails, dump water on your head, open the windows and feel the process of evaporation cool you all over. It makes for a bad hair day, but it beats the price a heat stroke will put on your vanity bill.)

The Arizona portion of the Juan Bautista de Anza National Historic Trail reaches roughly from the twin cities of Nogales (Arizona, and Mexico) on the east to Yuma and the Colorado River border with California on the west. In California, the trail continues to San Francisco.

Why take it at all? Because there's Nogales, Mexico, and its shopping at one end and Yuma with its historic sites and river recreation at the other. It's a chance to retrace a truly monumental trek through this region's history and prehistory including stops at ancient dwellings, aboriginal rock art galleries, a modern copper mine, and a missile emplacement. It's also the story of an amazing leader and a durable, doughty band of settlers. That's why.

■■■

First, a quick history lesson that'll help you appreciate sites along the drive.

In the 1770s, right around the time America declared its independence from England, the Spaniards had been in the New World for a couple of centuries and controlled Mexico and big chunks of what is now the U.S. Southwest and West. The Spaniards wanted to create an overland supply route connecting their holdings in the Mexican state of Sonora with their newly established, struggling settlements in California. Adding impetus was the knowledge that the Russians were coming, the Russians were coming.

Say what? Yep, real Russians. Russian expeditions were moving down from positions in the far north and beginning to encroach on the Spanish outposts in California. There also was a land-grab threat from other European powers wanting to establish colonies.

Enter Juan Bautista de Anza, a Spanish captain and a son of a Basque (people from a region straddling the Spain-France border). Anza, who was born in 1736 in Sonora (then part of what was called New Spain), was in charge of the Royal Presidio (fort) of Tubac in southern Arizona. He was busy fighting Seris and Apaches along the Gila River when he received permission to establish the desired route. In January 1774 he made a trail-blazing trip with 21 soldiers, five mule packers, a couple of servants, an interpreter, and a carpenter (more or fewer people, depending on the account) to prove that the desired route was possible.

On October 23 of the next year, Anza, sans air conditioning but blessed by autumnal weather, set off again from Tubac on an arduous 1,200-mile trek. With him went 240 people including 155 women and children; 13 big tents; 165 pack mules; 340 horses; 302 beef cattle; six tons of flour, beans, sugar, and chocolate; clothing; blankets; munitions; and horseshoes. The first night out, a woman died while giving birth, but she was the only one to perish en route unless you count the cows that were destined to become steaks and roasts along the way. On a happier note, there were three births and three marriages.

After traveling along the Santa Cruz and Gila rivers to Yuma, fording the Colorado River, and passing through California, the caravan reached Monterey on March 10, 1776. On March 28, a small contingent headed by now-Lt. Col. Anza reached the site where the Golden Gate bridge is located and founded San Francisco, then a place with no parking meters and now a city of milk, honey, conventional and unconventional lifestyles, computer millionaires, computer bankrupts, and median home prices considerably higher than the combined life-time earnings of all members of the original founding band of touristas.

There is some argument among the experts about whether to call the path of the expedition a trail or a route. We will go with the word "route," relying on the advice of a Tucson polymath named G. Donald Kucera, a techno-wizard who also can whip up a mean plate of huevos rancheros in the middle of the desert. Kucera is one of the leaders of a group of people dedicated to recreating the original trail on the ground rather than only on paper.

"The most one can say is that there is no remaining trace of the actual trail, only a corridor, and that the trail is somewhere around here and within the corridor," Kucera observed.

Mexico won its independence from Spain in 1821 but, some 25 years later, got into a fight with the United States, a conflict called the Mexican-American War; the United States took possession of much of the route's territory. In later years, the route got heavy use from the gold-digging Forty-Niners and from minimum-wage immigrants. Today, the federally designated historic route is administered by the National Park Service with the help of two volunteer, nonprofit organizations, the Anza Trail Coalition of Arizona and the Amigos de Anza in California. According to Kucera, very little of the route is owned by the feds. It passes through private, governmental, and tribal lands and is largely unmarked.

Congress authorized the Anza route in 1990. It is one of 12 national historic trails in the United States. Actually, DeAnza's original journey started in Culia-can, Sinaloa, Mexico, and there are plans to include the 600 miles of the route in Mexico into the first ever international historic route.

Patrick Fischer

Walking in History's Steps

The National Park Service offers a helpful and well-done Anza trail map and guide and lists Arizona and California places to explore the trail on foot or on a horse. Notable on that and other lists:

Trail between Tumacacori National Historical Park and Tubac State Historical Park: A 4.5-mile trail that connects the two parks. The trail is on an approximate alignment with the historic route and follows the Santa Cruz River, crossing it three times. There are interpretive ramadas along the way as well as shade from cottonwood, willow, and ash trees. Easy walking but no ATVs or mountain bikes.

Trail north from the Tubac park to Tubac Golf Resort: A 1-mile trek ending near a snack bar, rest rooms, and golf course.

Trail in Rio Rico: Another 4-mile section of trail. Trailhead reached by taking Interstate 19's Exit 17, turning east, and following Rio Rico Drive across the Santa Cruz River bridge where you should look for trailhead signs and parking on the left.

Santa Cruz River Linear Park: A river park along the Santa Cruz River in Tucson that offers a trail within the historic corridor. Runs from Irvington Road north to Ajo Way and from Silverlake to Grant Road on the west side of the river.

If you need more information, contact the Anza Trail Coalition of Arizona at (520) 325-0909; or check this Internet site: www.nps.gov/juba/recommend.htm.

[Costumed actors wait to play their roles in Anza Days celebration. ▲]

■ ■ ■

So much for the route's history. Let's get to it, starting on the sleeve known as Interstate 10 leading from Phoenix to Tucson. The freeway travels through the rich plant life of the Sonoran ranging from low-lying creosote bush to gigantic saguaros and even a man-made lake and racetrack called the Firebird International Raceway at Milepost 162B. Then comes the Gila River that was followed part of the way by the Anza expedition. At Exit 175, about a quarter-mile off the freeway, is the Gila (Indian) Arts and Crafts Center offering (for free) a museum and (not for free) a nice gift shop, and a restaurant. On display in the museum is a wall memorializing the exploits of Ira Hayes, the member of the tribe who was one of six Marines who were famously photographed raising the American flag at Iwo Jima. A decade later, Hayes, who had trouble dealing with his postwar celebrity, died of exposure after wandering away from a party.

In the vicinity of Milepost 210, vast groves (900 or more acres) of pecan trees flourish. No surprise, really, when you understand that this desert is amazingly fertile and needs only water to produce spectacular and varied crops including the famed Pima cotton.

Following that is Picacho Peak State Park and a face-to-face encounter with the uniquely shaped, smallish peak called Picacho. The distinctive, 3,400-foot volcanic mountain-of-sorts can be seen and readily identified from miles away. It was near this peak in 1862 that the farthest-west Civil War conflict was fought, ending in the wounding of five soldiers, the deaths of three others, and the retreat of the Confederates.

At the crest of an overpass at Milepost 246, there is an excellent view on your left of the Santa Catalina Mountains. The range, which has provided Tucson residents with a cool respite from desert floor heat for decades, is on the northern border of Tucson. (The attractions of Tucson and its environs as well as the road up Mount Lemmon, known formally as the Sky Island Scenic Byway or the Catalina Highway, are discussed in the preceding chapter.)

Interstate 10, which runs east out of Tucson, interchanges with I-19, the freeway that leads to Nogales and to the start of the Anza route. There are many attractions along the way, but we will get to those on the way back from Nogales. Of course, you can stop at any of them either going to or away from Nogales.

■■■

There are two cities named Nogales, one in Mexico, the other just across the border in the United States. The cultural and economic divides become quickly obvious. One of the best ways to deal with the one south of the border is to get a motel room in Nogales, Arizona, visit the Pimeria Alta Historical Society Museum on Grand Avenue, and then drive to near the border, park in a lot, and walk across the line. No passport or visa is needed to visit Mexico within 12 miles of the border. The Nogales Chamber of Commerce (see listing in the Where to Go section) has excellent information and advice for travelers who plan to cross the border.

It is useful to take several things on the walk into and around Nogales, Sonora: Money (dollars are fine), knowledge of the conversion rate, a bottle of water, a willingness to courteously bargain, a friendly technique for saying no to street vendors, a shopping bag, an appetite, and, most importantly, the understanding that you are in a foreign country with lots of nice, helpful people but also lots of poverty and the associated, inevitable corruption that infects underpaid public servants. Veterans of travel into Mexican border towns know that the words "bribe" and "mordida" mean the same thing. Most of all, take a headful of common sense and an awareness of your surroundings.

There are shops and shops and shops, a few good restaurants, grocery stores and bakeries with fresh products, shoe stores, drugstores with more reasonable prices for prescription drugs, ditto liquor stores. Nightlife is vigorous and, on some streets, rather explicit. Prices are generally good, sometimes spectacularly so if you know your items and can bargain. You can find a dentist and a doctor. If your command of Spanish *no es muy bueno*, fear not. English is commonplace, and virtually all of the shopkeepers and waiters are bilingual.

And yes, the beer is cold and good, the margaritas delicious, the chips and salsa fresh, and probably, also, the walnuts because "Nogales" means "walnuts" in Spanish, and they are grown in the area.

■■■

[Mission San Jose de Tumacacori stands framed by a mesquite tree in morning light.]

Randy Prentice

Pat Gorraiz

Sears Point

This petroglyph site offers a hardy little adventure for those who are in search of infrequently seen petroglyphs and who have a reliable four-wheel-drive vehicle, a pair of hiking boots, plenty of water, a daypack, and a cellular telephone. To try it otherwise in summer or after a heavy rain suggests someone who is brain-dead. Immediately after leaving Interstate 8 at Exit 78 (Spot Road), take a wide U-turn to the right onto the frontage road paralleling the freeway. There are no signs to Sears Point, and the concrete ends soon, replaced by gravel and loose sand. Two miles down this purported road is a dead end and, incongruously, a street sign designating Avenue 76E (no kidding). Take it left and head north into the largely untracked desert, past an understandably abandoned ranch and, eventually, if you don't get sidetracked onto other, small sand roads snaking about, you'll reach a ridge. Park and climb a faint trail on the east (your right as you face the ridge) side. It's 10 miles in, 10 miles out. www.blm.gov/az/trails/de_anza/sears_prehist.htm

[Petroglyphs are the main attraction at Sears Point. ▲]

Back on I-19 and returning to Tucson along the Anza route. At Exit 12 is a turnoff on State Route 289 that provides a beautiful and topographically exciting 11-mile side trip westward through rolling hills and mountains and canyons to the Pena Blanca Lake Recreational Area and shady campgrounds. The 52-acre lake, unhappily, is polluted by mercury from old mining operations, but it can be happily boated (if you bring a boat) and fished as long as no one eats the fish. Anza, by the way, never saw it, pristine or polluted. A dam created Pena Blanca in 1957.

Returning to the interstate, Exit 29 leads quickly into Tumacacori and the Tumacacori National Historical Park, administered, and splendidly so, by the National Park Service. It is a must stop for several reasons: An up-close-and-personal examination of the unrestored, colorful, cool, thick-walled, adobe church; a hike along the Santa Cruz River that is assumed to retrace Anza's steps; an informative 14-minute history video; some magnificent dioramas in a small but impressive museum; and, most of all, an overwhelming sense that you are walking through history. The river flows all year, partly courtesy of the Nogales sewage treatment plant effluent.

The pronunciation of this Indian word, incidentally, is "too muh KAH koh ree" and probably translates as "rocky, flat place." The Spanish built the church in stages, beginning in 1700 and completing it in 1797.

Across the street and nearby is the Santa Cruz Chili & Spice Co., a combined

Western museum and store selling packages of "chili and spice and everything nice." It was founded in 1943 and remains a popular, family-owned business that can be contacted at (520) 398-2591.

Three miles farther along are Tubac and the Tubac Presidio State Historic Park. The old presidio has a history that parallels Tumacacori's but, unlike Tumacacori, is now predominantly a shop-till-you-drop heaven for tourists engorged with history but in deep need of unloading disposable income at art galleries, craft shops, B and B's, and restaurants on items such as antiques, pots, clothing, jewelry, tiles, strings of chilies, cookbooks, etc., etc., etc. The Tubac Chamber of Commerce refers to it as a place "where art and history meet." If there were any combat during that meeting, history would lose. In short, it is now a shopping oasis in the desert and artists' colony, a mini version of Sedona.

But it is more than that. As surely as Sedona was born of beauty, Tubac and Tumacacori were built on faith. The famed Jesuit explorer Eusebio Francisco Kino began establishing missions in the area in the late 1600s and early 1700s as the keystone of Spain's effort to Christianize and control Indians in the area. He established Tumacacori in 1691 and Tubac, then a small Tohono O'odham Indian village, became a nearby mission. Anza was here and so were the Apaches, who considered the residents to be a natural resource ripe for raiding. The Tubac Presidio State Historic Park has a plentiful supply of informational pamphlets, a good museum, and an excellent video detailing the history of the presidio. The actual fort was established after a Tohono O'odham revolt in 1751, but nothing of the original structure exists above ground.

Through decades of different ownership and many battles, mostly with Apaches, Tubac rose and fell several more times over the years and eventually was deserted when the American Civil War resulted in the removal of all protective troops, subjecting the community to the resumption of Indian raids. It was resettled after the war, but it never recovered the dominance it enjoyed in 1860, when it was the largest town in what is now Arizona.

From Tubac the interstate leads to another historic site, this one also a paradoxical combination of the modern (sort of) with the ancient (sort of): an abandoned Titan missile silo. Its lifespan was short—about 20 years during the Cold War—and it is survived now by the Titan Missile Museum. For a fee, the traveler can watch yet another video, listen to a couple of lectures (one by a retired missileman who hangs onto his military crew cut but lost his personal battle of the bulge some years ago), climb down into the control room, and stare into the literal and figurative abyss of the silo that was home to 9.5 megatons carried in the nose of the 103-foot Titan II intercontinental ballistic missile that still stands there. Admission prices include the opportunity to wear a hard hat, a delightful fashion item, especially in 110 degrees. In 1982 this site, dating from 1963 when it was one of 18 in the area, was deactivated.

Between the missile site and Tucson is Exit 80 (Pima Mine Road) and the ASARCO Mineral Discovery Center, which is a fancy name for a visitors center and a one-hour bus tour of an adjoining, huge hole in the ground, about 2 by 2.5 miles across and 1,200 feet deep.

What is it? A hint: 60 to 75 percent of American copper (the estimate varies) comes from Arizona mines.

This one is a modern, still-operating, open-pit copper mine, and the tour guides offer encyclopedic knowledge about how to get a copper bracelet out of a pile of rock. Don't miss the giant trucks (bigger than some homes) and tires on display in the area around the center. The smell of pine oil during part of the tour comes from just that—pine oil used in a flotation process that separates copper from gunk. Be sure to ask the tour guide about the use of cattle—nicknamed ASARCOWS—to assist in restoration of the land.

Next up the line and just before Tucson is another famed mission established by Father Kino, San Xavier del Bac, also know as the "White Dove of the Desert." In addition to its stark color (white stucco over brick) and its Spanish colonial and Moorish architecture, the mission offers daily Masses and a variety of tourist facilities, including a museum. The first two churches at the mission are gone. The current one was built by Franciscans in the 1780s and 1790s. One of its twin steeples is unfinished, but there is disagreement about why that is so.

In Tucson just down the road, those determined to walk the walk of Anza and his band can leave the interstate at Irvington Road and head west across the Santa Cruz River. Immediately after you cross the bridge is a parking lot on the left (south) side. Park there, walk down to a riverside pathway. Head left on the pathway and you will find a sign indicating that you are on the Anza route. There are many other such spots in the Tucson area, but this one is the quickest to reach from the freeway. This segment of the trail, also known as Los Paseo de los Arboles, is planted with donated native trees and has been certified by the National Park Service and marked with the trail logo.

Interstate 19 links to Interstate 10 in Tucson, and the latter leads to the next major site, this one near Casa Grande and Coolidge, about 70 miles northwest of Tucson but well before Phoenix. At the interchange of I-10 and I-8, continue on 10 (I-8 leads to Yuma, but we will backtrack to this interchange for that leg) and aim for Coolidge. The Casa Grande Ruins National Monument can be reached by taking the exit for State Route 87 (about Milepost 211) and going north through Coolidge. If you're traveling on 10 from Phoenix, take Exit 185 and go east on State Route 387 for about 6 miles to State 287 and follow the signs to the monument entrance.

Casa Grande Ruins National Monument consists of the preserved remains of an ancient Hohokam farming community, including the magnificent, mysterious Casa Grande Ruins, or "Great House." The ruins are a tad out of the way for those bent on reaching Yuma, but for connoisseurs of prehistory, the site should not be bypassed.

■■■

Back to I-10, then to I-8 heading toward Gila Bend and Yuma. A lot of flat, hot desert driving leads you to Gila Bend, named for a bend in the Gila River and home to the Space Age Outer Limits Restaurant and Best Western Space Age Lodge, a 1960s landmark motel and restaurant inspired by Sputnik. About 14 miles west of Gila Bend, at Milepost 102, the exit takes you to a road for a 15-mile drive to the Painted Rock Petroglyph Site, one of those aforementioned aboriginal art galleries: ancient Hohokam petroglyphs depicting animals and humans and other phenomena carved and scratched into a small hill of rocks and interspersed with still more names and initials of still more 20th- and 21st- century bottom feeders.

[Mission San Xavier del Bac still opens its doors for Sunday church services.   ]

Laurence Parent

Petroglyphs were pecked into hard stone using other, sharp stones as chisels and heavier stones as hammers or, if the stone canvas was soft, they could be scratched in. Pictographs, on the other hand, were painted on the stone.

This little outcrop of rock slabs and boulders, one of 5,000 such rock art sites in Arizona, is circled by a short path and is elaborately engraved, mostly on the west side, with spirals (possibly a symbol of the emergence of life), anthropomorphs (humanlike figures), and simple and outlined crosses (possibly denoting the planet Venus). The park, if it can be called that, also has chemical toilets, ramadas, and campsites but no running water and only enough tree shade to shield the area's rattlesnakes from the sun. The Mormon Battalion, a volunteer U.S. Army unit made up of, duh, Mormons, passed this way in 1846 during its quest to establish a wagon route to the Pacific Ocean. Their idea was to demonstrate their patriotism and to establish a quid pro quo of military service in return for freedom from persecution. Didn't work.

On I-8 again, the Yuma County line is about 22 miles west, and a mile past that is Exit 78, the start of a side trip to Sears Point, an obscure, low-lying pair of volcanic rock piles decorated with still more petroglyphs. The Bureau of Land Management, which oversees the area, calls it "a very special area that lies at a crossroad of historical events and cultures."

After continuing west on I-8 for 11 more miles, take the Dateland Exit, stop at a restaurant on your left, and order a date or a prickly pear cactus milkshake. Or a piece of date cream pie. The treats are far more nourishing but less slimming than a hike across blistering volcanic rock to look at ancient art. And yes, near the restaurant is a 9-acre date grove; and yes, those are date palms you see; and yes, dates are sticky even when they are on the tree (or so the waitperson says).

Yuma and its gateway through a dramatic mountain pass is now 65 or so miles away, but before that is Milepost 63, the first angle for spotting the "sleeping giant." Take a look at a small mountain range ahead of you and on the right and look for the head of the reclining giant. A tip for those lacking imagination: His nose is the highest point and his open mouth is to the left, but the "mouth" will close the nearer you get.

■■■

Yuma and the Colorado River signal the end of the Anza route in Arizona. What did not await Anza and his gaggle of silly gooses who wanted to live on a California fault line was the now-current abundance of air-conditioned hotels, restaurants, and tourist draws highlighted by the un-air-conditioned Yuma Territorial Prison, one of Arizona's top attractions but one of its least attractive.

From Yuma, Anza went on to found San Francisco in 1776 and eventually was named by the King of Spain to be the governor of New Mexico. We're going to travel upriver, by road. ⬛

Casa Grande Ruins

T he Hohokam civilization of hunters and gatherers in the area traces back to around 79 A.D., a time when Vesuvius was blowing its top and burying Pompeii. About the time Mohammad, the founder of Islam, was born in 570, the Hohokam were at work improving an irrigation system of canals. By the time Columbus was born in 1451, the Hohokam culture had inexplicably disappeared. Why? Some say floods, some say disease, some say cultural breakdown, some just throw up their hands.

[A prehistoric gallery beckons at Painted Rocks Petroglyph Site.]

Tony Marinella

The Bridge and the Chariot, Lake Havasu City

Somewhere low on an imaginary scale of 1 to 10 measuring the agonies of travelers (No. 10 being something like reading a 12,000-word New Yorker essay about a birch bark canoe builder while trying to fall asleep on an unfamiliar and unforgiving mattress and No.1 being forgetting to retrieve your 98-cent flip flops from the motel room fridge) is the dilemma of what to do with yourself if you are alone, bored, and in a restaurant waiting endless minutes for your meal.

In that pathetic condition, the choice often is to stare off in the distance in search of great thoughts or fake interest in reading the contents label on the ketchup bottle at your table ("Wow, it has distilled vinegar and high fructose corn syrup. Who would have thought?")

In the exceedingly planned community of Lake Havasu City, along the Colorado River sort of midway between Yuma on the south and Hoover Dam on the north, the menu at a café in the London Bridge Resort has the answer. As you sit there staring through palm trees at the water below and the mountain range beyond, you can read a leaflet on the menu detailing the facts of the next-door structure that has made this Arizona city semi-famous: the legendary London Bridge that spans a channel off the river. It will tell you that:

The bridge, the world's largest antique, according to Guinness, was bought from the City of London for $2,460,000 in 1968 by Lake Havasu City's founder, the late Robert P. McCulloch, Sr. Its 22 million pounds of granite were shipped in 10,276 pieces and reconstructed over the next three years in Lake Havasu City. In London, it was 1,005 feet long, but in Lake Havasu it is 952 feet. The bridge lights were constructed from Napoleon's cannons.

There's more about the bridge, but we need to leave you something to read.

And that's not all. Whatever its other successes or failures, the resort, a massive complex of ersatz Englandiana, also offers a lobby that features

[Old London Bridge's granite blocks now span Lake Havasu. ▲   ]

a big pit containing "the world's only replica" of the ornate, carved, and gilded, 24-foot-long, eight-horse gold coach created in 1762 during the reign of King George III and used in subsequent coronations and to transport the sovereign to the opening of a new session of Parliament.

Oh, come on, now. It beats ketchup labels. And you can drive across the bridge.

The building at Casa Grande Ruins probably was constructed in the 1300s and was occupied for perhaps 50 to 75 years before it was abandoned. The ubiquitous Kino, relying on Pima Indian guides, was the first European to note the existence of the great house, in 1694. He went inside the walls and did what any good priest would do—said Mass.

The 11-room structure, now shielded from the elements by a modern, protective canopy, is four stories high and 60 feet long. It may have functioned in several capacities, including that of an astronomical observatory along the lines of England's Stonehenge; some scientists reason this to be so because its walls face the four cardinal points on the compass and various openings align with the sun and the moon at quite specific times. It is built of caliche mud, mostly clay and sand that solidifies into a concrete-like substance. The mud was put down in two-foot courses without support forms to hold it in place while it dried. The structure's wood beams came from as far as 50 or 60 miles away, presumably carted to the site on the backs of the workers. Maddeningly, some of the ancient walls that have withstood centuries of weather are scarred with the scratched-in names and initials of 20th- and 21st-century primitives who felt it appropriate to share their identities with the future and with us. Thanks so much.

Among other wonders also found at the site is what has been called, arguably, a ball court, a depression with mounded sides in which the Hohokam might have played some sort of game similar to those of the Maya. Other theories are that it was a partially filled well, a reservoir, a ceremonial chamber, or a dance platform. In the middle of one such pit, a polished green stone was found, possibly providing evidence to support the ballpark notion. There is no evidence, credible or otherwise, that the Hohokams had a sense of humor and stuck a green stone in the middle of an earthen cavity just because they knew that several centuries later it would cause arguing archaeologists to attack each other's intellectual viscera with sharp tongues and witty word processors.

The grounds of the ruins contain picnic tables, delightful shade ramadas, irrigated shade trees, and an abundance of pocket gophers, tiny rodents better known to the more dignified as ground squirrels. Exhibits in the visitors center explain the Hohokam culture and the ruins' history in plain language. ᛘ

Joshua Forest Scenic Parkway

Route	U.S. 93 between Wikieup and Wickenburg.
Mileage	128 miles from Kingman to Wickenburg, but the start of the official scenic road in Wikieup is only 54 miles to its end near Wickenburg.
Time to Allow	A half-day.
Elevation	3,300 feet at Kingman, about 2,000 at Wikieup and Wickenburg.
Overview	A startling landscape of giant Joshua trees, a magnificent gorge ignominiously called Burro Creek, and the handful of buildings that comprise Nothing, Arizona. Something about Nothing in a moment.

Joshua trees. This trip offers a look at dozens, nay, hundreds, of these huge, mean-looking, unlikely members of the lily family as you head south on U.S. Route 93 off of eastbound Interstate 40 out of Kingman. U.S. 93, reached by turning off on Exit 71, becomes the Joshua Forest Scenic Parkway and runs from its intersection with the interstate to Wikieup. At Wikieup it acquires the official designation of "scenic." The official scenic route lasts for 54 miles or until Wickenburg. And Wickenburg is 128 miles from Kingman. And one plus one equals ... oh, never mind.

There's a lot of pretty land to look at on both sides of the road on the way to the Joshuas' world. What's a lot? Example: A real estate sign offers your basic neighborhood lot (for this area, anyway). "For sale, 7,000 acres," it says.

It's a fascinating journey that follows the 1850 tracks of Lt. Amiel Whipple, who was surveying for a possible railroad route to the West Coast.

Along the way is a magnificent, deep gorge deceptively called Burro Creek and a less-than-magnificent two-building community where you can get gas, a tire, and, perhaps most importantly, a bathroom decorated with ribald graffiti.

Whatever its other attractions, the one reason to drive this route is to see the Joshua trees, so a word or two, or a thousand, about those plants seems appropriate here.

The Joshua tree, symbol of the Mojave Desert but also found in the Sonoran Desert, looks like the kind of tree that Dr. Seuss could have created for *Horton Hears A Who*. In fact, the Joshua tree is a giant yucca and belongs to the lily family. It can grow to between 30 and 50 feet high with a single trunk but many forks. The forks become branches ending in stiff, sharp-pointed clusters of long leaves.

English-themed shops line the shore at Lake Havasu City.

It got its name from Mormon pioneers who apparently linked its branches to the raised-in-prayer arms of Joshua of biblical fame. Its proper name is *Yucca brevifolia* and is one member of a genus of distinctive plants that provided Indians in the Southwest with soap, basket fibers, ropes, and even food. The yucca depends for cross-pollination on the small yucca moth. The small, white female moth visits the yucca's flowers by night in springtime, and when she is followed by many other yucca moths doing the same thing, the survival of the yucca line is guaranteed. Sort of moth-to-moth resuscitation.

At about Milepost 118 on U.S. 93, south of the interstate but before Wikieup and the start of the official scenic drive on Joshua Forest Scenic Parkway, a saguaro appears, a sure sign of dropping elevation. Just beyond is Luchia's restaurant, a clean and attractive store offering Indian jewelry, Mexican and American food, pies, pottery, old pawn, gifts, rugs, crystals and rocks, desert honey, and the fattest saguaro in the world, evidence that it does what saguaros do when watered: They suck it up.

Just outside of Wikieup is a roadside tablet announcing the presence of Big Sandy Valley, first explored in 1582 by Spanish traveler Antonio de Espejo and later by Lt. Whipple. Next up is Wikieup, with a trading post, bar, Subway franchise, and the start of the parkway. Wikieup is said to refer to the brush shelters or mat-covered homes of certain Indian tribes in Arizona and other states. At this point, saguaros and Joshua trees begin cropping up in abundance, interspersed with the occasional ocotillos. Just down the parkway are eye-popping Burro Creek Canyon and a nearby campground and pullout for a scenic view. At Mileposts 147 and 146, dramatic rock outcroppings and fields of boulder piles crop up.

Just past Milepost 148, appears Nothing, Arizona, an extremely unincorporated hamlet claiming a population of 4 and consisting of a little repair garage, a tiny store, two gas pumps, and a bathroom. A sign reports the town was founded in 1977 and is populated by a miniscule band of citizens who are "full of hope, faith, and believe in the work ethic. Through the years these dedicated people

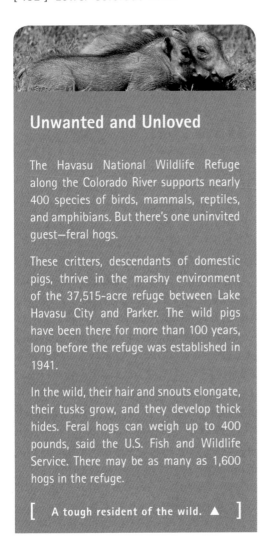

Unwanted and Unloved

The Havasu National Wildlife Refuge along the Colorado River supports nearly 400 species of birds, mammals, reptiles, and amphibians. But there's one uninvited guest—feral hogs.

These critters, descendants of domestic pigs, thrive in the marshy environment of the 37,515-acre refuge between Lake Havasu City and Parker. The wild pigs have been there for more than 100 years, long before the refuge was established in 1941.

In the wild, their hair and snouts elongate, their tusks grow, and they develop thick hides. Feral hogs can weigh up to 400 pounds, said the U.S. Fish and Wildlife Service. There may be as many as 1,600 hogs in the refuge.

[A tough resident of the wild. ▲]

have taken nothing, hoped for nothing, worked at nothing, for nothing."

Beyond Nothing is something: Milepost 163 and a major forest of Joshuas. The heavy stand of Joshuas in this area is one of three in the state, and an extensive forest of them also grows in southeastern California's Joshua Tree National Monument.

By Milepost 179, the Joshua population is thinning out, and at Milepost 192, headlights, which are to remain on in daylight to make cars more visible along the parkway, can be turned off. Wickenburg is just 7 miles ahead.

Wickenburg nestles in the Hassayampa River Valley, and your first stop should be the Chamber of Commerce, housed in a restored railroad station on Frontier Street, where an abundance of literature about the area can be found, some for free, some not. Also abundant are a lot of buildings dating to the early 1900s.

If there's a hurry to get on to Phoenix about 50 miles away, there is, nevertheless, one obligatory stop in Wickenburg: The Jail Tree, a large mesquite tucked incongruously behind a Circle K and sporting a sign that says, "The Jail Tree. From 1863 to 1890, outlaws were chained to the tree for lack of a hoosegow. Escapes were unknown."

Wickenburg, with a population heading well beyond 6,000, is on the northern edge of the Sonoran Desert and was founded in 1863 by an adventurer named Henry Wickenburg, a Prussian who came there looking for gold.

One story has it that Wickenburg bent down to pick up a vulture he had shot when he spotted gold in some rocks. That led to 80 mines including the founding father's Vulture Mine, source of more than $30 million in gold.

That doubtless made old Henry happy, but what he thought about Joshua trees is not recorded. You'll love 'em. ᴬᴴ

Where To Go
What To See
What To Do

Besides Yuma, these listings include attractions, annual events, and sources of touring information for communities and sites associated with the Juan Bautista de Anza Historic Trail, the strip North Along the River, the Lake Mead National Recreation Area, Other Western Arizona Communities, and the Joshua Forest Scenic Road.

Yuma

Information: The Yuma Convention & Visitors Bureau (800) 293-0071; www.visityuma.com) and the Yuma County Chamber of Commerce (928) 782-2567; www.yumachamber.org) each provides information for travelers, including lodging, dining, shopping, and traveling to one of the Mexican towns near Yuma. Visitors information center, 377 S. Main St.

Yuma Crossing State Historical Park: Site of the Yuma Quartermaster Depot used by the Army to store and distribute supplies for military posts in the Southwest in the 1860s. $. 201 N. Fourth Avenue. (928) 329-0471. www.pr.state.az.us/Parks/parkhtml/yumacross.html

Colorado King I Sternwheeler: Enjoy a narrated tour or dinner cruise along the lower Colorado River aboard a 57-foot-long sternwheeler. Kayak, canoe, and jet boat tours also available. $. Yuma River Tours, 1920 Arizona Ave. (928) 783-4400. www.coloradoking.com

The Peanut Patch: Offers behind-the-scenes look at peanut production. Also produces candy and sugar-free goodies available in the retail gift shop. Tour is free. 4322 E. County 13th St. Take Avenue 3E to East County 13th Street, turn east, and follow signs. Open Oct.-April; closed Sunday. Wheelchair accessible. (928) 726-6292.

Sanguinetti House Museum: Once the home of a pioneer merchant, it is now a regional museum in one of the city's oldest buildings. Exhibits tell the history of the lower Colorado River region from the 1540s to now. $. 240 S. Madison Ave. (928) 782-1841. www.yumalibrary.org/ahs

Yuma Birding and Nature Festival: Guided tours, field trips, and workshops highlight this annual celebration of the lower Colorado River area with its 380 species of birds and other wildlife. April. $. Various locations. (800) 293-0071; (928) 783-3061. www.yumabirding.org

[Picacho Peak's hillside blooms with brittlebush. ▲   ]

Yuma Valley Railway: Two-hour tour takes passengers along the lower Colorado River for a 22-mile round-trip. Run by volunteers. The train will be on the right. Rest rooms available on board. Open October-May, weekends only. $. From Fourth Avenue in Yuma, take Eighth Street west for about 10 miles (road becomes unpaved). (928) 783-3456. www.visityuma.com/attraction.htm

Yuma Art Center: Performing and visual arts center contains the historic Yuma Theatre built in 1912 and restored to the 1936 Art Deco style. Also contains a museum with four galleries and a gift shop. $. 254 S. Main in downtown Yuma. (928) 329-6607. www.yumafinearts.com

Quechan Tribal Museum at Fort Yuma: Discover Quechan Indian heritage and experience the site from where the U.S. Army protected the east-west trade routes in the 1800s. The tribe also operates a casino and RV parks. $. 350 Picacho Road. (760) 572-0661. www.cba.nau.edu/caied/TribePages/Quechan.asp

St. Thomas Mission: Founded in 1780 by Father Francisco Garces, this Catholic church was destroyed in 1855, then rebuilt in 1922. Located on the Fort Yuma Indian Reservation across the Colorado River from Yuma Crossing State Historical Park. Open during services, Sat. 4:30 p.m. and Sun. 10:30 a.m. Donation. (760) 572-0283.

Blythe Intaglios: Giant primitive earth figures scratched into the soil more than 2,000 years ago. One is a human figure 171 feet long. Free. Located in California, 15 miles north of Blythe just off U.S. Route 95. BLM Yuma Field Office, 2555 E. Gila Ridge Road. (928) 317-3200. www.recreation.gov/detail.cfm?ID=2050

Algodones Dunes: These rolling hills of sand are one of the largest dune systems in North America. Popular for hunting, hiking, and scenic views and off-road vehicle enthusiasts. Free. Located west of Yuma along Interstate 8, primarily north of the interstate. (760) 337-4432. www.blm.gov/ca/elcentro/ImperialSandDunes/index.html

Mohawk Dunes: Less desolate than the Algodones dune system in California, this desert landscape is filled with scrubby vegetation. Home to the endangered Sonoran pronghorn, the dunes stretch for 20 miles. Much of the dune system is located within the Barry M. Goldwater Air Force Range, a military testing area. Free, but permit required. Take Interstate 8 east from Yuma for about 42 miles to the Tacna exit; drive south to a dirt road that heads east for about 15 miles to the northern edge of the dunes. Information: Marine Corps Air Station Yuma, (928) 341-402l; Bureau of Land Management Yuma Field Office, (928) 317-3200.

Saihati Camel Farm: Tours of the breeding farm allow visitors to see a wide variety of animals but the farm specializes in camels. Open Nov. 1– May 31. $. 15672 S. Ave. 1E., Yuma. (928) 627-2553 .

Cocopah Indian Reservation: Located about 13 miles south of Yuma. Tribal enterprises include a casino, an RV park, and a golf course, Cocopah Museum and Culture Center, and Heritage Park. Museum exhibits explain family structures and traditional home life and include clothing, musical instruments, warrior displays, beadwork, and tattoo art. The Heritage Park features plants and trees that the Cocopah people use for ceremonies and daily subsistence. Donations. Gift shop sells beadwork, arts and crafts, tribal dolls, and Native American music on tapes and CDs. From Yuma, take the 16th Street Exit (U.S. 95), go south and follow the signs for San Luis, Mexico. About a mile past Somerton turn right (north) on Avenue G and follow the signs. (928) 627-2102. www.cocopah.com www.cba.nau.edu/caied/TribePages/Cocopah.asp www.itcaonline.com/tribes_cocopah.html

Tillamook Air Tours: Travel across the desert, date gardens, and an intaglio in a vintage 1928 biplane or a 1948 Stinson Reliant. Both are restored aircraft. Call for reservations. $. Located at the Somerton Airport on U.S. 95. (503) 842-1942. http://tillamookairtours.com

ANZA NATIONAL HISTORIC TRAIL

Phoenix to Nogales
Gila River Indian Community: See listings on Page 80.

Picacho Peak State Park: Five trails with varying degrees of difficulty, camping, picnic areas, ramadas, grills, restrooms, showers, electric hookups, RV accommodations, historical markers, and a playground. $. The park is located off Interstate 10 at Exit 219. (520) 466-3183. www.pr.state.az.us/Parks/parkhtml/picacho.html

Civil War Re-enactment: On April 15, 1862, the most significant Civil War battle in Arizona Territory broke out near Picacho Peak. Each March, more than 200 Civil War enactors play it out. $. Picacho Peak State Park.

Rooster Cogburn Ostrich Ranch: Visitors can mingle with and feed deer and ostrich at what's billed as the largest ostrich ranch in the United States. The gift shop sells ostrich products. $. Take Exit 219 from Interstate 10, then follow sign and take frontage road east 1 mile. (520) 466-3658. www.roostercogburn.com.

Tucson: See Page 130 for Tucson area listings.

Nogales-Santa Cruz Chamber of Commerce: A central source of information about attractions in Santa Cruz County and Ambos Nogales, the name that applies to the cities of Nogales in Arizona and Sonora, Mexico. Especially helpful to bird-watchers and travelers to Mexico. Online maps. (520) 287-3685. www.nogaleschamber.com

Pimeria Alta Historical Society Museum: Just one block from the international border, the museum focuses on the history of southern Arizona and northern Sonora, Mexico. Library, archives, photo collection, self-guided tours, gift shop. Closed Sunday. Free. From last exit on I-19 turn east on Crawford. Museum is in old Nogales City Hall. (520) 287-5402. www.nogalesmainstreet.com/blue.html

Nogales to Yuma

Anza Trail Information: www.nps.gov/juba www.nps.gov/tuma/Anzatrail.htm

Tumacacori National Historical Park: Showcases two of the oldest Spanish colonial missions in Arizona, San Jose de Tumacacori and Los Santos Angeles de Guevavi missions, both established in 1691. Also includes the San Cayetano de Calabazas mission established in 1756. Bookstore, museum, and visitors center; self-guided and ranger-led tours; birding. On weekends, usually September-June, demonstrators show visitors skills such as making tortillas, baskets, pottery, and paper flowers. $. During Anza Days (see Tubac listing below) in October, visitors with reservations can attend (without charge) a historic High Mass or Misa Mayor similar to those celebrated in the 17th and 18th centuries at the mission. Participants are required to dress in Spanish or Native American attire. Located off Exit 29 of I-19. (520) 398-2341. www.nps.gov/tuma

La Fiesta de Tumacacori: A traditional mariachi procession, a blacksmithing exhibit, piñatas, regional ethnic food, and live entertainment are features of this two-day event. December. Free. Tumacacori National Historical Park, 1891 E. Frontage Road. (520) 398-2341. www.nps.gov/tuma/special_events.htm

Tubac-Santa Cruz Visitors Center: Take Exit 34 from Interstate 19. The center is at 4 Plaza Road, Suite E. (520) 398-0007. www.toursantacruz.com

Tubac Presidio State Historic Park: Founded in June 1752 after the Pima Indians surrendered to the Spaniards. Listed on the National Register of Historic Places, the park has an underground archaeology display, museum, picnic area. $. (520) 398-2252. www.pr.state.az.us/Parks/parkhtml/tubac.html

Anza Days Cultural Celebration: Commemorates the 1775 Anza expedition that left from Tubac and founded San Francisco, Calif. Events include arts and crafts, entertainment, and re-enactments. October. $. Tubac Presidio State Historic Park, (520) 398-2704.

Tubac Center of the Arts: Over 3,500 square feet of exhibit space; includes a members' gallery, performance stage, art library, and gallery shop. Closed June-August. Located at 9 Plaza Road. (520) 398-2371. www.tubacarts.org

Tubac Historical Society Library: More than 3,000 volumes dedicated to Arizona and the Southwest. Closed May-Sept. Donations. 5 Placita de Anza. (520) 398-2020.

Old Presidio Traders: A family-owned shop selling works made by Zuni, Navajo, Hopi, Santa Domingo, Pueblo, Apache, and Tohono O'odham artists. 27 Tubac Road. (520) 398-9333; (866) 773-7434. www.oldpresidiotraders.com/index.html

Tubac Festival of Arts: This annual street festival showcases the work of hundreds of artists. February. Free. Downtown Tubac. (520) 398-2704.

Titan Missile Museum: Only museum in the world that has a Titan II missile from the Cold War era still in its silo. One-hour tour descends several flights of stairs, passes through a massive bomb-blast door in the belly of the silo, and ends at the launch command center. Visitors center, gift shop. $. Take Exit 69 from I-19, turn west on Duval Mine Road and follow the signs. (520) 625-7736. www.pimaair.org

Eloy: Eloy can be reached from Interstate 10 by taking Exit 211, which serves State Route 87. The Eloy Chamber of Commerce maintains Internet links to area attractions. (520) 466-3411. www.eloychamber.com. A National Park Service Internet site has online maps of the area including Eloy, Coolidge, and Casa Grande: www.nps.gov/cagr/pphtml/maps.html

Skydive Arizona: Billed as the "world's largest skydiving resort." RV hook-ups, bunk houses, camping, a sky dive school. 4900 N. Taylor Road, Eloy. (520) 466-3753. www.skydiveaz.com

Coolidge: From Interstate 10, Coolidge can be reached from Exit 210 and going north past Eloy or from Exit 185 and going east on State Route 387 to State 87. The Coolidge Chamber of Commerce lists the Casa Grande Ruins, beautiful sunsets, and cotton when it boasts of Coolidge. A section of its Internet site features the Gila River Indian Community. (520) 723-3009. www.coolidgeaz.org

Casa Grande Ruins National Monument: One of the largest prehistoric structures in North America, it was built by the Hohokam ("those who are gone"). The Hohokam were descendants of Archaic peoples who roamed the southwestern deserts beginning in about 5500 B.C. $. From Interstate 10, take Exit 211 and go north on State 87 or take Exit 185 north of the city of Casa Grande and go east on State 387 and follow the signs to the park entrance. (520) 723-3172. www.nps.gov/cagr

Coolidge Historical Museum: Located in the town's original jail building. Sunday, 1 p.m.-5 p.m., or by appointment. Donations. 161 W. Harding Ave. (520) 723-7186.

Golden Era Toy and Auto Museum: Your inner child can run wild here. Antique toys, Lionel trains, model planes, plus antique and classic cars. Open weekends Jan.-May. $. 297 W. Central Ave., Coolidge. (520) 723-5044; (480) 948-9570.

Blackwater Trading Post and Museum: Shop for Indian jewelry and crafts and view Hohokam and other Southwestern Indian artifacts that are on display. Donations. Located west of Casa Grande Ruins on the north side of State 87. (520) 723-5516.

Arizona Skydive Coolidge: Professional instruction, group jumps, bunk houses, and camping. Coolidge Municipal Airport. (888) 741-5867. www.arizonaskydiving.com

Greater Casa Grande Chamber of Commerce: Distributes visitors information on attractions, events, lodging, shopping and other travel topics. 575 N. Marshall St. Casa Grande. (800) 916-1515; (520) 836-2125. www.casagrandechamber.org

Casa Grande Valley Historical Society and Museum: The museum grounds have the Rebecca Dallis Schoolhouse, Heritage Hall (a historic stone church), and 3,000 artifacts to explore. Open mid-Sept.-mid-May. $. 110 W. Florence Blvd. (520) 836-2223. www.cgvhs.org

Casa Grande Art Museum: Housed in the historic Kratzka House, it features sculpture, water-color, multi-media, and Western art by local, regional, and national artists. Open Sept.-May, Wed., Sat. and Sun., 1 p.m.-4 p.m. Free. 319 W. 3rd St. (520) 836-3377.

Gila Bend Information: The Anza route continues west on Interstate 8 from its interchange with Interstate 10 at the city of Casa Grande. A sharp bend in the nearby Gila River prompted the town's name. (928) 683-2255. www.gilabendaz.org

Gatlin Archeological Park and Gila Bend Museum: Indian artifacts, a re-created stage stop and telegraph office, and large collection of Tohono

O'odham baskets. The museum sits within the confines of the 30-acre Gatlin Archeological Park, a Hohokam settlement near the Gila River. Botanical garden, and tourist information center on site. Donations. 644 W. Pima St. (928) 683-2255. www.gilabendaz.org.

Desert Sweet Shrimp Farm: Yes, they really are growing (and selling) shrimp out in the middle of the desert. Farm tours are available by appointment. Desert Shrimp Festival celebrates the end of the shrimp harvest season in October or November. Located off Old U.S. Route 80 north of Gila Bend. (623) 393-0136. www.desertsweetshrimp.com

Painted Rocks Petroglyph Site: You're on your own to view hundreds of ancient rock etchings and inscriptions left by passersby over the years. Facilities include tables, barbeque grills, steel fire rings, and a vault toilet for picnicking and primitive camping. No potable water. Campground host on site October-April. $. From Exit 102 on Interstate 8 approximately 12.5 miles west of Gila Bend, take Painted Rock Dam Road north for 10.7 miles to unpaved Rocky Point Road; turn left (west) and go 0.6 mile. Bureau of Land Management Phoenix Field office, (623) 580-5500. www.blm.gov/az/pfo/paint.htm

Dateland Palms Village Date Gardens: A gift shop sells varieties of medjool dates that are grown in the Dateland gardens. The Dateland Palms restaurant serves up date shakes as well as a variety of other date goodies. RV Park, pet kennels, and gas station. On Interstate 8 at Milepost 67. (928) 454-2772. www.dateland.com

NORTH, ALONG THE RIVER

Yuma to Lake Mead

Mittry Lake Wildlife Area: Fishing, wildlife-watching, hiking, boating, hunting and primitive camping. The area includes about 600 acres of water surface and 2,400 acres of marsh or upland terrain. Free. From U.S. Route 95 about 7 miles east of Yuma, turn north on Ave. 7E; go 9.5 miles and pavement ends; lake is about 0.5 mile further. The lake also can be reached via Imperial Dam Road off U.S. 95, but that is a more difficult route.
Bureau of Land Management Yuma Field Office, (928) 317-3200; www.blm.gov/az/yfo/mittry.htm; Arizona Game and Fish, www.gf.state.az.us/outdoor_recreation/wildlife_area_mittry_lake.shtml

Dome Valley Museum: About 15 miles northeast of Yuma, Dome Valley Road heads east from U.S. 95 for about 2 miles to Dome. The privately-run museum features an impressive farm-equipment collection, including some with antique status. $. (928) 785-9081. www.domevalleymuseum.com

Museum, Activity and Heritage Center: This is a facility of the U.S. Army Yuma Proving Grounds. It's easy to find. About 4 miles north of the Dome Valley turnoff, you'll come to two of the largest landmarks in Arizona. The locals call them "The Big Guns." One is an atomic canon; the other is a 210 millimeter artillery piece. They mark the T-intersection of U.S. 95 and Imperial Dam Road. Turn left (west) and in about a half-mile you'll come to an interpretive center with tanks and artillery pieces on display. Farther on, you'll come to the heritage center. About a million soldiers trained in this area during World War II. The heritage center focuses on telling the story of testing and evaluation of military equipment. The center invites visitors to "inspect the large array of shells and munitions; admire prize-winning models of military vehicles; study Army uniforms, equipment and photos from WWII up to the '21st Century Soldier;' and examine a vast array of photos and information on military vehicles, equipment and munitions ... ." Open Mon.-Fri. Free. (928) 328-3394. www.yuma.army.mil/heritage_center.htm

Imperial Dam: The dam on the lower Colorado River is just downriver from the southern boundary of the Imperial National Wildlife Refuge. The Bureau of Land Management leases land to Hidden Shores Village, which operates an RV resort primarily for long-term guests and people who have bought sites for RVs and mobile-home-type housing. About 40 sites are available to short-term RVers, and the resort's beach, boat-launching area and other facilities are available for day-use. $. (928) 539-6700. www.hiddenshoresvillage.com

Imperial National Wildlife Refuge: Situated in both Arizona and California, the 25,000-acre refuge for migratory birds sits along 30 miles of the lower Colorado River. About 3 miles north of Imperial Dam Road turnoff from U.S. 95, take Martinez Lake Road west for 13 miles and follow signs to visitors center operated by U.S. Fish & Wildlife Service. Visitors center has information about hiking, back road exploring, and view points. (928) 783-3371. www.fws.gov/southwest/refuges/arizona/imperial.html

Martinez Lake: Boat tours and rentals, birding, fishing, water skiing and wakeboarding, camping, lodging, and restaurants. Just south of the Imperial National Wildlife Refuge, this lake, a byproduct of Imperial Dam, is reached by Martinez Road (see previous listing). (800) 876-7004; (928) 783-4400; (928)783-0253. www.visityuma.com/martinez.htm www.martinezlake.com; www.yumarivertours.com

Kofa National Wildlife Refuge: Home to bighorn sheep and a stand of native palm trees, the refuge stretches for about 35 miles on the east side of U.S. 95 beginning about 10 miles north of the Martinez Lake turnoff. The name Kofa is a contraction of King of Arizona, once a notable mine in the area. Signs along 95 direct travelers to attractions in the refuge, including a

stone cabin and the half-mile-long Palm Canyon Trail. (928) 785-7861.
www.fws.gov/southwest/refuges/arizona/kofa.html

Quartzsite: This desert hamlet, which swells with tens of thousands of
visitors each winter, is located about 80 miles north of Yuma where U.S. 95
intersects with Interstate 10. Visitors come to buy, sell, and trade gems and
minerals and other swap-meet items. (928) 927-9321
http://www.qzchamber.com; www.ci.quartzsite.az.us

Hi Jolly Monument: A monument to the camel caretaker Hadji Ali, aka
Hi Jolly, who led a camel train as part of a 19th-century surveying expedition.
Annual Hi Jolly festival held in January. (928) 927-9321.
www.quartzsitebusinesschamber.com/calendar.html

Tyson's Well Stage Station Museum: Housed in an adobe stagecoach
station built in 1866, the museum highlights Quartzsite's history. November-
March. Donations. (928) 927-5229. www.quartzsitemuseum.com

Ehrenberg: Located on the Colorado River off Interstate 10 about 19 miles
west of Quartzsite, the town has businesses that cater to those seeking river-
oriented recreation. (928) 923-9601.
www.coloradoriverinfo.com/ehrenberg/chamber

Parker: From Ehrenberg, you can take the Parker-Poston Road through the
Colorado River Indian Reservation to Parker, staying within a few miles of the
river. Or you can drive east on Interstate 10 to Exit 17 at Quartzsite and go
north on State Route 95 (the continuation of U.S. Route 95) to Parker, a river
town that attracts water-sports enthusiasts. Parker Tourism Committee:
(928) 669-6511; (888) 733-7275. www.parkertourism.com; Chamber of
Commerce: (928) 669-2174.
www.parkerareachamberofcommerce.com/community_pi.html

Colorado River Indian Reservation: Headquartered in Parker, the
reservation extends mostly south from the river town. Besides a casino, the
tribe operates the nearly 1,300-acre Ahakhav preserve and park that offer
fishing, canoeing, swimming, birding, a 4.6-mile fitness trail, playground, and
picnic facilities; and a museum showcasing more than 10,000 years of
Colorado River Indian culture with exhibits about the Chemehuevi, Mojave,
Hopi, and Navajo cultures. (928) 669-6757. www.critonline.com

Poston Memorial Monument: On the Colorado River Indian Reservation,
this is a monument to the more than 18,000 people of Japanese ancestry who
were confined a short distance from here during World War II. Located
11 miles south of Parker on the Parker-Poston Road. Free. (928) 669-2174.
www.parkerareachamberofcommerce.com/community_pi.html
www.critonline.com/crit_contents/tourism

Buckskin Mountain State Park: Facilities for camping, hiking, basketball, volleyball, fishing, and boating. Located on State 95, about 12 miles north of Parker. $. (928) 667-3231. The park also operates the River Island Unit, (928) 667-3386, for tent campers.
www.pr.state.az.us/Parks/parkhtml/buckskin.html.

Bill Williams River National Wildlife Refuge: Here's an excellent opportunity to venture into a preserve that attracts dozens of species of migratory birds such as the yellow warbler, vermillion flycatcher, and summer tanager; and holds one of the last stands of cottonwood-willow forest lining the Colorado River. And yet you won't get too far off the pavement. Located along State 95 between mileposts 160 and 161. Check for road closures before driving into the refuge. (928) 667-4144.
www.fws.gov/southwest/refuges/arizona/billwill.html

Cattail Cove State Park: Campsites with electricity and water and campsites accessible only by boat. Swimming area, beach, boat ramp, picnic tables, grills, hiking trails, showers, and a dump station. Lies off State 95 just north of the Bill Williams refuge. (928) 855-1223.
www.pr.state.az.us/Parks/parkhtml/cattail.html

Lake Havasu City: The London Bridge, water-based recreation (bring your own equipment or rent it or take a cruise), resort-style vacationing, annual festivals—it's all here in what might be called the capital of Arizona's "West Coast." The Convention & Visitors Bureau has printed and online guides, maps, an events calendar, and lists of businesses that rent equipment for water fun or provide backcountry ventures. 314 London Bridge Road. (928) 453-3444. www.golakehavasu.com

Lake Havasu State Park: On the shoreline of Lake Havasu north of London Bridge, the park offers camping, boat launch ramps, picnic areas, swimming beaches, and hiking trails. $. (928) 855-2784.
www.pr.state.az.us/Parks/parkhtml/havasu.html

Lake Havasu Museum of History: Visitors can expect to see exhibits about the London Bridge, steamboats, the Chemehuevi Indians, mining. $. 320 London Bridge Road. (928) 854-4938.
www.golakehavasu.com/recreation.html#museum

Havasu National Wildlife Refuge: The refuge includes the Havasu Wilderness area. Although no motorized vehicles are allowed, visitors can walk throughout the acreage or canoe through the preserve, which stretches along the river from the Lake Havasu City area north to Topock Gorge at Interstate 40. Refuge office is located in Needles, Calif. (760) 326-3853.
www.fws.gov/southwest/refuges/arizona/havasu

Topock Gorge: The highlight here is canoeing and kayaking. Adventurers can enjoy the picturesque gorge and perhaps glimpse bighorn sheep along this slow-moving stretch of the Colorado. Take Exit 1 from Interstate 40 and follow the curve to the right and find Topock Marina on your left. Topock Marina, (928) 768-2325. www.topockarizona.com.

Golden Shores–Topock: Chamber of Commerce, www.goldenshores.net

Bullhead City: Water-based recreation prevails here, too, but with an added attraction: gaming. The glittering Laughlin, Nev., lies just across the river and you can reach it by car or water taxi. Bullhead City Chamber of Commerce: (928) 754-4121; (800) 987-7457. www.bullheadchamber.com. Other information sources: www.bullheadcity.com/tourism and www.visitlaughlin.com

Colorado River Historical Society Museum: Inspect the first telephone switchboard used in Bullhead City, an 1859 piano, and other local and Indian artifacts from the area's history. Gift shop. Closed July-August. $. In Bullhead City on the west side of State 95, half-mile north of the Laughlin Bridge. (928) 754-3399.

Hardyville Days Celebration: With this annual event, Bullhead City celebrates its roots, which trace to the long-gone river town of Hardyville. Live music, art, games, gunfighter shows, food, and rides along the Colorado River. October. Free. Various locations in Bullhead City. (928) 763-9400. www.hardyvilledays.com

Lake Mead National Recreation Area

Information: The National Park Service oversees this year-round playground where the daytime highs range from the high 50s in winter months to the 100s in the summer. Besides Lake Mead, the area is home to thousands of desert plants and animals. www.nps.gov/lame/

Katherine's Landing: Located on Lake Mohave, this recreation area and resort offers a swimming area, boat ramp, marina, campgrounds, RV park, motel, restaurant, store, ranger station, and visitors center. Campground contains rest rooms, showers, picnic areas, fire rings, and a laundry. There are also sites with full hook-ups at the resort. Located 6 miles north of Bullhead City off State Route 68. $. Ranger station: (928) 754-3272. www.nps.gov/lame. Resort: (928) 754-3245; reservations, (800) 752-9669.

Katherine's Mine: An abandoned mine and ghost town northeast of the marina. All that remains are rusted remnants and concrete slabs. Be careful. Much of the ground and old mining shafts are unstable and prone to collapse. Ranger station, (928) 754-3272. www.nps.gov/lame/hikekath.htm

Alan Bible Visitors Center: Interactive exhibits, maps, and information about Hoover Dame and the Lake Mead Recreational Area. Free. 4 miles east of Boulder City, Nev., at the junction of U.S. Route 93 and Lakeshore Road. (702) 293-8990. www.nps.gov/lame/visitorcenter

Historic Railway Trail: This old section of railway was used during the construction of the Hoover Dam. Spanning 2.7 miles one way, the path takes an easy stroll through four tunnels, eventually leading to the dam. Great views of Lake Mead and Hoover Dam. This trail also heads away from the dam on a 3.6-mile hike to Boulder City, via the old railroad grade. The trailhead lies 250 feet south of the Alan Bible Visitor Center. Open year-round. Free. (702) 293-8990.

Hoover Dam: Visitors center, guided tours, gift shop, and eatery. $. (702) 294-3517. www.hooverdam.com.

Valley of Fire State Park: Nevada's first and largest state park named after the sandstone formations created from shifting sand dunes. The visitors center offers interpretive programs in the spring and fall along with exhibits and souvenirs year-round. Two campgrounds with showers and running water (no hookups). Many hiking trails leading to sites such as Atlatl and Arch rocks. Located 6 miles from Lake Mead via Interstate 15's Exit 75. $. (702) 397-2088. http://parks.nv.gov/vf.htm

Lost City Museum: Established to house Ancestral Puebloan (Anasazi) artifacts from Pueblo Grande de Nevada threatened by the creation of Lake Mead. Includes reconstructed pueblos and a garden showcasing what was grown by the Puebloans. About 11 miles northwest of Overton Beach on Nevada Route 167. Visitors center. $. (702) 397-2193. http://dmla.clan.lib.nv.us/docs/museums/lost/lostcity.htm

Arizona Hot Springs Hike: This 6-mile round-trip hike leads to hot springs within White Rock Canyon. Visitors must climb a 20-foot ladder to reach the springs. From the Alan Bible Visitors Center, take U.S. 93 east for 8.4 miles. There is a dirt parking lot on the right marking the trailhead to White Rock Canyon. (702) 293-8990.

Willow Beach National Fish Hatchery: Visitors can tour the hatchery on a self-guided walk. Lies 14 miles south of Hoover Dam on U.S. 93 (Milepost 14). Free. (928) 767-3456. www.fws.gov/southwest/fishery/willowbeach.html

Chloride: Officially, this community is a ghost town. At least, it's listed in the book *Arizona Ghost Towns and Mining Camps*, published by *Arizona Highways*. The name was taken from silver chloride, the ore from which this town sprouted in the 1860s. If you're on the way to or from Hoover Dam and Lake Mead, you'll pass the signed turnoff (on the east side) to Chloride about

20 miles north of Kingman off U.S. 93. Drive another 4 miles and you'll enter a town with the look of an earlier century. The old Post Office (ZIP 86431) still functions and a variety of shops sell items that would have been in a 19th- or early 20th-century yard sale. Town folks hold a variety of festival-celebrations throughout the year. The largest is Old Miner's Day on the last Saturday in June. (928) 565-2204. www.chloridearizona.com

Other Western Arizona Communities

Bouse: Even the Bouse Chamber of Commerce recognizes that this town is barely a dot on the map. The chamber prominently and unabashedly places this question on its Internet site: "Where in the world is Bouse?" And here's the chamber's answer: "Bouse is located in the midst of the unspoiled Sonoran Desert of west-central Arizona. It peacefully sits in the shadows of the Plomosa Mountains, 27 miles southeast of Parker and the Colorado River, and 23 miles northeast of Quartzsite." That puts Bouse along State Route 72, about 22 miles northwest of U.S. Route 60. The town draws its name from Tom Bouse, an early-day settler, miner, and businessman. Bouse Chamber of Commerce: (928) 851-2174. www.bouseazchamber.com

Bouse Assay Office: Restored and opened as a museum and tourist information center, this site displays a variety of WWII military and historical mining equipment. Special group tours by request. To schedule a time to visit the museum other than the regular hours, call (928) 851-2174; (928) 851-2498.

Black Powder Shoot: Held at the Bouse Shooting Range on first and third Saturdays October through April. At Milepost 29.5 on State 72 south of Bouse. (928) 851-2142

Camp Bouse: Secret training site during World War II for night tank warfare. The base was located about 20 miles northeast of Bouse. A monument commemorating the base is located in town, on State Route 72 across from the A & C Mercantile Co. The second weekend of February, the town holds a reunion event that includes tours to the original camp site.

Bouse Fisherman Intaglio: The geoglyph or earth figure was created by ... well, there's no consensus. Some say Indians created it. When? The most common answer is "long ago." The figure includes a man with a spear that one myth says he stuck in the ground to cause the Colorado River to flow. Located on the Plomosa Road. Ask at the Bouse visitors center for directions.

Dobson Museum: There are no curators here. The museum includes several buildings and perhaps 10 acres filled with collectibles gathered for more than 35 years by Wendy Dobson and her late husband, Ace. Here's a sampling of what's on display: bottles, including opium containers and whisky jugs, gathered from dumps, homesteads, ghost towns, and old mines; farm tractors, trucks, implements, and tools; office equipment; books; kitchen utensils; clothing; cotton gins and water pumps; mining apparatus; and vintage motorcycles. Touring the place requires an appointment. Donations. Located about 40 miles east of Yuma. Take Exit 42 from Interstate 8, drive north to Tacna. (928) 785-4013.

McMullen Valley: The valley extends for about 35 miles from about 25 miles west of Wickenburg to the Granite Wash Mountains on its western end just north of Interstate 10. U.S. 60 runs through the valley, and it's framed by the Harcuvar Mountains on the north and the Harquahala Mountains on the south. Geographically it includes Aguila, Wenden, Salome, and Harcuvar. But its Internet site also takes in Hope, Vicksburg, Brenda, and the Alamo Lake area. Information: McMullen Valley Chamber of Commerce, (928) 859-3846. www.azoutback.com

Great Arizona Outback Chili Cook-off & Poker Run: Airplane rides (donations requested), scavenger hunt, live entertainment, folk dancing, beer garden, chili contest, classic car show, various types of poker runs, and salsa competition. Most events are free. February. Indian Hills Airpark, Salome.

Wellton: The town is east of Yuma at Interstate 8's Exit 30. It has several RV parks and a golf course and produces a variety of festival-type events such as the Tractor Rodeo, Pioneer Days, an old-fashioned 4th of July, and a fishing derby. Attractions include McElahaney Cattle Company Museum and the Pioneer Museum. (928) 785-3348. www.town.wellton.az.us

JOSHUA FOREST SCENIC PARKWAY

Information: The scenic road goes through a forest of Joshua trees along U. S. 93 between Wikieup and Wickenburg. www.arizonascenicroads.com/main.aspx

Bagdad Mine: Phelps Dodge Corp. offers tours of its open-pit copper mine at Bagdad by appointment only. The company town of Bagdad is about 20 miles from the scenic road. Take State Route 97 for about 16 miles to State Route 96. Turn left and go 4 miles to the town. (928) 633-3490. http://new.azcommerce.com/SiteSel/Profiles

Wickenburg

Chamber of Commerce: Information for tourists and travelers on topics such as lodging, dining, area attractions, birding, and dude and guest ranches, and outdoor tours. (928) 684-5479. www.outwickenburgway.com

Desert Caballeros Western Museum: The permanent collection includes works of famous Western artists such as Charles M. Russell and Howard Terpning. Exhibits also cover prehistoric Indian artifacts, Arizona gems and minerals, and dioramas of frontier life. $. 21 N. Frontier St. (928) 684-2272. www.westernmuseum.org

Del E. Webb Center: This 600-seat theater presents a diverse selection of music, dance, and drama. Season runs late October through mid-May. 1090 S. Vulture Mine Road. (928) 684-6624. www.delewebbcenter.org

Gold Rush Days: This "wild rootin'-tootin' western weekend" annually hosts one of Arizona's largest parades, plus a mucking and drilling contest, music, and two-day rodeo. February. (928) 684-5479. www.wickenburgchamber.com/events.asp

Bluegrass and Fiddle Festival: An annual two-day music bonanza with nationally known bluegrass bands. November. $. (928) 684-5479. www.wickenburgchamber.com/events.asp

Hassayampa River Preserve: A Nature Conservancy project. Foot paths lead through lush river bottom forests. Great bird-watching, especially by the pond and marsh habitat. Picnic area. $. Just southeast of Wickenburg on U.S. 60. (928) 684-2772. www.nature.org/wherewework/northamerica/states/arizona

Vulture Mine: Tour the ghost town of Vulture City and Henry Wickenburg's gold mine. $. From downtown, take U.S. 60 for 3 miles west to Vulture Mine Road, turn left and drive 12 miles. Open daily during the winter months; call for summer hours. (602) 859-2743; (928) 684-5479. www.wickenburgchamber.com/atractions.asp

Robson's Mining World: A re-created mining town boasting the world's largest collection of antique mining equipment. Belly up to their ice cream parlor or shop for antiques in their general store. Activities include gold panning, bird watching, and hiking. $. Open Oct.-May. Located off State Route 71, northwest of Wickenburg. (928) 685-2609. www.robsonsminingworld.com

Burro Creek Recreation Site: Camping, hiking, birding, swimming, picnicking. Facilities for RVs and tent campers. Cactus plants grow in a small, interpretive garden and are identified in a brochure available at the site. Located off U.S. 93; turnoff to the site is 1 mile south of Burro Creek Bridge. Camping fees. BLM Kingman Field Office, (928) 718-3700. www.blm.gov/az/watch.htm

The Colorado River flows through Lower Granite Gorge in the Grand Canyon. ▲
The Grand Canyon's lime-crested Havasu Falls cascades into turquoise pools. ▶

Kate Thompson

Arizona Strip Country
The Grand Canyon, Page, and Lake Powell

This chapter examines both the south and north sides of one of the world's great wonders and this state's biggest attraction, man-made or natural—the biggest magnet for travelers, biggest in size, biggest in scenic grandeur. Piercing this region are three scenic drives—one along U.S. Route 180 from Flagstaff to Valle Junction, another stretching west along U.S. Route 89A (the A stands for Alternate) from near Bitter Springs and the Vermilion Cliffs to Fredonia, and the third from Jacob Lake south on State Route 67 to the North Rim of the Grand Canyon. This magnificent chunk of northern Arizona reaches from Flagstaff on the south to Page and much-hated, much-loved Lake Powell on the north and to Fredonia on the west. Smack dab in the center of this stupendous area lies the Grand Canyon, Nature at its even-more-stupendous best, embarrassingly more dynamic than this or any other prose or poetry could hope to equal.

Tom Danielsen

Nature's Greatest Act of Deconstruction

F ires, plagues, hurricanes, tornadoes, volcanoes, and floods have all wrought apocalyptic change, but never have they left behind the unworldly beauty to be found in this giant fissure, this wide and deep slash inflicted on Planet Earth's face over 6 million years, give or take a million or so, by the forces of the once-mighty Colorado River, by wind, rain, erosion, and the unfathomable, immeasurable forces generated by geologic movements.

The first or the umpteenth look across and into this Canyon never fails to evoke awe. The views from the rims above or from the Colorado River at the bottom aren't even diminished by the abundant piles of dung left by the muscular mules that lug tourists up and down Bright Angel Trail or by the architectural leavings of Fred Harvey's men who built the big hotels and fancy restaurants that litter the edges.

Standing at one of the railings on the South Rim (the North Rim is coming up), this is some of what it's good to know while gaping at this grand gap:

The Canyon with its 600 or so side canyons is 277 miles long, a stretch that runs along the Colorado River from Lee's Ferry on the northeast to the Grand Wash Cliffs on the west. It averages 10 miles across on a straight line, rim to rim. That's as the crow flies. Hikers plodding down any of several trails to the bottom and staggering up trails to the other rim can expect to put something in the area of 24 miles of their pedometers, should they foolishly wish to tote even that amount of extra ounces. It's about 200 miles by road to go around one end of it from south to north.

The South Rim is at 7,000 feet above sea level, the North Rim 8,000. The river, which runs for 1,450 miles from its source in the Colorado Rockies to the mouth at the Sea of Cortes in Mexico, is about a mile down from the rim overlooks. It varies in width from 76 to 300 feet and its depth averages 35 feet. On that portion of the river that flows east to west, it is bounded by two huge dams and the lakes they created—the still-controversial Glen Canyon Dam and Lake Powell upriver near Page on the east and Hoover Dam and Lake Mead downstream on the west.

In the Grand Canyon National Park, it is illegal to approach or feed wildlife, as signs in the park inform. It is not illegal to feed yourself, however, and the South Rim offers a profusion of restaurants in addition to gorgeous lodges, a free shuttle bus service because parking is not always easy to find, campgrounds, hikes along the Rim or down into the Canyon, mule trips, ranger-guided activities, post office, taxis, gift shops, bars, banking, bookstores, coin-operated showers and laundry facilities, medical and dental services, religious services, and the biggest

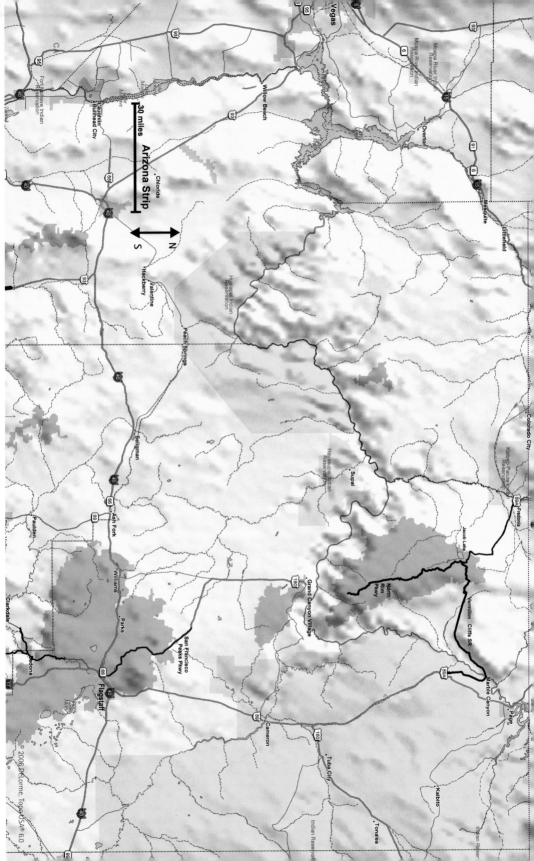

William Stone

aggregation of tour buses outside of a big bus station in a big city. On the Canyon bottom, there is Phantom Ranch where you can stay if you are willing to travel by foot, mule, or raft to get there. Ranch reservations are made up to two years in advance. For the less civilized and those who would prefer some time away from that day's portion of the 5 million humans who visit annually (but all of whom will appear to be there the day you visit), a tent and sleeping bag near the river on the Canyon bottom are highly recommended during warmer weather.

Oh, yes, the weather. It can and does change violently and abruptly in this high desert with summers generally hot (70s and 80s on the Rim but sometimes in the low 100s at the bottom) and dry (except for big thunderstorms) and winters freezing and snowy. Try spring and fall for the best shot at acceptable warmth (and not as many people as summer brings).

For non-triathletes, it is a wretched idea to think of hiking from either rim to the river at the bottom and then back to the rim in one day. The hike requires preparation, physical conditioning, water, and the recognition that this is a reversal of gravity's dictate that what goes up must come down: When you go down in the Canyon, you will have to come up, and that will be at the end of a day when you are likely to be more ready for bed than for a strenuous, long climb. The most popular trails off the South Rim are Bright Angel and Kaibab, and there are some 300 instances of illness, exhaustion, or injury on those trails every year. It will cost you a small fortune if the rangers have to get you back topside.

■■■

A brief, personal diary of one such autumnal hike, starting and ending at the South Rim:

Park vehicle; shoulder backpack weighing 45 pounds (much too much, but what would life be like at the bottom with only water, no Thermos of gimlets?); step to the Kaibab Trailhead at the Rim; look down, then prayerfully up; get weak in the knees; conclude it can't be done; start down the trail anyway under silent pressure from two companions suspected of being inclined to allege cowardice; hug the Canyon wall to avoid staring into the abyss; consider crawling across strips of trail with no cliff to cling to on either side; finally, begin to adjust and appreciate the magnificence and beauty of the rock formations and the river below.

Six hours later (thanks to indispensable flashlights and water canteens) hit bottom and the Colorado River; two quivering thighs, one sore back, one companion badly limping on damaged knee; unroll small tent and fall into deep sleep; awaken to smelly socks, pretty birds, and the ripple of a creek; spend another day and night exploring the bottom; late next morning begin trek back up different trail, Bright Angel.

[
The Desert View Watchtower stands against a darkening sky at the South Rim. ◀ Point Imperial in the Grand Canyon overlooks Saddle Mountain, Marble Canyon, and the Vermilion Cliffs. ▼
]

William Stone

Four hours later, decide to spend another night at a midpoint (Indian Garden) featuring a creek, potable spring water, lots of ferns, and a small campground; stare blankly but enviously at spindly, teenage lad sprinting up the trail toward the top, still four hours away by personal reckoning but much less for him; try to recall similar physical condition nearly a half-century ago but senility forbids; fix freeze-dry meal; kill the gimlets; relax.

Arise next morning, pack up, head out and up, grateful for walking stick and resentful of backpack; four hours later emerge proudly on the South Rim and stare with amazement at a coven of Texas tourists flashing the V for victory sign as they complete same route but . . . without backpacks and riding mules the entire way. Speculate that V stands for "Vicarious." Stagger to nearest big hotel bar, buy unmemorable but coveted bottle of cold beer, dump in some salt, drink it; head for car with head full of great memories.

■■■

Always leave the dance with the one that brung ya, it is said, and with that backwoods wisdom in mind we now take the wooded road that brung us here, State Route 64, and go east to Cameron on the Navajo Reservation.

Before Cameron, there are at least two more "must stop" sites. One, approximately 22 miles from Grand Canyon Village, is the Tusayan Ruins and Museum. Here you'll see the partially excavated ruins of a pueblo dating from about 1185 A.D. The other is the Desert View Watchtower, at 7,500 feet the highest point on the South Rim and the major overlook on the eastern end of the national park. The tower is a 1930s creation of an architect named Mary Colter who designed it for hotelier Fred Harvey's company to look like an ancient dwelling. Happily, this structure with its rock-faced steel frame does not excessively intrude on the natural scenery, but it does provide views on clear days of the Painted Desert to the east and the Colorado River flowing out of Marble Canyon to the north. Even more happily for some, it has among its offerings, ta-da, a gift shop.

About 35 miles after the watchtower comes the town of Cameron, site of a historic trading post, a nice lodge, an old bridge with a good view of the Little Colorado River Gorge, and the place to make a decision: Drive south on U.S. 89 to Flagstaff, or north on 89 and then east on U.S. Route 160 to Tuba City and into the Navajo and Hopi reservations, or drive north on 89 toward the town of Page, Lake Powell, and the Canyon's North Rim.

You've selected Page and Lake Powell, you say? Excellent choice.

Just when you think you are all wondered out from looking at wonderful sights, there are even more wonderful views ahead as we depart the Grand Canyon's South Rim and head for its north side and, 61 miles down a side road, the worst nightmare of any acrophobe's life—Toroweap Point, a peek into the abyss.

Along the way, one of Nature's finest canyons, this one named Glen, comes into a view, sort of, near the community of Page, but the original Glen Canyon is no more. One of man's great works, Lake Powell, has filled the late, great Glen Canyon with the dammed-up water of the late, great Colorado River. That all means important things to environmentalists, developers, farmers, and users of power. For the traveler, however, it means swapping the delights of hiking in a splendid canyon for the easy pleasure of house boating on an artificial lake that stretches for nearly 200 miles, more or less, the less defined by drought.

Travelers determined to see all of this need not fret about seeing some of the same wonders twice. There's much too much to be taken in at first sight, and a second viewing, in reverse, is worth the mileage unless you got a bad deal from a car rental agency. ⌘

[　　　A biker stops at Toroweap Point near the Canyon's North Rim.　　　]

Dugald Brenner

Connecting With the Canyon

Like millions of others, I caught my first glimpses of the Grand Canyon through the gaps in a row of tourists crowding the rails. Being a tourist myself, I could hardly blame those who had gotten there before me, but I did think: "This will ruin it." How can you appreciate this miracle of the natural world while trying to compete for space in a crowd? I felt more like a herd animal than a human being.

Published novelist and former journalist Donald H. Pfarrer, a Vietnam Navy combat officer, traveled from the Boston area to tour northern Arizona, including the Grand Canyon. These are his impressions.

> By DONALD H. PFARRER

When I made a place for myself at the rail my whole body felt a change. At first, I couldn't understand what sensation I was feeling, but as I let my gaze roam over the colors of the Canyon and probe its immensity, I slowly realized that I was somehow pro-jecting myself into the whole distance and depth of it. I had no feeling of danger, only one of reaching out and down.

David Muench

I think this explains, for me, the sense of profound surprise and

[Toroweap Point at the Grand Canyon.]

awe I felt. Verbal descriptions, photographs, and movies cannot do this to me. I never feel that I am reaching forward into a picture. Only the real Canyon can do that.

I was oblivious to the people around me. I was on the verge of the Canyon, feeling almost as if I were also in and over it.

This happened on the South Rim.

Three days later I reached the North Rim at Toroweap Point, where the sheer drop is 3,000 feet. I got down and crawled on my belly to the edge and looked down. The twisting Colorado River was emerald green flecked with white at the rapids, and I could hear the rushing of the water and see the rocks' colors of brown, rust, gray, and purple. I could look across, then down, then along the river's course, and again I felt myself reaching into the vastness.

The feeling was strong enough to convince me I had done the right thing to approach the Rim on my belly, and I was glad the wind was calm.

I did not regret the 2,000 miles I had traveled nor the money I had spent to lie on that shelf of reddish-brown stone. I will do it again some day. ∎

The Fun's for Real

A shot rang out.

Several shots, actually. This was a gunfight, after all. Not a real one, of course. Just blanks, fired for laughs as a stage setter and mood enhancer for the pending two-and-a-half-hour train ride from Williams, Arizona, to the big ditch that qualifies as Arizona's Number One tourist attraction.

Nothing like a little humorous gunplay in the morning to get your day off right. My 13-year-old son and I were still smiling at the horse manure jokes as we exited the Old West movie set next door to the Grand Canyon Railway station in the town of Williams.

We found our rail car and settled into our seats. It was hot, threatening to be a scorcher for the afternoon return trip to Williams. Luckily, when I made our July reservation months before, I failed to ask whether our vintage coach was air-conditioned. If I had known that it wasn't (the cars are heated in cooler months), I might have decided to take an Arizona highway to the Canyon instead.

Retired newspaper journalist Michael J. Sweeney, who lives on Vashon Island just off Seattle, Washington, took his teenage son, Joe, on the popular railroad trip on the Grand Canyon Railway from its origination point in Williams, (32 miles west of Flagstaff) to the South Rim of the Canyon. This is his account.

> By MICHAEL J. SWEENEY

Surprisingly, though, with every window open and the ceiling fans at takeoff thrust, the temperature wasn't too bad. Just like travel in the old days, I imagine, except the pall of smoke from the steam engine up front now stinks of fuel oil instead of coal dust. Even the return trip was bearable, if you don't mind being around sweaty people.

Although it's a relic, we were quickly reminded that the Grand Canyon Railway that runs regularly from Williams to the South Rim of the Grand Canyon still qualifies as a form of mass transportation, subject to all of the various rules and regulations governing this form of travel. As we all know, one of these rules requires that there be at least one crazy person, smelly person, or screaming baby on board each and every public conveyance at all times. The object, of course, being to vex, irritate, and annoy the other passengers. On this day, it was our special treat to be confined in a railroad car with a screaming toddler. This terminally unhappy little girl yelled almost non-stop for the entire trip north, pausing only once—all too briefly—to chuck her pacifier out the window. Thankfully, we were assigned a different car on the return trip. I'll take smelly people over screaming ones any day.

You can overnight at the South Rim and catch the train back tomorrow or next week if you wish. Most, however, make the trek as day-trippers, getting three hours at the Canyon to check out the sights before the train heads home. Three hours might not seem like much, but it actually was plenty of time to stroll the Rim, contemplate the wonders of Nature, walk a little way down one of the trails leading to the bottom, make good use of our binoculars, snap all the pictures we wanted, eat our sack lunches, buy ice cream and souvenirs, feed the squirrels, and even check out a hotel lobby or two.

A Grand Canyon backpacker pauses to admire Zoroaster Temple, a 7,128-foot butte consisting primarily of Coconino sandstone. The formation was named for the Persian religious leader who was active some six centuries before the birth of Christ.

Les David Manevitz

Rendezvous Days

The town of Williams celebrates its heritage each Memorial Day weekend with Rendezvous Days festivities that focus on history—not just the early 19th century, when mountain men like Bill Williams, for whom the town is named, hunted and trapped in the Southwest. You can also enjoy the traditional camp craft and black-powder marksmanship of early settlers, the Wild West gunfights of myth and legend, the nostalgic mystique associated with historic U.S. Route 66, a rodeo, and a parade.

The Bill Williams Buckskinners sponsor the Black Powder Shoot and trader's row during Rendezvous Days. Buckskinner Park, where the family-oriented event is held, offers a beautiful pine-covered camping area in the hills just south of town. Wearing period clothing and practicing the skills of the pre-1840 American pioneer, everybody seems to enjoy re-creating a simpler time.

Connecting with the past is a staple in Williams. When the steam whistle of the Grand Canyon Railway engine signals its departure mid-morning, seven days a week, it harkens back to 1901, when the 65-mile rail stub to the Canyon was built and Williams took on the appellation of "Gateway to the Grand Canyon."

Information: (800) 863-0546; (928) 635-4707 or (928) 635-4061; www.visitwilliams.com.

[The Grand Canyon Railway makes its run seven days a week between Williams and the Canyon. ▲]

Although it probably could be used as an example to help define the term anticlimax, the ride back to Williams turned out to be even more entertaining that the ride to the Canyon. This is when the outlaws who shot it out with the sheriff in the morning gallop up on horseback, board the train and proceed from car to car, "robbing" passengers of their pocket change (you won't get it back, but you don't have to surrender it if you don't wish to).

Everybody played along with this, of course, especially the kids, and by the time the train pulled into Williams for the night, we were all smiles again. Of course, the brass band playing on the platform didn't hurt, and neither did the fact that we arrived on schedule. ⋔

San Francisco Peaks Scenic Road

Route	U.S. Route 180 north from Flagstaff to State Route 64 at Valle.
Mileage	51 miles from Flagstaff to Valle.
Elevation	7,000 feet at Flagstaff, 7,500 at Canyon's Desert View to 4,200 feet at Cameron.
Overview	A drive through mountain grasslands, alpine forests, and piñon-juniper-sagebrush vegetation and running from mid-sized Flagstaff to seemingly limitless Grand Canyon with sights that are unrivaled in the world.

O n U.S. Route 180 just out of Flagstaff and heading north toward Grand Canyon (about 81 miles away) is a paved side road leading for about 8 miles up a heavily wooded, alpine route to the literal and figurative high point of this scenic drive, the San Francisco Peaks, home of the Arizona Snowbowl with some of the best snow skiing bargains in the state during Flagstaff's off-season. In summer, a ski lift offers scenic sky rides that take the visitor to an elevation of 11,500 feet and a view over 70 miles of scenery including the Grand Canyon and Flagstaff. In winter, the lift takes those with heavy coats, thick gloves, warm hats, and skis or snowboards to more than 30 fine ski runs and, in exceptional years, a couple hundred inches of dry powder snow.

The peaks are really just summits that form the crater rim of what was once a massive volcano that is now dubbed San Francisco Peaks. The highest of the peaks (and the highest point in the state) is Humphreys, at 12,633 feet. It and its buddies are there to play on, hike on, and ski on. They also, however, are the home of the Kachina gods to the Hopi and a cardinal point in the universe to the Navajo. They also are the magnificent remnants of a mountain that erupted several times during the past 3 million years, the last time about 220,000 years ago, and the experts say it could blow again some day. Don't let that thought disturb any plan to ski or climb it. In the end, we're all ashes to ashes anyway, and what better way to become a cinder than with a smile on your face while carving a track down through some deep powder.

The peaks are part of the 2,200-square-mile San Francisco Volcanic Field, as are 500 or so volcanic cones including Sunset Crater, Colton, Roden, and others with less well-known names. It is possible to hike some of these cinder cones, which are formed by lava blasting out of a volcano, cooling and leaving the cone of cinders, ash, and pumice around the volcanic vent. The sides of the cones go up—and down—at a steady and steep 33 degrees, the so-called "angle of repose" of cinders, which means that particular angle of slope is the maximum at which the cinders will remain in place. The footing for hikers is, as one *Arizona Highways* writer put it, like "walking on a field of ball bearings" and requires going into low range two-leg-drive.

The volcanic field is considered dormant but could reactivate and create another volcano some time in the future. There are seismometers around, but pending the unseemly rise of new volcanoes, it does not take sensors to figure out that it is a vast chunk of land dotted with lava rock and the benign remains of volcanic cones.

The Kachina Peaks Wilderness in the Coconino National Forest, with Kendrick Peak on horizon.

Tom Danielsen

After returning to U.S. Route 180 from the Snowbowl, this scenic route continues north to Valle. At about Milepost 235, not far past the turnoff to the Snowbowl, is a mini-site likely to provoke the question "what is that?" from someone in the car: "That" is the Chapel of the Holy Dove on the side of the highway, a sort of drive-in for one sort of soul food and housed in a tiny A-frame. The non-denominational place of worship is rustically and tastefully designed with a gravel floor, a door easily opened at all times by anyone, a pulpit, a Bible, a few pews, some wilted bouquets and scribbled messages everywhere—written directly on the tongue-and-groove wood slats that form the walls or on pieces of scratch paper pinned to those slats. Astonishingly, it also is remarkably free of gang graffiti.

A typical message reads:

"Lord, thank you for my family. If Coreen is pregnant, please send us a healthy baby. Help me to be a good dad to Sarah and Lacy and help me to be a good husband to Coreen. Help our world to know peace. The peace that only you can send."

At roughly Milepost 237, the route begins a cruise into patches of ghostly, blackened aspens and pines charred in a 1996 forest fire, one of many wildfires that have swept the area over the years. The officially designated scenic drive from there alternates between up and down grades, grassy flatlands, alpine stretches, and piñon-juniper forest until it ends just short of Valle. In Valle, U.S. 180 comes to a junction with State Route 64, which aims north for 27 miles to the touristy little town of Tusayan (it even has an IMAX theater) and, quickly, the entrance to a national park and ... the Canyon. ᛕ

Page and Lake Powell

T he big tuna in this chapter is the Grand Canyon, but failure to go on to Page and to explore adjoining Lake Powell means missing some nice bass in a damn big lake created by a much-damned dam. Although the lake is a mainstay, this is so-called slickrock country. The Navajo sandstone, formed from cemented sand, has eroded into smooth and rounded forms, largely devoid of plant life and looking ever so much like, well, slick rock.

In the opinion of environmentalists, Lake Powell, no matter how beautiful and impressive it might be, deserves its ultimate fate, predicted to be its strangulation on silt, sand, and stones from the Colorado and other tributary rivers and its disappearance in fewer than a thousand years, the victim of the very river it conquered. There's an irony in there somewhere. On the other hand, for those who would rather cruise up and down a lake in a luxurious houseboat or speed along it in a powerboat rather than hump into and along a canyon, the lake is a big improvement on Nature. Given this nation's penchant for obesity, there's probably another irony in that.

More about the lake, the dam that created it, and beautiful Glen Canyon that mostly drowned under it, in a moment. First, let's get from the South Rim of the Grand Canyon and the town of Cameron to the community of Page.

From Cameron, U.S. Route 89 leads 80 miles north to Page. Just out of Cameron the route enters the Painted Desert. The route quickly provides some delightful views into the Painted Desert's layers of color that decorate its ghostly, even eerie domes, buttes, and other formations rising up from nowhere to flaunt their pink, rose, brown, red, pale red, purple, and blue-greens. Continue on up the highway past Cedar Ridge and the view to the immediate east is of the impressive 1,800-foot-high Echo Cliffs and, on the horizon, the magnificent, 3,000-foot Vermilion Cliffs and the flat and fabled Paria Plateau. At the little community of Bitter Springs is a junction with some remarkable vistas. It is also the spot to take U.S. Route 89A west, a route that becomes the official Fredonia-Vermilion Cliffs Scenic Road leading to Jacob Lake, Fredonia, and the North Rim. That drive is described later in this chapter.

Continuing on U.S. 89 takes you through a short, eye-poppingly dramatic mountain pass through fortresses of towering red rocks, massive boulders, views of plateaus, a vista that looks down into Marble Canyon, and a vehicular passage through two huge cuts blasted by man through the center of cliffs ("We call 'em Big Cut and Little Cut," offered one motel clerk when asked.). Suddenly, just ahead, are Lake Powell, Glen Canyon Dam, and the hilltop town of Page,

Gary Ladd

Why Lake Powell?

Question: Why did we as a nation originally want Lake Powell?

Answer: Flood control downstream, power generation, water storage, agricultural irrigation, and, ultimately, economic development.

Question: Why do we want it now?

Answer: Same as above, plus Lake Powell's recreational opportunities.

Question: Was it a good decision?

Answer: Talk with any sybarite who has rented a houseboat for one point of view, then read the 1986 book *Cadillac Desert: The American West And Its Disappearing Water* by Marc Reisner for the opposing opinion, and decide for yourself. It is an issue that far transcends the limits of this touristy text. It's an argument of the values of ending flooding, storing water, and generating power versus the merits of refusing to use precious water for arguable goals and for preserving a magnificent, unspoiled wilderness for society at large. The fight is over; the preservationists lost that one, but they did succeed in putting an end to some moronic thoughts about erecting such dams in Grand Canyon itself.

[Water mirrors the sky at Padre Bay. ▲]

established in 1957 and now with a population about 7,000, a lot of them guides or guys who sell and repair boats and motors. If anyone in the vehicle is hungry, sleepy, or in need of divine guidance, the town offers 15 or so restaurants, about that same number of fast-food joints, at least a dozen motels and hotels, and a big testimony to the diverse forms faith takes: nearly 20 churches.

When the traveler has sated the needs of stomach, soul, and sleep in Page, there are several other attractions that merit attention, dominant among them the John Wesley Powell Memorial Museum in town, the Glen Canyon Dam-Lake Powell-Carl Hayden Visitor Center complex just down the road, and upper and lower Antelope Canyon (see story on Page 226).

The museum at 6 N. Lake Powell Blvd. collects and preserves the history of Page and the story of Maj. John Wesley Powell, a Civil War soldier who lost his right arm to amputation after it was struck by a mini-ball when he raised it to signal a charge during the battle of Shiloh. After that, he quite understandably decided to become a one-armed professor of geology at Illinois Wesleyan University. In May of 1869, however, he traded in his pipe and tweeds and set forth with nine other men in four boats. Even though the Colorado River's general course was known, not much else showed up on maps, so Powell decided to map it, study its geology, and confirm his theory that the river preceded the canyons (Grand, Glen, etc.) and then cut down through them as the plateau rose. He began in Green River, Wyoming, and fin-ished 99 days and 1,000 watery miles later at the Virgin River, now Lake Mead. After those months of struggle and adversity, including the loss of two boats and four men, Powell emerged a national hero for his pioneering exploration of the largely unknown.

The museum is a font of information about him, as well as Page, Glen Can-yon, and Lake Powell, with an extensive collection of literature, some excellent exhibits and displays, pet-rified dino tracks from the area, and, outside, Walt Disney's remarkable near-replica of a 16-foot pine rowboat Powell used during his ground-breaking first expedition (inexplicably, he did it again two years later). Disney used his version to make money from the *Ten Who Dared* movie re-creating Powell's trip. It costs a small fee to go inside this compact and diversified institution, and it's a bargain.

Next stop: the Carl Hayden Visitor Center, an imposing, architecturally pleasing structure adjoining the monumental Glen Canyon Dam and the Glen Canyon Bridge. There can be no better view of the great dam than from the panoramic windows of the center. And the people who created the huge relief map of the area and the displays explaining the river, the dam, what was Glen Canyon, the geology, and the history, both ancient and modern, deserve praise. The center bears the name of Carl Hayden, a powerful Arizona politician who gets much of the credit—or blame—for water development in the West.

The first blast of dynamite to create this dam across this big river coursing along the Colorado Plateau and through what was once beautiful, peaceful Glen Canyon occurred in October 1956 on a day that will live in infamy in the minds of some environmentalists. Ike, the famous general who became president, hit the button by remote control. The last bucket of concrete was dumped by project engineer Lem Wylie, about whom almost nobody remembers anything.

The dam stands 710 feet above bedrock, 583 above the original river channel. It is 330 feet thick at the foundation, 25 feet at the top. It is 1,560 feet long at the crest, and it and its powerhouse consumed almost 5.4 million cubic yards of concrete. The adjoining Glen Canyon Bridge over the river (now lake) is 700 feet above the water and the span of the bridge arch is 1,028 feet, the deck length 1,271 feet.

The lake, which started filling in 1963, reached capacity in 1980 (27 million acre feet or enough water to cover that many acres with one foot of water). Its maximum depth is 560 feet at the dam. In good times, it stretches 186 miles (163,000-acre surface area) and has had a gorgeous but now-shriveling 1,950-mile

[
A hiker stands silhouetted in the Paria Canyon-Vermilion Cliffs Wilderness. ◄ Rainbow Bridge, the world's largest natural arch, borders the Navajo Reservation near Lake Powell. ▼
]

Don B. Stevenson

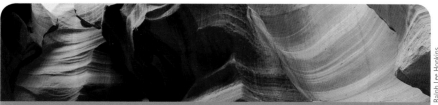

Ralph Lee Hopkins

Antelope Canyon

Just east of Page by a less than a handful of miles and fewer than five minutes are three smoke stacks of the coal-fired power plant called the Navajo Generating Station. The best way to ignore them is to venture into the nearby upper and lower passages of a natural phenomenon named Antelope Canyon. To get there, take State Route 98 from U.S. Route 89 to about Milepost 299 and follow the signs.

Actually, there are two canyons—Upper and Lower Antelope. Lower Antelope is a quarter-mile-long slot in the Colorado Plateau's floor that at times is barely shoulder-width wide. The breathtakingly beautiful passage can be walked in 15 minutes, and a flashlight is a handy tool to have for the trip. It isn't deep (the depth changes depending on whether windblown sand has raised the canyon floor or flooding has lowered it by washing the sand out one end). It also isn't strenuous, but you'll need to climb down and up stairways in the lower canyon; nor is it dangerous except . . .

. . . except in a flash flood such as one August of 1997 when 11 people— seven French, two Americans, one Swede, one English—drowned when they could not escape the water surging after a cloudburst 17 miles away. A wall of water rushed through the narrow slot, taking everyone with it without warning.

. . . and except when you are strolling through Upper Antelope, where you are in danger of tripping on any one of sometimes dozens of photographers' tripods. During long periods of time exposures, the tripods and the expensive cameras they support almost block parts of the dark, high-walled confines of this fantasy of color. The close quarters make bathing and the wearing of deodorant a useful civility to observe.

Stay out of the canyons on days when rain clouds are overhead or even on the horizon. Even then there may be a flood threat from a storm you can't see. There is no formal warning system for flash floods, although the guides try to monitor the weather in Antelope's watershed system.

[Antelope Canyon is one of the better-known slot canyons. ▲   ]

In 1931 a 12-year-old Navajo girl discovered the formation when she was sent out to find a missing herd of sheep. Since then, the spectacular, corkscrewed walls of the canyons have yielded incredibly colorful photos. The sandstone walls seem to glow, courtesy of the sunshine that falls in spots on the canyon floor from the small, spiraled openings above, creating a kaleidoscope of purples, reds, oranges, yellows, golds, and browns. As the sun moves across the mesa top, the most spectacular lighting appears around mid-day from May to August.

You can tour the canyons on your own or join tours conducted by outfits based in Page. The Navajo Tribe charges an admission fee.

shoreline of red sandstone formations. It is dotted here and there by big houseboats that have been deliberately beached on sandy shores to permit the renters to hike, swim, fish, or sleep in a tent or in the open air rather than on the boat. Tip: When beaching your houseboat, don't full power it onto the beach unless there are two or three strong men and women to help the boat's twin screws get it all the way back into the water; rather, gently ground it and spread the anchors.

What can you do on or around this, the country's second largest artificial lake? (Mead, downstream, is bigger.) You can hike, camp, take a motel room, eat like royalty, ride a bike, cruise up and down the lake in any of a large assortment of boats ranging from kayaks to big houseboats, explore any of the lake's 96 major canyons, fish for everything from bass to bluegill to northern pike if you bought a license, spend the night in any of several marinas that dot the huge lake, pay for a guided cruise, water ski, or simply sit in a deck chair on one of the houseboats and glory in the gorgeous red rock country that is the shoreline.

One target for those who choose to cruise: Rainbow Bridge, the world's largest natural bridge, about 50 miles (and four hours roundtrip) up the lake from the main marina, Wahweap, near Page and the Hayden visitor center. This incredible, sandstone arch, formed by water's flow, is 290 feet from base to top and spans 275 feet. It also can be reached by trails across the Navajo reservation, but that requires a permit from the Navajo Parks and Recreation Department in Window Rock, Arizona, (928) 871-6647.

Lake Powell: It's a great place to spend a day—or a month if you can afford it. And Page provides an excellent take-off point for a couple of scenic drives. So, anchors up. Let us depart Page, going south on 89 to the 89A junction and take 89A, the Fredonia-Vermilion Cliffs Scenic Road, west along the cliffs and toward Jacob Lake, Fredonia, and the Grand Canyon's North Rim. ⚑

Fredonia-Vermilion Cliffs Scenic Road

Route	From Flagstaff or Cameron, take U.S. Route 89 north to U.S. 89A at Bitter Springs. From Page, take 89 south to 89A. At Bitter Springs, go west on 89A to the communities of Jacob Lake and Fredonia.
Mileage	Bitter Springs to Fredonia, 85 miles.
Time to allow	One to two days.
Elevation	About 5,200 feet at Bitter Springs, 8,000 feet at Jacob Lake, and 4,700 feet at Fredonia.
Overview	Starting on the grassy plains of the Kaibab Plateau , the drive crosses the Colorado River at Marble Canyon, passes the ever-changing-color Vermilion Cliffs, and forges into the Kaibab National Forest in the midst of the Arizona Strip.

With the appropriately named Vermilion Cliffs sometimes in front of us, sometimes on the left and then on the right depending on the twists and turns of the road, we cross the Colorado River on Navajo Bridge about 14 miles along U.S. Route 89A from Bitter Springs. The bridge is one of only seven land crossings of the Colorado for 750 miles. There is a small but nice visitor center at the bridge, and it is possible to walk the old bridge over Marble Canyon while cars stream past on the nearby replacement. The view is of the bottom of the canyon 467 feet down and of its width, 600 feet. Just upstream in Marble Canyon is the official start of the Grand Canyon.

About 300 yards west of the bridge on the right is a road providing a quick side trip to Lee's Ferry, a famous spot not to be confused with Harper Lee of *To Kill A Mockingbird* or with Harper's Ferry, which is in West Virginia. Lee's Ferry was named for Mormon John Doyle Lee, who established the first Colorado River crossing there with ferryboats that operated from 1873 to 1928. Nearby is the Lonely Dell Ranch Historic District. ("Oh, what a lonely dell," exclaimed Emma, one of John's many and simultaneous wives, when she saw the valley for the first time). The district offers a look at western pioneer life in the late 1800s. River rafting trips (permits required) through the Grand Canyon start at Lee's Ferry and there are several amenities including: Emma's home, an old (1874) stone fort, hiking trails, a ranger station, campground, launch ramp, dock, fish-cleaning station, and 15 miles of upriver access.

Emma Lee, by the way, ended up running the ferry. Her husband, an adopted son of Brigham Young, was hiding out in the Glen Canyon area because the feds wanted him for his involvement in the Mountain Meadows massacre in Utah. At Mountain Meadows, Indians and Mormons killed some 120 settlers who were in a wagon train bound for California (Mark Twain once accused Brigham Young of ordering the massacre). Anyway, Lee was still on the lam even after establishing the ferry, but he eventually was busted in Utah in 1874. He confessed to his role in the slaughter, and three years later a firing squad did him in. In 1879, Emma sold the ferry enterprise to the Mormon Church for $3,000. The ferry ran continuously until 1929 when the Navajo Bridge was completed. Eventually, it was acquired by Coconino County and then by the National Park Service.

For anyone who is slightly disoriented by this time, Lee's Ferry is in a break among Glen, Marble, and Paria canyons and downriver from Glen Canyon Dam. The region was a natural corridor that connected Utah and northeastern Arizona

[Hikers check out the Coyote Buttes, reflected in a rainwater pool in the Paria Canyon–Vermilion Cliffs Wilderness.]

Ralph Lee Hopkins

Gary Ladd

An Ageless Spring

State Route 389 southwest out of Fredonia will, after 14 miles and a quarter-mile turn-off, land the traveler at Pipe Spring National Monument, a true oasis with a spring that provided water for thousands of years to aboriginal hunter-gatherers, then to traders, then to Mormon settlers, and finally to the National Park Service, which converted it into a tourist attraction drawing about 50,000 people a year. That's a mere one-hundredth of the total visitors to the Grand Canyon.

The original spring dried up in the 1990s, but the Park Service restored a flow (see "the Luxury of Cheese" on Page 232).

Pipe Spring is on the Arizona Strip, a huge landscape that lies north of the Grand Canyon. The Strip has served as a travel corridor for millennia and in the 1800s was dominated by members of the Church of Jesus Christ of Latter-day Saints. Still is; the area, stretching into Utah, remains heavily Mormon.

The Strip is one of several vast terraces that reach up to a high plateau in central Utah where rainwater and snowmelt flow south to the Vermilion Cliffs and surfaces at, among other spots, Pipe Spring.

In the 1850s, the Mormon Church urged its members to branch out from Salt Lake City in Utah, and some of them headed for the Arizona Strip. In 1863, one such settler, James Whitmore, moved sheep and cattle to the area and got title to 160 acres around Pipe Spring, where he built corrals and planted an orchard and vineyard. That in turn produced Indian raids, a lot of revenge fighting, and Whitmore's death. Mormon leader Brigham Young bought the land from Whitmore's widow and directed Anson Perry Winsor to manage it.

In 1868, Mormon militiamen built a small, stone cabin at Pipe Spring that was intended to hold off further Indian raids. Two years later, Young and Winsor began the work that led to completion of a small fort and courtyard, turning this remote outpost into a fortified cattle and dairy ranch. In the 1880s and 1890s, Mormon women and children hid out at the fort to save

[True to their name, the Vermilion Cliffs glow red at dawn. ▲   ]

their husbands from being federally prosecuted for polygamy.

The church sold the fortress-ranch in 1895 to private interests. In 1907, it was surrounded by the newly created, 120,00-acre Kaibab-Paiute Indian Reservation but remained in private hands. In 1923, the Pipe Spring site was purchased by the government and set aside as a national monument.

Today, it offers a visitors center with exhibits on Indian and pioneer life in the Old West, a short video of its history, regular guided tours, and a half-mile ridge trail with views of the Strip, Mount Trumbull, the Kaibab Plateau, and Kanab Canyon. Visitors also can stroll around the fort's buildings, corrals, garden, orchard, and duck-populated holding ponds created by the spring. There's even a woman wearing a bonnet and pioneer garb who demonstrates the creation of lace.

for Utah Mormons on the move. It also is the area where the major cliffs, Echo and Vermilion , meet and where the Paria River runs into the Colorado.

Back from Lee's Ferry and onto U.S. 89A is a landscape that continues to be dominated by the Vermilion Cliffs, which have strata variously described as red, magenta, "shadowed plum" (whatever that might be), pale vermilion, regular vermilion, gray, sandy, and even green. Whatever, they are big and colorful.

This also is the area where California condors, among the world's largest raptors, have been reintroduced into the wild, because the cliffs are ideal habitat for this endangered species. If you see something with a 9-foot wingspan flying about, it's not Batman and it's certainly not a robin. Count yourself exceptionally fortunate for the rare sighting.

We also are in the area of a path blazed by a couple of Spanish priests, Father (sometimes called Fray) Francisco Atanasio Dominguez and Father Silvestre Velez de Escalante. In 1776, the two Franciscan priests were leading an expedition in search of a direct route between Santa Fe in New Mexico and a new military garrison at Monterey, California. When they reached the Colorado River, at what is now the Lee's Ferry spot, they were trapped by the cliffs and the river, and they eventually were reduced to eating toasted cactus pads (now called nopales and not bad in a salad if you remove the spines first). Thus fortified, they hiked around a lot until they finally found a ford near what is now the Wahweap Marina on Lake Powell. That spot, now called the Crossing of the Fathers, lies these days beneath the lake's Padre Bay. An historical marker at Milepost 599 on 89A tells you this is part of the route.

Still on 89A, still in the Arizona Strip, the road runs past a couple of lodges, a field of giant boulders including one tiny home built into one of the boulders, and then begins a slow climb through a deep (but not high) mountain range of the

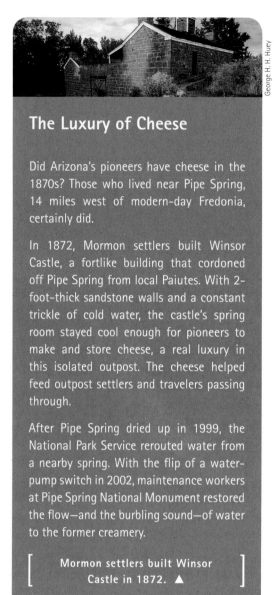

George H. H. Huey

The Luxury of Cheese

Did Arizona's pioneers have cheese in the 1870s? Those who lived near Pipe Spring, 14 miles west of modern-day Fredonia, certainly did.

In 1872, Mormon settlers built Winsor Castle, a fortlike building that cordoned off Pipe Spring from local Paiutes. With 2-foot-thick sandstone walls and a constant trickle of cold water, the castle's spring room stayed cool enough for pioneers to make and store cheese, a real luxury in this isolated outpost. The cheese helped feed outpost settlers and travelers passing through.

After Pipe Spring dried up in 1999, the National Park Service rerouted water from a nearby spring. With the flip of a water-pump switch in 2002, maintenance workers at Pipe Spring National Monument restored the flow—and the burbling sound—of water to the former creamery.

[Mormon settlers built Winsor
Castle in 1872. ▲]

Kaibab Plateau. About 12 miles before Jacob Lake, the desert terrain begins to take on the familiar look of piñon and juniper and eventually ponderosa pine as the road turns into a mountain route. This is a drive that should be taken in any season except winter, because the snows will obscure some of the beauty, because some of the roads will be impassable, and because most of the facilities will be closed.

A dozen more miles and the tiny community of Jacob Lake appears at the intersection of 89A and State Route 67. The latter highway is the officially scenic Kaibab Plateau-North Rim Parkway leading to the North Rim of the Canyon. (See story on Page 234.)

About 9 miles west of Jacob Lake, the highway passes Le Fevre Scenic Outlook on the left. Don't fail to stop here. You'll be rewarded with a great view of the broad Johnson Wash and the reddish Shinarump Cliffs, and the Vermilion Cliffs.

Some 21 miles farther along 89A is Fredonia, founded in 1885. Today's population hovers a little more than 1,000 people, enough to make it the Arizona Strip's largest community. It was settled by Mormon polygamists, who named it Hardscrabble, later changed to Fredonia. There is some speculation that the new name was a combination of "freedom" and "dona," the latter word translating roughly from the Spanish as "woman" or, very loosely, "wife." Polygamists, women, freedom. Got it. Very clever. Anyway, Today, Fredonia offers a sprinkling of motels, a gas station, a few restaurants, a community college, some closeted polygamists, and the main reason to drive this far: routes to Pipe Spring National Monument and Toroweap (see pages 230 and 233). It also is the gateway for a quick run into Utah and the community of Kanab. ᴀ🄷

Kaibab Plateau–North Rim Scenic Parkway

Route	State Route 67 from Jacob Lake to the North Rim of Grand Canyon National Park.
Mileage	45 miles.
Time to allow	One day minimum.
Elevation	Approximately 8,000 feet at Jacob Lake to 9,000-plus feet.
Overview	If you drove on the Fredonia-Vermilion Cliffs Scenic Road (U.S. Route 89A), you passed the start of the Kaibab drive, officially designated as an Arizona Parkway and a National Scenic Byway in the heart of the Kaibab Plateau. The drive leads to the North Rim of the Grand Canyon. Because of snow, the parkway can be driven only in late spring, summer, or early fall.

F or those who prefer a view of the Grand Canyon unobstructed by a forest of shoulders and legs, ignore the famous advice of Horace Greeley to go west. Instead, go north. That's north as in the North Rim of the Canyon, starting at the community of Jacob Lake.

Before leaving Jacob Lake, stop in the Kaibab Plateau Visitors Center on the west side of the highway and ask for directions to Rim viewpoints outside Grand Canyon National Park's North Rim. They are not difficult to reach and offer views into the Canyon with even fewer people then you'll find in the park. This side trip will be on graded gravel or dirt roads.

From Jacob Lake, go south for 45 miles on State 67. That's as far as you can drive, to the parking lot of the historic Grand Canyon Lodge perched right on the North Rim. Along the way, be on the lookout for Forest Service interpretive signs explaining the terrain and wildlife. If you do, you'll qualify as an insider by the time you reach the park.

People who live in this state generally think the North Rim is at least equal and probably superior in beauty to the far more popular and accessible (particularly in winter) South Rim. Getting there is part of the pleasure, so we'll talk a bit about that.

Jacob Lake was named for a 19th-century Mormon settler named Jacob Hamblin. There isn't much to this settlement except wonderful smells coming from the tall pines and spruce and fir and aspens flexing in the winds at this 8,000-foot elevation and other, enticing odors issuing from the kitchen exhaust vents of Jacob Lake Inn with its satisfying dining room and snack bar. The inn complex also includes motel rooms in individual cabins, a gift shop, and a service station. Outside are the Kaibab squirrels, semi-famous for the tufts of long hair on their ears and the white plumes that serve as their tails. They are found only on the Kaibab Plateau and only in ponderosa pine areas.

The inn is open all winter, as is U.S. 89A that runs past it. Other facilities along State 67, including the big lodge at the North Rim, are closed in the snowy months.

[Autumn gives a golden dressing to the Grand Canyon's North Rim.]

David Muench

The journey south from Jacob Lake to the Rim begins in alpine forest and reaches an elevation of nearly 9,000 feet, but it quickly emerges from the woods and into a large, flat, treeless area of grassy, high plains. It continues for several miles alternating between meadows and woodlands. About 25 miles south of Jacob Lake is a country store with gasoline and Kaibab Lodge. Shortly thereafter, you leave the Kaibab National Forest and enter the Grand Canyon National Park, with primitive camping 12 miles farther down the road. Wildlife in the area, including mule deer, elk, and bears, can sometimes be seen from the paved road leading through their homelands.

The easy, pretty drive ends at the Grand Canyon Lodge, which had to be rebuilt in 1937 after a fire. The big stone-and-wood structure offers the usual amenities for visitors but is notable particularly for its immense lobby and for its terrace that affords guests a wonderful place to sit and look.

The views are spectacular, and there are several self-guided trails to railed overlooks offering sweeping looks into the mile-deep Canyon with its changing colors and its endless array of buttes and spires. One short walk leads to Bright Angel Point, one of the best ways to stare into the awesome chasm. For those with packs and strong legs, the North Kaibab Trail leads to the Canyon bottom. It's a long, tough climb back up, but some hardy hikers even manage to go rim to rim.

Mark Larson

[Light pours into the Grand Canyon from the Cape Royal Overlook.   ]

The season at the North Rim generally stretches from about mid-May to mid-October, and although the crowds are far smaller and the development less obvious, reservations for overnight (or longer) stays, even in the campground, must be made well in advance, sometimes by as much as six months. (See Where to Go for details.)

Branching off State 67, there are lesser but paved roads leading to views rivaling those available anywhere else along the North Rim, with the possible exception of Toroweap. Arguably, the best of those is the Cape Royal Scenic Drive (look for the turnoff about 3 miles north of Grand Canyon Lodge) leading to Point Imperial, to Cape Royal, and, via a lovely half-mile hiking trail, a 50-foot-high natural arch in the sandstone that is called Angel's Window and that affords a dramatic look at the Colorado River far below.

This Cape Royal side road forks early on, with the left fork leading 8 miles to Point Imperial, the right fork 23 miles to Cape Royal. Take both and stop at all viewpoints; they are worth it. Royal has trailheads, but the trails are not for some great-granddads except those who reached that iconic status by age 60 or so. However, it is near here that the great-grandanybody-friendly trail to Angel's Window arch begins.

At 8,445 feet, Imperial is the highest vantage point from either South or North Rim. The Vermilion Cliffs are visible to the north, the rounded dome of Navajo Mountain to the northeast, the Painted Desert east. Cape Royal yields a view of the San Francisco Peaks to the distant south. ⚘

Where To Go
What To See
What To Do

Kerrick James

These listings include the South and North rims of the Grand Canyon, Cameron, Fredonia, the Havasupai and Hualapai Indian tribes, Page, Pipe Spring, and Williams. In addition to the Internet sites listed below, these sites will help you become more familiar with the Canyon's history: www.kaibab. org and www.grandcanyon.org (the Grand Canyon Association).

GRAND CANYON

South Rim

Information: The South Rim is open 24 hours a day, every day. When you enter the park, you will receive a park map and booklets with park information. While there are many Internet sites with Grand Canyon information, we suggest you begin with the following sites to help you plan a trip and bone up on the Canyon's natural history and history of people and events. Grand Canyon National Park, (928) 638-7888; Grand Canyon Chamber of Commerce, (888) 472-2696; (928) 638-2901. www.nps.gov/grca; www.grandcanyonchamber.org; www.kaibab.org

National Geographic Visitors Center/IMAX Theater: Obtain extensive information about the Grand Canyon and activities there. Express pay the park admission at the official pay station. Watch the giant IMAX movie on the Canyon that shows hourly every day of the year. In Tusayan, on State 64 just 2 miles south of the park entrance. (928) 638-2468. www.explorethecanyon.com

Canyon View Information Plaza: Located near Mather Point about 3 miles from the south entrance. An excellent place to begin a Canyon visit and receive an overview of park geography and recreational options. Rangers and outdoor and indoor exhibits provide information on topics such as ranger-guided activities, shuttle buses to viewpoints, day hikes along the Rim Trail or into the Canyon, bicycling, weather, and park attractions. www.nps.gov/grca/matherpt/index.htm

Grand Canyon Field Institute: A program of the Grand Canyon Association, the institute offers guided tours at Grand Canyon National Park led by expert instructors. Activities include backpacking, camping, hiking, and

[Rafters reap thrills at Sockdolager Rapid in the Grand Canyon. ▲   ]

whitewater rafting. Topics include geology, ecology, archaeology, history, and photography. $. (866) 471-4435; (928) 638-2485. www.grandcanyon.org/fieldinstitute

In-park lodging: Reservations for historic El Tovar Hotel and other lodges in the park and Phantom Ranch at the Canyon's bottom are handled by Xanterra Parks & Resorts. Reserve months in advance. $. (303) 297-2757; (888) 297-2757. www.grandcanyonlodges.com

Near-park lodging: A variety of lodging is available in Tusayan, at the park's southern entrance; Williams, about 60 miles south of the park; and Flagstaff, about 85 miles southeast of the park. For Tusayan information: (928) 638-2901, (888) 472-2696. www.grandcanyonchamber.org. For Williams: (800) 863-0546; (928) 635-1418. www.williamschamber.com. For Flagstaff: (928) 774-9541; (800) 842-7293. www.flagstaffarizona.org

Mule trips: Arranged through Grand Canyon National Park Lodges. One-day and overnight trips to Phantom Ranch at the Canyon's bottom. Mule trips fill up quickly and may be booked 11 months in advance. $. (303) 297-2757; (888) 297-2757. www.grandcanyonlodges.com/Mule-Rides-426.html

River boating and rafting: A number of river runners ferry visitors through the Canyon in rafts, dories, and other vessels during the April to October season. Trips run from three to 21 days. Make reservations well in advance. The park lists guidelines and concessionaires at www.nps.gov/grca/river. Also, the Hualapai Indian tribe offers trips. $. (928) 769-2216. www.grandcanyonresort.com

In-park camping: Two campgrounds and an RV park are located in the park. Mather Campground, open all year, is in Grand Canyon Village and offers tent and RV camping without hookups. Reservations recommended for March through November. Other times, sites are available on a first-come, first-serve basis. $. (800) 365-2267; (301) 722-1257. http://reservations.nps.gov. Desert View Campground is open mid-May through mid-October; on the park's eastern edge, about 26 miles from the village. Offering RV sites with hookups, Trailer Village is next to Mather Campground. (888) 297-2757 for advance reservations; (928) 638-2631 for same-day reservations.

Near-park camping: The Kaibab National Forest operates Ten X campground about 2 miles south of Tusayan off State 64. $. (928) 638-2443. www.fs.fed.us/r3/kai. A commercial campground, Camper Village, is located off State 64 about 7 miles south of Grand Canyon Village. $. (928) 638-2887.

Tusayan Ruin and Museum: An Indian ruin dating from 1185 A.D. and the adjacent museum hint at the way of life of a people referred to as Puebloan. Walk the ruin on your own or take a ranger-guided tour. Free. Located on the

South Rim's Desert View Drive (State 64) just west of the Desert View entrance. Free. (928) 638-7968. www.nps.gov/grca

Tusayan Ranger District: Hiking and camping information in the Kaibab National Forest. State 64, Tusayan. (928) 638-2443. www.fs.fed.us/r3/kai

Grand Canyon Backcountry Information Center: Get your permits and information here for hiking and camping down in the Canyon. Permits are granted only to requests by fax, mail, or in person. $. (928) 638-7875; (928) 638-7888. Fax, (928) 638-2125. Mail to Backcountry Office, Grand Canyon National Park, P.O. Box 129, Grand Canyon, AZ 86023.

Air Tours: There's nothing like seeing the Grand Canyon from the air, and helicopter and fixed-wing tours are available. $. Check with a travel agent or call the Grand Canyon Chamber of Commerce, (888) 472-2696 or (928) 638-2901, www.grandcanyonchamber.org; the National Geographic Visitor Center, air tours reservations, (928) 638-1144. www.papillon.com.

North Rim

Grand Canyon National Park/North Rim: Open about mid-May through mid-October, when snows usually close the highway to the North Rim. Most of the park's visitor facilities are closed in winter, although day use is possible when snowfall permits. North Rim Visitors Center, (928) 638-7864. General Canyon information, including weather information, (928) 638-7888. Campground reservations, (800) 365-2267.

In-park Lodging: Reservations for historic Grand Canyon Lodge are handled by Xanterra Parks & Resorts. Reserve months in advance. $. (303) 297-2757; (888) 297-2757. www.grandcanyonnorthrim.com

Near-park Lodging: Kaibab Lodge has cabins and a restaurant across the highway from a small general store and gas station. $. About 26 miles south of Jacob Lake on State 67. In season, (928) 638-2389; year-round, (928) 526-0924; (800) 525-0924.

In-park Camping: The North Rim Campground, located in the park, is open from mid-May to mid-October. Laundry and showers, for a fee, are nearby. Reservations are required, up to five months ahead. $. Online reservations can be made at http://reservations.nps.gov. Or call Spherix, (800) 365-2267; outside the United States, call (301) 722-1257.

Grand Canyon Backcountry Information Center: Get your permits and information here for hiking and camping down in the Canyon. Permits are granted only to requests by fax, mail, or in person. North Rim ranger station, (928) 638-7868. Main line, (928) 638-7875; (928) 638-7888.

Fax, (928) 638-2125. Mail to Backcountry Office, Grand Canyon National Park, P.O. Box 129, Grand Canyon, AZ 86023.

Near-park Camping: Camping is available outside the park on a seasonal basis. De Motte Park Campground is run by the Kaibab National Forest and is open early June to late September. $. It lies 25 miles south of Jacob Lake off State 67 and 7 miles north of the park's North Rim entrance. Dispersed camping also is available in the national forest. North Kaibab Ranger District, (928) 643-7395. www.fs.fed.us/r3/kai

Mule Trips: Mule trips are available from the North Rim (one-day and half-day trips) but do not go all the way to the river. Call Grand Canyon Trail Rides for reservations, (435) 679-8665, or write to P.O. Box 128, Tropic, Utah, 84776, or visit online www.onlinepages.net/conyonrides.

Cameron

Cameron Trading Post: Next to the Little Colorado River on U.S. 89. Motel, restaurant, stores, post office, service station, RV facilities. (928) 679-2231; (800) 338-7285.

Fredonia

Fredonia Chamber of Commerce: (928) 643-7241.

North Kaibab Ranger District: Information on hiking and camping in the Kaibab National Forest, including the Kaibab Plateau. (928) 643-7395. www.fs.fed.us/r3/kai

Havasupai Tribe

Havasupai Indian Reservation: The reservation lies in a large tributary canyon on the south side of the Colorado River, outside the boundary and jurisdiction of the National Park Service. Havasu Creek flows through the canyon and spills over four waterfalls before emptying into the Colorado River. The most spectacular of the falls—Havasu—drops in twin streams for about 120 feet into blue-green pools formed by minerals contained in the water. The falls and village of Supai can be reached only by an 8-mile hike or horse ride. Hiking is by tribal permit only. The tribe also manages a lodge in Supai, if you don't want to camp out. Permits and reservations available from Havasupai Tourist Enterprises, P.O. Box 160, Supai, Arizona 86435; (928) 448-2141. Lodge: (928) 448-2121. www.havasupaitribe.com; www.kaibab.org/supai/gc_supai.htm; www.public.asu.edu/~hbalasu/havasu.htm

Hualapai Tribe

Hualapai Indian Reservation: Grand Canyon West (on the south side of the Colorado River) is managed by the Hualapai Tribe. This land lies outside the boundary and jurisdiction of the National Park Service. The tribe operates a river-running outfitting service and a lodge in Peach Springs. It also operates or licenses motor and air tours of the Canyon below Peach Springs and of the Canyon's western end. (928) 769-2216. www.grandcanyonresort.com

Jacob Lake

Kaibab Plateau Visitors Center: For maps and trail, camping, and permit information for areas along the North Rim, this National Forest Service center is the answer. Open seasonally. (928) 643-7298. www.fs.fed.us/r3/kai

Jacob Lake Inn: Restaurant and lodging at the junction of State 67 and U.S. 89 and 89A. Jacob Lake. (928) 643-7232.

Camping: Run by the National Forest Service, Jacob Lake Campground is 45 miles north of the North Rim entrance. Open summers only, it does not have hookups and does not take reservations. $. (928) 643-7395. www.fs.fed. us/r3/kai/ On State 67, Kaibab Camper Village is a commercial campground in Jacob Lake that offers full hookups. In season, (928) 643-7894; off season, (928) 526-0924; outside Arizona, (800) 525-0924.

Page

Page-Lake Powell Chamber of Commerce: Information on local sights and services, tour bookings for lake and river tours, scenic flights, etc. (928) 645-2741. www.pagelakepowellchamber.org

Lake Powell Resorts and Marinas: Cruises, houseboat and powerboat rentals, accommodations. (928) 645-1150; (800) 528-6154. www.lakepowell.com

Glen Canyon National Recreation Area: The park is open for fishing, boating, boat camping, water-based recreation, summer ranger programs, full-day tours to Rainbow Bridge, four-wheeling on some of the park's back roads, backpacking in the Escalante or Orange Cliffs, exploring the lake's numerous side canyons by boat. Reservations highly advisable for the half- and full-day tours to Rainbow Bridge. Information: Carl Hayden Visitors Center in Page, (928) 608-6404; Bullfrog Visitors Center in Utah, (435) 684-7400; Lee's Ferry Ranger Station, (928) 355-2234. www.nps.gov/glca

John Wesley Powell Memorial Museum: Worth a visit for an interesting introduction to the first exploration of the Colorado River and the history of the area. Also serves as visitors information center and reservation agent for river and lake trips, scenic flights, and tours of Antelope Canyon. Closed weekends. $. Located at 6 N. Lake Powell Blvd. (928) 645-9496. www.powellmuseum.org

Antelope Canyon: The Navajo Nation and several Page companies offer tours of this red sandstone slot canyon and the surrounding area. Check with the Page-Lake Powell Chamber of Commerce (listed above).

Pipe Spring

Pipe Spring National Monument: (see Sidebar) $. (928) 643-7105. www.nps.gov/pisp

Williams

Williams Chamber of Commerce: (800) 863-0546. www.williamschamber.com

Williams Visitors Center: Jointly run by the Williams Chamber of Commerce and the Kaibab National Forest. Information is available on the local Williams area, the national forest, the Grand Canyon National Park, and northern Arizona. 200 W. Railroad Ave., Williams. (928) 635-1418. www.fs.fed.us/r3/kai/visit/visit.html

Rendezvous Days: Annual heritage festival that includes black-powder gun shoot and competition, a parade, live entertainment, crafts, food. Memorial Day weekend. Free. Downtown Williams. (800) 863-0546. www.williamschamber.com

Grand Canyon Railway: Departing from the historic Williams depot, the train chugs along to the Grand Canyon National Park. A museum, restaurant, hotel, RV park, and gift shop. $. 233 N. Grand Canyon Blvd. (800) 843-8724. www.thetrain.com

Elk Ridge Ski and Outdoor Recreation Area: Skiing, tubing, and snowboarding along seven trails. Activities such as horseback riding take place in warmer months. Lodging and rentals available. Thursdays are designated as ski-only days. $. 418 W. Franklin. (928) 234-6587. www.elkridgeski.com

Grand Canyon Deer Farm: A petting zoo with several types of deer, wallabies, pygmy goats, llamas, pronghorn antelope, and marmosets. Gift shop. Hours vary. $. 6752 E. Deer Farm Road. Off Interstate 40 at Exit 171, about 24 miles west of Flagstaff and 8 miles east of Williams. (928) 635-4073; (800) 926-3337. www.deerfarm.com

A soaptree yucca flowers near Bell Rock. ▲
Prescott treasures the Hassayampa Inn as a historical landmark. ▶

Up North
Flagstaff, Sedona, Prescott, and the Verde Valley

Heading north up the Interstate 17 corridor from Phoenix, the traveler moves out of the Sonoran Desert into higher country and finally the high country. Take note of the terrain as you pass Black Canyon City in the vicinity of Milepost 244. The freeway starts climbing smartly, and then it passes through a cut in the mountain. Before the cut, you're in desert land. As you come out the other end, you're in high plains, not far from a major Arizona valley, the Red Rock Country, and mountainous communities. Up here, the principal regions are Flagstaff, Sedona, Prescott, and the Verde Valley.

Robert G. McDonald

Chuck Lawsen

Northern Stars

B efore heading roughly north to and into the Grand Canyon as most travelers do, there are two suns, plus their attending small planets, in the north-central chunk of the state that keep people from driving directly from Phoenix to Arizona's biggest chasm: They are vibrant Flagstaff and its smaller, plusher, neighbor to the south, Sedona.

We will start in Flag, as it is commonly known, at 7,000 feet the urban handmaiden to the Grand Canyon. Big trees. Big vistas. Big mountains. Big university. Big history. Little-town feel.

No, a river does not run through it, but historic old Route 66 (or what is left of it) does. And there is an undeniable stream of vitality that courses through this old logging, ranching, and mining town that, over time, has become a cosmopolitan city offering a substantial industrial complex, plenty of frontier history, enticing theater, museums, art galleries, a historic downtown district, an 85-member symphony orchestra, Northern Arizona University, motels, and an epicurean abundance of restaurants.

One of the drives detailed in this chapter, the San Francisco Peaks Scenic Road, runs northwest on U.S. Route 180 past the peaks to just before the miniscule community of Valle, which probably should be pronounced "VAH yay" but more often is said simply "Valley" or even "Vail." We won't be there long enough to worry about it. From Valle, we will take State Route 64 to the South Rim of the Grand Canyon, then east to Cameron. At that point, the driver can return on U.S. Route 89 to Flagstaff ... or head for the Canyon.

There are many magnetic attractions in Flag, among them the splendid Museum of Northern Arizona, 3 miles north of the downtown on U.S. Route 180 (North Fort Valley Road), and the Lowell Observatory, 1 mile west of the downtown. The museum is mainly housed in a sturdy, attractive building, major parts of which were constructed of cinder block walls covered with basalt stone in 1935. It offers many permanent exhibits including the geology of the area, histories of the various Indian tribes, a dinosaur display, a bookstore, a fine gift shop featuring quality Indian jewelry and crafts, and, a changing extensive special exhibit.

The museum offers a regular series of lectures on such subjects as the Colorado Plateau's volcanoes, the Colorado River, the geology of the Grand Canyon, the mysterious disappearance of Glen and Bessie Hyde during their 1928 honeymoon trip through the Canyon, and on and on.

Just outside the heavy, old front door of this fine museum is the Rio de Flag Nature Trail beginning at a flagpole and following the rim of a small canyon

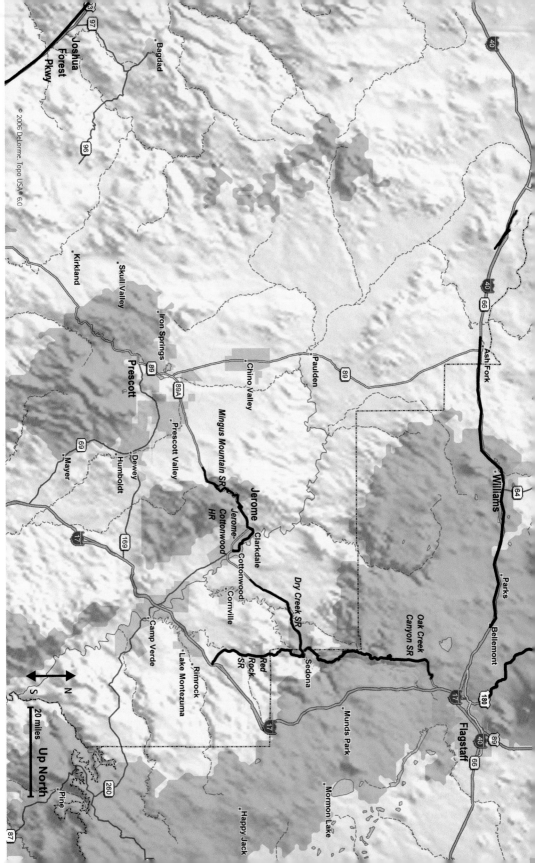

east, then descending on rock steps to the canyon floor leading to completion of a loop. Total distance: a half-mile and worth every bit of the modest time and effort expended. Unlike descending and ascending the Grand Canyon, it's easy to do this one on flabby thighs, sore feet, inappropriate shoes, and a couple of sips of water and still get back in time for lunch and supper.

Not far away, at 1400 W. Mars Hill Road, is the Lowell Observatory, one of the world's largest, privately operated, non-profit, research observatories. (And yes, it might as well be called West Pluto Road inasmuch as an astronomer assistant named Clyde Tombaugh made the first recognized sighting of Pluto while working at the observatory in February of 1930.) The observatory was founded in 1894 by Percival Lowell, who made the famous discovery of some linear features that he thought were the "canals," or artificial waterways, of Mars, which he interpreted as meaning the planet was or had been inhabited. Today, most everybody with any scientific credentials is sure now that he was wrong with the caveat that the planet once apparently had a lot of water.

But even if Pluto is not a planet (as is now debated) and Mars is not inhabited, the observatory complex can still claim many significant contributions to astronomy, including spectroscopic photographs by Y.M. Slipher that contributed mightily to the finding of an ever-expanding universe. Add to that this: Percival's first assistant astronomer, A.E. Douglass, was a pioneer of dendrochronology, the study of tree-ring dating.

Available to visitors: Daily tours, excellent visitor center exhibits, a planetary slide show, lectures, nighttime telescopic viewing, a scale model of the solar system and the inevitable gift shop. Outside, by the way, is the George Washington Tree, a ponderosa pine that started growing in 1732, the birth year of the guy with the lousy false teeth who decorates our dollar bills. **AH**

[The Archaeology Gallery at the Museum of Northern Arizona in Flagstaff exhibits artifacts of Native American culture.]

David H. Smith

Sedona-Oak Creek Canyon Scenic Road

Route	State Route 89A from Sedona north toward Flagstaff.
Mileage	30 miles from Sedona to end of official route and back to Sedona.
Time to Allow	Two hours.
Elevation	4,300 to 7,000 feet.
Overview	A quick trip through eight plant life zones, lots of splendid views down into the canyon, diversions including swimming and fishing for the young-at-heart, big and close cliffs on both sides of the road at the start. Fast, scenic way to Flagstaff from Sedona.

For those who entered Sedona from the south on State Route 179 or the southwest (State Route 89A from Prescott), and who have lingered there to empty their wallets and fill their stomachs, there's another direction to take that is a cinch to further sate the senses: north.

As it passes through Sedona aiming north toward Flagstaff, State 89A gets a new, official name, the Sedona-Oak Creek Canyon Scenic Road. It runs on a hairpin-curved, paved lane along Oak Creek, up through the beautiful, heavily vegetated Oak Creek Canyon, and onto a flat stretch of alpine forest and officially ends well short of Flag, as that city is commonly called by locals.

Though neither quite as amazing nor even remotely as rugged as the nearby Schnebly Hill Road, this route offers its own dramatic views and some things to do along the way.

It starts to climb dramatically just on the outskirts of Sedona with views of immense cliffs and drop-offs and then enters a forest canopy with the surrounding mountains closing in, narrowing the views.

First thing to do: Stop at Grasshopper Point just beyond Milepost 376, pay the vehicle fee, and hike a short trail to a small but relatively deep pool formed in a bend of the creek where you can swim under some overhanging cliffs. Next up along the road is Rainbow Trout Farm where even non-fisherpeople can catch a trout—for a price. A cane pole with cork bobber and the opportunity to cast some dough bait into the small, circular pond is likely to get your children a rainbow trout ranging from 8 to 30 inches. Cost of the fish and the fishing pole varies with the size of the fish. You also can assemble your own $400 Sage fly rod and flip out a fly, but that seems a bit like overkill. Fishing on public property along the creek also is permitted, but get a license if you want a rainbow in your pocket.

Finally, pull into Slide Rock State Park, fork over a modest fee for a carload, and in good weather prepare to get wet, at least your feet. If traveling in winter, bring a camera and skip the bathing suit. The ice formations are great for pictures, ghastly wading.

Slide Rock was originally a 43-acre homestead and apple farm created by Frank Pendley who came to the canyon in 1907 and planted his first apple orchard four years later. He also built some rustic cabins and catered to a giant-to-be busi-

Kerrick James

ness, tourism. The park property was purchased by the state of Arizona in 1985 and entered the list of the National Register of Historic Places in 1991. Once upon a time, it was possible to park along the road, climb down and slide into Oak Creek. Not now, not until you enter on a short side road, pay the fee, and park.

The park is named for famous Slide Rock, which is a short stretch of slippery, smooth rock in the shallow, 10- to 15-foot wide creek, a sort of gentle water chute created by Nature just so children and mildly adventurous adults can slide on their posteriors down the creek, bask in the sun, or just wade in the cool current. The park also offers other entertainments including outdoor grills, birdwatching, fishing, a nature trail, and, in season, apples (but do not pick your own).

Like Monument Valley, the park, the canyon, and the surrounding area have been the settings for many Hollywood Westerns, including *Broken Arrow* (starring the lanky James Stewart, 1950), *Drum Beat* (the quite short Alan Ladd and the very muscular Charles Bronson, 1954) and *Gun Fury* (the ever-lovely Rock Hudson and Donna Reed, 1953).

From there, this drive continues on up the canyon past numerous U.S. Forest Service campgrounds, a few homes and small businesses including a couple of restaurants and lodges tucked back in the trees, and hiking trails. It officially ends near a scenic viewpoint with parking at about Milepost 390 near the top of the Mogollon Rim and still roughly 15 miles from Flagstaff. At that point, the traveler can turn around and return to Sedona or motor on to Flagstaff and Interstate 40's mindless, high-speed access to Los Angeles or Chicago.

Best time to go: spring with its wildflowers and warming sun or fall with its vivid colors. Winter can mean snow and ice, summer definitely means tourists by the thousands. If you aren't sure what a tourist looks like, check your rearview mirror. Good-lookin' bunch, huh? ⋀

Schnebly Hill Road

Z owie, wowie, as a former, slightly off-center newspaper colleague was wont to say during times of excitement generated by anything from a poker game to a good kill shot during a racquetball match.

That's Schnebly Hill Road. Monument Valley with altitude. It is a zowie-wowie, but not officially scenic nor historic drive. The western end leaves State Route 179 less than a mile south of State Route 89A in Sedona, just below Tlaquepaque. The 13-mile, unpaved road heads generally east through, among, and atop the cliffs of the Mogollon Rim until it connects with Exit 320 on Interstate 17, which heads north to Flagstaff and south to Phoenix.

Named after the Schnebly family that settled the Sedona area—and Sedona was named after Sedona Schnebly—the road is a macho version of the paved Sedona-Oak Creek Canyon Scenic Road. It is wise to heed the sign near the start that says "Passenger Cars Not Recommended." The first 5 miles of passage are very rutted, more washboarded than six-pack abs, and very rocky.

Waders walk up Slide Rock to then rocket down its slippery slopes. ◄ The setting sun glints on a rock spire overlooking Sedona from Schnebly Hill Road. ▼

Chuck Lawsen

Have good tires, high undercarriage clearance, and the patience to drive no more than 5 or 10 miles an hour. Four-wheel-drive is not necessary, but taking a sedan or a big RV with low clearance would not be sensible. The last 6 miles to the freeway are, comparatively, a pussycat of a drive along good gravel.

The road's virtue is that it places the traveler in intimate contact with the spires, buttes, and cliffs of the red rock mountains that abut Sedona. The views ahead and behind are unbeaten in this state. At Schnebly Hill Vista, there is no need to go on the remaining 6 miles to the freeway unless you simply enjoy a mild, alpine drive or you would rather not face the return down hill to Sedona. ▯

Red Rock Scenic Road

Route	State Route 179 from Interstate 17 Exit 298 to Sedona.
Mileage	15 miles, interstate exit to Sedona.
Time to Allow	An hour, if in a hurry.
Elevation	About 4,200 feet.
Overview	This Arizona Scenic Road is designated as an All-American Road. Approaching Sedona from the south, the road makes its way among cliffs and sandstone sculptures that label the area Red Rock Country and draw New Agers and other seekers from throughout the world; this is an architectural and polychrome amazement of a drive.

A bsent one-way street signs, roads go both ways. And so it is with State Route 179, the Red Rock Scenic Road that leads from Interstate 17 into Sedona or, conversely, from Sedona to the interstate.

The reason for belaboring that obvious fact is that the traveler needs to know whether he or she prefers instant or delayed gratification. Translation: If you are in Sedona already and want to take State Route 179 south to the freeway, you will be immediately immersed in the glories of the red rocks that dominate Sedona. If, on the other hand, you are on Interstate 17 and take Exit 298 north to Sedona, it will mean several bends of the road and even several miles before you see much of those rocks.

Such a pleasant dilemma. However, for purposes of this discussion of what you will see out your windshield, we will take the latter course heading off the freeway and toward the town.

Before that happens, however, while driving north on Interstate 17 away from Phoenix, take Exit 289 east off the freeway and head along a delightful route for Montezuma Castle National Monument featuring an ancient cliff dwelling called Montezuma Castle and a nearby sinkhole full of water named Montezuma Well.

Randy Prentice

Hook 'Em and Cook 'Em

Fishing becomes a family activity at the Rainbow Trout Farm, 4 miles north of Sedona in Oak Creek Canyon. A nominal fee takes the place of a fishing license and includes equipment. Once you catch your fish, the bigger the fish, the higher the fee. For a small additional fee, the farm's crew cleans your catch and packs it in crushed ice. Propane grills and shaded picnic tables encourage cooks to prepare meals on the spot. The farm sells the unprepared grill kits, complete with seasonings, forks, and aluminum foil.

The Rainbow Trout Farm is at 3500 N. State Route 89A. Open daily all year, its hours vary. Information: (928) 282-5799.

[Fishing for a fee let's you have fun and eat your catch without the work of cleaning and cooking. ▲]

Somewhere around the 12th century, the Sinagua Indians lived in this area of the Verde Valley and, like many of the tourists of today, decided to stay. They farmed, hunted, and built homes.

It's quite a home, a towering cliff dwelling, several now-fragile stories of stone and mortar lodged under a cliff's sheltering overhang above Beaver Creek and boasting dozens of rooms. A second ruin, even bigger once upon a time, is at the bottom of the cliff. Overheard, this query from a senior citizen speaking to a woman, presumably his spouse: "Now, do I understand that they really built this?" An illogical question but an understandable one when you are standing below this splendid example of aboriginal architecture.

About 11 miles northeast of the so-called castle, and reached off Exit 293, is Montezuma Well, a sinkhole that is nearly 500 feet across and partly filled with water from the accompanying, 55-foot-deep lake. Both attractions offer visitor and picnic facilities. The monument has a visitor center.

One could reasonably ask: Why Montezuma's anything? It was a mistake committed, depending on which of several historical sources one consults, by either early settlers or U.S. Army scouts in the 1860s who apparently were persuaded that the castle was created by Mexico's Aztec emperor. It wasn't and he didn't. In fact, old Montezuma, who died in 1520 at age 54, wasn't even born until around the time the castle was abandoned and, as best anyone knows, never got anywhere near Arizona.

Back to the freeway and then off again on State Route 179, the Red Rock Scenic Road to Sedona 15 miles away.

This twisting, two-lane, paved highway begins in a terrain dominated by juniper, piñon pines, and grasses and then climbs. In a sense, it resembles another route in this chapter, the Dry Creek Scenic Road, in that its primary attraction is the mountain sculptures of red rock ahead. The beauty and grandeur all the way into Sedona are so apparent that they can be appreciated without your ever leaving the vehicle.

It doesn't take too many bends of the road through attractive, high-desert vegetation and compelling rock outcrops before famous Bell Rock, a vortex referred to elsewhere in this chapter, appears at about Milepost 305, rising out of the red soil of this area and sculpted in a sort of bell shape by wind and water. Next up is Cathedral Rock and, just up the road and just short of Sedona, the Village of Oak Creek, which is a popular retirement community and home to a stack of outlet stores.

Oak Creek reflects Cathedral Rock, glowing crimson at sunset.

Robert G. McDonald

Past Bell Rock, turn right on Chapel Road and travel a short distance to yet another example of man and Nature combining to produce magnificence: the Chapel of the Holy Cross. A wealthy Los Angeles sculptor named Marguerite Brunswig Staude teamed up with some San Francisco architects to create, in 1955-56, this austere yet awesome chapel that somehow manages to stand apart while simultaneously blending into its setting of two sandstone pillars called Twin Buttes. It is an inspiration, religious to believers, architectural to the secular, both to many. It is owned by the Roman Catholic Diocese of Phoenix and, yes, there is a gift shop.

And then get back on the highway until you reach Sedona, the end of this official scenic route and the beginning, at the other end of Sedona, of the Sedona-Oak Creek Canyon Scenic Road. ∰

Dry Creek Scenic Road

Route	State Route 89A.
Mileage	20 to 25 miles, Cottonwood to Sedona, depending on whether one takes the optional Red Rock Loop Road.
Time to Allow	A half-day.
Elevation	Between 3,500 and 4,300 feet.
Overview	A run that gets the tourist to Sedona through high desert and ending in dramatic, red and whitish sandstone and limestone mountains that draw visitors worldwide to this famous town. In Sedona, a world of choice ranging from scenery to shopping to supping. More vortexes than anyone has the energy to visit. Options for the leisurely drivers in no hurry to get to Sedona include Red Rock Loop Road or Dry Creek Road leading to other attractions including cliff dwellings, Boynton Canyon, Fay Canyon Arch, Vultee Arch, and others.

T he Dry Creek Scenic Road is and isn't.

The creek *is* usually dry, but the scenery along the highway *isn't* all that scenic when compared with what was behind and what is ahead. Mostly, it is a pleasant and short hitch from Cottonwood toward the quickly visible red and whitish rock monuments and mountains that encompass the Holy Grail of this area, Sedona.

The route begins in rolling hills about 10 miles out of Cottonwood until it reaches Milepost 363 or so, where the horizon yields its first views of the sandstone castles that await. You can barrel along this high-desert landscape toward Sedona, but you also can turn off just past Milepost 368 and take the Lower Red Rock Loop Road, which leaves State Route 89A, heads through Red Rock State Park with its visitor center and hiking trails, provides wonderful views of the red rock sculptures, and eventually rejoins State 89A at about Milepost 370. A mile farther,

Dry Creek Road can take the traveler to a natural arch called Devil's Bridge and even to the Palatki cliff dwellings and rock art of the Sinaguans.

Back on 89A, you are at the back door of Sedona, a mere 10,000-population town with acres of shopping, miles of towering red rock mountains, hundreds of artists and art galleries, thousands of tourists, the weight of the world in Indian jewelry, countless good restaurants, ample expensive and moderately priced lodging, and piles of books telling you where to find the nearest vortex. Staying on 89A will lead the tourist through the downtown and on to the Oak Creek Canyon Scenic Road and Flagstaff, but that is the next segment of this chapter.

If it is breakfast time, stop well before entering the downtown area at one favorite of the locals, the Coffee Pot Restaurant on 89A where, if you can find parking, you also can find Belgian waffles and huevos rancheros and "101 omelettes" ranging from "plain" and "cheese" through "zucchini, mushroom, spinach" and "smoked salmon and sautéed onion," all modestly priced. The place also makes a fine Tequila Mary.

Next stop farther along but still before downtown is a right turn off 89A onto State Route 179 and, in a couple of hundred yards, Tlaquepaque, the *ne plus ultra* of shopping centers in North America. It is a gorgeous collection of tasteful galleries, 40 or so shops, and several good restaurants set among giant cottonwood and sycamore trees, all housed within a beautifully walled, architectural dream of graceful arches, fountains, shady plazas, and flowered verandas. This landmark since the 1970s is named for a picturesque artists' colony in the Mexican city of Guadalajara and is pronounced with four, not five, syllables. Say *tlock ah POCK ay* or, sometimes, *tlockay-pockay*, but not *tuh lock ah pock ay*.

In December, Tlaquepaque offers a Festival of Lights that involves lighting 6,000 luminarias—traditionally, candles in sand-filled paper sacks, also called farolitos in some other parts of the Southwest and lamentably available in plastic versions—in the courtyards and walkways.

Tlaquepaque was born in 1971 in the Oak Creek floodplain (legal then, not now) by a Nevada developer named Abe Miller and was designed as an 18th-century Spanish Colonial village. It, along with the Chapel of the Holy Cross (discussed in the Red Rock Scenic Road section of this chapter), is one of those man-made creations in the Sedona area that prompted the earlier observation in the introduction that man and Nature can sometimes combine efforts to produce beauty greater than either's individual efforts.

On the other hand, it's distinctly not cheap, so bring your wallet.

So that's breakfast and shopping for today. Let's go back to yesteryear before we continue with the now.

Hundreds of years ago, long before settlers arrived in the Verde Valley in the late 1800s, our sensible predecessors, the Hohokam and the Sinagua Indians, found peaceful Oak Creek and the surrounding soil so hospitable to corn, beans, and squash that they stayed for a time. Centuries later, settlers arrived and, in 1902, the town was founded by a couple of Missouri brothers, Theodore C. and Ellsworth Schnebly. Old T.C. and Ellsworth persuaded the U.S. Postmaster to agree to name the settlement after T.C.'s wife, Sedona Schnebly, a Victorian woman of patrician background but pioneering courage.

Those with a sense of euphony can only be grateful that T.C. selected her first name, not her surname, to adorn the new town. Schnebly, Arizona? Sort of makes the nostrils flare. Bad enough that a spectacular nearby mountain road bears the name.

Leaping ahead by decades to the 1990s, planning began for this at-that-time unincorporated community that straddles two counties. That effort has made considerable progress in bringing some order to this now-sprawling city. Yes, more sewers, to be sure, but that's not nearly as exciting as one other, tiny example: Sedona is the only place in the world where McDonald's agreed to forsake its golden arches for the more compatible color of teal.

These days, there are the ordinances and council people and taxes and all the rest of the bureaucratic panoply of modern cities, but some things never change. Take pink Jeeps, for example. About 45 years ago, an itinerant trumpet player named Don Pratt wandered into the tiny town of Sedona and was earning somewhat of a living with a small band when he decided there was money to be made by offering tourists a trip into the heart of the red rocks in a Jeep, painted pink. (The Jeep, not the rocks.) Some years later, Pratt, a friendly, plain-spoken, unpretentious fellow who, in his later, more opulent years, snorted scornfully when waiters in a pricey restaurant wore white gloves while serving him, parlayed his pink Jeep enterprise profits into land development in the Sedona area and emerged a multi-millionaire. He died a wealthy man in 1995, but his Jeep enterprise continues, rivaled by several other Johnny-come-lately tours in four-wheel-drive vehicles decorated in primary colors. Pratt's original trip: a two-hour, hair-raising, entertaining Broken Arrow tour of the Coconino National Forest and its magnificent red rocks that still wows visitors. It's an easy way to tour this country without a backpack or aching thighs.

But for New Age spiritual seekers, there is far more to Sedona than jeep tours, wealthy retirees, artists, shopkeepers, musicians, and writers. There are, for sale, crystals, Birkenstocks, Kaveesha mystic oil massages, energy balancers, spiritual massage counselors and, at least not yet for sale, the granddad or grandma of all this ... vortices. Or vortexes, if you'd rather.

So, Mom, what's a vortex?

Well, kid, let's pick just one of many texts on the subject, all available in many locations and at many prices throughout this area. One, *The Sedona Vortex Experience*, by Gaia Lamb (the former Gayle Johansen) and Shinan Naom Barclay, a "Shamanic Humorist" who presents lectures and workshops, avers that a vortex is a "spiraling cone or funnel shape of awesome energy."

Sedona, it turns out, is a major power point on this planet, in other words, a vortex or a bunch of them. Turns out you can go to one of these whirling, eddying sources of energy and use Nature's "dynamic healing" to help you "clear, heal, and release old traumas, emotional scars and habituated thought patterns." There are prescribed ways to take advantage of this power of Nature, but first you have to get to a vortex. It's not difficult; There are lots of guides and maps to the various vortexes (or power points), but among the best known are Schnebly Hill Road, the Chapel of the Holy Cross, Coffee Pot Rock, and Bell Rock. At last notice, you could even take an air-conditioned van tour of vortex sites. Check the Yellow Pages.

Testimonials abound for these vortexes. One woman is quoted in the Lamb-Barclay pamphlet as declaring:

"I was driving across country, tired of the freeways ... I got off I-17, took 179 toward Sedona. When I saw Bell Rock I burst into tears. I pulled off the road, walked to the base of that great monolith, fell down, hugged the rocks and kissed the earth. I knew I was home."

One contrarian version of that, again quoted by the fair-minded Mesdames Lamb and Barclay, goes like this: "I sat down on a vortex and haven't been the same since."

In 1987, several thousand New Agers converged on Sedona for a "harmonic convergence" that was supposed to heal the planet. It didn't, but a lot of people who thought it significant that Sedona, spelled backwards, is Anodes (a common electronic contraption that loves electrons) conducted a peaceful festival. It caused no measurable commotion among most townsfolk with the possible exception of at least one widow who worried that the "longhairs" would break into her home.

[The Chapel of the Holy Cross blends into its environment.]

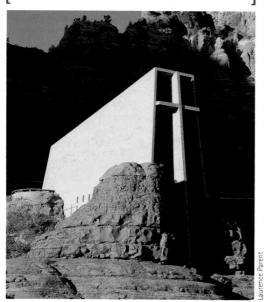

Laurence Parent

They didn't. Either way, whatever your level of credulity, visiting the vortexes is free.

Also free are the views of the famous red rocks, Nature's sculptures named Bell, Cathedral, Coffee Pot, and more, many more.

Take a breath of clean air, take a hike, take a Jeep or helicopter tour, take a break from driving, take a look at the 55-degree reading on the thermometer in January and 78 in October. You'll not see the like of many places like this again in a lifetime. ꬵꞪ

Mingus Mountain Scenic Road

Route	Interstate 17 from Phoenix to State Route 89A. At Exit 262 (Cordes Junction) left (or west) on State Route 69 to Prescott and State Route 89, north on State 89 for 5 miles, right on State 89A.
Mileage	68 miles Phoenix to Cordes Junction, 34 to Prescott, 33 to Jerome.
Time to Allow	Freeway to Jerome, two to three hours depending on stops.
Elevation	Between Prescott and Jerome, 5,300 feet to 7,800 feet.
Overview	A drive of great variety ranging from the easy beauty of pine-forested Prescott through the granite boulders of Granite Dells, up into more forest, followed by immense views of the San Francisco Peaks near Flagstaff and the Verde Valley and, finally, a steep drop into Jerome.

We begin in Phoenix, which we quickly depart after stocking up at an ATM (remember, we are headed for Sedona where you can buy a chair made out of iron straps and slabs of rock for a mere $3,800). We continue 60 miles north up Interstate 17 for the Cordes Junction Exit 262, turn west (that's left) on State Route 69 for Prescott, a charming, progressive, college town of close to 35,000 that, unlike so many other little communities in this area, does not depend on proximity to Sedona for its living or its identity.

But wait. Before that left turn, head right off the interstate and take a 2-mile detour to Arcosanti, a curious architectural work in progress over the last several decades and described as a "prototype arcology."

Say what? Arcology is a term coined by the Italian architect Paolo Soleri, a native of Turin but an Arizona resident since 1956, to describe "the concept of architecture and ecology working as one integral process to produce new urban habitats." When this futuristic, utopian "laboratory" is finished (if ever) it could house 6,000 people in a compact urban structure with large solar greenhouses on

25 acres of this 4,000-acre preserve in a valley called Paradise. In addition to the large structure, some parts completed, others abuilding, there is limited lodging, a café, a bakery, tours, a small but pretty gorge that abuts the project, and galleries offering windbells and wind chimes, Soleri sculptures, graphics, etc. A per person "donation" is suggested for those wishing to tour the project, which is open seven days a week from 9 a.m. to 5 p.m.

Back to the interstate and State Route 69 for 35 miles to Prescott along an attractive drive through little settlements, several times across the tortuous, entomologically named Big Bug Creek, alongside some small, rolling moun-

tains that resemble the topography in Montana or even Scotland and, when sun and clouds alternate, present a marvelous *sol y sombra* pattern. Just before Prescott is Prescott Valley, where an astonishing population of about 24,000 devotees of strip malls and fast food can lose whatever vestige of their minds remains in this abundance of instant gratification.

Richard Maack

Prescott: large town square (or plaza) with massive shade trees, small bandstand, and big bronze sculptures (including one by Solon Borglum, brother of Gutzon Borglum, the man who turned Mount Rushmore into a gallery of stone-faced presidents); Victorian homes; casinos; no downtown parking meters; the aura of a college town (two-year Yavapai College, four-year Prescott College, four-year Embry-Riddle Aeronautical University) such as a Shakespeare Festival in autumn and the café signboard suggesting "it's a perfect day for a banana split," a literary and gustatory twist sufficiently clever that it might even elicit a small smile from the dour and reclusive Mr. Salinger.

This mile-high town, named in 1864 for historian William Hickling Prescott and pronounced something like "press kit" is undeniably beautiful, historic and set among ponderosa pine-forested mountains where daytime summer temperatures usually hover in the 80s, winter in the 50s. It began life as the first Territorial capital of Arizona but lost that designation to Tucson, which then lost it to Phoenix, where it has stayed. In its early days, it also lost, over time, a 400-person chunk of its citizenry to Apaches and acquired a reputation as the place to get a drink, or two or three, at any of some 40 saloons along Montezuma Street, known otherwise as "Whiskey Row."

Among the extensive list of who's who characters who made Prescott their home at one time or another were the Earps, Wyatt and Virgil, and their gambling dentist buddy, John "Doc" Holliday. Virgil and his wife filed a timber claim there in 1878 and began harvesting timber. Wyatt and Holliday came along a year later, accompanied by Doc's girlfriend, the alluringly named "Big Nosed" Kate. Eventually, they all moved on to Tombstone and a 30-second shootout that will last forever in history. Virgil, wounded in the fight, eventually came back to Prescott where he ... raised hogs.

Victorian homes grace Prescott, which has more than 700 buildings listed on the National Register of Historic Places. ◄ Vacationers lounge outside Hotel Vendome. ▼

Kerrick James

There's a little something of just about everything in Prescott including, for the history fanatic with a couple of weeks to spare, three museums and 600 buildings on the National Register of Historic Places. For the urban visitor homesick for the bustle of the metropolis, there's even an almost-impenetrable line of vehicles arriving and departing the city during rush hours.

The problem with Prescott, if it has one, is that it is hard for the traveler to leave it, but leave it we must as we pursue the Mingus Mountain Scenic Road by taking State Route 89 north for about 5 miles, then right at a junction on State Route 89A through some dramatic rockscapes in an area called Granite Dells, a natural art gallery featuring giant boulders, picnic area, hikes, and an abundance of rock climbers who don't seem to mind risking paraplegia for the questionable pleasure of clambering up and over granite formations of Olympian proportions.

At Milepost 332 on State 89A, the official Mingus Mountain route begins its path toward Jerome, which is 33 miles from Prescott and is the start of a second route, the Jerome-Clarkdale-Cottonwood Historic Road.

The Mingus Mountain road climb begins quickly and is a classic version of so many of Arizona's high roads: At nearly every bend in these roads the topography changes—from high-plain prairie to heavy forest, from immense and uninterrupted vistas to narrow canyons, dramatic drop-offs, and rock sculpture. At various points along this particular road there are views of the magnificent Mogollon Rim, which is the southern edge of the Colorado Plateau (look north and up), the Verde Valley (look down) and the San Francisco Peaks near Flagstaff (look for snowcaps during winter).

Along the way, the signs advertise the Mingus Lake Recreation Area and Mingus Lake about 2 miles along a graveled byroad leading off 89A through a canyon. At the end of the 2 miles there is a pond, labeled Mingus Lake Fisheries Enhancement Project. If you fancy looking at some 3-inch trout, stop. Otherwise, turn around and head back to 89A and continue north toward Jerome on a serpentine road that reaches beyond 7,000 feet of elevation.

Mingus Mountain, at 7,743 feet at the top, is in the surrounding Prescott National Forest, and it is along the western slope of that mountain that the scenic route meanders upward through prairie and forest toward Jerome.

This route's end, a descent into still-mountainous Jerome, offers much visual drama. ⫞

[
A biker veers past foliage by Prescott's Granite Basin Lake. ▶
The Douglas Mansion at Jerome State Historic Park. ▼
]

George H. H. Huey

We Call It 'Press-Kit"

First things first. If you don't want to sound like you just fell off a tour bus, you must know that locals pronounce the city's name as "press-kit." Now that you have that down pat, you should be able to fit right in while visiting the charming and historic town that lies a mere 100 miles north of Phoenix and only 216 miles from Tucson.

The author is a graduate of Arizona State University and a veteran of the United States Marine Corps. He currently lives in Wales, with his wife Sara, where he is pursuing a master of arts degree in creative and media writing at the University of Wales Swansea, but he can't wait to get back to Phoenix so he can continue to explore the state.

> By CLINT VAN WINKLE

Kerrick James

Prescott was once the Territorial capital of Arizona and has more than 700 buildings on the National Register of Historic Places. So, history is never more than a stone's throw away. Visitors should begin their visit at Sharlot Hall Museum, the "largest museum in the central territory of Arizona," in order to gain a perspective of the town's rich past.

The Smoki Museum and Phippen Museum also delve into the region's heritage and offer visitors lessons about the area. Between Sharlot, Smoki, and Phippen, newbies will come away with a greater understanding of why Prescott is such a jewel of a city.

However, if museums aren't your thing, there is a truck-full of other activities to enjoy.

At a mile-high, 5,300 feet elevation, Prescott ranks as a haven for desert-dwellers seeking a reprieve from the summer heat. The town's center swarms with escapees there to enjoy the sweet pine tree aroma. Prescott is home to the largest stand of ponderosa pine trees in the world. The town enjoys an average summer temperature of 85 degrees and an average winter temperature of 50 degrees, making it the place to be during the hot summer months. And, taking advantage of the comfortable temperatures amongst the towering pines is easy since nearly 450 miles of multi-purpose trails meander through the region.

So, whether you fancy taking in the natural sights or brushing up on Western history, Prescott is a cool place to be. Ⅷ

Jerome-Clarkdale-Cottonwood Historic Road

Route	State Route 89A.
Mileage	10 to 11 miles.
Time to Allow	At least three hours if spending time in Jerome.
Elevation	5,435 at Jerome.
Overview	A look along a mountainous road at three towns with history, particularly in Jerome, as well as prehistoric Indian ruins and the gorgeous Verde Valley.

P utting personal pride of craft aside, nobody has described the lay of Jerome's land any better than Nell Murbarger, an expert on Western ghost towns. In her Ghosts of the Adobe Walls, she wrote:

On the drafty rump of Mingus Mountain, more than a mile above sea level, the weary old skeleton of Jerome roosts in the sun.

In the gunshot length between her north and south city limits lies an elevation range of more than a quarter mile. To this nearly perpendicular plane cling her houses—stilted and shored and braced and blocked. There are houses whose tenants must climb three flights of stairs to enter their own basements; houses where children at play in their backyards may look down on the roofs of their own dwellings.

This once-tough, now somewhat precious community has shape-shifted from an old mining camp into a ghost town and now into an artists' colony, a tourist must-see, and the southern tail of the big northern dog, Sedona. Jerome has a historic past, a vivid present, and probably a fruitful future uniquely its own. It is also, even though it is merely a continuation along State Route 89A from the previous route, a separate, officially designated trip, the Jerome-Clarkdale-Cottonwood Historic road.

Unlike the exaggerated beauty created by Nature and the white-knuckle roads created by mankind that make so many other official routes in this state compelling odysseys—Kingman to Oatman, Apache Junction to Roosevelt Dam, Oak Creek Canyon, for example—the delights of this short journey between Jerome

George H. H. Huey

Tuzigoot Ruins

Just outside Clarkdale, which is just outside Jerome and just before Cottonwood, are just some fine, prehistoric Indian ruins.

A thousand years ago or so, it was the home of a band of Sinagua Indians, who undoubtedly did not know that their remarkable, hand-built shelter would get this name centuries later from an Apache Indian (it means "crooked water" in Apache).

This village, constructed and occupied somewhere between the years 1000 and 1400 A.D., is on top of a low ridge that is about 120 feet above the fertile Verde Valley. Tuzigoot's population ranged between 50 and perhaps 225 at various times during its existence.

The National Park Service now administers the site, which includes a visitor center located at the start of a hard-surfaced, circular, quarter-mile, wheelchair-accessible hiking trail leading up to and through Tuzigoot's limestone and sandstone masonry ruin. In its heyday, the structure contained 86 ground-floor rooms and possibly 15 second-story rooms. A total of 408 burials have been found. Adults, who seldom lived beyond age 40, were buried in the hillsides with their heads covered by rush matting and bodies wrapped in cotton cloths.

At the top of the structure are excellent views of once-copper-rich Mingus Mountain and its colorful outcrops of argillite, malachite, and azurite.

The Verde Valley, in which Tuzigoot is set, was the home of about 50 major pueblo sites by the year 1300, probably selected because of plentiful pronghorn antelope, deer, and small game roaming the grasslands and the Verde River with fish and turtles and good crop irrigation.

[Sinagua culture indians occupied Tuzigoot for about 400 years. ▲]

and Cottonwood reside largely in the history of the communities that bookend it. For that reason alone it should be—and is—labeled historic rather than scenic.

So, let's first take a bare bones look at the erstwhile ghostly haunt of Jerome.

First to come into this area of the Verde Valley River were, of course, the Indians, in this case two peoples we now call the Sinagua (Spanish for "without water") and the Hohokam (Tohono O'odham for "those who have gone"). The Sinagua left their cultural and architectural footprints some 1,000 years ago in several places around here, most notably the nearby ruins of Tuzigoot. Then came Spanish explorers, followed in 1876 by American prospectors who knew they could transmute copper ore into green paper.

In those days, wherever the potential for big money was discovered on the land, four categories of humans could be expected to come quickly knocking: lawyers, financiers, prostitutes, and con artists.

Say hello to Eugene Jerome, a wealthy New Yorker who embodied two of those professions, law and finance. He also was a cousin of Winston Churchill's mother, for whatever that information is worth. So in the 1880s, Jerome put his money behind a mining operation in the vast copper deposit underneath, and a surveyor who was hired to lay out the town dubbed it Jerome. Eugene, who reportedly never visited this quirky, twisty-roaded community that hangs precariously off the 10- to 25-percent grade of the eastern side of Cleopatra Hill, sold it rock, riflestock, and whiskey barrel in 1888 to another mogul, Montana copper hotdog William Andrews Clark. Clark, whose name decorates the nearby planned community of Clarkdale, built a railroad into the town and sat back on a plush cushion of dividends paid to him by the United Verde Mine during the 1890s.

The mining camp of Jerome prospered into a boomtown, awash in mining money, bordello cash, saloon profits, and gambling IOUs. "The Wickedest Town in America," said one New York newspaper after surveying Jerome's multitude of bars, brothels, and casinos and turning a convenient blind eye to the Big Apple's original sins. This brawling life, further spiced or scandalized by mining deaths, several devastating fires, a jail that slid across the street and down the hill, mudslides, and scarlet fever and smallpox epidemics, went on, in greater or lesser degrees, until 1953 when the mine, about a billion dollars worth of Nature's underground bounty later, finally shut down.

What remained of the boomtown, which once had been the fifth-largest town in the Arizona Territory, turned ghostly after 1953. Remaining were only 50 to 100 diehards, still clutching to their hillside habitat, their low cost-of-living, and their great views. Somewhere around 1970, a modest revival began, propelled by beatniks, artists, writers, musicians, and the retired. Since then, the population of this picturesque and eccentric community has climbed to somewhere around 350.

Despite Jerome's history of big fires, historic buildings remain in abundance, including some museums and the big (really big with 8,000 square feet), white (really white) Douglas Mansion, now administered as the Jerome State Historic Park. It was built in the 1920s by "Rawhide Jimmy" Douglas, a mining magnate, and now contains an abundance of Jerome mining lore. There are restaurants, cafés, and dozens of shops peddling everything from the cheap and tawdry to the expensive and tasteful. There are limited overnight accommodations, but there are plenty for travelers who head down off this hill and toward Cottonwood, where we now go.

Immediately on the way out of Jerome in the first miles of the 6-mile drive along 89A to Cottonwood, the steeply dropping highway offers spectacular views of the Mogollon Rim, the Colorado Plateau, and the Verde Valley. At the bottom of the hill is Clarkdale, a community of about 3,500 that is on the National Register of Historic Sites; it was created in 1914 as a model planned company town accommodating the miners of Jerome. It is possible here to catch a ride on the popular Verde Canyon Railroad, which chugs slowly along the river and through a canyon to don't-blink-or-you'll-miss-it Perkinsville, a restful, 12-mile trip for sightseers and bird watchers wanting to spot a bald eagle nesting.

Back in Clarkdale, 89A runs quickly into Cottonwood, a great place to have a heart attack; despite a population of only about 10,000 (but growing), it sports a substantial medical community that serves the vast collection of retirees who have moved to the mild climate and splendid scenery of the Verde Valley and its towns, including Sedona and Jerome.

Cottonwood got its name from a circle of 16 of those trees along the Verde River. It offers all the modern conveniences, including accommodations for those who wish to explore the area and two downtowns, a new one along 89A and the original old town at, roughly, Broadway and Main that has been bypassed by the highway. If the vehicle of choice on this trip is a RV, the Dead Horse Ranch State Park along the Verde River off 10th Street has campsites, hookups, bird watching, and fishing.

Cottonwood began its community life around the 1870s as a campground for travelers to Oak Creek and Camp Verde and was one of three main crossings of the Verde River. It got its official name in 1885 and was laid out in 1908 by a couple of guys who pulled a drag through the brush to create a main street. ꟽ

[Homes are stacked over about 1,500 vertical feet on Jerome's Cleopatra Hill.]

George H. H. Huey

Romance Rides the Rails

Pamela Reed stood on one of the Verde Canyon Railroad's open-air viewing cars, gazing at the shimmering images of orange and gold cottonwood trees reflected in the Verde River some 150 feet below. The train paused on a sturdy wooden trestle constructed in 1912 over the basalt inner gorge of SOB Canyon, giving passengers a prime opportunity to snap pictures.

She turned toward the door connecting the cars as a flash of red caught her attention. Her boyfriend, David Tipescue, strode to her, a bouquet of roses and lilies cradled in his arms. She stood motionless as he dropped to one knee and asked her to marry him. He waited in silence along with the curious onlookers, couples holding hands, friends standing side-by-side. Reed nodded and whispered a choked affirmative. The crowd cheered and clapped as the newly betrothed couple embraced.

The author has contributed numerous feature articles to Arizona Highways, *conducted research into Arizona myths and legends, and written items for* "Taking the Off-Ramp," *the magazine's monthly presentation of Arizona oddities, attractions, and pleasures. She's the author of* Arizona off the Beaten Path *and* Fun With the Family (in Arizona).

> By CARRIE MINER

The romantic atmosphere found on the Verde Canyon Railroad's trips has provided the setting for countless proposals, anniversary celebrations, and even weddings.

The Verde Valley Railroad's 38 miles of track, built in 1912 at a cost of $1.3 million, became the lifeline of the mining communities of Clarkdale and Jerome. Now the railway takes visitors on a sight-seeing excursion through the rough-cut canyon to the Perkinsville Ranch before returning to Clarkdale (see Where To Go, Page 270).

The train runs year-around, but the autumn colors of the canyon's riparian forest make an especially stunning backdrop for wildlife watching in October and November. The deer, javelinas, and pronghorn antelope become more active during the fall, and migratory birds—mountain bluebirds, northern harriers, lesser night hawks, swifts, great white egrets, and herons—begin to arrive for the mild winter ahead. Year-round raptors like great horned owls, Coopers hawks, and American kestrels dominate the sky, but the 30 wintering bald and golden eagles elicit the biggest response from passengers on the train.

The train, pulled by two of North America's 12 remaining vintage FP7 locomotives, departs from the Clarkdale depot each afternoon. Upon leaving the yard and the mining operations, the train travels alongside the smoothly flowing

Verde River and past the remains of a Sinagua cliff dwelling tucked in a limestone cave about halfway up the canyon face.

A middle-aged couple, intent on their search for waterfowl, leaned over the open-air viewing car's rail and pointed excitedly at a great blue heron standing in the water. Farther downstream a bevy of ducks drifted on the surface, searching for mesquite pods and other edible treats. About 80 percent of the food for local wildlife comes from the Verde River, which makes the preservation of the canyon's riparian habitat a critical concern.

Biologists consider the cotton-wood-willow habitat one of the most productive ecosystems in North America, which explains why it draws some of the most diverse accumulations of birds found anywhere. It's also one of the most endangered habitats in North America, which makes the Verde River's long meander of trees ecologically invaluable.

The Verde Canyon Railroad skims the banks of the shimmering Verde River.

George H. H. Huey

The Verde Valley, in prehistoric times a shallow lake, shows the colors of multiple sedimentary layers, including white limestone and red sandstone deposits that are of the same geological stratum as the red rock formations around Sedona.

The Sycamore Wilderness harbors scattered Indian dwellings, petroglyphs, and old mines. The purplish-brown Tapeats sandstone, grayish-blond Martin limestone, and reddish-pink Redwall limestone dominate the canyon walls.

Fifteen-and-a-half miles down the track, the train entered a 680-foot-long man-made tunnel. Carved out of solid limestone, the tunnel supports itself except for the final 30 feet, which builders reinforced with steel beams.

During the final 4 miles, the railroad leaves the canyon and enters the Perkinsville valley where A.M. Perkins settled on a cattle ranch in 1900. Two years later, the railroad put in a water station to refuel the steam engines and dubbed the place Perkinsville.

At the community's peak, only 10 families lived in the area, then when the railroad switched to diesel locomotives in the early 1950s, the hamlet became a ghost town.

While passengers reclined in the cars' love seats and overstuffed chairs, the teal and white locomotive detached and traveled on a loop to the other end of the train to hook back up for the return trip.

The horn sounded, and the train began the return to Clarkdale. ᴀ́ʜ

Where To Go
What To See
What To Do

Richard Maack

The Up North region includes Flagstaff, Sedona, Jerome, Prescott, Chino Valley, and Verde Valley communities, including Camp Verde, Cottonwood, and Clarkdale. The communities are listed alphabetically.

Camp Verde

Camp Verde Chamber of Commerce: Camp Verde, located off Interstate 17 at State Route 260, resides along the banks of the Verde River, a 200-mile-long stream that runs through three national forests and offers a range of outdoor recreation. The town is about 55 miles south of Flagstaff and 85 miles north of Phoenix. The chamber's information includes lodging, area attractions, and guide and tour services. (928) 567-9294. www.campverde.org

Montezuma Castle National Monument: A 20-room, five-story ruin looks much as it did in the 1100s, when it was constructed in a large, cavelike overhang. The visitors center offers a library, bookstore, restrooms, and picnic area. Most of the area is wheelchair accessible. $. Near Camp Verde; take Interstate 17 to Exit 289, follow signs for 3 miles. (928) 567-3322. www.nps.gov/moca

Montezuma Well: Eleven miles from Montezuma Castle, a limestone sinkhole stretches 470 feet across; a spring supports a 55-foot-deep lake. The Sinagua people used this well to irrigate crops. Picnic area, two quarter-mile trails leading to well and ruins (well trail not recommended for wheelchairs). Free. Near Camp Verde; take Interstate 17 to Exit 293, follow signs for 5 miles. (928) 567-3322. www.nps.gov/moca/well.htm

Fort Verde State Historical Park: Dating back to the mid-1800s, this fort played a role during Gen. George Crook's campaign against the Apache Indians. Preserved original buildings furnished in traditional style from the 1800s. Every second Saturday in October, the park celebrates Fort Verde Days, with living-history programs and demonstrations relating to the years 1865 to 1891. Picnic tables, restrooms, RV and bus parking. Wheelchair accessible. $. Take Interstate 17 to State 260 (east), turn left on Main Street to 125 E. Holloman St. and turn left; park is on the right. (928) 567-3275. www.pr.state.az.us

Out of Africa Wildlife Park: Visitors can ride or walk through this preserve of roaming animals such as lions, tigers, panthers, hyenas, giraffes, wildebeests, zebras, and other animals from the African plains. The park is designed to give visitors a safari-type experience. $. Located on Verde Valley Justice Center Road off State 260 about 3 miles west of Camp Verde. (928) 567-2840. www.outofafricapark.com

Chino Valley

Chino Valley Area Chamber of Commerce: Chino Valley stretches along State Route 89 north of Prescott in the mountains of north-central Arizona. (928) 636-2493; (877) 523-1988. www.chinovalley.org

First Territorial Capital Celebration: Celebrates Chino Valley's role in Arizona history as the site of the first Territorial capital. Rodeo, parade, live entertainment, fireworks. Labor Day weekend. Memory Park.

[The county courthouse dominates Prescott's main square. ◄
At Montezuma Castle National Monument in the Verde Valley,
a Sinagua cliff dwelling remains. ▼]

George H. H. Huey

Clarkdale

Information: Clarkdale is located just northeast of Jerome near the junction of state routes 89A and 260.
www.azjerome.com/pages/clarkdale/clarkdale.htm

Tuzigoot National Monument: The 1,000-year-old pueblo built by the Sinagua people sits high on a desert hilltop. Once, the pueblo consisted of 110 rooms and two- and three-story structures. Visitors center and hiking trails. $. Fifty-two miles south of Flagstaff via State Route 89A. Or take State 260 west from Camp Verde. (928) 634-5564. www.nps.gov/tuzi

Verde Canyon Railroad: The scenic four-hour train ride, along a historic route from Clarkdale to the ghost ranch of Perkinsville and back, takes travelers past ancient ruins, geological formations, and eagle nests. $. 300 N. Broadway. (800) 320-0718. www.verdecanyonrr.com

Cornville

Page Springs Vineyard and Cellars: Scenic vineyards, wine-tasting room, and wine for sale. $. Take Exit 293 from Interstate 17. 1500 N. Page Springs Road. (928) 639-3004. www.pagespringscellars.com

Oak Creek Vineyards and Winery: Tasting room, gift shop, and vineyards. Closed Mon. and Tues. $. 1555 N. Page Springs Road. (928) 649-0290.

Cottonwood

Cottonwood Chamber of Commerce: Cottonwood is located just northeast of Jerome near the junction of state routes 89A and 260. (928) 634-7593. www.cottonwood.verdevalley.com

Dead Horse Ranch State Park: The cottonwood and willow riparian forest within the park is one of only 20 in the world. Numerous animal species live along the Verde River, which meanders through the park. Hiking trails, horse corrals, fishing, camping, hot showers, picnic areas. $. 675 Dead Horse Ranch Road. (928) 634-5283. www.pr.state.az.us

Flagstaff

Flagstaff Information: The Flagstaff Visitors Center, operated by the city, is a stop in itself because it's located in a historic train station. On the Internet site, the center's staff members share their secrets about enjoying the area. One E. Route 66, Flagstaff. (928) 774-9541; (800) 842-7293. www.flagstaffarizona.org. Another source is the Flagstaff Chamber of Commerce, (928) 774-4505. www.flagstaffchamber.com.

Northern Arizona University: The university has an art collection, changing exhibits, and other events and performances open to the public. Internet site includes campus maps. $. (928) 523-5661. http://events.nau.edu

Flagstaff Festival of Science: Each year the festival presents 10 days of events that center on a changing theme. Events include open houses at scientific institutions, interactive exhibits, excursions, hikes, and presentations. Opens in late September. Free. Flagstaff. (928) 774-9541. www.scifest.org

Arizona Snowbowl: Snowboarders and skiers can enjoy 32 trails on the San Francisco Peaks. Summer months allow for hiking, disk golf, and sky rides. Lodge and cabin, ski school, rentals. $. Located 14 miles outside of Flagstaff on U.S. Route 180. (928) 779-1951. www.arizonasnowbowl.com

Flagstaff Historic Tour: Guides dressed in period attire lead visitors past nearly 40 of the city's historic sites. Books, brochures, and maps available. Donations. 323 W. Aspen Ave. (520) 774-1330. www.flagguide.com/mainstreet/index.htm

Flagstaff Winterfest: Includes dog-sledding, concerts, snowmobile racing, snowboarding, cultural events, and a parade. February. Free. Further information: visitors center or chamber of commerce.

Wool Festival: Demonstrations on llama-, sheep-, and goat-shearing as well as spinning, dyeing, and camp cooking. June. Donations. The event is on the grounds of the Pioneer Museum, which is under the auspices of the Arizona Historical Society. The museum is located in the historic Coconino County Hospital for the Indigent, built in 1908. The museum grounds also include a barn and root cellar. $. 2340 N. Fort Valley Road. (928) 774-6272. www.arizonahistoricalsociety.org (click on Flagstaff).

Nordic Center: More than 40 kilometers of groomed cross-country trails allow visitors to snow-shoe, cross-country ski, sled, and take guided, snowy hikes. Lodging available. December to April. $. U.S. 180 at Milepost 232. (928) 220-0550. www.FlagstaffNordicCenter.com; www.fs.fed.us/r3/coconino/recreation/peaks/flagstaff-nordic-ctr.shtml

Museum of Northern Arizona: This museum's permanent and changing exhibits focus on the land, people and their arts and crafts, and plants of the Colorado Plateau. Besides exhibits, the museum sponsors programs and field trips throughout the year to focus on plateau topics. Its annual festivals includes ones dedicated to the culture of the Hopi and Navajo peoples. $. 3101 N. Fort Valley Road. (928) 774-5213. www.musnaz.org

Soar into Spring Kite and Activity Festival: Professional kite demonstrations, live music, carnival games, various kite-related events. April. Free. Sponsored by the city's Parks and Recreation Dept. Foxglenn Park, 4200 E. Butler Ave. (928) 779-7690. www.flagstaff.az.gov/index.asp?NID=60

Coconino Center for the Arts: Gallery has a 200-seat performance theater, rotating exhibits that showcase regional artists. Donations. 2300 N. Fort Valley Road. (928) 779-2300. www.culturalpartners.org

Walnut Canyon National Monument: The Sinagua occupied the area from about 1100 to 1250. Single-story ruins sheltered by limestone overhangs. $. Interstate 40 at Exit 204, 7.5 miles east of Flagstaff. (928) 526-3367. www.nps.gov/waca

Museum Club Roadhouse: Built in 1931 on old Route 66, the famous country-Western roadhouse and dance hall listed in the National Register of Historic places is the largest log cabin in the Southwest. Live music, Indian artifacts, and an extensive taxidermy collection. Free. 3404 E. Route 66. (928) 526-9434. www.museumclub.com

Riordan Mansion State Historic Park: The mansion, built in 1904 for two lumber baron brothers and their families, has 40 rooms. Tours, visitors center. $. 409 W. Riordan Road. (928) 779-4395. www.pr.state.az.us

The Arboretum at Flagstaff: The garden's 2,500 species of plants include an extensive collection of high-country wildflowers. Guided tours and interpretive trails run through the 200-acre mountain facility. Picnic areas and gift shop. Closed Nov. 1 through March 31. $. 4001 S. Woody Mountain Road. (928) 774-1442. www.thearb.org

Lowell Observatory: The privately owned observatory is best known for Clyde Tombaugh's discovery of Pluto. Astronomy exhibits, visitors center, tours. Daily; daytime and evening hours vary seasonally. $. 1400 W. Mars Hill Road. (928) 774-3358. www.lowell.edu

Hart Prairie Preserve: At the base of Mount Humphreys, the 245-acre preserve has a plethora of animals, old-growth ponderosa pine forest, and wildflowers to view. The buildings and lodge are listed on the National Registry of Historic Places. Nature walks, workshops, retreats. Closed Nov. through May. Free. 2601 N. Fort Valley Road. (928) 774-8892. www.nature.org/arizona

Lava River Cave: About 700,000 years old and the longest lava tube in Arizona invites you on a 1.5-mile roundtrip adventure that must be traveled with caution. Visitors should dress warmly since the temperature in the cave is around 30 degrees. Free. From Flagstaff: Northwest on U.S. 180 to Milepost 230, turn left (west) on Forest Service Road 245, turn left (south)

on Forest Service Road 171 to FR 171B; cave entrance is 300 yards east.
www.fs.fed.us/r3/coconino/recreation/peaks/lava-river-cave.shtml

Sunset Crater Volcano National Monument: Home to the Colorado
Plateau's youngest volcano. Trails allow visitors to explore volcanic
formations. Visitors center. $. From Flagstaff, take U.S. 89 north, turn right
on the Sunset Crater road. (928) 526-0502. www.nps.gov/sucr

Lamar Haines Memorial Wildlife Area: A spring-fed pond, an old
cabin, and petroglyphs highlight a visit to this birders haven. Free. From
Flagstaff, take U.S. 180 to the entrance to the Snow Bowl; trailhead for the
wildlife area appears on the right.

Jerome

Jerome Chamber of Commerce: www.jeromechamber.com

Gold King Mine and Ghost Town: Antique trucks, tractors,
construction and mining equipment displayed at this 100-year-old former
mining area. Gift shop. $. Jerome. (928) 634-0053. www.goldkingmine.net

Jerome Historical Society Mine Museum: Artifacts and displays
about Jerome's colorful past. Gift shop. $. 200 Main Street.
(928) 634-5477. www.jeromehistoricalsociety.org

Jerome State Historic Park/ Douglas Mansion: The Douglas Mansion,
listed on the National Register of Historic Places, is now a museum. Library,
artifacts, and exhibits about Jerome and the Douglas family. Picnic area. $.
In the town of Jerome just off State 89A, on Douglas Road.
(928) 634-5381. www.pr.state.az.us

Page Springs

Page Springs Hatchery: Arizona's largest trout-growing facility offers
tours, visitors center, and wildlife-watching area. Free. Located off State
89A 10 miles south of Sedona on Page Springs Road. (928) 774-5045.
www.gf.state.az.us/outdoor_recreation/wildlife_area_page_springs.shtml

Prescott

Information: Chamber of Commerce, (928) 445-2000. www.prescott.org;
City of Prescott, www.cityofprescott.net/visitors

Sharlot Hall Museum: Wide array of historical exhibits and pioneer-life
displays, including the 1864 governor's mansion. The museum hosts five
events annually: the Folk Arts Fair, Prescott Indian Art Market, the Arizona
Cowboy Poets Gathering, Prescott Book Festival, and Folk Music Festival. $.
415 West Gurley St., Prescott. (928) 445-3122. www.sharlot.org

Prescott Frontier Days: Prescott explodes with hoopla in the week that includes the Fourth of July. Festivities include the "World's Oldest Rodeo" first staged in 1888, a parade, golf tournament, 10K fun run, and rodeo dance. Make lodging reservatins early. $. Prescott. (866) 407-6336. www.worldsoldestrodeo.com

Smoki Museum: Museum, library, and trading post that focuses on Indian culture, art, and history. Each July the museum conducts an auction of Navajo rugs and other Indian art. $. 147 N. Arizona St. (928) 445-1230. www.smokimuseum.org

Arizona Shakespeare Festival: Each season, beginning in April the Arizona Classical Theatre stages classical productions at various locations. $. (928) 443-9220. www.azshakes.com.

Prescott Air Show: Features war birds, skydivers, current military aircraft. October. $. Prescott Municipal Airport. www.prescottairfair.com

Phippen Museum of Western Art: Artwork created by artists of theAmerican West. $. 4701 State 89 North, Prescott. (928) 778-1385. www.phippenartmuseum.org

Ken Lindley Complex: Large Prescott city park with playground, picnic tables, grills, snack bar, and the Mike Fann Community Skate Park for bikes, skateboards, and in-line skates. 702 E. Gurley St., adjacent to the Grace M. Sparkes Activity Center. www.cityofprescott.net/services/parks/parks.php

Prescott Valley

Information: Prescott Valley Chamber of Commerce, (928) 772-8857; www.pvchamber.org. Town of Prescott Valley, www.pvaz.net

Mountain Valley Park: A 69-acre city park with a skate park, Mountain Valley Splash aquatic center, ball courts, and more. 8600 E. Nace Road. (928) 759-3090. www.pvaz.net/Community/parks/facilities.htm

Sedona/ Oak Creek

Information: Chamber of Commerce, (800) 288-7336; (928) 282-7722. www.visitsedona.com. Also, www.sedona.net

Sedona International Film Festival: Showcases more than 100 independent films. A four-day event of panel discussions, awards brunch, entertainment, and a dance. February. $. Tickets needed in advance. Sedona. (928) 282-1177. www.sedonafilmfestival.com

Sedona Arts Center: The organization's palette remains full through the year with exhibits, workshops, and special events such as a plein air

festival, "first Friday" gallery walks, the annual Art and Sculpture Walk. $.
15 Art Bard Road. (928) 282-3809; (888) 954-4442.
www.sedonaartscenter.com

Sedona Jazz on the Rocks: The three-day event draws top jazz acts to
a festival atmosphere. September. $. The sponsoring organization also puts
on jazz programs throughout the year at various locations. (928) 282-1985.
www.sedonajazz.com

Tlaquepaque Arts and Crafts Village: Pronounced Tla-keh-pah-keh,
which means "best of everything" in Spanish, the authentically replicated
Mexican village allows visitors to walk down its cobblestone roads for a
unique shopping experience. 336 Route 179. (928) 282-4838.
www.tlaq.com

Sedona Heritage Museum: Exhibits and displays relating to the greater
Sedona area. $. 735 Jordan Road. (928) 282-7038.
www.sedonamuseum.org

Institute of Ecotourism: Offers weekly events and programs pertaining
to ecotourism. Also hosts children's activities. 91 Portal Lane.
(928) 282-2720. www.ioet.org

Chapel of the Holy Cross: The striking, slender building, built into a red
rock butte, offers stunning views of the valley below. The 90-foot cross is
the chapel's most prominent feature. Donations. 780 Chapel Road, just off
State Route 179. (928) 282-4069. www.sjvsedona.org/chapel.htm

Red Rock State Park: An herbarium teaches visitors about native plants
and animals along Oak Creek. Guided tours, numerous hiking trails, picnic
areas, and a visitors center. Hours vary seasonally. $. 4050 Red Rock Loop
Road. (928) 282-6907. www.pr.state.az.us

Slide Rock State Park: Known for the natural rock water slide. Birding,
swimming, hiking. Picnic areas, trails, volleyball courts, fishing. Hours vary
seasonally. $. 6871 N. State 89A. (928) 282-3034. www.pr.state.az.us

Williams
See Page 241.

Yarnell
Shrine of Saint Joseph of the Mountains: An inter-faith site with
life-sized statues depicting the biblical Stations of the Cross, retreat center,
and gift shop. Donations. From Prescott, go about 28 miles on State 89.
(928) 778-5229. www.stjoseph-shrine.org

A hiker sees the world unfold from a perch atop the Mogollon Rim. ▲
At Woods Canyon Lake, fishermen boat through the mist. ▶

Mogollon Rim Country
Payson, Pine, Strawberry, and Beyond

Pine forests and cliffs of sandstone and limestone create the major landscape currency in this region laced with lakes and streams. That, of course, suggests fishing, which is just fine in a dozen or more lakes stocked with trout. History, too, hangs around the Rim. You can hike or drive over routes that the U.S. Army followed to reach the famed Fort Apache during the Apache Wars. Or you can visit a town that was a central place in a bloody 19th-century feud involving two families and their supporters. Their enmity had something to do with the fact that one side consisted of cattlemen and the other was a sheepherder faction. Or you can just kick back and relax and maybe do a little antiquing in Payson, Pine, and Strawberry.

Nick Berezenko

Nick Berezenko

Four Seasons and Many Names

A little Arizona geology music, please, maestro, while we lecture briefly about a marvelous chunk of recreational land at the heart of the state.

What? Nothing comes quickly to mind? Then, perhaps Ferde Grofe's *Grand Canyon Suite*, even though the subject of this chapter is the Mogollon Rim country, which is one of the state's two most impressive landforms. The other is, of course, Grofe's, and our, Grand Canyon. With apologies to geologists, the major difference between the two is that one is up, the other down. The Rim is a formidable escarpment, which is up. The Canyon is a formidable ditch, which is down.

Some 600 million years ago, a period when the Earth's restless crust was uplifting, the 200-mile-long Mogollon Rim was created diagonally across the central part of the state as the southern edge of the great, four-state Colorado Plateau. (For convenience, you can think of a plateau as a huge mesa and a mesa as a big butte.) The Rim, or escarpment, begins in northwestern Arizona, heads south to below Flagstaff, then angles south and east all the way into New Mexico. The portion we care about in this chapter is that segment in the central part of the state that offers the most dramatic and obvious views of and from the Rim and that can be easily traveled by state routes 87 and 260. Find the town of Payson, the only incorporated community in the area, and you have found Rim Country.

The Rim got its name, as did the prehistoric Mogollon people who probably were the first to inhabit it, from a Spaniard, Juan Ignacio Flores Mogollon (pronounced MOE-gee-on or, as a popular but incorrect version would have it, Muggy-OWN). The presumed reason he was accorded that high honor was that he was the governor of the New Mexico area in the 1700s when that territory and what is now Arizona were under Spanish rule.

And just to confuse matters further, the Rim's midsection is sometimes known as the Tonto Rim. That is the area where one of the Rim's most famous denizens, novelist Zane Grey, hung out and where he placed some of his Western novels. That has spawned yet another name, Zane Grey Country. Furthermore, area chambers of commerce like to call it Rim Country.

Whatever it is called, this Massachusetts-sized land, mostly in the center of the state, reached easily on four-lane State Route 87 (also called the Beeline Highway) in 75 to 90 minutes north out of Phoenix or traversed east and west on State Route 260, is very nearly all things to all people. Why do travelers and residents love it? Let us count the ways:

High above the desert floor, its air is pure; its pine forests are never ending; its hiking trails are abundant, long, and exhaust-free; its lakes and streams are

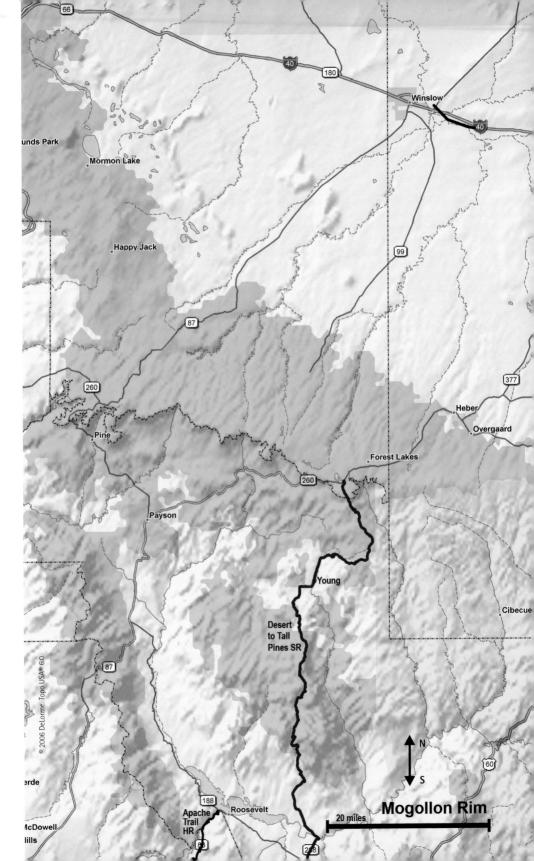

full of trout; it has four distinct seasons with summer a steady 15 or more degrees cooler than Phoenix (spring and fall are usually in the 80s, winter around 45 and up); precipitation averages 21 inches annually including a handful of snowfalls; its wildlife of elk, deer, turkey, javelina, antelope, bear, 239 species of birds, and an occasional puma is plentiful; its towns are small and friendly and full of re- tired folks (48 percent); it has a growing arts and antiques retailing business; and it has a regional medical center and nearly two dozen banks and related financial institutions.

Other amenities, such as where to rest your head or fill your tummy? There are more than 600 rooms available in lodges, cabin courts, national chain motels, and beds and breakfasts (half a dozen of the latter) in the area. To the 30 or more of those institutions, add a couple of dozen campgrounds, public and private, and food at another two dozen establishments from B (Beeline Café and Burger King) to T (Taco Bell) in the region. You can pick lodging ranging from a cabin in the woods to a motel room on the highway or a tent in a national forest. For precise help, contact the Rim Country Regional Chamber of Commerce in Payson at (800) 672-9766 or check the Internet at www.rimcountrychamber.com.

It is usually not apparent to the casual observer that the Rim is at hand; it is not as if one suddenly looks up and sees a great shelf, a vast drop-off stretching almost across the width of the state. It is generally more graduated, less dramatic than that, but at certain points, it can seem that way. One longtime resident of the desert below put it this way:

"As a child, when we drove to the Rim and onto it, I felt like I now imagine how Columbus might have felt as he pursued his immense journey: that he might be heading toward what the ancients claimed was a flat earth's drop-off into the eternal abyss. Approaching the top of the Rim, I truly felt I was at the edge of the Earth. Or, as a 4-year-old put it, 'Daddy. Stop the car. We're going to fall.'"

Childhood remembrances aside, if you fancy an easy hike through a cool, good-smelling, and quiet pine forest provided by any of three national forests that preserve the area, sitting on a ledge along the Rim and staring down at the boiling desert below, exchanging brief greetings with a deer, fly fishing for a suc- culent trout, sacking out in a cozy tent, cross-country skiing on powdery snow, backpacking, relaxing in a comfy lodge, or dumping some quarters in a slot at a casino that evening, it's the place to be. If none of that appeals, therapy and psychotherapeutic drugs are indicated. If you prefer the cacophony of horned taxis, screeching tires, and ringing cell phones, fly, do not drive, to Manhattan.

In a burst of adjectival enthusiasm, Don Dedera, writing in an *Arizona Highways* guide to the Rim, described it this way:

"To a traveler approaching it, the Rim seems slowly to ooze up from the primal basements of the planet, to block out the lower third of the sky. As you draw closer, the Rim asserts itself as sheer towers forming recesses, points and promontories. Bare rock pokes through the forest in rainbows of warm hues. As often as not, soft white or menacing cobalt clouds decorate a firmament so clear and baby blue it breaks your heart. Eagles in updrafts polish limey brows averaging 7,500 feet above sea level. As the gargantuan hulk leans on the human psyche, time slows to the syncopated clopping of the hooves of a walking cow pony. This is ranching country, relaxing country, wave-through-the-windshield country, unlocked-door country."

In short, he liked it. Nice sky, good views, pleasant people. But apparently and inexplicably not satisfied with his own descriptive feat, Dedera then offers this translucent, just-shy-of-opaque quotation from another excellent Arizona writer, Charles Bowden, discussing the Rim:

"Here, the edge of the great stone wafer to the north slowly erodes backward into itself and spills soil onto the deserts below. The dissolving edge pulsed with periods of uplift, warped with faulting, and wound up higher than either the plateau to the north or the deserts to the south. The lip has shed the more recent rock of the geologic clock and is down to Precambrian stone, material a billion or two years old."

So, with that, let us move away from lovely hyperbole and back to the hard core:

The major town in the area, as we have noted, is Payson, with a population that's nudged past 15,000 and is growing steadily at an annual rate of about 3.5 percent. Others of significance include Pine, Strawberry, Star Valley, Kohl's Ranch, and Christopher Creek.

[Ponderosa pines cling to the Mogollon Rim's Poison Springs Point.   ]

Nick Berezenko

The first humans to populate the Rim were the prehistoric Mogollons, who arrived from New Mexico somewhere around 300 B.C. and mysteriously vanished (probably absorbed into other cultures) by 1500 A.D. They were succeeded by the Tonto Apache Indians (still there and now the proud owners of a popular casino on their land), followed in the 1870s or thereabouts by ranchers, miners, military, and other sorts of pioneers.

Nick Berezenko

Payson in its youth (it was founded in 1884) was mostly a center for ranchers and loggers, but it is now home to people who appreciate four distinct but mostly mild seasons, unsullied air, unhurried pace of life, and the great outdoors at their doorstep. Five bucks at some cafes will get you a big buckaroo of a breakfast including a huge, homemade biscuit sliced in half and sluiced with thick and flavorful gravy, two slices of bacon, one egg, hash browns and a cup of coffee, all served by what seems to be an abundant population of women approaching their golden years and who can be counted on to call you "hon."

Payson in those old days was a rough and ready community with an ample supply of saloons and even its own fort (McDonald) built to offer protection from Apache raids. These days, it is a growing vacation and retirement community, but it's still easy to get a beer. A short distance north and west on State 87 and just under the Rim are the communities of Pine (settled in 1879 by Mormons and now full of artists) and Strawberry (3 miles west of Pine), both higher in elevation than Payson. These little towns offer historical buildings and an abundance of antique or specialty shops.

Star Valley is 4 miles east of Payson on State Route 260 and got its name from a squatter named, yes, Star. He married an Apache woman, but that wasn't much help to him because he was killed by the Apaches. Kohl's Ranch, a rustic resort, is 18 miles east of Payson, and Christopher Creek is a tiny, pine-filled community 22 miles east of Payson and also was named after an early settler.

Two trails along this portion of the Rim deserve particular attention: the Crook Trail and the Old Rim Road, often confused with each other. In 1872, famed Indian fighter Gen. George Crook and his troops began building a trail between a fort in Prescott on the west with Fort Apache far to the south and east, the aim being to put some military clamps on Apache warriors and legendary Apache leader Geronimo. It became the third major road in northern Arizona and it can be found—and hiked—today. It generally parallels and occasionally overlaps the Rim Road with its spectacular views from points along the Rim. Small chevrons nailed to trees mark spots where the trails overlap, and some of Crook's original blazes on pine trees remain. Maps and other information on these trails are available from the Payson Ranger Station of the Tonto National Forest. The station is located on the south side of State 260 on the eastern edge of town.

An explorer pauses at the towering girth of Tonto Natural Bridge. ◀ Hikers wind through the misty Waterfall Trail in Tonto Natural Bridge State Park. ▼

Nick Berczenko

We end this discussion of the Rim with a teaser, particularly appropriate if the traveler is on his or her way to or from the vortices and crystals of Sedona: In 1975, a tree-thinning crew saw a strange light coming from the edge of the Rim.

Or so it is said.

The crew investigated and found a disc-like spacecraft hovering near the tops of the tall pines. One of the crew went toward the ship but was knocked down by some mysterious force. His colleagues beat it, and he and the craft disappeared. He turned up four or five days later with a splendid tale of a trip on a flying saucer.

Or so it is said.

Moral: Regardless of wherever you find yourself at any given moment on the Rim, you are within comfortable driving or hiking distance of an attraction created by Nature, by mankind, or by Venusians. ▥

Tom Danielsen

Tonto Natural Bridge

"Excuse me, sir," said the middle-aged woman, "but would you please wait on the trail for a few minutes? My mother is up the trail ahead of you, and she is having some problems and needs privacy."

Well, sure, what the heck. Just one more unpredictable phenomenon in one of the most amazing of Nature's constructions in Rim Country, the Tonto Natural Bridge in Tonto Natural Bridge State Park, a 160-acre gem of a park under the Rim with a magnificent bridge created partly by the flow of Pine Creek eroding its way through the rock and limestone.

The bridge is believed to be the largest natural travertine bridge in North America. The span is 183 feet high over a 400-foot-long tunnel measuring 150 feet at its widest. The location of the small valley was documented in 1877 by a prospector who saw the bridge while he was running from Apaches and hid in a cave there for two nights and three days. He later claimed squatter's rights and brought his relatives, the Goodfellows, over from Scotland.

Visitors can stand on the bridge or hike down into the shade, creek, and slippery rock under the bridge to explore this geologic wonder. Swimming and wading in that creek is possible. Picnic tables, grills, trails, rest rooms, and a gift shop are at the site.

As for the up and down climb, the one down is steep but made easier and less dangerous by the existence of manufactured steps and handrails. The one up, on the opposite side of the creek, is somewhat less arduous but still a problem for those with health problems. On a recent trip out of the depths below the bridge, one overweight, sixtyish grandmother required, alternately, periodic privacy or a portable, canvas chair on which to rest at several points along the climb, all the while being supplied with bottles of water provided by a bucket brigade of indefatigable grandchildren scurrying to and from a fountain atop and to the side of the bridge above.

Lest anyone be concerned, she eventually inched her way to the top, the family SUV, and the public facilities.

[Visitors can enjoy the cool grotto below Tonto Natural Bridge. ▲]

Taking the Beeline

The 75-mile drive north from metropolitan Phoenix on State Route 87 out to Payson is not one of the state's officially designated scenic routes, but it could be. It is remarkably scenic, unofficially, of course.

The road, called the Beeline Highway, leads quickly to two man-made alterations of the desert: canals, those concrete versions of an arroyo but, unlike an arroyo, always full of water. The highway first crosses the Arizona Canal, which diverts water from the Salt River to the thirsty maw of the greater Phoenix area. About 4 miles farther is the Central Arizona Project Aqueduct, a 335-mile canal that begins at the Colorado River on Arizona's western border and ends southwest of Tucson. It delivers about 2 billion gallons of water a day to southern Arizona's towns and farms. Arroyos were created over centuries and cost nothing; the CAP canal required 20 years and $2.5 billion.

At Milepost 188 (Shea Boulevard) is a turnoff to the community of Fountain Hills, which claims to have the world's highest fountain, shooting water 560 feet up every 15 minutes during certain hours. Three mileposts farther is the Verde ("green" in Spanish) River, the headwaters of which are in the Chino Valley between Prescott and Ash Fork. The drive then enters the Tonto National Forest, a nearly 3-million-acre wonderland of some lush, saguaro-creosote bush-prickly pear Sonoran Desert but then becoming mostly pines and peaks. The highway begins to climb into bewitching vistas of moonscapes, boulder fields, valleys, foothills, and, eventually, the community of Sunflower, an old cavalry watering station, and 7,153-foot Mount Ord, named for a mid-1800s general named Edward O. C. Ord but probably known to intimates as Ed.

The terrain begins changing here, at about Milepost 225, from lower Sonoran Desert to upper Sonoran and the imminent end of the battalions of saguaros, the last one occurring just before Milepost 230. Some 20 mileposts farther is a dramatic view of the Mogollon Rim, the natural wow that separates Arizona's central highlands from the Colorado Plateau.

Just at the junction with State Route 188 is a rest stop offering a bathroom break for humans and pets and machines dispensing cups of coffee and hot chocolate as well as something for the nutritionally-depraved: alleged chicken soup in a coffee cup, the age of neither the chicken nor the broth stated.

Along much of this portion of State 87 are several descending mountain grades, usually of 6 percent but sometimes slightly greater. That's the approximate equivalent of an advanced beginner or beginning intermediate run on a ski hill. ▥

From Desert to Tall Pines Scenic Byway

Route	State routes 260 and 288 and Forest Service Road 512.
Mileage	80 miles.
Time to Allow	Four hours from State Route 260 to Globe.
Elevation	2,000 feet at Salt River to 7,600 on the Mogollon Rim.
Overview	Beautiful, scenic, climbing paved road through lush Sonoran Desert from Phoenix to mountain community of Payson and then east on State Route 260 to impressive Mogollon Rim views and Young Road. From there, mostly narrow and sometimes-steep dirt road down through pine forests, historic and unincorporated town of Young, the Sierra Anchas, and the sight from above of Roosevelt Lake before ending in Globe.

The "From Desert to Tall Pines Scenic Byway" stretches mostly over an unpaved route between State Route 260 on the north and Roosevelt Lake on the south. We begin by taking State 260 east out of the middle of Payson into a tantalizing, tortuous, pine-lined way past Preacher Canyon, named for an unnamed missionary who came this way in the 1880s, singing gospel songs and carrying a loaded, double-barrel shotgun, presumably for unbelievers and guys wearing black hats.

At Milepost 264 is a magnificent view of the Mogollon Rim, that line of cliffs extending across Arizona and formed by the usual shaping force of uplift and the plastic surgery of erosion some 25 million years ago. To its immediate north lies the Colorado Plateau.

Just ahead on State 260 stands Kohl's Ranch, once a working ranch and now a restaurant-motel-lounge-gift shop combo. Zane Grey one lived and worked near here. Then comes Christopher Creek and, soon, a most-welcome variation on the omnipresent "watch for elk" signs throughout the northern parts of the state. This one is a sequence of four signs, a clear theft from the famous Burma-Shave roadside campaign of decades past. They read, in a poetically challenged rhythm that initially grinds and then grows on you, "They saw an elk"..."Oh what a thrill"... "Until they smashed it"... "On the grill."

Milepost 282 offers a short trip to Al Fulton Point, on the right, and its panoramic look at the Mogollon Rim from on its edge. Across the highway, a decent road also will take the would-be camper to the popular Woods Canyon Lake and a recreation area with campgrounds and small lakes.

Just past Milepost 284, the scenic drive officially starts at Young Road (Forest Service Road 512), an unpaved 26 miles in a generally southern direction toward the pleasant valley community of Young.

Young Road offers peaks, valleys, typical mountain hairpin curves, steep drop-offs, beautiful pine forests, and back roads into wilderness areas that should not be driven in your father's Oldsmobile unless he was possessed of bravado and possessed a Bravada. And while we are on the subject of driving automobiles on gravel roads, it is best to stay a respectable distance behind any other vehicle traveling the Young Road unless you don't care if your windshield looks as if it just emerged from a rock-throwing episode.

Nick Berezenko

Zane Grey Country

Although the first inhabitants of central Arizona's Mogollon Rim Country likely would disagree if they were still around, their turf probably can be called Zane Grey Country without too much concern about contradiction except from the Apaches who came later and are still very much around.

Nobody's old enough to remember the prehistoric Mogollons, but lots of people remember the famous Western author of the enormously popular *Riders of the Purple Sage* (1912) and 84 other novels, many of them centered on this area. Those who don't recall reading at least one of his books are mostly likely to be (pick one or more) people who prefer Louis L'Amour, people who never read a melodramatic Western tale, teenagers, or those who have spent their sentient years struggling to remember what Proust remembered.

Grey, who was born in 1875 and died in 1939, was a dentist by education and writer by inclination. He had a cabin built in this area in the early 1920s, but it was destroyed by the Dude wildfire in 1990. A replica, however, has been built adjacent to the Rim Country Museum in Payson (see Page 293 in Where To Go).

[Visitors can view a replica of writer Zane Grey's cabin. ▲]

Young is a tiny community plunked down in Pleasant Valley and tethered to history and frontier celebrity by the single strand of a bloody feud that, by comparison, makes the more-famous gunfight in Tombstone read like a water-pistol squabble.

An Arizona Department of Commerce profile of Young describes it as mostly "a retirement and second-home community" with half of the population 50 years old or older. Mountains surround Young in the heart of the Tonto National Forest at about 5,000 feet. It has the deserved reputation of being a peaceful community, but its history is bounded at both ends by violence. Young began in the 1880s as a cattle-ranching community, but between 1887 and 1892 it was the scene of a running gun battle between two families, the Grahams and the Tewksburys and their respective supporters. The end result was the deaths of somewhere between 20 and 50 people—the most often cited number is 30—during what is now called, sans irony, the Pleasant Valley War.

The war was, arguably, the outgrowth of one of those hoary, old cow versus sheep flaps, plus the death of a Navajo sheepherder, and no one was ever convicted of anything. Zane Grey did a fictional account of the feud in a book entitled *To The Last Man*, and the names of a couple of participants in a few of the gunfights—Commodore Perry Owens and Jim Roberts—have passed into the gunslinger hall of fame. In one gun battle, Owens (Commodore was his first name, Sheriff his rank) shot four times and nailed four men, three of them fatally. He eventually metamorphosed into a successful mercantile businessman and died peacefully in 1919. Roberts, also a peace officer, shot five men in feud-related battle. He died in 1934 of a heart ailment.

Parker Canyon unfolds in the Sierra Anchas. ▼ A Salado Indian doorway peers into history in Pueblo Canyon in the Sierra Ancha Wilderness. ▶

Nick Berezenko

Many are the tales that emerged from that feud between the Tewksbury and Graham families, but one demands yet another recounting. Don Dedera, a former *Arizona Highways* editor, described it this way in some of his published writings:

"The last Graham to die was Tom. He was shot in the back (August 2, 1892) while driving a wagonload of grain to Tempe. His young widow had his six-shooter in her handbag, and when the courtroom was concentrating on testimony at a hearing for the alleged killer, she shoved the pistol into the side of the suspect and pulled the trigger. Misfire. The hammer caught on the fold of cloth."

From Young it's all precipitously downhill to the end of this scenic route. The road offers a spectacular view of the vast Sierra Ancha (or "wide mountains" in Spanish), a mountain range in the Tonto National Forest. It is

Jeff Snyder

crowned by Aztec Peak, the highest point in the range at 7,733 feet. The Sierra Ancha Wilderness covers nearly 21,000 acres about 15 miles south of Young and 36 miles north of Globe. It contains awesome canyons and views worth frequent stops when you can find a pullout on the twisty road. You'll pass several rugged Forest Service roads. One of them, FR 487 on your left, leads to Workman Creek and its 180-foot falls, an area of old uranium mines.

Workman Creek was named after Herbert Wertman, at onetime a packer in an Army pack train and who lived below the falls in the 1880s. He was notable for being more than 6 feet tall and weighing perhaps 140 pounds, which means he had a waistline measurement that was the male equivalent of Scarlett O'Hara's 17 inches. He also had long, blond hair tied with a blue ribbon, the sort of information everyone who visits the area should know. The transmogrification of Wertman to Workman can only be explained by the effect of time on pronunciation and its spawn, spelling.

At its southern end near Roosevelt Lake, the road becomes State Route 288, which links with State Route 88, which takes you to U.S. Route 60 near Globe where you can pick up another scenic drive—the Gila-Pinal Scenic Road stretching about 40 miles from the Globe-Miami area westward to Superior and Florence Junction (see Page 74). ⫴

[Cascading maple leaves blanket Workman Creek in the Sierra Anchas.]

Claire Curran

Where To Go
What To See
What To Do

Nick Berezenko

Listings here include the Coconino, Tonto, and Apache-Sitgreaves national forests, lands of which account for most of the Mogollon Rim. Also included are the communities of Christopher Creek, Payson, Pine, Strawberry, and Young. Northern Arizona University has an interesting overview at www.cpluhna.nau.edu/Places/mogollon_rim.htm.
The Arizona Game and Fish Department lists lakes and streams at www.gf.state.az.us/h_f/where_fish_mogollon.shtml.
And this Internet site will be handy: www.rimcountry.com

National Forests: The Mogollon Rim lies in parts of three national forests, which offer extensive recreational opportunities and programs. Here are telephone numbers and links to the forests' Internet sites: Coconino, (928) 527-3600;
www.fs.fed.us/r3/coconino/recreation/mog_rim/rec_mogollon.shtml.
Tonto, (928) 474-7900; www.fs.fed.us/r3/tonto.
Apache-Sitgreaves, (928) 333-5966; www.fs.fed.us/r3/asnf/recreation

The narrow channel of Blue Ridge Reservoir is good for fishing. ▲
Devil's Chasm, a Salado cliff dwelling, clings to the rock face in Tonto National Forest. ▼

Jeff Snyder

Christopher Creek

Christopher Creek: Between Payson and Forest Lakes, this small community offers lodges and campgrounds, two restaurants, a market with a post office, towing station, and repair shop, and access to trails within the region. No gas stations, but visitors can fill up at Star Valley or Forest Lakes, each about 18 miles away. From Payson, head east on State Route 260. Rim Country Ranger Station, (928) 474-7900.

Payson

Woods Canyon Lake Recreation Area: Among towering stands of old-growth ponderosa pine trees, the 52-acre lake offers boating and fishing. Seven developed campgrounds nearby. A seasonal store, boat rentals. A 5-mile trail meanders along the lake's shoreline. Open from around Memorial Day to around Labor Day. $ for camping. Take State 260 east from Payson for about 30 miles; turn left (north) onto Forest Service Road 300 and drive 3.5 miles to entrance. (928) 537-8888; (877) 444-6777. www.fs.fed.us/r3/asnf/recreation/campgrounds; www.reserveusa.com

[A pair of boaters enjoys gleaming, golden serenity as sunrise hits Woods Canyon Lake. ▼ A hiker admires cascading ribbons of water along Waterfall Trail. ▶]

Nick Berezenko

World's Oldest Continuous Rodeo: Held in Payson every third weekend in August since 1884. Professional rodeo cowboys from around the world compete. Parade. $. (800) 672-9766. www.rimcountrychamber.com

Shoofly Village Ruins: Occupied from around 1000 to 1250 A.D. by Indians with ties to the Hohokam and Salado cultures. The ruins contain 87 rooms with a surrounding quarter-mile, paved path. Wheelchair accessible. Picnic area with grill and ramada. Free. Located just northeast of Payson; take State Route 87 to Houston Mesa Road, go northeast and follow signs. (928) 474-7900.

Rim Country Museum: A complete view of Rim Country history and culture. Historic buildings show exhibits spanning from ancient cultures to Western novelist Zane Grey, who wrote about the region. Guided tours available. $. Green Valley Park. (928) 474-3483. www.rimcountrymuseums.org

Museum of Rim Country Archaeology: A branch of the Rim Country Museum, it displays petroglyphs, murals, pottery, tools, physical anthropology, and hands-on exhibits. Visitors can take a self-guided tour

Nick Berezenko

or call ahead for a guided tour. Wheelchair accessible. $. 510 W. Main St. (928) 468-1128.

Tonto Creek Hatchery: Established in 1936 by the Game and Fish Department, the hatchery breeds rainbow, cutthroat, Apache, and brook trout. Visitors can take a self-guided tour. Visitors center offers historical information. Wheelchair accessible. Free. Located about 20 miles northeast of Payson, via State 260 east for 17 miles, turn left on Forest Service Road 289, and follow for 4 miles to hatchery. (928) 478-4200. www.gf.state.az.us/h_f/hatcheries_tonto_creek.shtml

Highline National Recreation Trail: Skirting the base of the Mogollon Rim, a 51-mile trail is used by hikers, mountain bikers, and horseback riders. Stretching from just south of Pine to east of Christopher Creek, the trail offers views. Free. The western end begins at Pine Trailhead (15 miles north of Payson off State 87) and continues eastward to the 260 Trailhead (27 miles east of Payson off State 260). Payson Ranger Station, (928) 474-7900; Rim Country Chamber, (928) 474-4515, (800) 672-9766. www.fs.fed.us/r3/tonto/recreation/rec-hiking-trail_detail-highline.shtml

Fossil Springs Wilderness: Flowing at 20,000 gallons per minute, the springs support a diverse riparian environment friendly to many different species of birds and trees. Day-hike, swimming holes, trails. Free. Located about 30 miles southeast of Camp Verde; take Forest Highway 9 and Forest Service Road 708. (928) 477-2172; 928-567-4121. www.fs.fed.us/r3/coconino/recreation/red_rock/fossil-spgs-wild.shtml

Tonto Natural Bridge State Park: Possibly the largest travertine bridge in the world stands at 183 feet tall. Tunnel and waterfall viewed from several different paths. Trails leading down to the bottom of the canyon are steep and reveal ferns and deposits of travertine forming stalagmites and stalactites. Visitors center, ramadas with picnic tables and grills, historic lodge, museum. Partial wheelchair accessibility. Hours vary seasonally. $. Located about 10 miles northwest of Payson via State 87. (928) 476-4202; gift shop (928) 476-2261. www.pr.state.az.us

Pine-Strawberry

Pine-Strawberry Museum: In a chapel built in 1917, exhibits show artifacts from Indians and pioneers. Tours can be scheduled by calling in advance. Wheelchair accessible. Hours vary, so call ahead. Free. Fifteen miles north of Payson, off State 87. (928) 476-3547. www.pinestrawhs.org

Strawberry Schoolhouse: The oldest school structure in Arizona was built in 1885 in one day. The one-room log structure shows photographs of early pioneers within a restored interior. Wheelchair accessible. Open seasonally, call ahead for hours. Free. In Strawberry; take State 87 north to Fossil Creek Road; head west for about 2 miles. (928) 476-3095. www.pinestrawhs.org/schoolhouse.htm.

Llama Buddy: Explore the Mogollon Rim with a llama hiking buddy through Fossil Creek Llamas, which operates a ranch near Strawberry, 110 miles northeast of Phoenix. The company offers overnight pack trips and day hikes through Rim Country, with the gentle creatures carrying your gear, often while humming little llama tunes. (928) 476-5178. www.fossilcreekllamas.com.

Young

Young: A small settlement in Tonto National Forest best known for the infamous Pleasant Valley War fought for five years by the Grahams and Tewksburys. Every third weekend in July, roping, a parade, and arts and crafts displays in the community center. Museum is open all day long during the weekend event. Free. Eighty miles northeast of Phoenix via State 87 north to Payson, east on State 260 for 33 miles, then on partly unpaved Young Road south for 23 miles. Pleasant Valley Ranger Station, (928) 462-4300; Pleasant Valley Library, (928) 462-3588. http://new.azcommerce.com/SiteSel/Profiles

[A kayaker glides across a glassy pond in the Mogollon Rim area.   ]

Morey Mibradt

Pacheta Falls roars with runoff from a monsoon storm. ▲
Blue lupines fringe a ponderosa pine tree. ▶

Jack Dykinga

The White Mountains
Nature at Her Best

When writers of Western stories and movies describe the high country, they surely draw on east-central Arizona's White Mountains for inspiration. It's all here: astounding scenery decorated with summer green, autumn gold and red, winter white, and the many colors of wildflowers in spring, summer, and fall; forests that flow up and down mountains before giving way to grassy meadows; trout lakes reachable by fine roads or lakes that require some back-country driving; small towns with fine digs for those wanting lodges and classy RV parks; towns established in the 1800s by Mormon pioneers; and, of course, history and a sense of the Old West.

Jack Dykinga

Getting 'High' on Arizona

W e are entering Arizona's high country, a place to get high on the dizzying elevation, the intoxicating views, and an array of attractions and activities.

It's also the place where low-desert folk go to escape the heat, or catch a fish, or hike a mountain trail, or ski, or just shack up next to a wood stove in winter and an outdoor barbeque pit in summer.

The elevations encountered on the three designated scenic drives discussed here generally range, with a couple of modest exceptions both up and down, between an altitude of 5,000 and 10,000 literally breathtaking feet.

Enough suspense. We are entering the magical White Mountains, a 2,000-square-mile fairyland of snowy mountains in winter, golden aspens in fall, green meadows in summer, and wildflowers in spring. If enough of the mountains' intoxicating elements are consumed, some people might think the land is populated by sasquatches, tree trolls, pine sprites, woodland wizards, and elves. But such creatures rarely, if ever, are seen.

There also are some magical fish (read: they inexplicably shook the hook) that share more than 25 lakes and 800 miles of rivers and streams with trout, bass, bluegill, catfish, and walleyes. For those who are without gills or fishing tackle, there is birding, boating, hiking, camping, horseback riding, downhill and cross country skiing, tours of prehistoric Indian ruins as well as historical and cultural sites, mountain biking, mountain climbing, and canyon gawking. Also, you may spot bears, elk, deer, bobcats, wolves, and other wildlife, besides the customary abundance of cows and horses.

It's great and gorgeous Nature at her best, perhaps the state's finest array of outdoor vacation activities that can be found in such a concentrated area. It also makes for great driving along the three officially designated scenic roads—the Coronado Trail Scenic Road, the White River Scenic Road, and the White Mountain Scenic Road—that afford views of natural wonders ranging from the Petrified Forest to the Salt River Canyon to the Mogollon Rim, that magnificent escarpment that forms the southern edge of the massive Colorado Plateau.

Did we neglect to mention golf? The area's got game, on good courses, in all directions and highly recommended for all those who don't want to play with that rude threesome of dehydration, heat stroke, and heat exhaustion often encountered on or about the sixth of any 18-hole adventure into the 100- to 115-degree summer days of Phoenix or Tucson. Summer temperatures in the high country generally range between the 60s and the mid-80s.

Golf, of course, is only half a word, sort of like ham sans eggs. So the other half of Golf is Retirement. At the risk of reading like a chamber of commerce

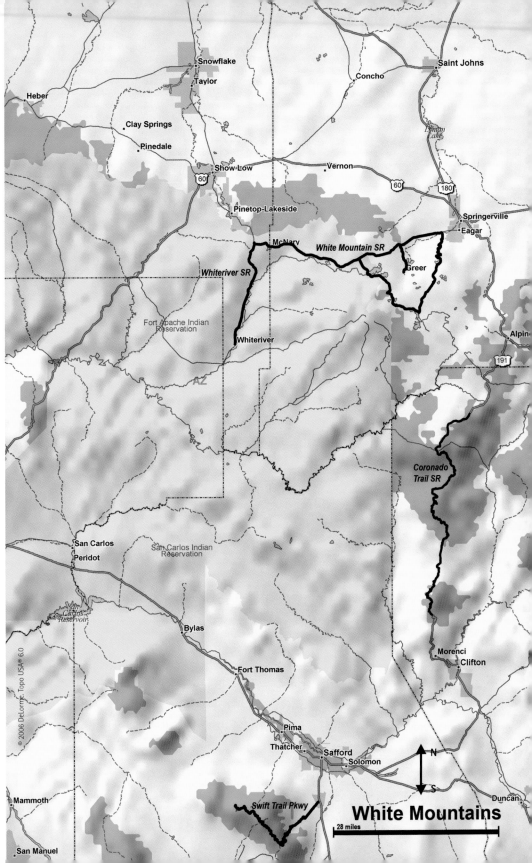

Heber
Snowflake
Taylor
Saint Johns
Concho
Clay Springs
Pinedale
Lyman Lake
Show Low
Vernon
US 60
180
Pinetop-Lakeside
Springerville
Eagar
McNary
White Mountain SR
Greer
Whiteriver SR
Whiteriver
Alpine
191
AZ
Fort Apache Indian Reservation
Coronado Trail SR
San Carlos
Peridot
San Carlos Indian Reservation
Bylas
San Carlos Reservoir
Fort Thomas
Morenci
Clifton
Pima
Thatcher
Safford
Solomon
Duncan
Mammoth
N
S
Swift Trail Pkwy

© 2006 DeLorme. Topo USA® 6.0

San Manuel

28 miles

White Mountains

promo, travelers who are at or near that golden (if only 10 karat) age should look carefully at some of the towns along these routes, communities such as Springerville, Eagar, Pinetop, Lakeside, McNary, Snowflake (named for two guys, Snow and Flake, rather than that stuff you've had to shovel from your driveway), Alpine, Greer, Show Low (yes, from a historic poker game), and Nutrioso (a Spanish combination of "beaver" and "bear"), just to name a few. They offer great scenery, wonderful climates, good restaurants, and, lastly, good people who will welcome you ... and your good money.

That said, let's get in the saddle of our 210 horses and hit the trails. ◪

Jeff Snyder

Coronado 'Found' the White Mountains

Francisco Vasquez de Coronado was another one of those fire-in-the-eyes, half-nutso Spaniard conquistadores who apparently got bored with their home lives and their golf games at 16th-century Costa del Sol courses and decided it would be more fun and more profitable to thrash around in the forests and deserts of the Southwest, which then was the frontier of New Spain.

In Coronado's case, he began plowing through eastern Arizona and New Mexico in 1540, searching for the mythic Seven Cities of Cibola and gold. He apparently was a man who, in one of those glorious epiphanies, decided to believe in himself. He shouldn't have. He failed to find either the cities or the gold, although in fairness he did open up the Southwest to colonization. That last feat, however, was not particularly popular with some elements of the indigenous population that were getting along just fine, thank you.

Coronado's dubious triumph is the approximate historical equivalent of the 1968 Harvard-Yale football game that ended in a tie, 29 to 29. Because Yale had gone into the game with a string of six victories and appeared unbeatable, the Harvard newspaper headline proclaimed: "Harvard Beats Yale."

Coronado also "found" Arizona's White Mountains, which in those days were a lot of dense pine forest and big bears (and still are). These days they are finally producing lots of tourist gold because of what the area has to offer, including still more gold in the autumnal aspens. His route, following the paths of ancient Indian traders, is now memorialized as the Coronado Trail Scenic Road running from Springerville on the north to Morenci and Clifton 120 miles south.

[Shade encloses the Black River. ▲   ]

A Place to Escape

There are millions upon millions of skiers and snowboarders in the United States, but there still is room at the top to experience the thrill of aloneness.

In the grip of an escapist mood, take the lift, then, to the top of Sunrise Peak in Arizona's Apache Indian country on a winter's weekday. On shameless display in the near and the distant are the barely credible splendors of the state's eastern terrain. Far below, in the murmuring lodge, hidden and forgotten for the moment, are the many people enjoying the indoor amenities.

But one stands alone at the top, leaning on poles, listening. On such a day, in such a mood, there is a special ecstasy in hearing the wind burst through the pines, driving the sound of humankind ahead of it and away ... away. The sun's rays that split the trees and whitened and brightened the mountainside with their depressingly cheery enzymes and bleach are gone now, sealed off by a darkening monolith of cloud heavy with snow.

[Guests at X Diamond Ranch meander past agave plants.]

David H. Smith

The flakes begin to fall, gently and sparsely at first, then heavily, layering the hair and the eyebrows and the parka. The pines catch them, the wind frees them. The tracks of the past weekend's skiers and boarders, the long loops of linked turns, the tight coil of a wedel, begin to disappear.

It is time to go, to chase the wind on one traverse, embrace it on the return in the winding descent. The skis are running smoothly now, cutting cleanly through the forgiving hardpack on a turn, sending off sprays of powder in the short schuss.

The slope gentles and the sounds, forgotten during that first concentration on control, unblur, separate: the clicking of the skis against each other, the harsh whisper of metal edges slicing a patch of crust, the breath coming harder, the rustle of parka as poles are planted and released.

Ahead is a field of moguls, a goose-pimpling of the smooth slope where countless skiers have unsheepishly followed each other's winding spoor, throwing up snow on the turns until mounds are created.

Up to the first mogul. The skis unweight by themselves, the turn comes easily, the skis point down and head for the next. Knees flex, absorbing the jolts.

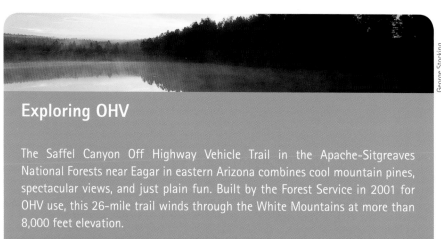

George Stocking

Exploring OHV

The Saffel Canyon Off Highway Vehicle Trail in the Apache-Sitgreaves National Forests near Eagar in eastern Arizona combines cool mountain pines, spectacular views, and just plain fun. Built by the Forest Service in 2001 for OHV use, this 26-mile trail winds through the White Mountains at more than 8,000 feet elevation.

Accessible from various points, the Saffel Canyon OHV Trail is perfect for shorter trips. The south trailhead near Pat Knoll has rest rooms, a covered area, parking lot, and a "tot lot" for beginners. Wildlife viewing, spectacular scenery, old cabins, and breathtaking views lure riders to this mountain trail.

Be prepared for rain during summer, and in fall enjoy the golden aspens.

To get to the trail from State Route 260 south of Eagar, take Forest Service Road 285 south for about 3 miles. At Forest Service Road 74, marked 76 on older forest maps, turn left (east) at the sign indicating the way to the OHV trail. The well-marked northern trailhead is about one-half mile down the road. The southern trailhead near Pat Knoll is another 18 miles south on Forest Service Road 285.

Information: Apache-Sitgreaves National Forests, Springerville Ranger District, (928) 333-4372.

[Dawn silhouettes the shoreline of Luna Lake. ▲   ]

Suddenly, the balance is gone. It is a fall. Down, down into the powder that has not been flattened along the side of the trail. Snow in the eyes, the mitts. The bindings holding the feet to the skis have released, freeing the unbroken limbs from their tethers.

It is not a time to hurry. The snow is soft, even warm. Haven't we been told this is how old Eskimos used to die, deliberately and consentingly buried in dry, warm mounds of snow, slipping painlessly off to a frozen, permanent sleep? Is that really, wonderfully true? Is death the ultimate meaning of life?

Such idle speculations are interrupted by the professionally solicitous ski patrolman, the only other person on this patch of the slope. He passes, slows, and asks if everything is all right.

Of course. Of course. It has never been more right. ▥

White River Scenic Road

Route
A straight shot on State Route 73 south from Hon-Dah to Whiteriver, the designated scenic portion. From there, continue to historic Fort Apache and, if wished, a loop on U.S. Route 60 leading back north to Show Low.

Mileage
Officially, 11 miles one way, starting at Hon-Dah but 60 or so miles round trip from Hon-Dah to just beyond Fort Apache and return to Hon-Dah.

Time to Allow
At least four hours, depending on time spent in Fort Apache, located south of the end of the official route.

Elevation
5,000 to 7,000 feet.

Overview
The officially designated scenic portion of the drive is nearly a dozen miles, and portions of it are colorful in the warmer seasons. The unofficial continuation leads to historic Fort Apache and some ancient ruins.

This short, straight drive on State Route 73 between Hon-Dah on the north and the community of Whiteriver on the south has the least visual excitement of the four designated scenic trips in this eastern section of the state. But, in this case, the cliché that less is more (sometimes) could be applied if one were in a generous mood.

The "more" is the bookends: a fancy, modern casino at one end, a well-preserved, very old Army fort at the other. The "less" is the drive in between.

Travelers can begin this drive after a night in any of several pleasant towns in the immediate area including Show Low, Pinetop-Lakeside, and Hon-Dah. Show Low, population about 8,000 and elevation about 6,300 feet, is an old town that has gotten rid of most of its wrinkles and liver spots courtesy of some extensive cosmetic surgery. It is now a modern, wide open, airy, clean community with many businesses and nice landscaping, a far cry from its founding in the 1870s. As its name suggests, it was born during a poker game in 1876 between an Indian scout and his partner. The men decided to settle their differences over ownership of a big ranch that was, in effect, the town site. Rather than dueling Colts, they began a winner-take-all card game of seven-up at a kitchen table. After it had dragged on for hours, one man said to the other something on the order of "show low and you win." The other man drew a winning deuce of clubs, and you can't get lower than that. The card is now the name of a street there.

Hon-Dah, the start of this designated drive, isn't really a town; it's a big, White Mountain Apache-owned casino-convention center-resort at about the intersection of state routes 260 and 73. The name, in the Apache language, is said to translate as "welcome to my home." There are big rooms with TV, a bar, a restaurant, a heated, open-air but roofed hot tub, ditto for the swimming pool, an RV park across the street and ... slot machines, those money-grubbing backbones of all casinos. Five hundred of them: nickel slots, quarter slots, dollar slots, progressive slots, video poker slots, video blackjack slots, and

Robert G. McDonald

even some live poker. The casino also offers live entertainment and an ominous reminder of the perils of getting caught up in the betting atmosphere: an ATM on the floor. The only other perils are to the lungs and heart from the miasma of cigarette smoke and to the ears from the bonging, banging din of some sort of tuneless, mindless electronic music, if music is what it can be called. The casino is open 24 hours a day, every day.

Even if your agenda ignores gaming, a stop in the lodge's lobby is worth at least 30 minutes. The décor draws its inspiration from the White Mountain Apaches and their homeland. Off in one corner of the lodge a small museum (free) displays many interesting artifacts and offers a short film from which you'll learn the basics of Apache culture.

■■■

So let's hear it for fresh air as we head south on State 73 for the 11-mile designated route ending north of the community of Whiteriver, headquarters for the White Mountain Apache Tribe and site of an airplane runway long enough to accommodate Air Force One. We'll then continue south for a short distance to Fort Apache and, lastly, the Kinishba ruins.

The White River (yep, the river name contains two words, the town only one) escorts the route on its way south, the river largely hidden from the road until just outside Whiteriver when the river gorge comes into view, river and all. Along the route but off to the west is a site said to be the grave of Alchesay, a revered White Mountain Apache chief who scouted for the U.S. Army in the 1870s and

Gold aspens brighten a stand of spruce, fir, and pine at Ord Creek in the White Mountains. ◄ Glowing scenery unfolds at sunset from Baldy Peak. ▼

Robert G. McDonald

Jerry Jacka

Fort Apache

Just beyond the official reach of the White River Scenic Road is the Grail of this trip, Fort Apache, but you don't need some Arthurian Sir Bors or Sir Lancelot to lead your quest. Just stay in the saddle of your noble, white SUV charger and continue a few miles down State Route 73 past Whiteriver to where the highway bends sharply to the right. There, turn left (there's a Fort Apache sign at this junction) and you'll be at the fort within a mile.

More than 20 old buildings, some beautifully crafted from stones, fill this 288-acre historic Army fort established in 1870. First named Camp Ord, it became Camp Mogollon, then Camp Thomas, then Camp Apache, then Fort Apache. All that between 1870 and 1879, and please memorize the sequence for the written test to come.

Fort Apache was a military post until 1922, when the government converted it to an Indian boarding school, but many of the old homes and other structures can be visited, including a particularly splendid one thought to have housed General George Crook, commander of the Military Department of Arizona in the 1870s and 1880s. Crook's quarters even offer some items for sale including a popgun for $20, a most useful item in this wild country. The fort played an instrumental role in a variety of campaigns against Indians, including the Victorio Campaign in 1879, the Battle of Cibecue in 1881, the Geronimo Campaign from 1881 to 1886, and the Mexican Border Campaign against Pancho Villa in 1916 and 1917.

Also on the site you'll find the Apache Cultural Center with good displays of photos, gear, history, tools, and cultural practices. Also, take the self-guided tour to see prehistoric petroglyphs and a re-created Apache village. One exhibit

[Theodore Roosevelt once stayed at Fort Apache's officers' quarters. ▲]

extensively discusses the Sunrise puberty ceremony. The young Apache woman at the entrance desk said she had avoided the physically exhausting, four-day affair because it was expensive and, anyway, she had grown up in Phoenix. She estimated that between 60 and 80 percent of young Apaches, herself included, do not speak Apache, but that it is being taught in Head Start classes.

Across and down the circular road, well within walking distance of the fort complex, lies the fort cemetery, populated by headstones. They announce the presence of the remains of many U.S. Army-employed Indian scouts, Indian children, and even Corydon Cooley, the scout who lost his claim to ownership of Show Low in a poker game.

Information: See Fort Apache Historic Park listing in Where To Go, Page 325.

was awarded the Medal of Honor for his wartime activities. Don't look for signs for the grave; they are as elusive—if they exist at all—as Apache warrior bands during those Indian-Army wars. By the way, on the Army rolls, Alchesay was A-1, a name that the tribe gave to one of the many lakes on the reservation. It's about 10 miles east of Hon-Dah on the south side of State Route 260.

Overall, the drive is in the midst of the Fort Apache Indian Reservation, also known as the White Mountain Indian Reservation, a land of 1.6 million acres, dense pine forests separated by meadows, 26 lakes, and 800 miles of streams. While attractive, the heavily timbered route makes no demands on anybody's powers of description unless side roads to fish hatcheries or distant lakes get your adrenalin pump thrumming. If that is the case, the William Creek National Fish Hatchery, run by the U.S. Fish and Wildlife Service, can be reached via a side road about 5 miles south of Hon-Dah.

Just beyond the end of the designated drive is Fort Apache, a worthy and historic destination.

A short distance down the road from Fort Apache are the Kinishba ruins ("brown house" in anglicized Apache), a couple of peculiar structures built and occupied by the Mogollon people between 1250 and 1400 A.D. and somewhat restored in the 1930. These days, a rather modern stovepipe juts out of the main building. The ruin is reached a couple of miles down a rutted, dirt road called Kinishba Road (go left at both forks) running northward off of State 73. A small sign tells visitors it is a sacred site to the Apaches and urges that it be treated with respect, a nice but futile sentiment that has failed miserably to prevent the accumulation of rubbish. But still, history and culture linger at this place.

At this point, head back to Hon-Dah, which also is the starting point of this drive. Or continue west on State 73 to U.S. Route 60—about 15 miles—and then north for about 25 miles to Show Low. ⎈

White Mountain Scenic Road

Route	A straight line west to east (or the other way around if you wish) on State Route 260 between Hon-Dah and Springerville with a loop part way along down State Route 273 to Sunrise and Big Lake and State Route 373 to Greer, then back on State Route 261 to State 260, continuing east.
Mileage	About 60, loop included.
Time to Allow	Two to four hours, depending on side trips and dawdling.
Elevation	Ranges between 7,000 and 9,000 feet.
Overview	A particularly nice drive in any season, particularly fall when colors are ablaze. Takes the sightseer to lakes, mountains, forests, and even a big casino.

P icture this, or better yet, see it in person and photograph it: an Ivory Soap Day, 99 and 44/100ths percent purely white beauty. A winter day under a cloudless, blue sky, a golden sun, and new, powdery snow gently drifting off the drooping boughs of the big pines and floating on the breeze across the windshield like dimestore glitter.

Yeah, get these days all the time in winter, the locals will say.

A half-hour away from Hon-Dah (the casino and starting point of the official White Mountain Scenic Road, a mostly flat, high-country route that ends 40 miles to the east in Springerville-Eagar), is good skiing and snowboarding at Sunrise Park. Don't care for snow? Came here to get away from the drifted driveway back east? Stay on this road, State Route 260, to Springerville and take a right on U.S. Route 191. A couple or three hours and 120-plus miles or so farther south is the warm Sonoran Desert. To the west is Phoenix, a half-day distant.

But all that's for wusses. We've been there, south on the Coronado Trail, in this chapter, so we will stay on this scenic route instead. Golf can come another day.

Each season offers different reasons for this drive, all of them beautiful and, in summer, cool.

Immediately outside Hon-Dah, heading east on State Route 260, the scene that stretches for several miles is a mixture of big pines, alluring meadows, lakes near and far off either side of the road, hiking trails (rather inaccessible in winter), and some aspen groves that turn to butter in autumn. Utter but ever-changing beauty. The drive captures the essence of the White Mountains, a particularly apt name in the snowy months when even the brown grasses on the surrounding mounds and mountains are either dusted by winter's talcum or buried under a white, downy comforter.

The highway quickly passes through the tiny community of McNary, then at 11 miles from Hon-Dah, the entrance to Big Bear and Little Bear lakes. Next, and quickly so, is the intersection of 260 with State Route 473 and an 8-mile run to the south for Hawley Lake with fishing, cabins, camping, boat rentals, and groceries.

Eighteen miles from Hon-Dah is A-1 Lake, just off the highway. The lake's bureaucratic name came from the identification number the U.S. Army gave to Alchesay, the Apache chief and war hero who scouted for the military. Then it is time for the skiers and boarders in the vehicle to start rustling up their gear, because State Route 273 is at hand. This loop road takes you south to the Sunrise Ski Park, its nearby marina, and a sledding hill. State 273 eventually connects with State Route 261 and with the nearby and popular, 575-acre Big Lake, featuring a visitor center, campgrounds, store, and boat rentals—all closed in winter as are many of the lesser roads in the area. Heading back north, 261 rejoins 260, the main path to Springerville.

At about this point, 25 miles past Hon-Dah, at Milepost 382, the pine-dense view opens up on a descending highway that reveals the quite attractive Round Valley, home of Springerville and Eagar.

On 260 just east of the 273 turnoff to Sunrise and Big Lake is State Route 373, leading 5 miles into a dead end in the captivating resort town of Greer, buried deep in the big pines of the Apache National Forest and stretching for less than a mile alongside the Little Colorado River. The town is guarded from expansion by the federal land on all sides.

Greer sits in a valley, but it's a high valley at 8,500 feet of elevation. It got its name from a Mormon pioneer named Americus Vespucius Greer and was settled in 1879. The population of this little community in winter may reach "about 122" according to one resident. In summer, however, the population explodes to between 5,000 and 6,000, she said. That might seem improbable until a drive through the area reveals a population of restaurants, lodges, cabins, and grand resorts adequate to the needs of just about any town smaller than Phoenix or Tucson.

Nearby is Molly Butler Lodge, built in 1910 and self-described as the oldest lodge in the state.

Another 12 miles down the highway, always looking into the Round Valley below, are Springerville and Eagar, the official end of the White Mountain Scenic Road.

It ends too soon—40 (or more for side trips) miles of driving in this exquisite country aren't enough. ▟

Annual goldeneye carpets a meadow near Springerville and the end of the White Mountain Scenic Road.

David Widmaier

Law of the Gun

Cattle rustling, outlaws, Indian raids, shoot-outs, rough and tumble sheriffs, disputes over water rights—they were part of the Old West and of an area in the White Mountains of eastern Arizona centered on the twin communities of Eagar and Springerville.

Documentation for this survival-of-the-fittest world can be found in a collection of newspapers and artifacts on display in a museum at the X Diamond, a combination resort, Western museum, and historic working ranch a few miles west of Eagar.

Turn south from State Route 260 just west of Milepost 391, at the sign that says "Museum." Shortly thereafter, County Road 4124 winds down into a narrow valley carved out long ago by the Little Colorado River. For several miles, the river channels between rugged lava cliffs and the foothills of the White Mountains. The ranch spreads out about 2 miles up the valley, where the river first emerges from the high country.

Andy Marshall was born in Maine in 1947 and dreamed as a youth of going West. He has now lived in the region for more than 30 years, many of them on the Navajo reservation. His careers have included teaching, economic development, entertainment, sales management, and financial services. He has explored remote locations in the Southwest and lives with his family in Springerville in the White Mountains, where he has taught language arts at a charter school, and prefers, in winter, to hike without gloves, an uncommonly foolish act.

> By ANDY MARSHALL

A constant river flow, fed by winter snows and summer monsoons, keeps the valley fertile with heavy timber carpets, home to deer, elk, bear, and a wide variety of birds. Native bushes and cacti grow up the fractured lava cliffs, ponderosa pines thrive along the river, and different grasses flourish on the valley floor. It is common to see hawks circling the river as it bubbles around curves in the canyon. In winter, the valley is slightly warmer than the high country, and in summer mountain breezes stir the air. Warm, summer days bring monsoon clouds that shade the valley and rumble a warning—or promise—of the afternoon thunderstorms.

The valley's climate, water, rich soil, and natural shelter attracted pioneer ranchers in early Territorial times. Now, it is a hideaway offering respite from urban pressures, and it must have been an oasis to the earliest inhabitants as well: There are significant Indian ruins on the ranch grounds. ▥

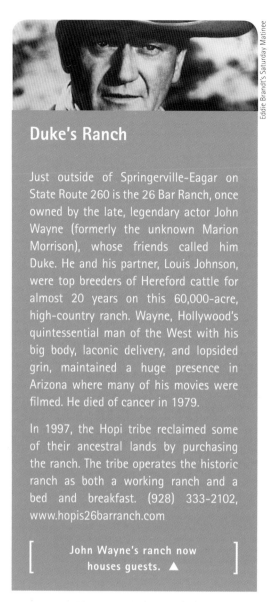

Eddie Brandt's Saturday Matinee

Duke's Ranch

Just outside of Springerville-Eagar on State Route 260 is the 26 Bar Ranch, once owned by the late, legendary actor John Wayne (formerly the unknown Marion Morrison), whose friends called him Duke. He and his partner, Louis Johnson, were top breeders of Hereford cattle for almost 20 years on this 60,000-acre, high-country ranch. Wayne, Hollywood's quintessential man of the West with his big body, laconic delivery, and lopsided grin, maintained a huge presence in Arizona where many of his movies were filmed. He died of cancer in 1979.

In 1997, the Hopi tribe reclaimed some of their ancestral lands by purchasing the ranch. The tribe operates the historic ranch as both a working ranch and a bed and breakfast. (928) 333-2102, www.hopis26barranch.com

[John Wayne's ranch now houses guests. ▲]

The X Diamond has been in the same family for 120 years and maintains its original style and appearance while developing a Western museum. Amenities include fly fishing, horseback riding, hiking, tours of the ruins, and even a beauty salon. Guests can schedule a tour of the partially excavated ruins and sometimes participate in a field school where local experts provide hands-on training in archaeology and supervised digging at the excavation site. Few experiences compare with finding a 900-year-old potsherd or other artifact and properly documenting it for preservation in the museum.

The museum at the ranch consists of original, well-maintained buildings displaying collections from the early Territorial days and artifacts from the ruins. Pioneer life was not all work, and there are many elegant, high-fashion ladies' dresses on hand. There also is a collection of rare player pianos and other 19th-century musical instruments that played their roles in the life of this valley that was a farming and cattle-ranching center during the Apache wars with the U.S. Army.

When you depart this peaceful place, drive slowly along the grassy plain atop the lava cliffs. It is not hard to see where the river flows out of its confining valley and begins to course north across the high desert. A herd of graceful pronghorns can sometimes be seen along the road. Take some time for the view of the White Mountains to the south and the sweeping vistas of the Colorado Plateau to the north before leaving.

Information: (928) 333-2286. www.xdiamondranch.com ⋒

Coronado Trail Scenic Road

Route	U.S. Route 191.
Mileage	About 125 miles from Springerville to Clifton and Morenci. Top stops: Hannagan Meadow and the Morenci mine tour.
Time to Allow	Up to six hours.
Elevation	6,800 feet at Springerville; 8,000 at Alpine; 9,100 at Hannagan Meadow; 4,800 at Morenci.
Overview	An Arizona Scenic Road and a National Scenic Byway, the paved trail is beautiful but tortuous (someone once counted 460 curves). It stretches south from Springerville through valleys and mountain forests to the mining towns of Morenci and Clifton. Snowy in winter; daytime travel recommended.

1 f coming into eastern Arizona from Tucson or other parts of southern Arizona, it makes sense to drive to Morenci and then head north to Springerville. Coming in from Phoenix or Interstate 40, it is more logical to do it the other way around, and that latter way is the one we'll use. If you choose the former, turn this book upside down.

Springerville: Sounds like a TV comedy series named for a town full of dogs. Canine population unknown. Humans, several thousand. It was named for Henry Springer, an Albuquerque merchant who came here in the 1870s and opened a store. Its adjoining twin town of Eagar was named for three brothers who came in 1870. Both communities have long and colorful histories dominated by Mormon pioneers, but also stained by the arrival of gangs, notably the Clantons. They came to the Round Valley area (originally known in Spanish as Valle Redondo) after their shootout at the O.K. Corral in Tombstone. Then in the late 1880s, skilled gunman Sheriff Commodore Perry Owens (Commodore is part of his name, Sheriff his title) cleaned out most of the bad guys.

While in the Springerville-Eagar area, there are several attractions to visit–if you can make the time–before setting off on the Coronado route. Springerville is the unlikely site for a Mormon museum featuring a remarkable art collection ranging from the Renaissance to the early 20th century. That collection includes an engraving credited to Rembrandt; some 18th-century Italian pen and ink drawings; elaborately inlaid antique furniture; a French porcelain and German glassware collection, including two Baccarat crystal bottles reportedly given by Napoleon to one of his generals; a set of Austrian china; and an assortment of French pin boxes with miniature paintings on the lids.

Much of the collection was willed to the Mormon church in Springerville by Renee Cushman, a world traveler who once lived in Springerville but was not a member of the Church of Jesus Christ of Latter-day Saints. You'll find the museum in a wing of the Springerville meetinghouse on the north side of the Mormon church, and viewing is by special appointment only (see Where To Go).

The biggest tourist draw in Springerville—you can tell by the road signs pointing you in that direction—is the Casa Malpais Archaeological Park.

First the pronunciation. Some locals and some tourists call it Kah-Sah Mal-PIE. To be technically correct, which could open you up to untutored challenges, say Kah-Sah Mal Pa EES, or "House of the Badlands" in Spanish. Why badlands? Probably because the original Spanish-speaking settlers of Round Valley (where Springerville is located) called the land north of Springerville the badlands, and Casa Malpais is on the edge of those badlands.

Casa Malpais is an ancient, 14-acre site now owned by the city of Springerville. The Mogollons, mountain people who lived in the Arizona and New Mexico border area and who flourished for 1,100 years, lived here. The Mogollons left Casa Malpais some 600 years ago for reasons best known to them but the subject of much speculation now; most theories center on climatic change. Modern Hopi and Zuni Indians claim an ancestral relationship to the ruin.

The remains of this big, masonry pueblo, dating back to about 1266, include, to borrow from a city brochure, a great kiva complex, several masonry compounds, an enclosing fortified wall, several isolated rooms, catacombs, sacred chambers, grinding area, rock art panels, a calendrical system, and trash middens. It exists on five volcanic terraces and is reached by a modest climb, not wheelchair-accessible, along a rocky path leading past underground catacombs, a network of still-below-ground rooms, and through a natural stone channel that serves as a sort of stone stairway to the upper terrace.

This gated National Historic Landmark site is on Papago Street about 2 miles and several hundred yards of roadbed east of Springerville's downtown. It can be toured with a guide by contacting the Casa Malpais Museum and Visitor Center, 318 E. Main St.(see Where To Go).

In passing, the site looks out over the Round Valley Ensphere, described as the only high school domed football stadium in the United States. It also looks out over a portion of the White Mountain Volcanic Field near the headwaters of the

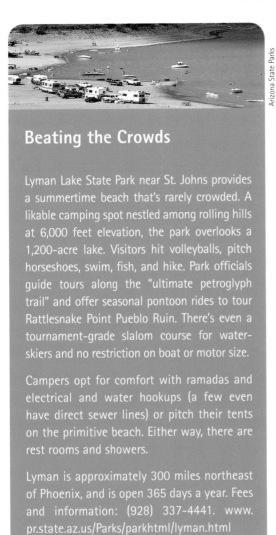

Arizona State Parks

Beating the Crowds

Lyman Lake State Park near St. Johns provides a summertime beach that's rarely crowded. A likable camping spot nestled among rolling hills at 6,000 feet elevation, the park overlooks a 1,200-acre lake. Visitors hit volleyballs, pitch horseshoes, swim, fish, and hike. Park officials guide tours along the "ultimate petroglyph trail" and offer seasonal pontoon rides to tour Rattlesnake Point Pueblo Ruin. There's even a tournament-grade slalom course for water-skiers and no restriction on boat or motor size.

Campers opt for comfort with ramadas and electrical and water hookups (a few even have direct sewer lines) or pitch their tents on the primitive beach. Either way, there are rest rooms and showers.

Lyman is approximately 300 miles northeast of Phoenix, and is open 365 days a year. Fees and information: (928) 337-4441. www.pr.state.az.us/Parks/parkhtml/lyman.html

[**The Lyman Lake beach offers summer "noncrowds." ▲**]

Little Colorado. The volcanic field is a 1,100-square-mile patch (think all of Rhode Island and more) of lava mesas, more than 400 cinder cones, and some deep canyons. The volcanoes started erupting there about 3 million years ago. They have quit for now.

Before departing Springerville, we go to the statue of a 10-foot-tall woman in frontier dress, a sunbonnet, and carrying a baby in the crook of her left arm and the barrel of a rifle in her right hand. Another child is hanging onto her skirt and right leg. One of 12 identical such monuments created in the late 1920s and early 1930s to honor the women who traveled into the unknown land of the West and helped settle it, she is the product of a drive by the Daughters of the American Revolution and a then-county judge named Harry Truman to get Congress to acknowledge the women pioneers. Her identical sisters are planted in Maryland, Pennsylvania, West Virginia, Ohio, Indiana, Illinois, Missouri, Kansas, Colorado, New Mexico, and California.

The Madonna and her sister statues were cast in something called algonite, a concrete-like conglomerate of several elements including cement. They are said to look out over historically significant spots. In the Springerville case, she is on Main Street next to the McDonald's, an institution whose fries and burgers have contributed to the creation of a living population with concrete arteries.

■ ■ ■

When done with Springerville-Eagar, it is time to select from among the scenic-historic routes discussed in this chapter. If you must pick only one, the

Coronado Trail Scenic Road is the longest but the best for an overview of the pine forests, the aspen meadows, the mountain ranges, the valleys, and the vistas offered by this part of the country, not to mention the conspicuous abundance of hiking trails and developed campsites off just about any road or side path. Be warned that the long drive must go slowly because of steep grades and numerous hairpin turns. If you get carsick easily, this drive is not for you.

With that in mind, head for U.S. Route 191, which can be reached either out of Springerville or Eagar and becomes the Coronado Trail beginning near Eagar. Coming up on the right a few miles south down the highway is a narrow, winding side road that runs for 5 pretty miles into the state-owned Sipe White Mountain Wildlife Area, a 1,362-acre, somewhat-protected home for elk, deer, eagles, waterfowl, and native fish. There is a beautiful stone building at the end of the drive that serves as a visitor center and as the starting point for a 1.5-mile loop hiking trail to a scenic overlook. Nearby is the Glen Livet reservoir.

Kerrick James

Back out on U.S. 191, the road leads through alpine hills, meadows, and valleys to Nelson Reservoir, a 60-acre lake paralleling the highway for about a mile. The lake offers a stock of trout, some picnic tables, toilets, and boat ramps (electric motors only, please) and is wheelchair-accessible. To the southeast is a good view of the rounded Escudilla Mountain, an 11,000-foot, old volcano, the third-highest mountain in the state. It is believed to have been named by Coronado or one of his party for a soup bowl of his native Spain. The mountain is a wilderness area, once home to grizzly bears and now the center of 5,200 acres of hiking trails and great views.

Next and quickly so is the community of Nutrioso, which yields its tiny charms to those willing to take a quick loop off and then back on 191. The first settlers here killed a beaver ("nutria") and then a bear ("oso").

Eight miles farther is the community of Alpine, at 8,000-foot elevation a gateway of sorts into major fishing and hiking country. It was founded in the 1870s by Mormons and is just north of the Blue Range Primitive Area, a fine wilderness divided by the Blue River and populated by wildlife and wild mountain-bikers.

The next 25 miles takes you through the beautiful passage between Alpine and Hannagan Meadow and resembles a vast, overly vegetated Christmas tree farm on growth hormones—dense stands of towering, healthy pines with rarely a break or vista.

■■■

Before Hannagan Meadow, however, is one of several spots designated by signs as a "wolf recovery area." A small road off to the right takes the driver along a pleasant, forested route into an area of protection for the Mexican gray wolf, an endangered species of wolf that has been reintroduced into eastern and southeastern Arizona. The U.S. Endangered Species Act protects the big carnivore (up to 90 pounds) from being shot—with certain exceptions. This beautiful animal

The Blue River, snaking through eastern Arizona, is also a prime birding spot. ◀ The endangered Mexican wolf is the rarest subspecies of gray wolf in North America. ▼

G. C. Kelley

likes mountainous oak wood-land, pine, and grassland habitat and preys largely on deer. The wolves were exterminated by a combination of federal, state, and private campaigns that began in earnest in 1914 when Congress appropriated $115,000 to hire hundreds of federal hunters assigned to kill wolves, mountain lions, coyotes, grizzlies, and other predators in the United States.

The mountain lion can run 44 mph, jump 20 feet, and vertically leap 8 feet.

Tom Vezo

The current newage of wolf enlightenment isn't all that popular with some ranchers, but they are now up against environmental and ecological groups with resources and some political clout with pols, depending on the national administration.

The road, which can be taken in a short or long burst, is quite pretty and the potential for seeing a wolf, unless you fancy yourself to be Little Red Whatever, is a magnetic draw. Chances are you won't, but what if you did?

■ ■ ■

At Hannagan Meadow, the forest parts to reveal a small, pretty meadow on one side of the road and the Hannagan Meadow Lodge on the other. A lodge employee, a woman with a friendly manner and a Gothic taste for eye makeup set on stun, proclaims that she has sat on the lodge porch in the evening and watched a wolf chase a deer across the meadow. There is hardly a better place to stay and dine in the midst of all this forested splendor unless you are determined to drive on to Morenci and Clifton.

The old story has it that back in the 1890s a fellow named Bob Hannagan, who ran cattle in this area, got about $1,200 in debt to some local residents. They finally chained him to a tree in the meadow and kept him there until some relatives paid his obligation.

So we leave Hannagan Meadow and say a delighted hello, a short drive down 191, to a vista point that must not be skipped. It is called Blue Vista, at 9,184 feet of elevation. There is a nature trail and there are limited facilities, but never mind that. Step to either side of the parking area and look out onto and down on what are likely the most spectacular views of ridges, meadows, mountains, peaks, and valleys anyone will ever see. Even Mount Graham, 70 miles to the south, is visible. Not even a panoramic camera can capture what the eye can. The setting is the Blue Range Primitive Area and the edge of the Mogollon Rim, which is the southern drop-off of the Colorado Plateau.

A long descent begins now, heading toward the mining community of Morenci and the end of the official Coronado Trail. Along the way are numerous campgrounds reached by short drives off 191, including ones offering some privacy called Juan Miller Campground and Honeymoon Campground. Assuming you prudently do not choose to let your gaze wander as you drive, all designated view points including the Blue Range and the Red Mountain Fire Interpretation overlooks are worth a stop, both for the views and for the informational signs to tell you what you are seeing.

When the mileposts get into the 180s, the descent changes back to an ascent of this mountainous road and then returns to a downward grade. Chase Creek Scenic Vista has a particularly useful panoramic map describing the horizon and the land below. Just below, near Milepost 175, is the "Natural Arch," a delicate, small but delightful natural hole in the big rock formation above and to the left.

At about Milepost 173 on this winding descent into Morenci, the scars and residue of copper mining begin to dominate and culminate in a drive along the Phelps Dodge Corp.'s Morenci open pit copper mine, man's version of the Grand Canyon. The visual impact is explosive. Stretching 3 miles from rim to rim, this deep, gaping, terraced hole in the earth is the biggest open pit copper mine in the United States, an abyss that inspires horror in the eyes of some, admiring awe in others. Either way, it is quite impossible not to be impressed (or clinically depressed) by the ability of corporate America to reshape Nature's America. (Mine touring information: see Where To Go.)

Much of the old town of Morenci is buried under debris from the pit because it got in the way of the search for ore. Phelps Dodge, which owns the area, built a new town, complete with a nice mall, finishing it in 1969.

Below and beyond Morenci and its clusters of exceedingly modest hillside houses is historic and architecturally fascinating Clifton (an old mining town with wonderful old buildings) and, 40-plus miles farther, Safford and the start of the designated Swift Trail Parkway up Mount Graham, part of the Phoenix chapter of this book.

So it is that at about Milepost 172 in unincorporated but corporately dominated Morenci that the Coronado Trail Scenic Road comes to an end, and we leave Morenci saying with Julius Caesar, veni, vidi but not vici. I came, I saw, but I did not conquer because there was no point. Phelps Dodge Corp. already has done that. ⌘

Where To Go
What To See
What To Do

Listings for the White Mountains include Alpine, Clifton, Greer, Heber and Overgard, Hon-Dah, Morenci, Pinetop and Lakeside, Show Low, Snowflake and Taylor, Springerville and Eagar, St. Johns, the White Mountain Apache Tribe, the Apache-Sitgreaves National Forests, and other sources for information about Graham and Greenlee counties.

Information

White Mountains: www.wmonline.com; www.whitemtns.com www.fs.fed.us/r3/asnf

Graham County Touring: Northeastern Graham County touches the southern end of the White Mountains region. (888) 837-1841; (928) 428-2511. www.visitgrahamcounty.com

Greenlee County Touring: The eastern White Mountains region includes Greenlee County. (928) 865-3313. www.co.greenlee.az.us/History/PointsofInterest.aspx

Apache-Sitgreaves National Forests: Sprawls over 2 million acres north of Clifton and south of Springerville and noted for high altitudes (9,100 feet at some camping areas), and for its 24 lakes and 450 miles of streams. (928) 333-4301. www.fs.fed.us/r3/asnf

Alpine

Alpine Area Chamber of Commerce: It maintains a lodging list, including bed and breakfast inns, motels and lodges, cabins, guest ranches and retreats, and RV parks. (928) 339-4330. www.alpinearizona.com

Escudilla Mountain: Don't let this be a turnoff, but Congress declared No. 308 to be a national recreational trail. The mountain, and Terry Flat below it, present some of Arizona's finest scenery, but their remoteness keeps them from being too heavily visited. Aldo Leopold, a forest ranger and pioneer conservationist, wrote in *A Sand County Almanac* that Arizona's last grizzly bear—his name was Bigfoot and he had a taste for cows that doomed him— was killed at Escudilla. The 3-mile 308 trail goes nearly 1,300 feet up to the 10,912-foot summit of Escudilla, Arizona's third-highest mountain. If you make it to the top, you can go even higher on a fire tower and see all the way to the Peaks at Flagstaff to the northwest or Graham Mountain near Safford to the south. Free. From Alpine, take U.S. 191 north for 5.5 miles to Forest Service Road 56; turn right and follow 56 for 3.6 miles to Terry Flat; take the left fork to the trailhead. Alpine Ranger District, (928) 339-4384. www.fs.fed.us/r3/asnf/recreation/trails/alpine_trails/trl_alp_escudilla.shtml

Luna Lake: Wildlife watching, hunting, trout fishing, hiking, and boating at an elevation of 7,880 feet. Camping facilities and boat ramp. Located 3 miles east of Alpine off U.S. 180. Alpine Ranger District, (928) 339-4384. www.fs.fed.us/r3/asnf/recreation/campgrounds www.gf.state.az.us/outdoor_recreation/wildlife_area_luna_lake.shtml

Clifton

Cliffside Jail: In 1878, Margarito Verala built Clifton's city jail by blasting a hole into the side of a granite cliff. To celebrate, he "shot up" the town and subsequently became the jail's first prisoner. The jail is open to visitors and a restored Copper Head locomotive from the 1880s sits next to it. On U.S. 191. (928) 865-3313. www.co.greenlee.az.us/History/PointsofInterest.aspx

[A field of brown-eyed susans blooms in the White Mountains. ◀
Luna Lake reflects the mist in Apache National Forest. ▼]

George Stocking

Greenlee County Historical Society: Indian artifacts, a rock collection, as well as early pioneering and mining displays. Brochures available for the historical walking tour. Gift shop. Tues., Thurs., and Sat., 2 p.m. to 4:30 p.m. 315 Chase Creek. (928) 865-3115. www.co.greenlee.az.us/History/HistoryHomePage.aspx

Greer

Greer Business Association: www.greerarizona.com

Butterfly Lodge Museum: The restored 1913 hunting lodge was the home of author James Willard Schultz and his artist son Lone Wolf. The home is on the National Register of Historic Places and still contains the original furnishings. Artifacts and works from both father and son are on display. Open Memorial Day through Labor Day, Thur.-Sun. $. Southeast corner of State Route 373 and County Road 1126. (928) 735-7514. www.greerarizona.com/history.htm; www.wmonline.com/butterflylodge.htm

Greer Days: An annual celebration featuring a lumberjack competition, 5K walk/run, chili cook-off, parade, boat races, live entertainment. June. $. Greer. (928) 333-2123. www.springerville-eagarchamber.com

Heber/Overgaard

Chamber of Commerce: Maintains a list of area attractions and lodging, including cabins and RV parks. 2774 Hwy 260, Overgaard. (928) 535-5777. www.heberovergaard.org

Buffalo Museum of America: Life-sized stuffed bison, a Buffalo Bill exhibit, *Dances with Wolves* movie prop, paintings. Closed Wed. $. 2269 Hwy 260 East, Overgaard. (928) 535-4141.

Hon-Dah

Williams Creek National Fish Hatchery: Self-guided tours. Raises the threatened Apache trout, along with rainbow, cutthroat, brown, and brook trout. Picnic facilities, restrooms, and an interpretative display. Closed weekends. Free. For the Williams Creek Unit, take State 73 for 4.1 miles south of State 260 at Hon-Dah; turn left (east) at the hatchery's directional sign; go almost 1 mile and turn right at T-junction and go 9 miles. The Alchesay Unit is located 9 miles north of Whiteriver off State 73. Williams Creek: (928) 334-2346. Alchesay: (928) 338-4901. www.fws.gov/southwest/fishery/AWCNFH.html

Morenci

Morenci Mine Tour: The Phelps Dodge Morenci Copper Mine is one of the world's largest open pit mines. The 2.5-hour tour begins at a spectacular overlook, from which huge, huge ore-hauling trucks look like dots. Fri. and Sat. 8:30 a.m. and 1 p.m. $. (877) 646-8687. www.phelpsdodge.com/Community-Environment/MorenciMineTour.htm

Pinetop- Lakeside

Pinetop-Lakeside Chamber of Commerce: 102-C W. White Mountain Blvd, Lakeside. (928) 367-4290. www.pinetoplakesidechamber.com

White Mountain Bluegrass Musical Festival: A weekend full of entertainment by nationally known bluegrass musicians. August. $. Pinetop. (928) 367-4290 or (800) 573-4031. www.pinetoplakesidechamber.com

Native American Festival Art Show: Authentic handmade art work from some of the top Indian artists in the Southwest. Jewelry, paintings, baskets, and rugs. July. $; Pinetop-Lakeside. (928) 367-4290; (800) 573-4031.

Mogollon Rim Interpretive Trail: The easy, level, mile-long, mostly paved trail (No. 615) loops at the very edge of the rim and is equipped with interpretive signs. Pacific and Bebb's willow trees, water plants, and sedges flourish along an irrigation ditch. Free. Located off State 260 between Show Low and Pinetop-Lakeside, about 3 miles north of the Lakeside Ranger station. After passing Camp Tatiyee, look for the Mogollon Rim Trail sign. Park and walk through the "V" and follow signs. Apache-Sitgreaves National Forest, (928) 368-5111. www.fs.fed.us/r3/asnf/recreation/trails/lakeside_rd/trl_lak_mogorim.shtml

Show Low

Chamber of Commerce: Information on area attractions and events such as the annual Show Low Days Still Cruizin Car Show. (888) 746-9469 or (928) 537-2326. www.showlowchamberofcommerce.com

Show Low Historical Society Museum: Displays of Show Low's early families and pioneers. Open April 15 through Oct. 20. Donations. 541 E. Deuce of Clubs, Show Low. (928) 532-7115. www.showlowmuseum.com

Snowflake/Taylor

Snowflake/Taylor Chamber of Commerce: Provides printed and online information about the area's history, attractions, events, and lodging. (928) 536-4331. www.ci.snowflake.az.us/visitors-tourism.htm

Stinson Pioneer Museum: Reflects the history of early Snowflake. The adobe home was the residence of William J. Flake and two rooms have been restored to show the living conditions of pioneer families. $. 100 E. 1st St. South.

Snowflake Historic Homes Tour: The city has more than 100 historical buildings, with 45 of them listed on the National Registry of Historic Places. Several of the buildings are restored, and eight offer historical exhibits and are open to the public. Horse-drawn wagon trips for groups by appointment. Closed Sun. and Mon. $. (928) 536-4881.

Mormon Temple: The granite temple has Navajo rugs and pottery, original paintings, decorative Indian patterns painted on ceilings throughout the temple and large murals. Call first. Free. 1875 W. Canyon Drive. (928) 536-6626.

Springerville/ Eagar

Springerville-Eagar Regional Chamber of Commerce: Provides printed an online information about the area's history, attractions, events, lodging, and other travel information. (928) 333-2123. www.springerville-eagarchamber.com

Renee Cushman Art Museum: Features works by Rembrandt and Tiepolo. Also has art and furniture from the Renaissance to the early 20th century. By appointment. 150 N. Aldrice Burk (the LDS Stake House), Springerville.

Casa Malpais Museum and Visitor Center: Tours begin daily at 9 and 11 a.m. and 2 p.m. $. 318 E. Main St., Springerville. (928) 333-5375. www.wmonline.com/attract/casam.htm

Madonna of the Trail Statue: Dedicated in 1928, the pioneer woman holding a baby is one of 12 Madonna statues in the United States placed by the Daughters of the American Revolution. Main Street, Springerville, across from Post Office.

Little House Museum: Hours vary. $. Diamond X Ranch. Located 7 miles west of Eagar on South Fork Road, then 3 miles south of State 260. (928) 333-2286. www.xdiamondranch.com

Eagar Daze: Annual event celebrating the Town of Eagar's history features one of the few logging events held in the Southwest. A barbecue, live entertainment, junior rodeo, dog show, dance, more. The first weekend in August. Free. Eagar. (928) 333-4128 ext. 228 or 230. www.eagar.com/rec_events.htm

St. Johns

St. Johns Regional Chamber of Commerce: Provides printed an online information about the area's history, attractions, events, and other travel information. (928) 337-2000. stjohnschamber.com

Apache County Museum: Artifacts, exhibits, and displays relating to the region. Closed weekends. Donations. 180 W. Cleveland. (928) 337-4737.

Top of the Mountain Grand Prix: 200 cars participate in the three-day event. Live entertainment, food, and midway activities. Labor Day weekend. $. Call St. Johns Chamber of Commerce for tickets, (928) 337-2000.

San Juan Fiesta: Horseshoe tournament, car show, live entertainment, cake walk, golf tournament, parade, more. June. (928) 337-2000.

White Mountain Apache Tribe

Information: Office of Tourism: The tribal Internet site includes information about permits that tourists will need and recreational opportunities and attractions. (877) 338-9628. www.wmat.nsn.us

Fort Apache Historic Park: Those who thrill to the bugle call of Western history shouldn't miss this key remote outpost from 1870. Walking tours of the historic buildings. $. From Pinetop, take State 73 through Whiteriver to its intersection with Indian Route 46. Signs at the intersection guide visitors to the park. (928) 338-4525. www.wmat.nsn.us/fortapachepark.htm

White Mountain Apache Cultural Center and Museum: Exhibits and displays focus on the history and culture of the White Mountain Apache Tribe. Closed weekends. $. Located in Fort Apache Historic Park (listed above). (928) 338-4625. www.wmat.us/wmaculture.shtml

Kinishba Ruins: Required permit available at White Mountain Apache Cultural Center (listed above). Located 6 miles southwest of Whiteriver off of State 73. Turnoff marked by sign. Stay left at forks. Ruins are 2 miles from paved road. (928) 338-4625. www.wmat.us/wmaculture.shtml www.wmonline.com/attract/ftapache/kinishba.htm

Sunrise Park Resort: More than 65 ski runs, 10 lifts including a quad, terrain park, 100-room lodge, cross-country skiing, children's "ski-wee" area. In summer months, the resort has mountain bike rentals, horseback rides, lift rides, and marina at nearby Sunrise Lake. Located east of Hon-Dah off State Route 273. Owned and operated by the White Mountain Apache Tribe. Snow conditions and reservations available at (800) 772-7669. www.sunriseskipark.com

Outdoor Adventures: Apache guides are available to escort individuals or groups for hiking, swimming, rock climbing, and rappelling often over waterfalls. Information: Hon-Dah Ski & Outdoor, (928) 369-7669; (877) 226-4868. http://162.42.237.6/wmatod/outdoorshop.shtml

The Yei Bichei formation is a series of rocks representing Navajo dieties. ▲

Indian Country
Navajoland and Hopiland

The Navajo and the Hopi reservations account for virtually all of the land in northeastern Arizona, the region between New Mexico on the east and U.S. Route 89 on the west, from Interstate 40 on the south to Utah on the north. The expanse embodies ruggedly beautiful terrain blending plateaus, mesas, and buttes; canyons and valleys; and mountains and meadows. It lies within the Colorado Plateau, a 130,000-square-mile province that has been populated for at least 12,000 years but with a geologic age of 500 million years. Aside from scenic treats, Indian Country preserves cultures with origins in prehistoric times. To the people of these cultures, the land holds great spiritual value and important links to their past.

Marc Muench

Don B. Stevenson

Nurturing Heritage

A brief conversation with a Navajo official:

QUESTION: How do you say "welcome" in the Navajo language? Is it pronounced "yah tah hey"?

ANSWER: Well, yeah (chuckling). If you're John Wayne. Try this: ya ah tay. So, *Yá'át'ééh*, ya'll.

And welcome to The Rez, 27,000 square miles of home for nearly 200,000 Navajos (Dineh or Diné, "The People," as they call themselves) and blanketing the northeastern quadrant of Arizona as well as parts of adjoining southeast Utah and northwest New Mexico.

Tucked in among and surrounded by all that Navajo land is the 9,000-member Hopi tribe, mostly concentrated on three mesas and 2,400 square miles. The two tribes are neighbors, but they don't always like one another, particularly in these litigious days, on the bureaucratic level. One (the Navajo) even observes daylight-saving time, while the other (the Hopi) sticks with the state of Arizona and refuses.

The Navajo reservation is the largest in acreage in the United States, and the Navajo population, with another 75,000 members (those with at least one-quarter Navajo blood) off reservation, is the among the largest tribes in population

We all remember at least one of those clichés about the weather: If you don't like what's happening right now, wait a few minutes and it will change. Ditto for driving through the shape-shifting landscapes of the Navajo and Hopi Indian reservations.

Discussing this land in an *Arizona Highways* guide to northeastern Arizona, writer Tom Dollar had this to say about the morphing terrain: "The remarkably varied physiography of Indian Country encompasses barren, eroded hills; slumped cliffs and cones; and rain-severed gullies of the Painted Desert. It also includes the wind-sculpted buttes of Monument valley, the pine forest atop Navajo Mountain, the watery immensity of Lake Powell, the lava-capped summits of the Hopi mesas and the enchanted Petrified Forest." So if you aren't enthralled by the scene of the moment, keep driving. A few miles down the road it will change.

A Navajo publication says : "...this is a land of great contrasts. Embracing this diversity, Navajos relate to the land as their mother. The Navajo believe they're an extension of Mother Earth, and thus are also a part of her beauty. Because of this belief, the Dineh treat the land with utmost respect."

In addition to the scenery, vast change can be observed among the people and their ways. The pickup has largely replaced the horse, and the supermarket

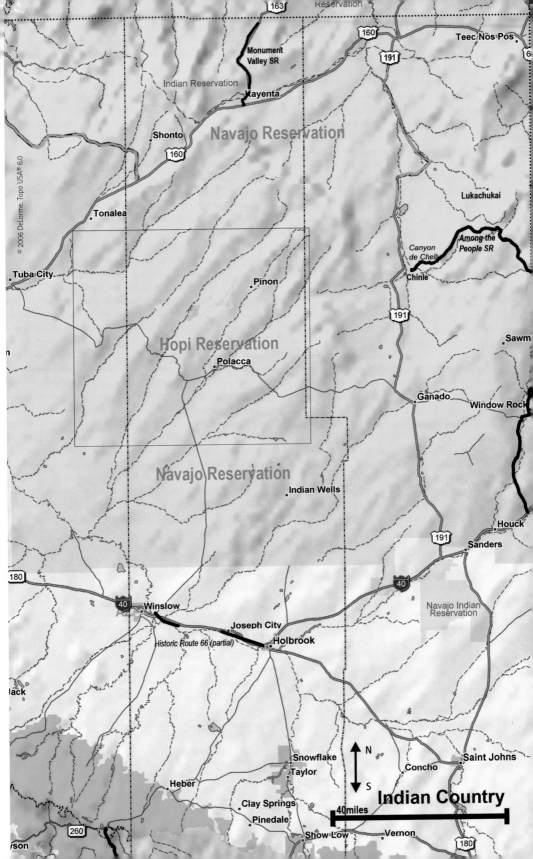

163
160
Teec Nos Pos
6
Monument
Valley SR
Indian Reservation
Kayenta
191
Shonto
Navajo Reservation
160
Lukachukai
Tonalea
Among the
People SR
Canyon
de Chelly
Tuba City
Chinle
Pinon
191
Hopi Reservation
Sawm
Polacca
Ganado
Window Rock
Navajo Reservation
Indian Wells
Houck
191
Sanders
180
40
Winslow
Navajo Indian
Reservation
Joseph City
Historic Route 66 (partial)
Holbrook
lack
N
Snowflake
Saint Johns
Taylor
Concho
Heber
S
Clay Springs
Indian Country
Pinedale
40miles
260
Show Low
Vernon
yson
180

© 2006 DeLorme. Topo USA® 6.0

has mostly supplanted the trading post. Sadly, the Navajo language, made famous by the Navajo code talkers who baffled the Japanese during World War II, has fallen into disuse among many of the young. That same Navajo publication subtly puts the concern about change this way: "Today, the Navajo Nation is striving to sustain a viable economy for an ever-increasing population ... *while nurturing its cultural heritage*" (italics added).

A cowboy-booted guide leading a tour of Canyon de Chelly (said da SHAY) unintentionally captured the changes concisely. After a brief lecture on prehistoric farming, he was asked how the Indian families still living, farming, and herding in some of the traditional ways in the bottom of the canyon get their food supplies today. He answered: "They go to the grocery store."

But the old ways are still there, to be seen and heard and enjoyed. So see, hear, and enjoy, but do it with respect: Don't litter, don't remove artifacts, don't hike off trail, don't four-wheel or ATV-drive on backcountry roads and trails, do get a permit to fish and, oh, yes, leave the bikini in the suitcase. Things haven't changed that much yet.

This is a huge land of huge differences: Awesome wind-and-rain-carved sculptures but vast stretches of bleakness; immense wealth in coal and oil and natural gas but big cargo-pants pockets of poverty; modern motels and primitive hogans; mutton stew and Caesar salads; professional golfer Notah Begay of Stanford University and sheepherders who speak only Navajo; CPAs and gang bangers; and exquisite silver and turquoise jewelry. Winter brings blowing snow and an average monthly temperature of 30 to 40 degrees in January; summer sees a searing sun and average mercury readings in the 90s in July. Those are only averages; the extremes are much colder and much hotter.

It is a kaleidoscopic land best depicted in superlatives, both in words and pictures. The splendors include volcanic ruins, some dinosaur tracks for the kids to examine, Navajo National Monument and its ancient ruins called Betatakin and Keet Seel, Monument Valley, Canyon de Chelly, and, finally, the Hubbell Trading Post in Ganado and another in Keams Canyon on Hopi land.

You must go there. Soon, before hitting Phoenix or Tucson, because the cultural interface between the old ways and the modern here continues to crumble. Someday, only the land will testify to what was.

■■■

About food . . .

The junk and fast varieties are widely available, but traditional chow should not be missed, specifically Indian fry bread, in an amazing array of permutations, and mutton. Fry bread, which resembles a puffy tortilla, is a dinner-plate-sized slab of flat, circular bread dough fried to a swollen, flaky, and golden appearance. You can get it in the form of the popular Navajo taco (covered with beans, meat, cheese, lettuce, and chile) or you can get a vegetarian variation. It also comes

[**A stream bends through Keet Seel Canyon on the Navajo Indian Reservation.**]

William Stone

plain with other dishes such as mutton stew. For those with an empty notch or two still on their belt, it can be converted to dessert by slathering it with honey or dappling it with powdered sugar. It even can be filled with mutton. As for mutton, you can find it in great slabs in supermarkets on the reservation, or it can be purchased in restaurants in several forms including stew and steaks. To spare you the embarrassment of having to ask what it is, mutton is sheep meat, specifically that of a ram or ewe that was at least a year old at time of slaughter.

And lodging . . .

Modern motels can be found in all the population centers, usually with air-conditioning and often with HBO. Under development by tribal tourism officials is a program to encourage the creation of bed and breakfast facilities. As of this writing, hogan-style B&Bs could be found in Tuba City, Tsaile, St. Michaels, and Fort Defiance. Conventional ones are in Many Farms and Tuba City. Call the Navajo Tourism Department at (928) 871-6436 in Window Rock for an updated list.

And personal conduct . . .

1. Thou shall not worry overmuch about finding a gas station. There are plenty and usually within a half-tank's drive. 2. Thou shall not drive without plenty of drinking water. 3. Thou shall not carry a *concealed* weapon. 4. Thou shall not forget to pack some dog/cat chow and a bowl for water if you care at all for homeless canines and felines. 5. Thou shall not take pictures of Indians without

their permission nor, as mentioned earlier, shall you drive on obscure back roads or hike in the backcountry without a tribal permit. 6. Thou shall not call tribal officials to complain about uncollected road kill. They already know it's a problem. 7. Thou shall not carry booze with you anywhere on the reservation, and, as a corollary, thou shall not get mad when the waitperson says you can't have a martini with your mutton steak. Liquor is illegal on the reservation. 8. Thou shall spend at least a few bucks on native food. 9. Thou shall not ask where all the teepees are. The traditional dwelling of the Navajo is the hogan, a six- or eight-sided log and earthen structure now giving way to lumber yard construction materials and mobile homes, but still a frequent sight. 10. Even if demanded by your spoiled male child who missed his Ritalin dose today, thou shall not fork over $73.50 for a tomahawk in a trading post (read: gift shop) if said feathered weapon bears a "Certificate of Authenticity" tag and then the words "genuine reproduction."

[Modern Navajo weavings drape the Rug Room at the Hubbell Trading Post.   ]

George H. H. Huey

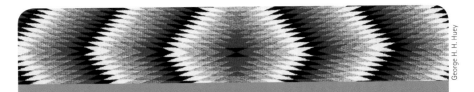

George H. H. Huey

A Trading Post of Old

Twenty-eight miles west of Window Rock on State Route 264 and near the town of Ganado is the nation's oldest known trading post, and it's a real one with creaking wooden flooring, a place where Indians can still buy groceries and other supplies as well as swap their artwork and crafts, particularly rugs, for cash. The Hubbell Trading Post also is a national historic site operated by the National Park Service.

There is a credible argument that the days of the trading posts of old are mostly gone, victims of supermarkets, department stores, shopping malls, fast food joints, auto-parts dealers, catalog outlets, and better transportation. That argument holds that nowadays many so-called trading posts are mostly just gift shops catering to tourists and doing little or no trading.

That argument seems largely true. Certainly, it describes the mostly missing trader of old, a man who was part medic, part arbitration specialist, part mortician, and part supplier of food, weapons, and household supplies in return for Indian rugs, baskets, blankets, furs, and jewelry.

Billy Malone wasn't all those things, but he was some of them when he was the trader at Hubbell for more than two decades. (Northern Arizona University recorded an oral history with Billy before he left Hubbell: www.nau.edu/~cline/speccoll/exhibits/traders/oralhistories/malone.html.)

Well known as a specialist in rugs, Billy amassed pile upon pile of gorgeous weavings he purchased from the locals. That's not all he bought, but rugs constituted a major share of his inventory. He also gave no-interest loans and groceries on credit to artisans who were working on big projects but needed some money to finish them. On the late morning when he discussed his work, he had already purchased three baskets, jewelry from four silversmiths, moccasins, and several rugs.

Why did the native artists sell to him? "Well, I think you work up a working relationship with someone, and they're happy with what you are paying them. We pay a fair price."

The retail price range for the rugs?   ▶

[The "eyedazzler" pattern explodes off this Navajo rug. ▲   ]

"Anywhere from $75 to $50,000. Here's a $50,000 one right here, 7 by 14 feet, hand-carded and plant dyed."

Will it sell? "Yeah."

"And here's a 15-inch by 15-inch round rug for $295, made by a 99-year-old woman."

Billy smiled as he fondled the rugs, even though Hubbell profits go to the National Park Service.

The Hubbell got its name from John Lorenzo Hubbell who bought the post in 1878 and ran it for a half-century, along with 24 trading posts and other businesses in Indian country. He died in 1930 and is buried next to his wife on nearby Hubbell Hill.

Engulfed by Navajoland is the much smaller Hopi tribe, which is concentrated in a dozen villages on top of or at the base of three high mesas clustered along a 12-mile stretch of Hopi tribal land in the southeastern portion of the Navajo reservation and straddling the two Arizona counties of Coconino and Navajo.

The Hopi, who are classified as Pueblo Indians, have lived in northeastern Arizona for at least a thousand years. They are unquestionably friendly but also somewhat private, formal, and reserved. There are restrictions on visitors, and the traveler who wishes to see life on First, Second, and Third mesas is expected to seek guidance and be most respectful of the people by putting away the camera and tape recorder unless given specific permission. On Third Mesa, incidentally, is Old Oraibi, which dates back to the year 1150 and is said to be the oldest continuously inhabited village in North America.

The Hopis and the Navajos throughout their history have engaged one another in serious disagreements over water, mineral resources, and, mostly, which tribe can use what land. The combat has moved to the U.S. Congress and to the federal courts and in 1962 even produced a court decree that said the two tribes should find a solution such as joint use of grazing land surrounding Hopi villages. Predictably, that didn't work, so Congress in 1974 partitioned a joint-use area into halves and told Hopis on the Navajo half to leave and Navajos on the Hopi half to do the same. Equally predictably, that didn't work either. The conflicts continue, although Indian officials like to insist that it is more of a government-to-government flap than a person-to-person one.

Those who are not bent on speeding through the lands of the Hopi and the Diné will encounter a multitude of outlets—stores, trading posts, roadside stands—for the many arts and crafts produced by the tribal artisans and artists—painters, sculptors, carvers, jewelers, weavers, potters, and basket makers. The dominant forms are magnificent, hand-woven rugs and other colorful weavings often created using natural plant dyes; baskets; turquoise, coral, and silver jewelry; and sand paintings.

Perhaps because of the sheer size of the Navajo land and its population, there is an unfortunate tendency to pay less attention to the Hopi tribe, which has its own, distinct history and language and is noted particularly for its kachina carvings, its incredible jewelry featuring silver overlay, its pottery, and its basketry. The famous silver overlay technique, introduced in the 1930s to the Hopi by the Museum of Northern Arizona in Flagstaff, relies on a design cut into a sheet of silver that is then soldered, or overlaid, onto a second surface. The recessed area is then oxidized and brushed with fine steel wool. Hopi kachinas, according to writer and scholar Bernard Fontana, are the "living essence of plants, animals, and such inanimate objects as the moon." There are some 300 of them, and the carved dolls that sell for as much as $15,000 apiece are likenesses of these kachinas. ᛁᛁᛁ

A biker takes a reflective moment atop a sandstone arch on the Navajo Indian Reservation.

Kate Thompson

The Art of the Hopi

Tradition: An all-important word among the Hopi Indians

Tradition—including the creation of beautiful arts and crafts—links the present and the ancient past. The cliff-dwelling ancestors of the Hopis made intricately designed pottery and tightly woven baskets. They fashioned jewelry from shell and turquoise, pecked designs into or painted them onto cliff walls, and wore clothing woven from native-grown hand-spun cotton.

Like their ancestors, today's Hopi artists work in a variety of media, including painting, basket and textile weaving, sculpting, and the making of pottery and jewelry. However, they are probably best known for their kachina carvings.

Kachinas are part of the Pueblo culture, particularly the Hopis'; kachinas carved by non-Puebloans are never authentic and usually are not particularly well done.

Kachina carvings were originally made to be given as gifts to girls during ceremonies. Through the years, some recipients began to sell their kachinas. This led to carving kachinas strictly for commercial purposes. Kachina art continues to evolve. Today many artists create exemplary works from one solid piece of cottonwood root, with no accoutrements added, and flowing free-form from the natural shape of the wood.

Most Hopi artists learn their skills at an early age, often from family members. Perhaps the most important artistic influence for youngsters is that making pottery or jewelry, weaving baskets, carving kachinas, or painting is simply something that most everyone does.

Although there are many wood sculptors and several ceramic sculptors among the Hopis, today's Hopi sculptors who work in stone or bronze can be counted on one hand, but they are excellent craftsmen.

Textile weaving also is not widespread among the Hopis today. Hopi men, the traditional weavers, are skilled craftsmen; however, when traders began bringing supplies into Hopi country in the 1800s, the craft began to decline. Items such as kilts, sashes, robes, and belts—which are still woven by a number of men—are sometimes sold to other Hopis for use in ceremonies, but they are not readily available to tourists or collectors.

Overlay jewelry, a traditional style for which the Hopis are noted, involves cutting a design from a flat sheet of silver or gold, then soldering it onto a solid piece of metal that forms a background. Recessed areas are oxidized, and raised surfaces are either highly polished or given a lustrous satin finish.

Although this is the predominant style of jewelry fashioned by Hopi artisans, some also create gold or silver pieces that require a variety of techniques, including fabrication, tufa casting, lost-wax casting, and stamp work. Several Hopi jewelers use diamonds, and many set other precious and semiprecious stones into their jewelry.

Like most Hopi art, jewelry designs usually include traditional Hopi symbols and ceremonial images. Tradition, spirituality, and art are so entwined that one cannot be isolated from the other.

All Hopi art symbolizes a way of life that has continued for centuries, a part of their heritage and their tradition. Tradition, heritage, culture. All words that are greatly overused when speaking of the Hopis. Yet there seems to be no way to avoid them.

(Condensed from an *Arizona Highways* article by
Indian art expert Lois Essary Jacka.)

Created by Anthony E. Honahnie, this is an acrylic painting of *Earth God*, a diety who intercedes between the worlds of the living and the dead.

Jerry Jacka

Flagstaff to Kayenta

F lagstaff figures into four of the regions in this book as a hub, crossroad, or starting point. Previously, we regarded the mountain community as a gateway to the Grand Canyon and as a star of Arizona's "Up North." In the next chapter, Flagstaff becomes one of the cities along Old Route 66. Here, Flagstaff serves as the starting point for a venture in Indian Country along the western border of Navajoland.

In this role, Flagstaff leads us into a land of buttes, mesas, and plateaus—all formations that are, generally speaking, flat on top. Also, it's a land of spires, pinnacles, canyons, prairies, pine forests, and sand. And speaking of sand, this is sandstone country, a soft, red rock chopped, hollowed, spun, toppled, and carved by wind and rain over the centuries into fantasy formations that have captivated photographers since long before Hollywood and Technicolor ruled this most visual of worlds.

Twelve miles after leaving Flagstaff on U.S. Route 89 north, just past Milepost 430, a loop road leaves U.S. 89 and goes east for 2 miles to a visitors center and roughly the place where, in the years 1064 or 1065, prehistoric local hunters and farmers became the only people in the southwestern United States to have ever seen a volcanic eruption. It is the area of the Wupatki and Sunset Crater Volcano national monuments, both administered by the National Park Service. Because those 11th-century people had never been subjected to the *Sturm und Drang* of a rock concert, one can only speculate about their enjoyment of the warning tremors, the noise, and then the fountaining of lava and rain of debris.

Sunset Crater, quite visible from, and near to, the loop road, is now a 1,000-foot volcanic cinder cone, the most recent volcanic creation in the 6 million years of volcanic activity in the 2,200-square-mile region called the San Francisco volcanic field, now dormant—but not dead. Sunset Crater got its name because red and yellow oxidized cinders were released by the vent in about 1250 and fell onto the rim. The colors of the cinders reminded folks of, duh, a sunset.

Climbing on the cone itself is prohibited, as is backcountry camping, but you can walk around the cone. The closing of the crater to climbers to protect it from scarring came about when Congress in 1930 made it a national monument. Two years earlier, a film crew had planned to create a landslide there, but a group of local citizens put a stop to that.

After leaving the Sunset Crater visitors center, the paved loop heads north (and eventually west back to U.S. 89) through great fields of lava flows, lava rocks, and lava cinders, tributes to the Earth's ability to spit up and spew its bile in this region. Passage through this area leads in about 20 miles to Wupatki National Monument, a 56-square-mile area of ancient pueblos populated, probably, by the ancestral Sinaguans but also bearing elements of Ancestral Puebloan (or Anasazi) and Hohokam traditions.

The Wupatki ruin was heavily populated during the 1100s and grew into a three-story, 100-room pueblo with a community room, ball court, food storerooms, and a nearby spring (now dry). The monument area also contains several smaller dwelling ruins, including Lomaki Pueblo a half-mile off the road, Wukoki Pueblo reached by a 2.5-mile spur road, and Citadel and Nalakihu pueblos adjoining the loop road.

[Late afternoon light cloaks the cinder cone slopes of Sunset Crater.   ]

Chuck Lawsen

For the most part, visitors can walk among the ruins, step into the rooms, and marvel at the architecture and way of life in these prehistoric farming communities. You also can buy the Wupatki Trail Guide brochure available at the visitors center, a great stop where one of the informational exhibits reports that the height of the average male living in Wupatki was 5 feet, 5 inches tall, the average female 5 feet, 1 inch. The average age at death was 35. Makes you instantly feel taller and destined to live long and prosper.

On the self-guided trail around this "stabilized" and "reconstructed" ruin (note the steel supports holding up some tottering walls), don't miss the blowhole, a hole in the ground that the Hopi Indians call the "wind spirit." It is a crevice in the Earth's crust that inhales and exhales, sometimes up to 35 miles per hour, and specialists speculate how Wupatki residents put it to use, if any.

■ ■ ■

Not far distant from Wupatki as the turkey buzzard flies and easily seen from the Cinder Hills Overlook of the Sunset Crater monument is a crater called the Roden, which faces a future nearly as dramatic as its explosive birth eons ago. Roden Crater is a work in progress, a 300,000-year-old volcano with an adjoining smaller cone that are owned and are being transformed by an artist named James Turrell. The crater, which has been experiencing a gigantic, artistic root canal, and Turrell, who has supervised this grand and decorative dentistry, are both well known in the art world even if not around Flagstaff.

According to a handout distributed by the Turrell-linked, non-profit Skystone Foundation in Flagstaff, this is "the artist's pivotal work" and the "transformation of the dormant volcano ... into an observatory will lead visitors into the experience of seeing the commonplace of their world in an extraordinary way." Construction to reshape the crater's bowl and to build an 850-foot tunnel and subterranean concrete spaces has been underway since 1999. The spaces "will create an opportunity to view in an intensified way the infinitely variable interaction of light and space and to track the passage of planets, stars, sun, and moon. Roden Crater will allow visitors to become intimately connected with the earth and sky."

The Roden, which overlooks the Painted Desert, can be reached by vehicle by taking a dirt road that branches off the Sunset Crater-Wupatki loop road. The turnoff, leading southeast, is a little more than halfway between Sunset, and Wupatki. After 10 miles, the dirt road comes to Indian Route 15 (also called Leupp Road); turn left (east), go about a mile and turn left (north) onto Indian Route 70, which in 8 miles takes you to the Grand Falls of the Little Colorado River. Before that site, you come to Roden. The Grand Falls, by the way, is quite a sight when the river is flowing, generally during the spring runoff or summer monsoon season.

Another way to reach Roden begins at a stoplight on U.S. 89 about 10 miles before the turnoff to Sunset Crater. Turn right (east) on Townsend-Winona Road, go 8 miles to Indian Route 15 (Leupp Road) and turn left; then go about 10 miles to Indian Route 70 and turn left (north).

■■■

Back on U.S. 89 after leaving Wupatki, the town of Gray Mountain (elevation 6,305 feet) shows up quickly. It offers the usual trading post/gift shop but, more notably, a genuine Navajo taco. And still on matters of the palate, it's the last place you can legally get a cocktail or a beer before you enter the officially dry Rez.

Within yards is the line of the Navajo Reservation. It's time now to drive especially carefully, because sheep, horses, and cattle roam freely throughout much

A Navajo ranger leads a group as they explore the Betatakin ruin
at Navajo National Monument.

Nick Berezenko

of the reservation and apparently have been told they have the right of way. Best not to hit one.

Still going north, the next stop is the town of Cameron, with its historic trading post established in 1916. The post now offers a tasteful and elaborate gift shop with an abundance of hand-crafted items, often a rug-weaving exhibition with a honest-to-gosh real Navajo weaver weaving an honest-to-gosh rug, a gallery of Indian history, an AAA-approved motel (the word "lodge" seems more popular), a restaurant, an RV park, and a good view of the Little Colorado River Gorge. Near the viewpoint you'll see the 1911 swayback suspension bridge that is now closed but that was built originally to accommodate travel over the gorge. There are good Navajo tacos here, too. Order the smaller version unless you are sharing or have a huge appetite.

From here, it's 16 miles to U.S. Route 160. Turn right (east) and head for Tuba City. But first, just after the intersection, at about Milepost 316, there is a primitive sign advertising dinosaur tracks at Moenave. It involves a short turnoff and loop trip back, but sure enough, there they are: footprints preserved in rock. Also there, most likely, will be a Navajo mom and pop and a kid or two who will "volunteer" to lead you in the paths of the dinos. Negotiable tips expected.

Tuba City is a population center offering a truck stop (at the southwest corner of U.S. 160 and State 264) with an excellent Navajo taco and a trading post (turn left at the intersection)—all the conveniences, in fact. Tuba City is where Lori Piestewa, the only Native American female member of the U.S. Armed Forces to be killed in combat (Iraq), lived.

Continuing about 22 miles along 160, at about Red Lake, drivers find two large, sandstone pillars next to the highway. They are called "Elephant's Feet." It really should be "Elephant's Legs." Tsk.

Another 30 miles on 160 brings you to an intersection with State Route 564, which leads left to a beautiful, 9-mile drive with overlooks into the extravagant beauty and wonder of Tsegi Canyon. At road's end, lie some dramatic lessons in prehistory—the Navajo National Monument with its Ancestral Puebloan cliff dwellings of 13th-century Betatakin ("ledge house" in the Navajo language) and 10th-century Keet Seel ("remains of square houses"), all under the dominion of the National Park Service.

From the visitors center with informative displays, including a re-created, old-style hogan and a sweathouse, you can take several short trails, including a 1-mile round-trip hike to a site that overlooks the 135-room village of Betatakin. The ruin sits on a 370-foot-wide ledge under a 450-foot-high sandstone roof. Ranger-led tours of Betatakin can be arranged between Memorial Day and Labor Day, but it's a moderately strenuous, five-hour tour involving a 5-mile round-trip hike. The hike back up is the equivalent of climbing the steps of a 70-story building. It's worth it if you have hiking boots, a daypack with at least two quarts of water, and a good heart and lungs. One morning tour is conducted for 25 first-come, first-served hikers, who often start showing up at the visitors center around sunrise to get one of the free tickets.

Keet Seel is quite another matter: Reaching this 160-room village perched high up on a natural shelf takes a strenuous 17-mile round-trip hike from the visitors center on the rim to the canyon floor along steep, rocky switchbacks, sand dunes, and shallow streams. It can be done as a long day hike or, better, an over-nighter. Reservations must be made, and there is a required orientation lecture. (See Where To Go on Page 352.)

Incidentally, at the base of the cliff is a 70-foot, creaking ladder that leads to the ruin. Getting to the streets and rooms of this largest such ruin in the United States means climbing that ladder. A blindfold might help. ⋔

[**Betatakin, which was built by Ancestral Puebloans, has 135 rooms.**   ]

Tom Danielsen

Kayenta-Monument Valley Scenic Road

Route	U.S. 163, from Kayenta to famed Monument Valley.
Mileage	About 28 miles.
Time to Allow	At least one day, preferably two. If possible plan a trip that includes a sunrise and a sunset, the times when the colors are at their best.
Elevation	About 5,800 feet at Kayenta; an average of about 5,100 feet at Monument Valley.
Overview	The Navajo people call this place *Tsé Bii' Ndzisgaii*, which means "stretches of treeless areas or clearing among the rocks. Navajo mythology views the valley as a huge hogan, the traditional Navajo dwelling. The valley encompasses about 600 square miles, of which about 100 are a Navajo tribal park.

F rom Kayenta, at the intersection of U.S. routes 160 and 163, it's a short hop up 163 to Monument Valley and Goulding's trading post, lodge, and museum. But first, if you want to eat and soak up a little history, visit the Kayenta Burger King, which displays artifacts of the famed Navajo Code Talkers of World War II. A son of one of the talkers established the display.

Just north of Kayenta, the incredible rock formations of Monument Valley begin to show on the horizon, starting with Owl Rock on the left and El Capitan (a 1,500-foot-tall volcanic neck also known as Agathla) on the right. Unlimber the Nikon, for this is a land that, like the Grand Canyon, best yields it aesthetic splendors not to Technicolor writing with the pen or the word processor but to the eyes of the human and the lens of the camera. The shapes and the names of these astonishing rock formations match: Mittens, Totem Pole, Three Sisters. These "icons of the American West" as writer Rose Houk called them, will not last forever. The forces of wind and rain and volcanoes that created them eventually will erode them into nothing.

Monument Valley can be enjoyed out a car window from a distance or up close on horseback or foot. There is a 17-mile, s-l-o-w road through the formations, and guided tours also can be arranged at the visitors center so you can take in hogans, ancient cliff dwellings, and petroglyphs. Besides Goulding's (www.gouldings.com), lodging, camping, and restaurants are available in Kayenta. The tribe operates a campground at the park (see Where To Go).

Goulding's just across the border in Utah got its start in 1924 when Harry Goulding opened it. It is no longer a true trading post, but it does offer amazing views, a small airstrip, gift shop, restaurant, and a lodge tucked up against the imposing Big Rock Door Mesa. The old structure that housed the trading post is now a museum that is strong on prehistoric Native American artifacts and on modern North American artifacts such as John Wayne and John Ford.

In the late 1930s, Goulding got Hollywood film director Ford to make movies in this area, including *Stagecoach*. Other movies shot here include *My Darling Clementine*, *The Searchers*, *How The West Was Won*, *The Trial of Billy Jack*, and *The Legend of the Lone Ranger*. Memorabilia of Wayne's acting exploits and a small shack where he stayed can be found in and just outside the museum complex. ▥

[The Mittens at Monument Valley, with Merrick Butte in the background.   ]

Tim Fitzharris

Dinétah (Among the People) Scenic Road

Route	Indian Route 64 at Chinle east to Indian Route 12 near Tsaile; south on 12 to Window Rock; a quick jog west on State Route 264; south on 12 to Interstate 40 at Lupton.
Mileage	About 100 miles, plus side trips.
Time to Allow	At least one day, preferably two.
Elevation	About 5,500 feet at Canyon de Chelly (Chinle); 7,300 at Wheatfields Lake; 6,200 feet at Lupton.
Overview	Beginning at the rim of Canyon de Chelly, an ancient homeland that's still populated, the drive takes you through the heart of Navajoland on an unparalleled trip into Indian history and Navajoland scenery.

B efore leaving Chinle, spend a day, better two, exploring the floor and the north and south rim overlooks into Canyon de Chelly (said da SHAY), a 130-square-mile monument that photographers, anthropologists, and world travelers consider one of the world's most beautiful canyons.

If plans don't permit a stay of that length, an hour or two will cover the first two overlooks on either rim, and four hours will allow for an informative and entertaining guided tour of part of the canyon floor starting from its mouth near Chinle. Plaques at the several overlooks tell various stories about this canyon, including a particularly grisly one. It recounts the story of the fatal plunge of an Indian woman fighting off a Spanish soldier, who had climbed to her tenuous ledge where she had sought shelter from rifle fire below. Caught in her grip, he also took the fatal fall.

Along the south rim drive lies Spider Rock, an 800-foot-tall, white-topped sandstone pillar. In Navajo mythology, the column is the home of Spider Woman, who taught the Navajo people how to weave. She also is said to come down at night to take unruly children back to her home and devour them. Their littered bones create the white atop the rock.

LeRoy DeJolie

The Long Walk

If you talk to an older Navajo for awhile, sooner or later a reference will be made to the Long Walk. To the Navajo it is as bleak and memorable an event as the Civil War is to old families in the Deep South.

The Long Walk refers to an episode in which the U.S. Army forced an estimated 9,000 Navajos off their homeland and marched them 300 miles from Fort Defiance in Arizona to Fort Sumner on the Pecos River in New Mexico.

The Navajos had lived in *Dinetah*, the land bordered by their four sacred mountains, since before Columbus discovered America: to the east, in southern Colorado, Mount Blanca; on the south, Mount Taylor in New Mexico; on the west, the San Francisco Peaks in the Flagstaff area; on the north, Mount Hesperus, also in Colorado.

After rumors spread that gold was to be found in the southern Rocky Mountains, the Navajos were viewed as an impediment to efforts to reap riches. Gen. James H. Carleton, the military governor of the New Mexico Territory (which then included Arizona), issued General Order 15 to rid the region of Navajos. The Army, in the winter of 1864, burned hogans, destroyed crops and livestock and rounded up Navajos, killing those who resisted. The Indians were force-marched to Fort Sumner. It was not until 1868 that they were allowed to return to their homeland.

[Returning Navajos wept at the sight of Mount Taylor. ▲   ]

Signs at the overlooks caution drivers to lock their vehicles and secure their valuables because of the prevalence of theft. The sites also are popular with seemingly abandoned but friendly beggar dogs seeking a handout and water. Please oblige them.

A variety of canyon tours are available (ask the rangers at the National Park Service visitors center) and include ones by horseback, by foot, and by four-wheel-drive and giant six-wheel-drive vehicles. You can choose to ride in a Jeep, a Korean War-vintage truck, a big Dodge pickup, a Unimog (something like a Humvee), or even your own 4WD vehicle. Traffic on the canyon floor, not counting livestock, can resemble a busy country road during the day, and there are dozens of stands where native craftspeople offer their artistic works for sale.

Why a guide except on the rim drives? Because flash floods, quicksand, and dry but deep sand can make unguided travel quite dangerous. Also, with the exception of a 2.5-mile round-trip hike from one overlook on the south rim down to the spectacular ruin called White House, a guide is required. The canyon does not follow a straight line; a short distance from the mouth, it forms into an intersection shaped like a V on its side with Canyon de Chelly on the south and Canyon del Muerto ("canyon of death") on the north.

The canyon, with its sheer walls of sandstone, its many cliff houses, its petroglyphs and pictographs, and its sandy bottom covered with giant cottonwood and tamarisk trees, ranges in depth from 30 feet at the mouth to more than 1,000 feet 15 miles away. It has been a home and occasionally a refuge

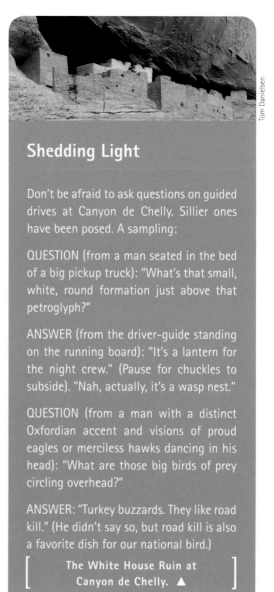

Tom Danielsen

Shedding Light

Don't be afraid to ask questions on guided drives at Canyon de Chelly. Sillier ones have been posed. A sampling:

QUESTION (from a man seated in the bed of a big pickup truck): "What's that small, white, round formation just above that petroglyph?"

ANSWER (from the driver-guide standing on the running board): "It's a lantern for the night crew." (Pause for chuckles to subside). "Nah, actually, it's a wasp nest."

QUESTION (from a man with a distinct Oxfordian accent and visions of proud eagles or merciless hawks dancing in his head): "What are those big birds of prey circling overhead?"

ANSWER: "Turkey buzzards. They like road kill." (He didn't say so, but road kill is also a favorite dish for our national bird.)

[**The White House Ruin at Canyon de Chelly.** ▲]

and fortress to native people for perhaps 3,500 years. It was in this canyon that Kit Carson and the U.S. Army conducted the infamous "scorched earth campaign" that led to the "Long Walk" of the Navajo people taken to captivity in New Mexico. Today, its floor remains the permanent or seasonal home for approximately 40 families in del Muerto and 35 in de Chelly.

Daytime temperatures April through November range from 60 degrees to 90; in daytime winter, 45 to 60. The altitude is 5,500 feet. Campgrounds, several modern motels, a few restaurants, and plenty of fast-food outlets can be found in and around Chinle.

■■■

After you've taken your fill of the canyon, strike out east on Indian Route 64. You'll be moving along the north rim, Canyon del Muerto. Next stop: the town of Tsaile, site of the main campus of Diné College, which when it opened in 1969 was the first Indian-owned college in the United States. The campus includes a cultural center and a museum that tell the story of the Navajos and display fine examples of their arts and crafts. From the highway, look for the four-story Hatathli Center, shaped like a stylized hogan.

In another few miles, Indian Route 64 connects with Indian 12. Turn right (south) and begin a 50-mile drive in a desolate area of Arizona and New Mexico punctuated with multicolored buttes and boulders. There are only a few scattered settlements between Tsaile and Fort Defiance, during which you'll pass Wheatfields Lake, a nice place for a break. By the time you reach Fort Defiance, established in 1851 as a collection of adobe and log buildings but now long gone, you'll understand why soldiers stationed there nicknamed it Hell's Gate or Hell's Hollow, because the area was so isolated.

A tree cholla frames a hogan and cottonwoods along Chinle Wash by Sliding House Ruins.

Randy Prentice

Nine miles of driving south brings you to Window Rock, the capital of the Navajo Nation named for a sandstone formation with a hole (window) cut by erosion. Here you can wander through a huge outdoor marketplace filled with native arts, crafts, and food. You'll find it at the intersection of Indian 12 and State Route 264. Elsewhere in Window Rock are the Navajo Nation Zoological and Botanical Park and Navajo Tribal Museum (see Where To Go).

The drive on Indian 12 then coincides for a few miles with State 264 to a junction where 264 continues west and 12 bears southward. A mile west of the junction lies St. Michael's mission and museum, a bucolic place that documents the Franciscans' work with the Navajos. Return to 12 for a 25-mile drive to Lupton and Interstate 40. ▥

Where To Go
What To See
What To Do

Marc Muench

The roads on the Navajo and Hopi reservations lead to prehistoric sites as well as to tribal and other sites that focus on preserving the cultures of these people.

Navajoland

Information: The 27,000-square-mile Navajo Indian Reservation lies primarily in Arizona, with Window Rock the capital, but Navajoland also extends into Utah and New Mexico. These two Internet sites provide excellent overviews of tribal history, culture, and other highlights: www.navajo.org/history.htm; http://cpluhna.nau.edu/People/navajo.htm

Tourism Office: Through printed brochures and an Internet site, the office provides detailed information on attractions such as Monument Valley, Canyon de Chelly, and Antelope Canyon near Page; the on-going marketplace at Window Rock and spot markets and sales around Navajoland; exhibits featuring Navajo arts and crafts; places to buy Navajo-style food; lodging, including where you can stay overnight in a hogan, the traditional Navajo dwelling; and guided tours, maps, and directions. Based in Window Rock. (928) 871-8504. www.discovernavajo.com

Parks and Recreation: This branch of tribal government operates several parks and other recreational sites. This office (or one of its satellites listed in the town of their location) is the one to contact for permits for hiking, camping, fishing, and other required permits. (928) 871-6647. www.navajonationparks.org

Navajo Nation Hospitality Enterprise: The enterprise owns and operates three Quality Inn lodges in Tuba City, Window Rock, and Page, and runs the Navajo Travel Center on Interstate 40 at Exit 325. In addition, the enterprise is associated with tour operators. (623) 412-0297. www.explorenavajo.com

Cameron

Visitors Center: Information and permits for hiking and other outdoor activities in the western portion of the Navajo Nation can be obtained here. The western area includes the Colorado River, Marble Canyon, Jackass

Canyon, Salt Trail Canyon, Totahatso Point, Rainbow Bridge trails, Cove Mesa, and Coal Mine Canyon. At the junction of U.S. Route 89 and State Route 64. (928) 679-2303. www.navajonationparks.org/permits.htm

Cameron Trading Post: Located along the Little Colorado River, the post was established a few years after a suspension bridge was built across the river in 1911. The post sells authentic Navajo rugs and jewelry, Pueblo pottery, and Hopi Kachina dolls, and memento items. Visitors can also explore the history behind Indian art and Old West memorabilia in the gallery. The post has a lodge and RV park, a restaurant that features Navajo food such as fry bread, and a secluded garden laced with colorful flowers

Monument Valley stretches beyond Hunt Mesa. ◄ A ray of light beams in through the smooth orange rock of Antelope Canyon. ▼

Marc Muench

and sandstone walkways. Located 54 miles north of Flagstaff on U.S. 89. (800) 338-7385. www.camerontradingpost.com

Little Colorado River Tribal Park: Navajo merchants crowd the scenic overlook of the steep, sandstone walls that rise from the Little Colorado River. Besides a flea market-type atmosphere, ramadas, tables, and fireplaces are available along the cliff edges for visitors. Free. 9.4 miles west of Cameron on State 64 (928) 679-2303. www.navajonationparks.org/htm/littlecolorado.htm

Chinle

Canyon de Chelly National Monument: A guide and permit are required for entering the canyon, except for hiking to White House Ruin. A drive along the canyon rim offers scenic overlooks; maps and overlook information at the visitors center, located on Indian Route 64 about 3 miles east of U.S. Route 191. (928) 674-5500. www.nps.gov/cach

Fort Defiance

Good Shepherd Mission: The Episcopal church operates a 48-acre compound that includes an art gallery and the Hozho' retreat center for groups and individuals. Church services are conducted in both English and Diné (Navajo language). (928) 729-2322. www.goodshepherdmission.org

Ganado

Hubbell Trading Post: The Hubbell Family operated this post for nearly a century before selling it to the National Park Service. There's no charge to tour the compound. One mile west of Ganado on State Route 264. (928) 755-3475. www.nps.gov/hutr

Greasewood Springs

Keith J. Boyd Memorial Rodeo: Billed as the "Biggest Little Show in the Southwest," it is one of many annual rodeos sponsored by the All Indian Rodeo Cowboys Association. May. $. Greasewood Springs. www.aircarodeo.com

Kayenta

Navajo National Monument: Two of Arizona's largest ruins are preserved here, Betatakin and Keet Seel. Tours are offered to the Ancestral Puebloan ruins that are over 900 years old. An overlook offers views of Betatakin. Ranger-led tours are the only way visitors can approach the ruins. Visitors center, campgrounds, and replicas of ancient hogans and sweat lodges. Free. State Route 564 turns north off U.S. Route 160 at Black Mesa and leads to the visitors center. (928) 672-2700. www.nps.gov/nava

Monument Valley Navajo Tribal Park: You may recognize the stunning red sandstone landmarks from the many Western movies that were filmed at Monument Valley. Parts of this region are sacred to the Navajos, so stay on the park's loop road. Guided tours. Visitors center. $. From Kayenta, north on U.S. Route 163 for about 45 miles. (435) 727-5870. www.navajonationparks.org/htm/monumentvalley.htm

Lake Powell

Antelope Point Marina and Resort: On Lake Powell, a marina, full-service boat launching ramp, hotel resort, boat tours, boat rentals, campgrounds, swimming beaches, cultural center. BIA Highway N22B, Mile Marker #4, Navajo Nation. $. (800) 255-5561. www.lakepowellhouseboating.com

Antelope Canyon: Self-guided and guided tours of the upper and lower canyons are available. Closed November-March. $. Located east of Page off State Route 98. (928) 698-2808. www.navajonationparks.org/htm/antelopecanyon.htm

Lupton

Tee-Pee Trading Post: Shaped like a giant tee-pee, this throwback from the Route 66 era sells Southwest souvenirs. Located off Interstate 40 at Exit 359. (928) 688-2266.

[White House Ruin stands out in Canyon de Chelly.   ]

David Muench

Teec Nos Pos

Four Corners Navajo Tribal Park: Stand in four states all at once at the only place in the United States where four state lines intersect. A plaque with the state seals of Arizona, Utah, Colorado, and New Mexico marks the location. Crafts and art can be purchased at the tribal park. $. Off U.S. Route 160. (928) 871-6647. www.navajonationparks.org/htm/fourcorners.htm

Tsaile

Hatathli Museum and Gallery: Housed at Diné College, the first Indian-owned community college in the country, the museum and gallery hosts Indian exhibits. Navajo rugs, silverwork, baskets, pottery, and literature on sale. Free. (928) 724-6654. www.explorenavajo.com/attractions.asp

Window Rock

Navajo Tribal Museum: The museum offers a glimpse into the rich culture and history of the Navajo people. Auditorium, outdoor amphitheater, library, and authentic Navajo hogan. Closed Sun. Free. Window Rock. (928) 871-7941. www.wnmu.org/mcf/museums/nnm.html www.discovernavajo.com

Keshmish Festival: Highlights the works of Indian artists, as well as cultural events and entertainment. November. Free. Navajo Nation Museum.

Music Festival: Each year in June. Navajo Tribal Museum.

Navajo Nation Fair: This premier Indian fair boasts an all-Indian rodeo, Miss Navajo competition, battle of the bands, rides, fireworks, concerts, and a powwow. September. $. Navajo Nation Fairgrounds, Window Rock. (928) 871-6478 / 6647. www.navajonationfair.com

Navajo Nation Zoological and Botanical Park: The only tribally operated zoological and botanical park in the United States has animals native to Navajoland and important to Navajo culture. Exhibits on culture. Free. Window Rock. (928) 871-6573. www.discovernavajo.com

Navajo Veterans' Memorial Park: In the shadow of the massive Window Rock sits a tribute to all the Navajos who have served in the U.S. military, including World War II's code talkers. Free. (928) 871-6647. www.navajonationparks.org/htm/veterans.htm

St. Michael's Mission and Historical Museum: The museum, housed in the original 1898 Franciscan mission, delves into Navajo culture and the role religious influences played. Free. Located off State 264 about 3 miles west of Window Rock. (928) 871-4171. www.discovernavajo.com

Hopi Tribe

Information: The 1.6-million-acre Hopi reservation consists of three mesas and several villages, each with an autonomous government. Surrounded by Navajoland, the Hopi reservation is a political and cultural island amid the plateaus, canyons, mesas, and mountains of northeastern Arizona. State 264 cuts east-west through the reservation, and State Route 87 serves it from the south and Interstate 40. Hopi lands usually are usually open to visitors under certain restrictions. For example, only guided tours are allowed in some areas; and sketching, photographing, videotaping, audio recording, carrying alcohol, and traveling outside non-designated areas are prohibited. (928) 734-3283. www.hopi.nsn.us www.nau.edu/~hcpo-p

Hopi Art: www.hopi.nsn.us/artisans.asp

First Mesa: Hand-coiled pottery is a renowned product of First Mesa villages, which lie above the community of Polacca, located on State 264 about 11 miles west of Keams Canyon. Walpi, the oldest of the three villages on the mesa, is high above the desert floor on a narrow strip of land just 150 feet across at its widest point. Many consider Walpi the best destination on the Hopi reservation. Next to Walpi is Sichomovi, which has Punsi Hall visitors center, the starting point for First Mesa guided tours. Tewa is the third of the First Mesa villages. Punsi Hall closed weekends. (928) 737-2262. www.hopi.nsn.us/village1.asp

Second Mesa: Located 10 miles west of First Mesa are the villages of Shongopavi, Mishongnovi, and Shipaulovi. In Shongopavi, Hopi artisans have mastered silver overlay jewelry and coiled plaques. The other two villages occupy the eastern portion of Second Mesa. The Hopi Cultural Center and a hotel are located on this mesa. The cultural center has a museum and is also the tourism headquarters for the area. $. (928) 734-2401. www.hopiculturalcenter.com; www.hopi.nsn.us/village2.asp

Third Mesa: Oraibi, Kykotsmovi, Hotevilla, Bacavi, and Moencopi sit atop Third Mesa, which is 10 miles west of Second Mesa. Moenkopi, divided into Upper and Lower Moenkopi, is also considered part of Third Mesa, although the village is 40 miles away from the mesa. Third Mesa villages are known for their textile weaving, wicker baskets, and plaques. The seat of Hopi tribal government is Kykotsmovi, but the real gem of Third Mesa is Old Oraibi, the oldest continually inhabited settlement in North America. (928) 734-3283. www.hopi.nsn.us

The neon lights of Café 66 glow at night along the main street in downtown Williams. ▲ Children feed burros in Oatman. ▶

David H. Smith

Historic Route 66
A Trip Across Arizona

Historic Route 66 is one of three routes designated "historic" by the Arizona Department of Transportation's Parkways, Historic and Scenic Roads Advisory Committee and Transportation Enhancement office. That's not to say that the road has no scenic value. In places, the scenery ranks among the best in the state. In this chapter, we start at the Arizona-New Mexico border on the east and drive all the way across the state on Historic Route 66, where it exists, and on Interstate 40. Many towns along the way have stretches of road lined with restaurants, lodgings, and tourist attractions in the style of the old road's early days.

Kerrick James

Get Your Kicks

A n entire forest has surely perished to meet the paper needs of all the authors who have written about getting kicks and kitsch on "Historic" Route 66. The need has become an obsession more compelling than the actual kicks, whatever they might be, and at least equal to the seductive qualities of the kitschy, ubiquitous souvenir coffee cup bearing the famous road sign that is just one "6" short of being deemed demonic.

Driving the old Route 66 *is* a kitschy kick. There is so much to see and write about. So first, a little about the history and reputation of Route 66 before taking it across the state.

Route 66 (or Highway 66 or U.S. 66) is really that, a route, not a road like its successor, Interstate 40. It ran—and runs—east and west for roughly (and that describes its past and current condition) 2,500 miles between Chicago and Los Angeles and was pieced together out of a collection of roads unified mostly by highway signs for a decade, until 1938, when it finally was paved the entire way. For the record, although it was conceived years earlier, it was officially born in 1926 and officially died in 1984, survived by I-40. Portions of it live on in several states including Arizona, where it ranges between a point near Lupton on the east and a point just south of Oatman near the California border on the west.

Along the way, it disappears and reappears periodically, braided into the freeway here and there and ambling through towns such as Holbrook, Joseph City, Winslow, Winona, Flagstaff, Williams, Ash Fork, Seligman, Peach Springs, and Kingman.

The consensus of Route 66 cognoscenti is that the road developed its large and still-growing fan club for two big reasons:

One was a 1947 song, *Get Your Kicks On Route 66,* written by an actor-musician-composer named Bobby Troup and popularized by such melodic maestros as Nat "King" Cole, Bing Crosby, and, eventually, The Rolling Stones. Troup, who was re-married to an actor named Julie London, died in 1999 at age 80. His lyrics, whose quality falls somewhere between a poem by Edgar Guest and rap by anyone, begin, "If you ever plan to motor West," and contain the much-quoted "Don't forget Winona." That's an unforgettable reference to a forgettable hamlet just east of Flagstaff and just off I-40. However, Winona is worth visiting if only for the niacin rush of nostalgia.

The second was the immensely popular television show *Route 66,* which began in 1960 and ended four years later. It starred Martin Milner and George Maharis as two guys in a Corvette cruising for adventure on Route 66. The series, which

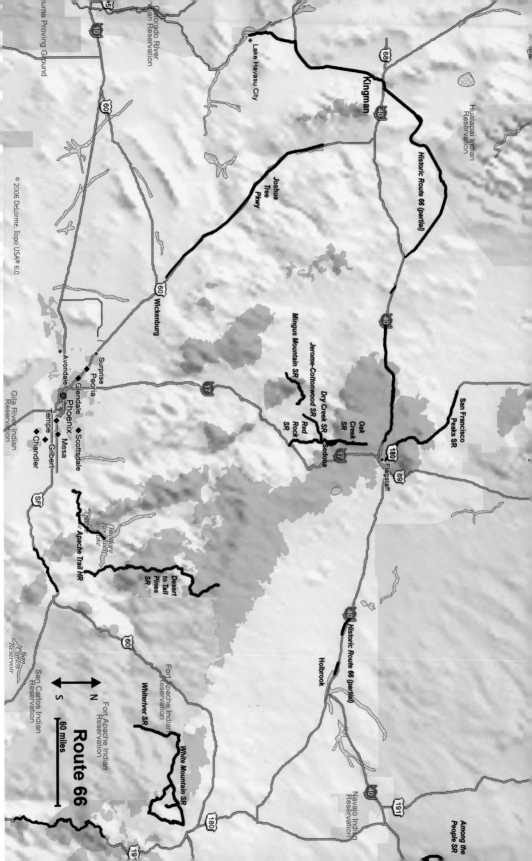

made its way overseas, probably accounts for a goodly share of the current popularity of the real Route 66 with Europeans, particularly Germans on motorcycles.

Never forgotten by Route 66 fans is the fact that the route made the ebb and flow of Americans from east to west and back again far easier. It attracted everyone from truckers to migrant farm workers and got some of its heaviest use in times of tumult such as the Oklahoma dust bowl disaster, the Great Depression, and the end of World War II's gasoline rationing. Think Steinbeck and *The Grapes of Wrath*.

Parts of Route 66 have been designated "historic" by the Arizona Parkways, Historic and Scenic Roads program, and it is the scenic portion running, erratically, between Flagstaff and Oatman that is of dominant interest.

■■■

It is delightfully impossible to encapsulate in a sentence or a paragraph the historic and scenic wonders of a route that traverses the approximately 380-mile width of the state, through canyons, over mountains, across flat desert, up and down basin-and-range country, past grasslands and fields of cactus, and, always, through the colorful history of this state.

First we will take up the eastern portion of old Route 66 running from I-40's junction with the community of Lupton on the eastern border and ending, roughly, in Winona just east of Flagstaff.

Second, we will take the path from Flagstaff to Kingman. Throughout the length of this segment of road—sometimes I-40 and sometimes old Route

[A vintage gas pump still stands along Historic Route 66 in Seligman.]

Tony Marinella

66—you'll pass through some blink-once-and-it's-behind-you communities such as Bellemont, Parks, Williams (blink three times there), Ash Fork, Seligman, Peach Springs, Truxton, Hackberry, and, finally, Kingman.

Third, after Kingman, yet another chunk of the Old 66 route, also officially designated as a historic drive but scenic, too, heads south in a dramatic run into colorful, tiny, touristy Oatman and on into California. The Kingman-Oatman leg is the tail of this beloved old dog of a highway. The tail wags its way around the hairpin turns of a mountain pass from outside of Kingman southwest to Oatman and becomes an acrophobic crawl along which you'd better not blink at all. ⵑⵑ

Kitsch Everywhere

Route 66 kitsch? You want it? You got it—everywhere.

Here's just a partial list of what is available at countless shops along Route 66, much of it bearing the famous road sign that resembles a badge or shield, some of it just the numbers 66 and still others the sign and a slogan such as "The Main Street of America" or "The Mother Road."

The list: a flashing neon highway sign dubiously suitable for the bathroom or the den, a deck of cards, sweatshirts, T-shirts, lapel pins, key chains, postcards, tapes, books, videos, refrigerator magnets, stickers for your bumper or whatever, hats in many variations but especially the billed ones you can wear backwards as a fashion accoutrement to baggy shorts, and coffee cups. There's much more, of course, but you get the idea.

Probably the ultimate use of the sign as a marketing device is a car dealer in Kingman whose lot faces the highway and who, on this day, put prices on used car windshields that all ended in, guess what, 66. Thus, $5,966, $3,566, $9,966, etc.

[
An old-style gas station operates in Hackberry. ▲
Buildings in Williams are decorated for Christmas. ▼
]

Chuck Lawsen

Historic Route 66 (Lupton to Flagstaff)

Route	Interstate 40 and stretches of the old Route 66 in towns along the way.
Mileage	160 miles.
Time to Allow	One or two days, depending on the length of your stops.
Elevation	About 6,200 feet at Lupton; about 7,000 feet at Flagstaff.
Overview	The drive on Interstate 40 is a National Scenic Byway. The state Historic Route 66 includes paved and unpaved pieces of the old road in towns including Holbrook, Joseph City, Winslow, Winona, and Flagstaff. Directions: www.historic66.com/arizona and www.theroadwanderer.net/route66AZ.htm

N ear the Arizona-New Mexico border, a series of extremely big, extremely yellow signs bloom along the roadside, in the heat of summer and the cold of winter. They proclaim the approach of a Chief Yellowhorse trading post, this one tucked into a beautiful, smooth rock outcrop. Notable for its array of tourist trinkets, the shop also offers giant teepees, which, of course, have nothing to do with the Navajo people upon whose reservation this business is located and whose members once sheltered in hogans, not teepees or wigwams. Asked once about that incongruity, the "chief" replied that lots of tourists wouldn't know a hogan from a hoagie, but everyone knows that a teepee means "Indian." Or words to that effect. (Chief Yellowhorse died in 1999 and a son runs the trading posts.)

A little farther into Arizona, Exit 357 at Lupton leads to Indian Route 12, which will take you to the Navajo Nation's capital, Window Rock, about 30 miles north. Straight ahead on I-40 leads to more touristy trading posts including Ortega's ("hand tooled leather purses" and "truckers welcome," raising certain questions about the propensities of some drivers of 18-wheelers). Still ahead is Fort Courage, which encourages God to bless America and which sells kachina dolls and T-shirts.

The Puerco (Spanish for "pig") River flows (sometimes) on your left and, generally on the right and periodically, are stretches of old paving that are the remains of old Route 66.

At Exit 311, a half-mile trip leads to a National Park Service visitors center that provides a splendid introduction to two wonders of this country: the Petrified Forest National Park and the Painted Desert, which is part of the park. Overnight camping and backcounty hiking require permits, but there are no established campsites in this exquisite, Technicolor, high-desert chunk of land decorated with reddish, beige, gray, and white formations. A 28-mile park road offers overlooks across great vistas of the Painted Desert.

Petrified wood fragments and pebbles lie strewn in Petrified Forest National Park.

Mark Miller

As for the petrified wood, visitors will be told repeatedly—in person and with signs and literature and an informative film at the visitors center—do not take a chunk of it, not even a teensy bit of it. It's illegal. You can buy all you want of this mineralized wood at shops that abound in the region. It weighs about 200 pounds per cubic foot, and it rates a seven on a 10-point scale of hardness.

The Painted Desert is generally thought of as the northern section of the Petrified Forest National Park, but that is not accurate. The desert actually forms a huge crescent with boundaries that are open to argument. For those with more than a passing curiosity, excellent printed discussions of how the Painted Desert and petrified wood came to be created are contained in voluminous and authoritative literature, some of it published by the Petrified Forest Museum Association and available at the visitors centers. Included are extensive treatises on the discoveries of the remains of small dinosaurs, crocodile-like reptiles, giant amphibians, and ancient pueblos and cultures that once inhabited the area.

Speaking of dinosaurs, dino sculptures as well as chunks of broken, petrified logs dot the sides of the interstate the rest of the way into Holbrook, which has its own Dinosaur Park. One small, ancient beast, re-created in green and inexplicably sporting a brand on its haunches, can even be found on the grounds of the Wigwam Motel on Route 66 in Holbrook. The motel was constructed in the 1940s and is a fascinating—if less than luxurious—example of Route 66 kitsch at its peak. Accommodations consist of concrete teepees complete with bathroom mirrors that slant at the same acute angle as the teepees. A different classic or soon-to-be antique car is parked outside each unit, and you can find a small but interesting collection of memorabilia in the office lobby. If your taste, your destination, or the time of day dictate another place to stay, you can still wander around and stare.

Back on I-40 and still retracing Route 66, the trail leads to Exit 257 and State Route 87 and a short drive to Homolovi Ruins State Park and its four Ancestral Puebloan, or Anasazi, pueblos that were occupied between 1250 and 1450 A.D.

Four more miles of interstate driving brings you to the modern town of Winslow, and beyond that, at Exit 230, a pair of ghost towns. The scene is midway between Winslow and Flagstaff, and the names are Canyon Diablo and Two Guns. They are not far off I-40. The Canyon Diablo community (3 miles north of the exit) was created as a railroad town in 1880 when the advancement of the rail line had to be halted until a trestle could be constructed over Canyon Diablo. It is said to have been remarkably lawless and contained saloons, gambling houses, and brothels, all of which closed once the trestle was completed over the canyon a decade later. Equally raffish and lawless was Two Guns (south of the exit), where, it is said, a man named Two Gun Miller opened a store and subsequently shot another man who sought to open a competing store. Self-defense, said a jury of Miller, who lived in a cave in the canyon and was mean to archaeologists.

Such ancient lore prefaces the highly civilized environs of Flagstaff and the next segment of the drive along Historic Route 66 to the shores of the Colorado River. ₥

[Dawn lights the ruins at Homolovi State Park.]

Randy Prentice

Historic Route 66 (Flagstaff to Kingman)

Route	Intermittently along Interstate 40 and Route 66.
Mileage	150 miles.
Time to Allow	All day.
Elevation	Nearly 7,000 feet at Flagstaff, about 3,300 at Kingman.
Overview	Always fascinating scenery ranges from high-desert plains to dense pine forests on a weave of I-40 and the famous Historic Route 66 including several stretches of old 66's much-repaired concrete that took Depression-era migrants west and spawned a popular song and even more popular TV show. Large stretches are designated as historic under the Arizona Parkways, Historic & Scenic Roads program.

F lagstaff's downtown is not only historic, it's vibrant despite a sprawl of shopping centers and chain stores on its outskirts. It got its name in 1881, according to one account, after a party of adventurers heading west plopped down on a July 4 and stripped a pine tree upon which they affixed the U.S. flag. The tree became a marker, and the area was dubbed Flag Staff by subsequent travelers and ranchers. The name eventually was merged into one word. That's one version, anyway. There are several others, most of them nominating some other tree, post, or pole that has attracted the allegiance of the tale-teller.

Tourist draws, in addition to Route 66, include the 1925 train depot designed in revival Tudor architecture, several old Victorian structures, Northern Arizona University, Pioneer Historical Museum, the Coconino Center for the Arts, the superb Museum of Northern Arizona, and the Lowell Observatory, which was created in 1894 to search for signs of intelligent life on Mars. The observatory has made many contributions to modern astronomy including the discovery of Pluto. Details of these attractions are in Where To Go in the Up North chapter of this book beginning on Page 268.

Because it is cold and snowy in winter, Flagstaff just barely escaped being Hollywood. In 1913, movie mogul Cecil B. DeMille arrived in Flagstaff to scout it out for a movie called *Squaw Man* but disliked the weather so much that he sent a telegram to associates in New York decreeing: "Flagstaff no good for our purpose. Have proceeded to California." Thus was the present Tinsel Town born and Flagstaff spared.

■ ■ ■

Upon leaving Flagstaff, the Route 66 signs point toward Bellemont. Leave I-40 and take the frontage road, which is Route 66. This is in the Kaibab National Forest, and it is a beautiful forest of pines and some birch. A sign tells drivers that some of the road ahead is "primitive." That means dirt, interspersed with blacktop and, eventually, a delightful but short stretch of the old, much-patched concrete that was once the Mother Road. A stop at Parks reveals a concrete-block building offering a post office, a hair dresser, a feed and mercantile store, and a Healing Hands massage/herbal/aromatherapy emporium.

Less than a half-mile farther west is the Parks General Store, which, according to the local lore offered by two resident merchants, once had to move its windows and doors to the opposite side when Route 66 was slightly re-routed years ago.

Continuing along old Route 66 past the Parks General Store, the roadbed for one delightful but short stretch returns to the old, tar-smeared but original two-lane concrete ribbon that is the Grail of roadies. Then blacktop, then more original concrete. At Deer Farm Road, it's time to follow the sign back to I-40 nearby, but not until taking the time to read the sign at that junction that

[Christmas lights adorn a steam engine in Flagstaff on Route 66.   ]

Tom Bean

recounts the legend of Route 66 and reveals that this short stretch of the road was completed in 1931, paved eight years later with the concrete that is still there, and, in 1964, supplanted by I-40.

I-40 leads quickly (about 4 miles) to Exit 165; you can head north on State Route 64 to the Grand Canyon or turn left and take Route 66 to the town of Williams, a friendly town that can guarantee tourists they will never be more than half a football field away from a motel as they drive through, heading west. There are several reasons for all those motels, including Route 66 itself, a downhill ski area, an easy and short drive to the Grand Canyon's South Rim, and the century-old Grand Canyon Railway offering an all-day round-trip to the Canyon (and featuring food, music, a mock train robbery, and a sense of what it was like to travel by train in the early 1900s).

Out of Williams, I-40 leads to Exit 146 and the turnoff to Ash Fork and the very brief resumption of Route 66. Twenty-two miles farther along I-40 is Exit 123 and Seligman 2 miles away. A long, flat stretch follows out of Seligman with good views of mesas, low-lying mountain ranges, and plains.

The historic route continues out of Seligman and leads well away from the interstate toward Grand Canyon Caverns, an astonishing, dry series of crystal-line chambers deep underground and accessible now by elevator after paying an admission fee. In 1927, a woodcutter discovered them when he was on his way to a poker game and almost fell down a hole leading to the vast, dark cavity. The guided tour of the caverns includes a look at the preserved remains of Bob, a 5-year-old, 30-pound bobcat who fell down one of the surface holes in about 1850 and whose mummified remains, ah, remain.

No smoking in the cavern, by the way, and, even more sadly for smokers, no gum chewing. "People stick it on the fragile crystals of the walls," the guide will tell you with a hint of scorn.

Peach Springs, Truxton, and Hackberry pass by quickly (one blink each) as Route 66 continues its way into sprawling Kingman with its abundance of motels (at least 66 of them, it seems), restaurants, and gas stations. Kingman lies roughly in the middle of the longest stretch, about 160 miles, of Route 66 and calls itself the "Heart of Historic Route 66." The sprawling, old railroad and mining town offers the Mohave Museum of History and Arts, golf courses, and quick trips to the old mining town of Chloride, Hoover Dam, the Grand Canyon, and the real but transplanted London Bridge.

There is some lore holding that Clark Gable and Carole Lombard were married in a small Kingman church, but the tale has as many skeptics as adherents.

Two final notes about Kingman: It is located in an ancient volcanic crater, and its main drag, Andy Devine Avenue, aka Route 66, is named after the late character actor in oater movies whose voice had the combined qualities of a castrato speaking through a throatful of gravel. ▥

Historic Route 66 (Kingman to Oatman)

Route	Kingman to Oatman.
Mileage	26 miles.
Time to Allow	Most of a day, assuming a return to Kingman.
Elevation	3,300 feet at Kingman, a few hundred feet lower at Oatman.
Overview	This exciting, scenic, partly mountainous drive is included in the state's Historic Route 66 designation. It arrives at an old, gold-mining town full of tourists, shops, wild burros, cold beer, and a narrow main drag, all a couple of gallons of gas away from the California border on the Colorado River.

F or those who fear heights, Route 66 from Kingman to the old gold-mining town of Oatman unarguably qualifies as a nightmare.

It also qualifies as the most beautiful, astonishing, vertiginous section of the entire route, one that should be driven in a small, foreign, convertible sports car with wide tires, a low center of gravity, the top down, and the CD player booming with Bach's "Toccata and Fugue in D Minor."

Or, lacking such a vehicle or a taste for old Johann Sebastian, you can just roll down the windows of your SUV, put on Eminem (that's what he's doing to you), and obey the speed limit signs. It's still a kick.

If it's springtime, the roadside and the surrounding lands are filled with the blues, purples, golds, yellows, and whites of wildflowers, a soothing prelude to the Gothic stretch of road to come.

Route 66 follows Andy Devine Avenue through Kingman to Andy Devine Avenue West (turn left) and Oatman, which is 26 eyebrow-lifting, hair-raising miles to the south. Four miles after that turn, head right to Route 66 or Oatman Highway. Turn left after you pass I-40 and continue toward Oatman, now 22 miles away. The direction signs are quite explicit.

Big yuccas begin to spring up and ahead loom the Black Mountains. Rock spires, split rocks, boulder fields, and mountain vistas follow. Wild burros (descendants of burros left behind when mines mostly played out and the miners left) and bighorn sheep can wander onto the road, assuming they have not fallen into any of the abandoned mine shafts that dot the countryside. Back in the 1930s, a U.S. Bureau of Land Management sign at Milepost 34 says, refugees from the Depression went so far as to hire locals to tow their Model T and Model A Fords over the mountainous grades ahead and through Sitgreaves Pass at 3,550 feet. Later, in wartime, the road became a military route and, still later and continuing to the present day, a tourist vacation road.

The highway is crisscrossed by several dry washes, appropriately signed with warnings not to drive into them during or for a while after rains, lest a flash flood sweep everyone away.

The beautiful drive through gorgeous countryside soon begins to be a climb, and the road seems to narrow (but only seems that way) as it works its way into the Black Mountains and its 15-mph switchbacks.

About 20 miles out of Kingman, a saguaro appears, a sure sign that despite the mountain road ahead, the overall elevation is dropping. Farther on, about 3 miles northeast of Oatman, is Gold Road, an old mining community dating back

[**Cholla cacti blanket the terrain outside Oatman.**   ]

Neil Weidner

to the early 1900s but now populated mostly by weeds and ghosts among the mine shafts and fallen walls.

The drop into the old gold mining town of Oatman comes quickly, offering a view of a natural pinnacle called Elephant's Tooth and a look at a population of a few hundred people who rely on tourists for a living. The old town, which began as a tent city and had some 12,000 residents during its golden days, features some

[**Historic Route 66 winds through the Black Mountains.**]

George Stocking

of the original buildings, lots of gift shops and cafés, and, most notably, the wild burros who wander the main street seeking and getting handouts, mostly carrots. The visitor is warned that the burros can, and will, kick and bite, but mostly they are far more interested in taking a veggie donation.

■■■

The town was founded in the first decade of the 1900s and by the early 1930s had produced nearly 2 million ounces of gold. The mines were closed in about 1942, wartime, when gold was not considered an essential element. Oatman, originally named Vivian, was later re-dubbed to memorialize the Oatman family that was killed in 1851 along the Gila Trail well west of Tucson and nowhere near the current community of Oatman.

The Oatmans, members of a Mormon splinter group from Illinois, consisted of Roys and Mary Ann and their seven children. The farming family was on its way to a promised land in Arizona when it was set upon by 19 Yavapais as the family was camped on a mesa near the Gila River.

Six Oatmans were fatally bludgeoned including mother, father, and four of the children. Lorenzo, 14, badly beaten and bleeding, escaped the Indians and wolves and eventually was rescued. Olive, 13, and Mary Ann, 7, were taken captive, tortured, and turned into slaves. They were traded later to more kindly Mojave Indians, but the weaker Mary Ann subsequently died. In 1856, the Mojaves released Olive, who was by then bearing indelible blue tattoos on her chin, courtesy of her captors. She was turned over to a U.S. Army post commander in trade for four blankets, white beads, trinkets, and a horse.

In 1865, Olive married a banker, adopted a baby girl, and lived for three decades in Sherman, Texas. She died of a heart attack in 1903 at age 65. Her survivors might have included two children born to her and a Mojave chief's son, but that speculation has never been proved.

Leaving history where one commonly finds it, behind, and returning to Oatman and the present day, the question arises of what to do in this town? Watch a mock gunfight on the weekends, buy a bauble or two or three, and examine the old Oatman Hotel, a two-story adobe dating back to the 1920s and, according to some, the place where Clark Gable and Carole Lombard stayed briefly after their wedding, purportedly in Kingman. There's always the chance of running into a filmmaker shooting a Hollywood movie. Oatman was the area chosen for films such as *How The West Was Won* and *Foxfire*, among others.

At the southern end of town, a road sign tells you that Golden Shores is 18 miles away, on the Arizona side of the Colorado River that divides this state from California, and the town of Needles, 22 miles down road.

Route 66 continues toward that junction of states, but our scenic tour does not. Say goodbye to Historic Route 66. ﬄ

Where To Go
What To See
What To Do

The information listing below covers Historic Route 66 from a national and an Arizona perspective. Following that are listings for communities and attractions listed geographically east to west.

Information: The nonprofit National Historic Route 66 Federation (909) 336-6131; www.national66.com) includes history, photographs, and other information. The Historic Route 66 Association of Arizona (928) 753-5001; www.azrt66.com) has compiled profiles of many towns and attractions along the route. Each May, it sponsors a weekend-long "fun run" from Seligman to Topock/Golden Shores for "street legal" vehicles. Another Internet site, www.historic66.com, includes directions to and descriptions of old roadway segments.

Lupton to Flagstaff

Lupton: The Painted Cliffs Welcome Center is a convenient first stop for travelers entering Arizona from the east on Interstate 40. Operated by the Arizona Office of Tourism, the center stocks complete touring information and maps. Exit 359. (928) 688-2448.

Holbrook

Information: Sometimes referred to as the gateway to the Petrified National Forest and Painted Desert, the town traces its history to 1881 when cattle ranches and railroads were the mainstay. The historic Navajo County courthouse here was built in 1898. Visitors packets include directions for a historical walking tour. (800) 524-2459; (928) 524-2459. www.ci.holbrook.az.us

Navajo County Historic Courthouse: The old courthouse houses a museum of Apache, Navajo, Hopi, and pioneer artifacts. Indians perform at the courthouse every weekday in June and July. Free. 100 E. Arizona. (928) 524-6558.

Petrified Forest National Park: Millions of years old, colorfully mineralized stumps and logs dot the park. The world-renowned Painted Desert lies within the park, as do the Painted Desert Inn Museum and the

[The Grand Canyon Railway's vintage locomotive
lingers at the Williams depot. ▲]

petroglyph-covered Newspaper Rock. Working archeological sites, visitors center offering a hands-on geology exhibit, tours, and movie. $. South entrance off U.S. Route 180, 19 miles southeast of Holbrook. North entrance at Exit 311 of Interstate 40 east of Holbrook. (928) 524-6228. www.nps.gov/pefo

Museum of the Americas and Dinosaur Park: Life-sized dinosaur replicas and a collection of pre-Columbian artifacts can be found at this privately owned museum. $. 3 miles east at Interstate 40 Exit 292. (928) 524-9178; (888) 830-6682.

Joseph City

Rock Art Canyon Ranch: A family-owned cattle ranch with guides that take visitors to view thousands of petroglyphs located on cliffs and boulders in Chevelon Canyon. The ranch also has a museum. May 1 through Nov. 1. Reservations. $. Located south of town. (928) 288-3260. http://new.azcommerce.com/SiteSel/Profiles

Winslow

Information: For information on Winslow area attractions, call (928) 289-2434 or the numbers listed below. www.winslowarizona.org/visitorinfo.html

Old Trails Museum: Exhibits focus on Route 66, the Ancestral Puebloan (Anasazi) culture, the Santa Fe Railroad, vintage clothing, ranch life, and antique bottles. $. Downtown. (928) 289-5861.

Standin' on a Corner: Each fall, Winslow throws a festival named for a line in the song *Take it Easy*. The line, "Standin" on a corner in Winslow, Arizona," put the town on the map. A downtown park features a two-story mural depicting the scene. www.standinonthecorner.com

Homolovi Ruins State Park: Considered sacred to the Hopi Indians, this site holds four 14th-century pueblo ruins. Visitors center with bookstore and museum. Campground. Restrooms and showers are available, along with picnic areas, grills, and day-use ramadas. $. Located north of Exit 257. (928) 289-4106. www.pr.state.az.us/Parks/parkhtml/homolovi.html.

La Posada: Considered one of the great railroad hotels, this hacienda-style building was once the favorite stop of travelers on the Santa Fe Railway. Designed by Mary Elizabeth Jane Colter, it opened in 1930. After 27 years it closed and eventually was converted for use as an office. Now, much of La Posada has been restored. $. 303 E. Second St. (Route 66). Reservations, (928) 289-4366. www.laposada.org

Meteor Crater: Around 50,000 years ago, a meteorite slammed into the surface of the Earth, leaving a crater nearly 600 feet deep and 4,000 feet wide. You can view the crater from the visitors center or take a guided half-mile tour skirting the rim. Gift shop, rock shop, interactive learning center, and a theater showing movies on meteor collisions and impacts. Food. Wheelchair accessible. $. Exit 233 from Interstate 40; go south for about 6 miles. (800) 289-5898; (928) 289-5898. www.meteorcrater.com

Flagstaff to Kingman

Flagstaff: See listings on Page 270.

Williams: See listings on Page 241.

Ash Fork: Ash Fork Commission for Tourism and Economic Development, (928) 637-2442; (928) 637-2269. Also, www.azrt66.com

Seligman: (928) 422-3939. www.azrt66.com

Peach Springs

Hualapai Indian Reservation: (928) 769-2590. www.itcaonline.com/tribes_hualapai.html

Grand Canyon Resort: Owned entirely by the Hualapai tribe, the resort has a Wild West town, Indian village, horseback tours, lodging, wagon rides, Grand Canyon tours, and more. (877) 716-9378. www.destinationgrandcanyon.com

Grand Canyon Caverns: An elevator descends 21 stories into one of the largest dry caves in the world. Hiking, biking, lodging, cocktail lounge, tours. In Peach Springs on Historic Route 66, 22 miles west of Seligman, and 60 miles east of Kingman. (928) 422-3223. www.gccaverns.com

Hualapai River Runners: After taking a motorized boat trip down the lower Grand Canyon from Diamond Creek, rafters ride a helicopter back to Peach Springs. (928) 769-2219 or (888) 216-0076. www.grandcanyonresort.com

Kingman

The Powerhouse Tourist Information and Visitor Center: 120 W. Route 66. (866) 427-7866. www.kingmantourism.org

Historic Route 66 Museum: Learn everything you ever wanted to know about the famous route. Free. Powerhouse Visitor Center, 120 W. Route 66. (928) 753-9889. www.kingmantourism.org/route66museum

Mohave Museum of History and Arts: Exhibits and displays about northwestern Arizona. Also oversees Bonelli House (listed below). $. 400 W. Beale St. (928) 753-3195. www.kingmantourism.org/to-do-and-see/museums/mohave-museum-history-arts.php

Bonelli House: Dating to 1915, it's an example of Anglo-Territorial architecture. 430 E. Spring St. (928) 753-3175. www.kingmantourism.org/to-do-and-see/kingman-attractions/bonelli-house.php

Andy Devine Days Parade and Community Fair: Celebrate Kingman's Western heritage as well as actor Andy Devine. September. Downtown Kingman. (928) 757-3850.

Hualapai Mountain Park: A county park in the forest allows visitors to hike, picnic, watch a variety of wildlife, camp, or rent cabins. From the Powerhouse Visitor Center in Kingman, head east on Andy Devine Avenue (Historic Route 66), turn right onto Hualapai Mountain Road and follow it for 14 miles to Hualapai Mountain Park. (928) 757-3859. www.mcparks.com/hmp

Oatman

Oatman-Gold Road Chamber of Commerce: (928) 768-6222 or (928) 768-3839. www.oatmangoldroad.com

Bitter Creek Outlaws: Wild West-style gunfights. Daily, 11 a.m. and 3 p.m. with additional show at 1:30 on Monday and Thursday. Free. (928) 279-0205. oatmangold.com/bittercreek/oatman.htm

Gold Road Mine Tours: Stand 500 feet directly under Route 66 on a one-hour mine shaft tour. Gold panning also offered. $. East of Oatman 2.5 miles on Route 66. (928) 768-1600; www.goldroadmine.com

Oatman Town Burros: Wild burros wander the downtown area looking for a handout.

Topock/Golden Shores: (928) 768-1110. www.azrt66.com/day3.htm#shores

History on the Go

Willard Clay

Historical markers, compiled by the Office of Roadside Development, chronicle the centuries of progress, activity, victory, and destruction that occurred throughout Arizona. Though not every milepost included corresponds to a physical sign, they designate areas of special value.

Some historical markers serve as memorials to fallen heroes, some stand proudly in front of state facilities, while others indicate the vicinity of major battles. From the Mormon Battalion's epic trek across the untamed desert, to the surrender of Geronimo, to the plight of ordinary pioneers who faced unknown dangers in uncharted territory, these simple markers stitch moments of time together through the threads of Arizona highways. As you drive along U.S. and state routes, signs will alert you that a marker is upcoming. The markers are listed here from the smallest to the largest route number and by milepost (MP).

INTERSTATE 8

MP 0 (Business Loop)

Yuma Crossing: From 1850 to 1877, all travelers crossing the Colorado River used the ferries. Several operated between the mouth of the Gila River and Pilot Knob. Steamboats arrived on the river in 1850, and the first railroad bridge was built in 1877.

MP 0 (Business Loop)

Blue Star Memorial Highway: A tribute to the armed forces that have defended the United States of America.

MP 0.2 (Business Loop)

Territorial Prison: Built to house the bad men who were the terror of Arizona when it was one of the last frontiers. Escape from the prison was difficult, but confinement in the stark, sun-baked cells was even worse.

MP 14.5

El Camino Del Diablo (The Devil's Highway): This early route from Sonora, Mexico, to California follows the path taken by Father Eusebio Kino

[
Crescent Lake is one of the gems in the Apache National Forest in the White Mountains.
]

in 1700. He was seeking to discover if California was an island or part of the mainland. The parched desert along this route has claimed hundreds of lives, particularly during the California gold rush of 1849.

INTERSTATE 10

MP 305 (Business Loop)

Mormon Battalion Trail: On Dec. 4, 1846, on its way to California to protect U.S. interests during the war with Mexico, the battalion camped on the San Pedro River before turning west toward Tucson.

MP 364 (Business Loop)

Old Fort Bowie: Known as the "Guardian of Apache Pass" and overlooking the only spring for miles, Fort Bowie was established in 1862 after the Battle of Apache Pass, the largest conflict in Arizona's Indian wars. In that battle, Apaches massed under Cochise and Mangas Coloradas attacked the pass, but were routed by California volunteers firing howitzers.

MP 182.2

Gila River Indian Reservation: Originally established in 1859, the government opened the first Indian school here for Pimas and Maricopas in 1871 with the Rev. Charles H. Cook as teacher. The reservation encompasses the location of the Pima villages, friendly resting places for travelers during the Mexican War and the California gold rush. The reservation also was the birthplace of Ira Hayes, a Pima Indian who was one of the U.S. Marines in the famed flag-raising at Iwo Jima.

MP 219

Mormon Battalion Trail: The Mormon Battalion camped here Dec. 17, 1846, en route to California. During the war with Mexico, on one of the longest infantry marches of record, the soldiers were the first to unfurl the U.S. flag in Tucson.

MP 219

Battle of Picacho: This is the site of the westernmost action, April 15, 1862, between Confederate and Union forces in the Civil War.

MP 320

Apache Peace Treaty Ratification: On Oct. 12, 1872, 4 miles southeast of here at Council Rocks near Dragoon Springs, Gen. O. O. Howard and Cochise, chief of the Chiricahua Apache Indians, ratified a peace treaty. It ended years of warfare between that tribe and the white settlers. Cochise's stronghold was hidden deep in the Dragoon Mountains beyond.

INTERSTATE 17

MP 242

Black Canyon Highway: Black Canyon Highway construction began in 1947 under Gov. Sidney P. Osborne and was completed in 1961 under Gov. Paul Fannin.

MP 284

Copper Canyon Route to the Verde Valley: In January 1865, nine men and one horse entered the Verde Valley through Copper Canyon to launch the first successful Anglo-American irrigation project in northern Arizona. Cattle lost to Indian raids exceeded the value of the first year's crops, but the intrepid pioneers persevered.

MP 285

Camp Verde: The oldest settlement in the Verde Valley, this was the site of the historic Fort Lincoln, established in 1864 to protect the settlers from marauding Apaches. Four of the fort buildings may still be seen, one of which houses the Fort Verde Museum.

INTERSTATE 19

MP 4 (Business Loop)

Blue Star Memorial Highway: A tribute to the armed forces that have defended and continue to stand ready for the United States of America.

MP 5 (Business Loop)

Kitchen Memorial: Born in Tennessee in 1823, Pete Kitchen—pioneer, rancher, stockman, miner, and Indian fighter—came to Arizona in 1854 and established a 1,000-acre ranch that supplied meat and other products to Army camps, Tucson, and other nearby settlements.

MP 9

Ghost Town of Calabasas: In the 18th century this was a Tohono O'odham (Papago) Indian village visited by Jesuit missionaries. It later became the site of Spanish mines, a huge Mexican cattle ranch, and a military outpost. During the Civil War, it was the location of Fort Mason, and in the 1880s, it was a wild railroad construction camp.

MP 22

Tubac: Spain planted its flag here in 1737 and erected a garrison in 1752 to protect church missions. Later, Spain lost the post to Mexico. Settled by the Mormons in 1852, it was an American mining center by 1856. Tubac was a self-governed post on a lawless frontier and issued its own paper money, boletos, redeemable in silver. It also boasted the first American newspaper in the region. Apache raids caused its abandonment from 1861 to 1864.

MP 59 (Business Loop)

San Xavier del Bac Mission: Originally founded by Jesuits in April 1700, the mission was sacked during the Pima Revolt in 1751, then restored in 1752. After the Franciscans took over in 1768, Apaches raided it that same year. Work on the present structure spanned from 1785 to 1798. It was abandoned in the Mexican revolt from Spain 1822, but priests returned in 1859 after the Gadsden Purchase. It withstood an earthquake in 1887 and was restored twice in the 20th century. It stands as one of America's most beautiful missions in active use today.

MP 62 (Business Loop)

First Municipal Airport in the United States: The first plane landed in Tucson on Nov. 20, 1919, by pilot Swede Myerhofer.

INTERSTATE 40

MP 163 (Business Loop)

Bill Williams Mountain: Standing at 9,264 feet elevation, this mountain was named for a colorful mountaineer, guide, and trapper who is generally credited with being the first American to explore northern Arizona, circa 1830 or earlier. Williams lived at different times among the Osage and Ute Indians and earlier had been a Baptist circuit rider in Missouri. He was killed by Indians in 1849.

MP 266

Sunset Crossing on the Little Colorado River: This was the crossing for Beale's camel expedition in 1858 on the military road from Fort Defiance to Fort Mohave and was a simple rocky ledge through a river bed filled with dangerous quicksand. It was used by military travelers and the Mormon immigrants who arrived in northern Arizona in 1876. It was the main means of crossing of the river until the railroad was built in 1882.

MP 358

Dominguez–Escalante Expedition: In November 1776, a party of Spanish explorers and Indian guides passed through this area on the way to the Zuni mission in what is now New Mexico. Franciscan fathers Francisco Atanasio Dominguez and Silvestre Velez de Escalante had left Santa Fe hoping to find an overland route to the presidio at Monterey. However, cold weather and rugged terrain forced them to turn south and return to Santa

Fe. While they never succeeded in finding a shorter route to California, the priests explored much new territory in the present states of New Mexico, Colorado, Utah, and Arizona. They were the first Europeans to discover a crossing of the Colorado River after wandering for miles along the rim of the seemingly impassable Marble Canyon Gorge. The explorers tried bringing the Christian religion to the Hopis in Oraibi, 100 miles west of here. Their conversion efforts were not well received, but the Hopis saved them from starving. They camped near this location on Nov. 16, 1776, in a snowstorm. They had but one more day's ride before reaching the mission in Zuni.

U.S. ROUTE 60

MP 18

Last Camp of Hi Jolly: Born in Syria circa 1828, Jolly died in Quartzsite Dec. 16, 1902. He came to this country Feb. 10, 1856, and worked as a camel-driver and scout for more than 30 years as an aide to the U.S. government.

MP 19

Tyson Wells Old Stage Station: This was a stage stop between Ehrenberg and Wickenburg and points east. Travelers in the 1870s and 1880s made their first stop here on eastward journeys from the Colorado River. "No grass but good water," an early desert guide indicated. Accommodations were extremely crude.

MP 56

Salome: This desert town was made famous by the humor of Dick Wick Hall, operator of the Laughing Gas Station. Hall's publication, *Salome Sun*, was filled with exaggerated tales of the adaptation of animal and plant life to the desert environment, such as his frog that was 7 years old and never learned to swim.

MP 106

Wickenburg Massacre: In this vicinity, on Nov. 5, 1871, the Wickenburg-Ehrenberg stage was ambushed by Mohave Indians. John Lanz, Fred W. Loring, P. M. Hamel, W. G. Salmon, Frederick Shoholm, and C. S. Adams were killed. Mollie Sheppard died later from her wounds.

MP 107

Vulture Mine: This mine was discovered in 1863 by Henry Wickenburg. To supply the needs of the subsequent mines and protective military camps, the Salt River-irrigated agricultural industry was developed. The Vulture Mine produced $10 million in gold and was the greatest single factor in the settlement of central Arizona. Its discoverer died by his own hand in 1905 at the age of 86.

MP 109

Crypt of Henry Wickenburg: Born Dec. 21, 1820, died May 14, 1905.

MP 166

Original Site of Phoenix: In the winter of 1867-1868, a party led by Jack Swilling dug a canal from the Salt River to irrigate fields in this vicinity. Helling's Mill on the bank of the canal, plus a few neighboring stores, became the center of the Phoenix settlement. Three years later, a new town site was surveyed and established to the west.

MP 168

First Farm Dwelling in the Valley: In the spring of 1868, S. (Frenchie) Sawyer built the first farm dwelling and harvested the first cultivated crop, barley, in the valley. These same fertile acres had been irrigated centuries before by Indians who abandoned their canals and lands.

MP 170

Dedication: Erected in 1941 by the Maricopa Chapter of the Daughters of the American Revolution, dedicated to the pioneer spirit of our early settlers.

MP 171

Governor Hunt's Tomb: Here lies the burial vault of Gov. George W. P. Hunt, 1881-1934. Waiter, miner, merchant, banker, legislator, and president of Arizona's Constitutional Convention, as well as the state's first governor, he served through seven terms beginning in 1912, the year Arizona became the 48th state. He was an ambassador to Thailand from 1921-22. Entombed with him are his wife, her parents, Mr. and Mrs. Jessie W. Ellison, and Mrs. Hunt's sister, Miss Lena Ellison.

MP 171

Hayden's Ferry: Started in 1872, the ferry conveyed travelers across the Salt River during its flood stages. Named for Charles Trumbull Hayden, probate judge, miller, merchant, farmer, freighter and civic leader, who was an early resident of Tempe and father of U.S. Sen. Carl Hayden.

MP 171

Moeur Park: This plaque was erected by the Tempe Garden Club in memory of Honor Anderson Moeur, wife of Gov. B. B. Moeur, for her untiring efforts toward beautification of our highway and the creation of this park.

MP 171

State of Arizona Tempe Bridge: An impressive result of prison labor assistance, this bridge was constructed 1910–1913.

MP 195

Dedication: Erected in 1938 by the Dons Club of Phoenix to commemorate the legend of the Lost Dutchman Mine.

MP 204

Jefferson Davis Highway No. 70: Erected 1943 by United Daughters of the Confederacy of Arizona.

MP 223

Picket Post Mountain: A lookout point during Indian wars. Soldiers protected Pinal City and the Silver King Mine from Apache raiders. It was the home of Col. William Boyce Thompson, mining magnate and founder of the Boyce Thompson Arboretum at the foot of the mountain.

MP 246

Miami–Superior Highway: Built in 1919, this stretch of highway runs 21 miles and cost $1 million to construct.

MP 248

Old Dominion Mine: Included in this historic copper mine are the Globe Ledge silver claims. Discovered in 1873, it was the first to yield profitable ore in the Globe-Miami district. The Old Dominion included many other early claims. Production ceased in the 1930s due to subterranean flooding and the lowered price of copper.

MP 265

McMillenville and Ghost Mining Camp: In 1874, silver was discovered in what became the fabulous Stonewall Jackson Ledge. The discovery brought boom conditions that lasted less than 10 years. An Indian attack on the camp was repulsed in 1882.

MP 297

Becker Butte Lookout: Dedicated to the memory of Gustav Becker of Springerville, Arizona, 1850-1940. Pioneer merchant, trail blazer, road builder, and a father of U.S. Highway 60. "His was a long life, founded on the golden rule."

MP 387

Madonna of the Trail: National Society Daughters of the American

Revolution dedicated this memorial to the pioneer mothers of the covered wagon days.

STATE ROUTE 64

MP 268

Grand Canyon Airline Tragedy: In 1956, a TWA Super Constellation and an United Airlines DC-7 collided over the Painted Desert, killing a total of 128 passengers and crew from both aircraft.

STATE ROUTE 66

MP 52

Dedication: In honor of Lt. Edward Fitzgerald Beale (1822-1893), who commanded the exploration of a wagon route to the Colorado River, taking the only camel train in American history 1857-1858. Beale's survey was then followed by a railroad survey, 1858-1859. The route of Atlantic and Pacific Railroad was built across Arizona in 1882-1883, the tracks reaching Kingman in the spring of 1883. State Route 66 closely follows Beale's original survey.

MP 276

The Old Fort: A group of Mormon colonists, led by William C. Allen, settled here March 24, 1876. They erected a fort of cottonwood logs and mud on this site. It was first known as Allen's Camp. In 1878, the name was changed to St. Joseph in honor of Joseph Smith, the Mormon prophet. In 1923, the name of the town was changed to Joseph City. It is the oldest Mormon community in Arizona.

MP 325

Navajo Springs: On Dec. 29, 1863, during a snowstorm, Arizona Territorial Governor John N. Goodwin and other officials arriving from the east by wagon train took their oaths of office and raised the U.S. flag just inside the new territory's border with New Mexico.

STATE ROUTE 69

MP 247

The Woolsey Trail/Old Black Canyon Road: The old stage and freighting route first used in 1865 connected Prescott and southern Arizona. It can be seen on the opposite side of the canyon and was originally called the Woolsey Trail, then later the Black Canyon Road.

MP 280

Old Fort Woolsey: Site of Woolsey Ranch, known as Old Fort Woolsey because of engagements in this locality between Indians and pioneer settlers. Also known as "Half-way House" by stagecoach drivers and travelers. Named for Col. King Woolsey, who served in the first, second, seventh, eighth, and ninth Territorial Councils.

MP 283

Old Orchard Ranch: Home of Sharlot M. Hall, pioneer Arizona poet. This homestead and ranch established in 1882 was the inspiration for some of the most tender, most expressive poetry written in Arizona. Here Miss Hall, appointed Territorial historian, composed many of the works included in Cactus and Pine and Poems of a Ranch Woman.

MP 293

Prescott: Founded in 1864 on Granite Creek, it was a source of placer gold and once Arizona's Territorial capital. In frontier days, the oldest rodeo in the West began here.

U.S. ROUTE 70

MP 273.1

Apacheland/Old San Carlos: The Old Indian Agency, of the bloody Apache War days, was covered by the waters of San Carlos Lake. Upon completion of the Coolidge Dam in 1928, the Old Indian Cemetery was covered with a cement slab. Buildings were moved several miles north to a new San Carlos.

MP 302

Geronimo: Named for the rebellious medicine man who led the Chiricahua Apaches on their last raids, to surrender, and finally into exile in Florida and Oklahoma. This was also the site of original Camp Thomas, established in 1876 to keep Geronimo's tribesmen on their farmlands along the Gila River.

MP 341

The Gila Valley: Site of numerous events, including the route of Coronado in search of fabled Seven Cities of Cibola in 1540. James O. Pattie and other famous trappers ventured along the Gila River in 1825-26. Gen. Stephen W. Kearny and Lt. W. H. Emory were led by Kit Carson to California in 1846 and Apache Indian hunting grounds here were colonized by Mormons in 1879.

MP 344

Solomon (Solomonville): County seat of Graham County 1883-1915.

Named for Isadore Elkan Solomon, a settler who, in 1876, burned charcoal to supply fuel to the Lesinsky Brothers Copper Smelter near Clifton.

MP 347

Gila Valley: In 1846, General Kearney's Army of the West, guided by Kit Carson, followed the Gila River from New Mexico to California, occupying that region during the Mexican War and thus opening the southern snow-free route to the Pacific coast.

MP 353

Wright Memorial: In memory of two of the many pioneers of the Gila Valley, Lorenzo and Seth Wright, who were killed 1 mile north of this spot by Indians. The Indians had stolen 45 horses from some settlers. While pursuing the them, the Wrights were ambushed on Dec. 1, 1885.

MP 364

Merrill Memorial: In memory of Horatio Harris Merrill, born Jan. 3, 1837, and his daughter, Eliza Ann Merrill, born July 27, 1881, who while traveling by team and wagon from Pima, Arizona, to Clifton, Arizona, were ambushed and killed by Indians on Dec. 3, 1895.

STATE ROUTE 73

MP 333

Kinishba Ruins: Derived from a modernized version of Apache words, Kinishba roughly translates to "brown house." This area was home to the Ancestral Puebloan, or Anasazi, people between 1300 and 1400.

STATE ROUTE 75

MP 392

Apache Grove: This area served as a resting place for Apache War parties during the raids of the 1880s. Near here, Felix B. Knox, a cattleman and gambler, stayed behind to face Indians while his wife, children, and hired man escaped in a buckboard. Out of respect for his valor, the Indians did not mutilate his body.

STATE ROUTE 77

MP 80

Canada del Oro: For early travelers, the road through this canyon was one of the most dangerous in Arizona. Indians attacked lone riders and wagon trains along this route from Tucson to Old Camp Grant on the San Pedro

River. Despite the canyon's name, very little gold was ever found here.

MP 161

El Capitan Pass: This pass was used by Kearny's Army of the West in a march to California in 1846, guided by Kit Carson. It was described in a journal of the trip as "Carson's old trail." The pass led around the impassable canyon on the Gila River where Coolidge Dam later constructed.

STATE ROUTE 79

MP 115

Tom Mix Memorial: In memory of Westerns movie actor Tom Mix (Jan. 8, 1880-Oct. 12, 1940), whose spirit left his body on this spot and whose characterization and portrayals in life served to better fix memories of the Old West in the minds of living men.

MP 136

Poston's Butte: The final resting place of the "Father of Arizona," Charles D. Poston, born in Kentucky in 1825. Poston was Arizona's first delegate to Congress and is buried in accordance with his wishes. It was to have been the site for Poston's temple to the sun, but that effort failed, and he died in poverty in Phoenix in 1902. Not until years later were his remains brought to the place called Parsee Hill, but known to local residents as Poston's Butte.

STATE ROUTE 80

MP 301

Mormon Battalion Trail: Capt. P. C. Merrill camped near here on Dec. 18, 1846. He returned to San Pedro in 1877.

MP 314

Pioneer Memorial: In memory of unidentified veterans, pioneers, and settlers.

MP 316

Boothill Graveyard: Boothill is home to many infamous gun fighters. Buried here are the remains of Tom McLowery, Frank McLowery, and Billie Clanton, killed in the Earp-Clanton battle on Oct. 26, 1881, near the O.K. Corral in Tombstone.

MP 343

The Lavender Pit: This open pit mine was named the Lavender Pit in honor of Harrison M. Lavender, 1890-1952.

MP 389

San Bernardino: This Mexican land grant dating from 1822 stretched on both sides of the international boundary. It was a stopping place for the Mormon Battalion in 1846 and for thousands of gold-seekers in following years. Also the home ranch of John Slaughter, Arizona sheriff from 1884-1922.

MP 406

Geronimo's Surrender: "Near here, Geronimo, last Apache chieftain, and Nachite with their followers, surrendered, on Sept 6, 1886, to Gen. Nelson A. Miles. First, Lt. Charles B. Gatewood with Kieta and Martine, Apache scouts, risked their lives to enter the camp of the hostiles to present terms of surrender offered to them by General Miles. After two days, Gatewood received the consent of Geronimo and Nachite to surrender. The surrender of Geronimo in Skeleton Canyon, on that historic day, forever ended Indian warfare in the United States."

STATE ROUTE 82

MP 16

Johnny Ward Ranch: On Jan. 27, 1861, Coyotero Apaches raided the ranch of John Ward, taking his livestock and abducting his 12-year-old stepson, Felix Ward, later known as the scout Mickey Free. Ward blamed the raid not on the Coyotero Apaches but on Cochise's band of Chokonens of the Chiricahua Apaches. The event spawned a hunt for Cochise, in what would later be referred to as the Bascom Affair, named after George N. Bascom, the lieutenant dispatched to round up Cochise and his men. Bascom double-crossed Cochise and killed some of his family, so Cochise swore vengeance against all whites.

MP 19

Mowry Mine: It was originally worked by Mexicans. The mine was purchased for $25,000 in 1860 by Lt. Sylvester Mowry, a West Point graduate. Mowry, later accused of Confederate sympathies, was imprisoned in Fort Yuma. The mine was taken by the U.S. government. Mowry died in London on Oct. 15, 1871.

MP 40

San Ignacia del Babocomari Mexican Land Grant: On Dec. 25, 1832, for $380, Ignacio Elias and his sister Eulalia purchased 123,068 acres of rangeland stretching almost to the San Pedro River on the east and to the Canelo Hills and Sonoita Creek on the west. Only 34,707 acres was allowed by the U.S. Court of Private Land Claims. It was the largest land grant approved in Arizona.

MP 294

Camp Crittenden: Established on Aug. 10, 1867, it was named Camp Crittenden in honor of Col. Thomas A. Crittenden of the 32nd U.S. Infantry. The camp was abandoned June 1, 1873. It was established to protect the settlements of Babocomari, Sonoita, and Santa Cruz valleys from Indians, including Cochise.

STATE ROUTE 84

MP 181

Barony of Arizona: James Addison Peralta Reavis, the "Baron of Arizona," was a brazen forger who claimed over 12 million acres of central Arizona and western New Mexico as an old Spanish land grant. He and his family lived here in royal style until his fraud was exposed. From the barony he went to federal prison in 1895.

STATE ROUTE 85

MP 123

Mormon Battalion Trail: Honoring the Mormon Battalion, which passed here on Dec. 27, 1846, on its way to California, in the service of the U.S. Army in the war with Mexico.

MP 145

Gadsden Purchase: Until Dec. 30, 1853, the Gila River (1 mile north) formed the international boundary between the United States and Mexico. Through the Gadsden Purchase, territory south of that boundary became a part of the United States, creating the present international boundary.

MP 193 (West Washington Street)

Arizona State Capitol: Completed in 1900 at a cost of approximately $136,000, this building was designed by James Riley Gordon of San Antonio, Texas. It served as the first Arizona-owned seat of government during the late Territorial days and in its transition to statehood in 1912. The original structure is 184 feet long and 84 feet deep. The exterior is constructed entirely of Arizona products: grey granite from the Salt River Mountains, tufa from Yavapai County, and malapia rock from Camelback Mountain for the foundation.

MP 195 ((West Washington Street)

Carnegie Public Library and Park: The Carnegie library was erected in

1907-1908 and refurbished in 1986.

STATE ROUTE 86

MP 94

Quijotoa: This site was named after the Tohono O'odham (Papago) word meaning "mountain shaped like a carrying basket." The discovery of a pocket of gold and silver ore led to an impressive boom here in 1883. The desert has reclaimed the original site and its suburbs of Logan City, New Virginia, Brooklyn, and Allen City. The mine was a complete failure, with only a tiny pocket of riches being found on the mountain.

STATE ROUTE 87

MP 190

Grave of Dr. Carlos Montezuma (Wassaja): Wassaja, a Yavapai Indian, was taken captive at the age of 6 by Pima Indians. He was sold to a white man who educated him as a physician. As Dr. Carlos Montezuma, he had a practice in Chicago and became a champion of Indian rights. But he died of tuberculosis in a brush hut near here in 1923, refusing all medical care.

MP 190

Camp Reno: From 1866 until 1868, this outpost of Fort McDowell served as a departure point for military expeditions against the Tonto and Pinal Apache Indians.

MP 191

Fort McDowell: This important military post protected central Arizona settlements from the Tonto Apaches during the Indian Wars, 1865 to 1886. Its function as a post ended in 1890 and it became a reservation in 1891.

MP 291

Battle of Big Dry Wash: Near here, on July 17, 1882, was fought the last big battle of the Apache Wars. Fourteen cavalry troops, commanded by Capt. A. R. Chaffee, encircled a group of renegade Coyotero Apaches led by charismatic medicine man Na-ti-o-tish. This followed a week of raiding and slaughter by the Apaches, who had escaped from the White Mountain Reservation. Most of the hostiles were killed. Lt. Thomas Cruse won the Medal of Honor in this battle.

STATE ROUTE 88 (THE APACHE TRAIL)

MP 208

Canyon Lake: Originally formed by the Mormon Flat Dam, a water-storage reservoir was built later by the Salt River Project in 1925.

MP 229

Apache Lake: Originally formed by the Horse Mesa Dam, a water-storage reservoir was built later by the Salt River Project in 1927.

MP 241

Roosevelt Dam: Roosevelt Lake, formed by the Theodore Roosevelt Dam that the Bureau of Reclamation built from 1905 to 1911, became a water-storage reservoir for the Salt River Project.

STATE ROUTE 89

MP 252

Henry Wickenburg Memorial: Henry Wickenburg, the discoverer of the fabulously rich Vulture Mine and the man for whom the town of Wickenburg was named, came to Arizona in 1862. Legend tells us that this intrepid frontiersman, a native of Russia, found the gold in chunks of rock he was throwing at a recalcitrant burro. Development of the mine led to brisk milling activity along the Hassayampa River with subsequent growth of the town of Wickenburg, which at that time became one of the largest in the Territory.

MP 289

Ruins of Walnut Grove Dam: Although 135 feet at the base and standing 110 feet. high, this dam weakened and collapsed during the night of Feb. 22, 1890. The rushing water took more than 50 lives and swept away everything in its path. Damage extended as far downstream as Wickenburg. The dam was never rebuilt.

MP 306

Prescott: The mile-high city is the former Territorial capital of Arizona and present seat of Yavapai County. Founded in 1864 and named for historian William Hickling Prescott, Prescott is situated on Granite Creek, an early source of placer gold.

MP 312

Memorial Park: This park is dedicated to the veterans of all United States wars in recognition of their courage and sacrifice in the service of our country.

MP 333

Del Rio Springs: This site of the original Camp Whipple was established in December 1863. From Jan. 22 to May 18, 1864, the offices of the Territorial government of Arizona were operated from tents and log cabins here, before being moved to Prescott, the Territory's first permanent capital.

MP 346

Historic 35th Parallel: For ages, a route traveled by Indians, missionaries, and trappers. The U.S. Army survey of 1851 was completed by Capt. Lorenzo Sitgreaves. In 1854, Lt. Amiel W. Whipple, along with scientists and troops, made a topographical survey for a railroad to the Pacific. From 1857 to 1859, Lt. Edward E. Beale, with his camel corps, explored the way for a wagon road route of the Santa Fe Railroad.

MP 346

Dedication: A tribute to the armed forces that have defended the United States of America.

STATE ROUTE 89A

MP 344

Jerome Blast Furnace: This blast furnace was in use in 1882. The smelter site at that time was where the big open pit is now. This little furnace used coke for fuel. The nearest source of supply was Wales, England, more than half-way around the world. Small sailing vessels carried the coke across the Atlantic ocean and around the horn of South America to San Francisco. From there is was transported by railroad to Ashfork, Arizona, where it was loaded into mule-drawn freight wagons and hauled 60 miles over the mountains to Jerome.

MP 344

Prescott Granite: This rock was used in drilling contests. Great skill and stamina were required in both single and double jack drilling. In the team drilling contest held on Sept. 16,191, one contestant, Jim Kennedy was injured when his partner's sledge handle broke and the hammer struck him in the head. His team won, but Kennedy died from the injury.

MP 377

Indian Gardens: In 1876 or 1877, Jim Thompson built a log cabin here and began cultivating the old Indian gardens where the Indians had grown corn and squash long before Oak Creek was known to white men. Thompson remained here at his Indian gardens guest ranch until his death in 1917.

U.S. ROUTE 89

MP 466

Cameron (Originally Tanner's Crossing): Named for one of Arizona's first U.S. senators, a pioneer in development of trails and copper mines in Grand Canyon. Near here was the site of Tanner's Crossing of the Little Colorado River on the Mormon Trail from Utah, via Lee's Ferry to settlements in Arizona and Mexico.

MP 540

Glen Canyon Bridge: One of the world's highest steel-arch bridges stands 700 feet above the Colorado River. It took two years to build, costing $4 million.

MP 540

Glen Canyon Dam: Dedicated by the first lady, Mrs. Lyndon B. Johnson, on Sept. 22, 1966.

MP 540

Lake Powell: Maj. John Wesley Powell led scientific exploration parties down the Green and Colorado Rivers in 1869 and in 1871-72. Years later, Powell became a leader in government science programs, headed the U.S. Geological Survey and the Bureau of American Ethnology, and advocated enlightened land and water conservation policies which resulted in the passage of the Reclamation Act of 1902. To commemorate his courage and years of public service, the reservoir behind Glen Canyon Dam has been named Lake Powell.

MP 549

Glen Canyon National Recreation Area: Established in 1958, this area surrounds Lake Powell and expands 186 miles along the old Colorado River channel behind Glen Canyon Dam.

MP 549

Glen Canyon Bridge: Constructed from 1957 to 1959 to facilitate construction of Glen Canyon Dam and for public use as a part of U.S. Highway 89.

U.S. ROUTE 89A

MP 537

Navajo Nation: A six-yoke team of oxen once climbed the historic Dugway Trail up from Lee's Ferry.

MP 537

Navajo Bridge: Finished in 1928, the arch of this bridge stands at 616 feet and has been placed on the National Register of Historic Places by the United States Department of the Interior.

MP 538

Lee's Ferry: John D. Lee settled here in December 1871 and 13 months later established ferry service 6 miles upstream from this bridge. After her husband's death, Emma Lee, 1875 to 1879, had Warren M. Johnson run the oar-driven ferry until the Church of the Latter Day Saints purchased her interest. Coconino County operated the ferry from 1910 to 1928.

MP 557

Dominguez and Escalante Expedition: Fatigued by a 30-mile ride, the Spanish padres picked their way down the north slope of the Kaibab Plateau toward the light of Paiute campfires near what is now Coyote Spring, 15 miles north. The timid natives fled from the approaching Spaniards. No white man had ever been in this region. Coaxed to return, the Indians brought piñon nuts and two roasted rabbits for the hungry explorers. During the night, a medicine man performed his healing ritual for an ailing Spaniard. Dominguez and Escalante were furious over a Catholic's participation in the pagan rites. After admonishing their companion for his frail faith, the fathers implored the Indians to cease their ceremonies, be baptized, and embrace Christianity. The expedition was unique in the history of the West. Searching for a safe overland route from Santa Fe to Monterey, the padres were determined to establish rapport with tribes along the way. They did not reach Monterey. However, their regard for the natives allowed them to travel the 1,700 miles without a shot being fired or a word of anger uttered between Spaniard and Indian.

MP 609

Pipe Springs National Monument: Fifteen miles southwest of here is historic Pipe Springs, early pioneer outpost and first telegraph station in Arizona.

MP 610

Dominguez and Escalante Expedition: A worn and hungry band of Spanish explorers made camp at Johnson Wash, 6 miles to the east, on Oct. 21, 1776. Fathers Dominguez and Escalante called it Santa Barbara. They found no water for their horses or men and had been subsisting on meager supplies of piñon nuts and prickly-pear cakes obtained in trade from the local Paiutes.

The Spaniards had already spent nights without water and with only minimal nourishment. Lorenzo de Olivares was nearly mad with thirst after eating too many of the salty cactus cakes. He disappeared that evening, stumbling up the wash. Having worried about their companion all night, the padres found him the next morning at some small pools near the base of the Red Shinarump cliffs to the north. The territory known as the Arizona Strip confronted the expedition with some of its most brutal difficulties. Wandering first southeasterly and then north, without the aid of native guides, they struggled through a harsh and rutted land searching for the Ute crossing of the Colorado River. Dominguez and Escalante returned to Santa Fe in January 1777, after exploring much of what is now the Four Corners region, but failing to open a land route to Spanish settlements at Monterey.

MP 612

Blue Star Memorial Highway: A tribute to the United Forces who have defended the United States of America.

STATE ROUTE 90

MP 314

Fort Huachuca: Situated on the southern route to the Pacific Ocean in 1877. It brought law and order to Arizona Territory, protecting settlers, miners, travelers, and immigrants. Its troops won the surrender of Geronimo. General Pershing and General Wood served here. As the Army's electronic proving ground, Huachuca remains on active status.

MP 318

Fort Huachuca: Established in 1877 as the southern link of a military chain across Arizona to prevent Apache from raiding into Mexico, it also has been an important training center for Army field operations continuing into this century.

MP 329

Mormon Battalion Trail: Their campsite was here in December 1846. They were forced to herd wild horses and black bulls when the animals overran the camp.

STATE ROUTE 92

MP 340

Mormon Battalion Trail: The battalion camped here on Dec. 9, 1846. They first camped on the San Pedro River.

U.S. ROUTE 93

MP 28

Ghost Town of White Hills: Eight miles northeast along this road are the ruins of White Hills, once a mining boom town. A six-year wonder, from 1892 to 1898 the mine produced $12 million in gold and silver. The mineral discovery was one of the few credited to an Indian, a Hualapai named Jeff. White Hills had 12 saloons and two cemeteries. Water was nearly as expensive as whiskey.

MP 67

Junction, Union Pass Road: Over this road pioneers freighted from Hardyville, head of navigation on the Colorado River, to Mohave County and Yavapai County settlements. Hardyville was established in 1864 by "Capt." W.M.H. Hardy, a pioneer, ferryman, merchant, postmaster, stockman, miner, trail blazer, road builder, and legislator. Today's community of Bullhead City traces its origins to the settlement.

MP 123

Big Sandy Valley: The first exploration was most likely conducted by early Spanish explorers, like Espejo, from 1582 to 1589. The valley was later explored by a party under Lt. Amiel W. Whipple in 1854. It was considered an important agricultural, horticultural, mining, milling, and smelting area in early days. McCrackin Mine, discovered by Jackson McCrackin and H. A. "Chloride Jack" Owen, on Aug. 17, 1874, sits 18 miles south.

MP 160

Bill Williams River: The Santa Maria River combines with the Big Sandy to form Bill Williams River, which was explored as early as 1605 by the Spanish. Named for an early trapper and mountain man, the river yielded beaver to intrepid trappers who came west from Santa Fe. The combined stream empties into the Colorado River.

MP 174

Camp Date Creek: Originally established in 1867, this camp became Date Creek Agency in 1871, where Mohaves were given food rations in vain attempts to stop their raids. Here, in 1872, General Crook's troops killed eight Indians who were thought to have participated in the Wickenburg Massacre of stagecoach passengers.

STATE ROUTE 95

MP 234

Oatman Mining District: In the Black Mountains, 15 miles east, is the Oatman Mining District. Many original buildings still exist in the ghost town site. The Tom Reed, United Eastern, Gold Road, and other mines produced more than $30 million of gold from the early 1900s into the 1930s.

MP 247

Bullhead Community Park: Commercial steamship transportation on the Colorado River was of great importance from 1852 through 1877 and served the mining communities of northern Arizona. Cargo was unloaded at Hardyville, one and a half-miles south of this point, sometimes returning downstream with barge loads of local ore. Bull's Head Rock, from which Bullhead City derived its name, was located upstream from this point and, since 1953, has been covered by the waters behind Davis Dam. Bull's Head Rock was once used as a navigation marker and was located at a point where the Mohave Indians forded the river, as it was free of quicksand.

U.S. ROUTE 160

MP 344.3

Utah Pioneer Trails: Erected to honor George A. Smith, Jr., a member of Jacob Hamblin's party of nine Mormon missionaries and explorers. Smith was wounded with his own revolver by Indians on Nov. 2, 1880, presumably to avenge the recent killing of Indians by white men. He died while being carried on horseback to reach medical aid. His companions, to save their own lives, left his body wrapped in a blanket, unburied.

U.S. ROUTE 180

MP 380

Lyman Dam on the Little Colorado: The original dam at this site was destroyed in the spring floods of April 1915, with the loss of eight lives and severe damage to farmlands. It was rebuilt with loans from Arizona.

MP 427

Bushvalley Fort: Here stood the old Bushvalley Fort built in 1879 for protection against renegade Apaches.

STATE ROUTE 188

MP 242

Seiber Memorial: Al Seiber, veteran of the Civil War and for 20 years a leader of scouts for the U. S. Army during the Arizona Indian troubles, was killed on this spot on Feb. 19, 1907, by a rolling rock during construction of Tonto Road. His body is buried in the cemetery at Globe.

U.S. ROUTE 191

MP 38

Chiricahua National Monument: The monument includes a campground and museum. "The Wonderland of Rocks" started as an old lava flow that has eroded over the years until thousands of pinnacles, balanced rocks, and grotesque rock forms crowd canyons and mountain slopes. These mountains were the home of the Chiricahua Apaches, the most famous of whom was Geronimo.

MP 163

San Francisco River: In January 1825, a trapper named James O. Pattie ascended this river and, with one companion, trapped 250 beavers in 14 days. This was the first known penetration of the Arizona region by American citizens.

MP 164

Clifton Cliff Jail: Blasted from solid rock, this cavelike jail confined many of the bad men who crowded into the district in the boom days. Local tradition says that the first inmate in 1881 was the miner who built the jail. It was contributed to the town by the Lesinsky brothers, who built the first copper smelter on Chase Creek.

MP 170

Ruins of Metcalf: First claims were located here in 1872 by Jim and Bob Metcalf. Arizona Central Yankie and Montezuma claims were later grouped with Shannon and Longfellow Mines to form Copper Mountain Mining District. H.A. and Charles Lesinsky built the first smelter in 1873 and then produced Arizona's first railroad, a narrow gauge line running up Chase Creek Canyon.

MP 233

Clifton-Springerville Highway/The Coronado Trail: This scenic byway stretches across more than 120 miles of some of Arizona's most diverse landscape, from desert to alpine meadows.

STATE ROUTE 260

MP 234

General Crook Trail: Each mile was marked on this trail from Camp Verde to Camp Apache by the soldiers under Gen. George Crook, conqueror, but also friend of the Indians. First traversed in 1871, the road was improved and used by wagons in 1874. It was the principal supply route from Fort Whipple, at Prescott, to Camp Verde and Camp Apache.

MP 268

Zane Grey's Cabin: An Ohio-born dentist, Zane Grey spent many years under the Mogollon Rim, writing *To the Last Man* and a dozen other westerns with Arizona settings and characters. His prolific writings popularized the American cowboy as a taciturn, romantic figure. The cabin burned during a 1990s forest fire.

MP 357

Cooley Mountain: Named for Corydon E. Cooley, a Virginian who was an officer in the New Mexico Union Volunteers in the Civil War. He was also a guide, scout, and Indian interpreter. Cooley served the U.S. Army in campaigns against the Apaches, yet was respected as a friend by the natives. He married Mollie, an Apache girl, and was co-founder of Show Low. Cooley's Cienega Ranch became the town of McNary.

STATE ROUTE 264

MP 323

Spindle Mill: Near here, in 1879, Mormon colonists built Arizona's first woolen mill, hoping to utilize Hopi and Navajo wool and labor. The Mormons intended to build a new industry to supply the early settlers. The Spindle Mill operated only a short time, its abandonment signaling failure of the Mormon missionary movement among the Hopi.

MP 472

Chief Hastele Memorial: This site is dedicated in memory of Chief Hastele (circa 1810-1890), the great Navajo leader who proved himself a true friend of the Mormon people in bringing peace and goodwill to both Anglos and Indians. He was an honored friend of Jacob Hamblin, Latter-day Saint missionary, Indian guide, and peacemaker, who was sometimes known as the "Buckskin Apostle." Chief Hastele was also famed for his integrity and deep concern for truth, as exemplified by his oft-quoted statement, "My heart is clean."

STATE ROUTE 287

MP 193

Ghost Town of Adamsville: In the 1870s, a flour mill and a few stores formed the hub of life in Adamsville, where shootings and knifings were commonplace. Most of the adobe houses have since been washed away by the flooding Gila River.

Special Interests

SPECTATOR SPORTS

Professional

Arizona Cardinals: The oldest continually operated National Football League (NFL) team in the nation. Home games at Cardinals Stadium in Glendale, south of Glendale Avenue and Loop 101. Season: August- December. (800) 999-1402; www.azcardinals.com

Arizona Diamondbacks: Major League Baseball's 2001 World Champions. Home games at air-conditioned, domed Chase Field, 401 E. Jefferson St., in downtown Phoenix. Season: April-October. (602) 462-6500; http://arizona.diamondbacks.mlb.com

Phoenix Suns: National Basketball Association (NBA). Home games at U.S. Airways Center, 201 E. Jefferson St., in downtown Phoenix. Season: October-May. (800) 462-2849; (602) 514-5444; www.nba.com/suns

Phoenix Coyotes: National Hockey League (NHL). Home games at Glendale Arena, 9400 W. Maryland Ave., Glendale (just off Loop 101 at Glendale Ave.). Season: September-April. (623) 463-8800; www.phoenixcoyotes.com

Arizona Heat: Women's softball team in the National Pro Fast Pitch League. Home games at Hi Corbett Field, east of downtown Tucson in Reid Park. Season: May-August. (520) 296-9595; www.arizonaprofastpitch.com

Phoenix Mercury: Women's National Basketball Association (WNBA). Home games at U.S. Airways Center, 201 E. Jefferson St., in downtown Phoenix. Season: May-September. (602) 252-WNBA; www.wnba.com/mercury

Arizona Rattlers: Arena Football League (AFL).Home games at U.S. Airways Center, 201 E. Jefferson St., in downtown Phoenix. Season: January-May. (602) 514-8383; www.azrattlers.com

Phoenix Roadrunners: East Coast Hockey League (minor league hockey). Home games at U.S Airways Center, 201 E Jefferson St., in downtown Phoenix. Season: January-April. (602) 462-4625; www.phxroadrunners.com

[Spring training at Phoenix Municipal Stadium. ▲]

Arizona Sting: National Lacrosse League (NLL). Home games at Glendale Arena, 9400 W. Maryland Ave., Glendale (just off Loop 101 at Glendale Ave.). Season: January–April. (480) 563-7825; www.arizonasting.com

FBR Open: One of the oldest events on the Professional Golf Association (PGA) tour. The tournament is held in late January or early February at Scottsdale's Tournament Players Club, 17020 N. Hayden Road. (602) 870-0163; www.phoenixopen.com

Chrysler Classic of Tucson: PGA Tour event held in February at Omni Tucson National Golf Resort & Spa in the Catalina Foothills. (520) 571-0400; www.tucsonnational.com

Safeway International Golf Tournament: Ladies Professional Golf Association (LPGA). Held in March at Superstition Mountain Golf and Country Club, located off U.S. Route 60 east about 13 miles east of Power Road. (602) 495-4653; www.safewaygolf.com

Tucson Sidewinders: The Arizona Diamondbacks Triple-A affiliate plays in the Pacific Coast League. Their season starts in April and runs through September. Tucson Electric Park, 2500 E. Ajo Way, Tucson, (520) 434-1021; www.tucsonsidewinders.com

Cactus League: A dozen Major League Baseball teams conduct spring training in Mesa, Peoria, Phoenix, Scottsdale, Surprise, Tempe, and Tucson beginning each February. The Cactus League Internet site, www.cactusleague. com, maintains schedules, ticket-ordering, and locations (with maps) of each ballpark used by the teams.

Arizona Fall League: The Surprise Scorpions, Mesa Solar Sox, Peoria Saguaros, Phoenix Desert Dogs, Peoria Javelinas, and Grand Canyon Rafters make up the league that consists of 180 of baseball's top prospects. (480) 496-6700; www.minorleaguebaseball.com

Arizona Summer League: Arizona Brewers, Arizona Rangers, Arizona Royals, Mesa Angels, Mesa Cubs, Peoria Mariners, Phoenix Athletics, and Scottsdale Giants are "Rookie" minor league baseball teams that play in the Summer Arizona League. Each team plays 56 games from June through August. (208) 429-1511; www.minorleaguebaseball.com

Collegiate

Arizona State University Sun Devils: The maroon and gold compete in NCAA division I-A in numerous sports: Football, wrestling, volleyball, baseball, water polo, etc. Tempe; (480) 965-2381 or (888) 786-3857; http://thesundevils.collegesports.com

University of Arizona Wildcats: Arizonans love the Wildcats' athletic teams, which compete in NCAA division I-A: Football, basketball, softball, baseball, etc. Tucson; (520) 621-CATS or (800) 452-CATS; www.arizonaathletics.com

Northern Arizona University Lumberjacks: NAU teams compete in NCAA Division I-AA: Football, soccer, basketball, volleyball, tennis, cross-country, golf, swimming and diving, track and field. 1 Skydome Drive, Flagstaff; (928) 523-5353; http://nau.newtier.com

Fiesta Bowl: Top-rated Division I-A college football teams come to town to play in a Bowl Championship Series (BCS) game. January. Cardinals Stadium, Glendale; (480) 350-0900; www.tostitosfiestabowl.com

Insight Bowl: Chase Field transforms into a football field once a year for an action packed Division I-A football match-up. December. Chase Field, Phoenix; (480) 350-0900; www.insightbowl.com

Racing Sports

Phoenix International Raceway: Home to NASCAR'S Subway Fresh 500, the Busch Series Bashas' Supermarkets 200, the Grand-Am Cup Phoenix 200, and the Grand American Rolex Sports Car Series Phoenix 250. 455 N. Third St., Phoenix; (602) 252-2227 or (866) 408-7223; www.phoenixintlraceway.com

Firebird International Raceway: The world-class facilities accommodate the super stars of drag racing. Professional races, including boat races at Firebird Lake, take place year round. 20,000 S. Maricopa Road, Chandler; (602) 268-0200; www.firebirdraceway.com

Southwestern International Raceway: A National Hot Rod Association (NHRA) sanctioned track that provides tons of high-speed drag racing excitement. 11300 S. Houghton Road, Tucson; (520) 762-9700; www.sirace.com

Thunder Raceway: Quarter-mile dirt-track racing begins in May and runs through September. Races include: modifieds, pro stocks, dwarf cars, mini stocks. sprint cars, mini sprints, southwest late models, and midgets. 4701 E Deuce of Clubs, Show Low; (928) 242-1384; www.thunderraceway.com

Speedworld Motorplex: Year-round drag racing at this NHRA-sanctioned track. 19421 W. Jomax Road, Wittmann; (623) 388-0039; www.speedworldmotorplex.com

Yuma Speedway Park: Features a 3/8-mile semi-banked clay oval and a 300-foot sand drag strip. 3450 W. County 15 Street, Yuma; (520) 726-9483.

Central Arizona Raceway: Claims the 3/8-mile clay oval is the fastest in the state. Pinal County Fairgrounds; (520) 723-8888; www.centralazraceway.com

Canyon Raceway: A mile-long dirt oval track that hosts stock cars, mod lites, and midgets. 9777 W. Carefree Highway, Peoria; (602) 258-7223; www.canyonraceway.net

Canyon Off-road Park: Moto-cross and quad racing at an owner/rider-operated facility. Off Carefree Highway and 99th Ave., Phoenix. (623) 434-4363; www.copracing.com

Ocotillo Raceway: Mile-long dirt supercross track that includes a "mini monster track." Eloy; (520) 743-7727; www.gohuge.com

Arizona Cycle Park: The Classic Series held at this National Championship MX track is "Arizona's most prestigious and longest running series." Litchfield Park.; (623) 853-0750; www.arizonacyclepark.com

Mount Graham Motorsports Park: Motorcycle and ATV dirt-track racing. Safford; (928) 651-7601; www.excservices.com

Phoenix Greyhound Park: Live greyhound racing seven nights a week. Fine dining is available on site as well. 3801 E. Washington St., Phoenix. (602) 273-7181; www.phoenixgreyhoundpark.com

Tucson Greyhound Park: Live dog races have taken place here for more than 60 years. The track simulcasts other racing events, including horse racing, as well. 2601 S. Third Ave., Tucson; (520) 884-7576; www.tucdogtrak.com

Apache Greyhound Park: Dog racing, simulcasts, and one restaurant. 2551 W. Apache Trail, Apache Junction; (480) 982-2371.

Turf Paradise Race Course: Live thoroughbred horse races take place from September through May. The 1,000-seat, air-conditioned clubhouse simulcasts races year round. 1501 W. Bell Rd., Phoenix; (888) 942-1101 or (602) 375-6478; www.turfparadise.com

Rillito Park: Live quarter horse, thoroughbred, and Arabian horse racing occurs from January to March. Two restaurants are on site. 4502 N. First Avenue, Tucson; (520) 293-5011; www.thepepper.com/tucson_horse_racing.html

Yavapai Downs: Live thoroughbred and quarter horse racing Memorial Day through Labor Day. 10401 Highway 89A, Prescott Valley; (928) 775-8000; www.yavapaidownsatpv.com

Southern California Speedboat Club's Thanksgiving Regatta: Power boat racing on the Colorado River that is hosted by Blue Water Resort and Casino. Parker; (888)-243-3360; www.bluewaterfun.com

Jet Jam Racing Series: A personal watercraft extravaganza. Lake Havasu City; (928) 764-2210; www.dsmevents.com/jetjam/home.htm

American Power Boat Association National Watercross Tour: Makes stops in northwest Arizona. (586) 773-9700; www.apbapwr.com/schedules.htm

Rodeos and Horse Shows

Horse Shows in The Sun: An Arizona winter circuit of hunter/jumper horse shows that takes place for six consecutive weekends. Tucson; (845) 246-8833; www.hitsshows.com

La Fiesta de los Vaqueros (Celebration of Cowboys): Nine days of ropes, bulls, and the top rodeo cowboys in the world. February. Tucson; (800) 964-5662; www.tucsonrodeo.com

Scottsdale Arabian Horse Show: For more than 50 years, the top owners, breeders, and trainers converge on Scottsdale for a first-class horse show. Vendors will also be on hand to sell food, jewelry, and artwork. February. (480) 515-1122; www.scottsdaleshow.com

Parada del Sol Rodeo: A weekend of concerts and rodeo excitement that has been held for more than 50 years. A parade and a family-friendly block party take place in Old Town. March. Scottsdale; (480) 990-3179; www.scottsdalejaycees.org/paradadelsol/rodeo.htm

Sonoita Quarter Horse Show: At the Santa Cruz County Fair Grounds. May. Sonoita. (714) 444-2918; www.sonoitafairgrounds.com

Pine Country Pro Rodeo: The PRCA comes to northern Arizona for this event. June. Flagstaff; (928) 779-7685 x4838.

Prescott Frontier Days: The unique distinction of "World's Oldest Rodeo" goes to Prescott, a city that first hosted "cowboy contests" on July 4, 1888. Late June/early July. (800) 358-1888; www.worldsoldestrodeo.com

Payson Rodeo: The "World's Oldest Continuous Rodeo" has continually been held the third week of August for more than 122 years. August. (800) 672-9766; www.rimcountrychamber.com/rodeoPageN.htm

Florence Junior Parada: Little cowboys and cowgirls between the ages of 5 and 18 compete in the "oldest continuous running junior-sanctioned rodeo in the world." November. Florence; (520) 868-9433; www.town.florence.az.us

San Carlos Apache Tribe's Veteran's Memorial Rodeo: Fair and festivities surround a weekend of roping and riding. November. (800) 272-2438; www.apachegoldcasinoresort.com

Gold Rush Days: This "wild rootin'-tootin' western weekend" hosts one of Arizona's largest parades as well as a mucking and drilling contest, music, and a two-day rodeo that features rodeo cowboys from all over the country. February. Wickenburg; (928) 684-5479; www.wickenburgchamber.com/events.asp

Navajo Nation Fair Rodeo: An All Indian Rodeo Cowboys Association (AIRCA) event for more than 60 years. September. Window Rock; Navajo Nation Fairgrounds; (928) 871-7052.

Miscellaneous Sports

Arizona Roller Derby League: The Bad News Beaters, Brusiers, Smash Squad, Surly Gurlies, and the Tent City Terrors compete in the all-female, roller skate free-for-all. Most bouts take place at Castle Sports Club in Phoenix: 11420 N. 19th Ave; (602) 331-2582 or (877) 725- 8849 for tickets; www.azrollerderby.com

Arizona Boxing Commission: Oversees and regulates boxing. 1110 W. Washington St., Suite 260, Phoenix; (602) 364-1727.

Rage in the Cage: Hosts mixed martial arts bouts throughout Arizona. The fights take place in a 16-foot octagonal steel cage. Brausa Academy, 1932 E. University Dr., Tempe, Arizona; (480) 232-2098; www.rageinthecage.com

King of the Cage: Brazilian Jiu-Jitsu, wrestling, Muay Thai, boxing, and more as athletes compete in the professional mixed martial arts events. Apache Gold Casino and Resort, San Carlos; (800) 2722438; www.apachegoldcasinoresort.com or www.kingofthecage.com

ARIZONA CASINOS

www.azindiangaming.org

Ak-Chin Indian Community: Harrah's Ak-Chin Casino, 15406 Maricopa Road, Maricopa; (800) 427-7247; www.harrahs.com

Cocopah Indian Tribe: Cocopah Casino, 15136 S. Avenue B, Somerton; (800) 237-5687. www.wincocopahcasino.com

Colorado River Indian Tribes: Blue Water Casino, 11222 Resort Drive, Parker; (888) 243-3360. www.bluewaterfun.com

Fort McDowell Yavapai Nation: Fort McDowell Gaming Center, north of Fountain Hills on State Route 87 and Fort McDowell Road; (800) 843-3678; www.fortmcdowellcasino.com

Fort Mojave Indian Tribe: Spirit Mountain Casino, 8555 S. Highway 95, Mohave Valley; (888) 837-4030

Gila River Indian Community: Wild Horse Pass Casino, Maricopa Road, 1 mile west of Interstate 10, across from Firebird Lake; (800) 946-4452; www.wingilariver.com. Vee Quiva Casino: 51st Ave. and Estrella, Laveen; (800) 946-4452; www.wingilariver.com. Lone Butte Casino, 1200 S. 56th St., Chandler; (800) 946-4452; www.wingilariver.com

Pascua Yaqui Tribe: Casino of the Sun, 7406 S. Camino del Oeste, Tucson; (520) 879-5450; www.casinosun.com. Casino del Sol, 5655 W. Valencia Road, Tucson; (520) 838-6506; www.casinodelsol.com

Quechan Indian Tribe: Paradise Casino, 540 Quechan Drive, Fort Yuma; (888) 777-4946; www.paradise-casinos.com

Salt River Pima-Maricopa Indian Community: Casino Arizona at Salt River, 524 N. 92nd St., Scottsdale; (480) 850-7777; www.casinoaz.com. Casino Arizona at Talking Stick, 9700 E. Indian Bend Road, Scottsdale; (480) 850-7777; www.casinoaz.com

San Carlos Apache Tribe: Apache Gold Casino, U.S. Route 70, San Carlos, east of Globe; (800) 272-2438; www.apachegoldcasinoresort.com

Tohono O'odham Nation: Desert Diamond Casino I, 7350 S. Nogales Highway, Tucson; (520) 294-7777; Desert Diamond Casino II, 1100 W. Pima Mine Road, Sahuarita; (866) 332-9467; Golden Has:sañ Casino, Highway 86, Why; (520) 362-2746. For all three, www.desertdiamondcasino.com

Tonto Apache Tribe: Mazatzal Casino, State Route 87, Payson; (800) 777-7529; www.777play.com

White Mountain Apache Tribe: Hon-Dah Casino, located at the junction of State Routes 260 and 73; (800) 929-8744; www.hon-dah.com

Yavapai-Apache Nation: Cliff Castle Casino, 555 Middle Verde Road, Camp Verde; (800) 381-7568; www.cliffcastle.com

Yavapai-Prescott Indian Tribe: Bucky's Casino, State Route 69 and Heather Heights, Prescott; (800) 756-8744; Yavapai Casino, 1500 E. Highway 69, Prescott; (800) 756-8744. For both, www.buckyscasino.com

MISCELLANEOUS

Old Time Fiddlers Contests: Several music festivals featuring fiddlers contests, bluegrass music, and similar jamborees are held in various Arizona locations, usually in February through September. www.arizonaoldtimefiddlers.org

Dude Ranches: Arizona Dude Ranch Association, P.O. Box 603, Cortaro, AZ 85652. www.azdra.com. The Dude Ranchers' Association., P.O. Box 2307, Cody, WY 82414. (307) 587-2339; www.duderanch.org

Shooting Sports: The National Shooting Sports Foundation: (203) 426-1320; www.wheretoshoot.org

Golf: The Arizona Golf Association maintains a directory. (602) 944-3035 or (800) 458-8484; www.azgolf.org/main/index.asp

Ice Skating Rinks

Phoenix Area

Alltel Ice Den: 120,000 square feet with two rinks. Classes and hockey leagues. 9375 E. Bell Road, Scottsdale; (480) 585-7465; www.coyotesice.com

Arcadia Ice Arena: Classes, open skating, and hockey sessions. Southeast corner of 38th Street and Thomas Road; (602) 957-9966; www.arcadiaice.com

Oceanside Ice Arena: Classes, hockey leagues, broomball, and public sessions. 1520 N. Hayden Road, Tempe; (480) 947-2470; www.iskateaz.com

Desert Schools Coyotes Centers: Facilities in Chandler and Peoria offer hockey, classes, and public skating. 7225 W. Harrison, Chandler; (480) 598-9400. 15829 N. 83rd Ave., Peoria; (623) 334-1200; www.polariceent.com

Ozzie Ice: A hockey-training facility for young players. 10436 N 32nd St, Phoenix; 602-493-4667; www.ozzieice.com

Tucson Area

Arizona Skate Center Inc.: 3970 West Ina Road, (520) 572-7528.

Polar Ice Tucson: Home of the Tucson Chilly Peppers of Tucson Women's Hockey League. 7333 E. Rosewood St., (520) 290-8800; www.polaricetucson.com

Gateway Ice Center: Classes, youth hockey leagues, and broom ball. 4759 E. Camp Lowell Drive; (520) 290-8800; www.gatewayicecenter.com

Other Areas

Jay Lively Activity Center: Classes, hockey, and broomball. 1650 N. Turquoise Drive, Flagstaff; (928) 774-1051.

Outdoor Ice Skating Rink: Williams sets up a public rink during winter next to the Williams visitors center; (928) 635-0273; www.williamschamber.com

Index

George Stocking

[Spider Rock, an 800-foot sandstone pillar, towers above Canyon de Chelly. ▲]